OAKLAND COMMUNITY COLLEGE
Orchard Ridge Campus
27055 Orchard Lake Road
Farmington, Michigan 48024

GENERATIONS
AN INTRODUCTION TO DRAMA

GENERATIONS

AN INTRODUCTION TO DRAMA

EDITED BY

M. S. BARRANGER, *Tulane University*

AND

DANIEL B. DODSON, *Columbia University*

HARCOURT BRACE JOVANOVICH, INC.
New York   Chicago   San Francisco   Atlanta

© 1971 BY HARCOURT BRACE JOVANOVICH, INC.

All rights reserved. No part of this publication may be
reproduced or transmitted in any form or by any means,
electronic or mechanical, including photocopy,
recording, or any information storage and retrieval system,
without permission in writing from the publisher.

ISBN: 0-15-529534-9

Library of Congress Catalog Card Number: 77-153747

Printed in the United States of America

COVER PHOTO BY ZOË DOMINIC: 1967 production of Ibsen's *Ghosts*
by the Royal Shakespeare Company at the Aldwych Theatre.

Preface

One of the most popular themes in world drama has been the conflict between youth and age—the confrontation of generations. What currently is known as the generation gap disturbed the Greece of Sophocles, the France of Molière, the England of Shakespeare, and the post–World War II America of Arthur Miller. In its ritualistic origin, drama, in fact, derived from the futile attempts of the old to resist the encroachment of youth.

The seven plays in this anthology are drawn from the whole span of Western drama, and in each a version of the generational conflict is inherent in the theme and central action of the play. In each play youth is attempting to free itself from the restrictions imposed upon it by the authority of the prevailing power structure: parental, political, or social.

Each playwright has chosen to emphasize certain characteristic perspectives of the struggle. In Lorraine Hansberry's *A Raisin in the Sun* youth is impatient to be freed not only from the black ghetto of racially segregated America, but also from the strength and wisdom of the older generation in order to achieve a different ideal of manhood. In Shakespeare's *Romeo and Juliet* the passionate love of two young people is sacrificed to the willful patterns set by their families. In Sophocles' *Antigone* youth confuses piety and self-will in a struggle with political expediency. The struggle is played in various moods: in sheer absurdism in *Picnic on the Battlefield*, in illness and insanity in *Ghosts*, in high comic exaggeration in *The Miser*.

In order to enhance the relevance of the theme for today's students, we have reversed chronology, beginning with the contemporary and working back in time. This reverse order will, we believe, help the student to identify easily and quickly with both the language and the characters.

Generations is suited for use in either a thematic or a genre course. Its seven plays not only cover a wide span of time, but represent tragedy, comedy, and farce. The brief introduction preceding each play gives helpful background information about author and play. Detailed questions following the plays can be used for review or for suggestions on ways of thinking about content and structure. Ideas for writing assignments appear at the end of the book.

We hope that the special emphasis on the relevance of drama to the problems of today's youth will make *Generations* especially valuable for an introduction to the study and understanding of the world's drama.

M. S. B.
D. B. D.

January 1971

Contents

PREFACE v

INTRODUCTION 3

A RAISIN IN THE SUN
LORRAINE HANSBERRY 5

ALL MY SONS
ARTHUR MILLER 87

PICNIC ON THE BATTLEFIELD
FERNANDO ARRABAL
Translated by Barbara Wright 153

GHOSTS
HENRIK IBSEN
Translated by Michael Meyer 171

THE MISER
MOLIÈRE
Translated by H. Baker and J. Miller 229

ROMEO AND JULIET
WILLIAM SHAKESPEARE 281

ANTIGONE
SOPHOCLES
Translated by Dudley Fitts
and Robert Fitzgerald 373

STUDY GUIDE 413

SUGGESTED TOPICS FOR PAPERS 427

GENERATIONS
AN INTRODUCTION TO DRAMA

Introduction

A Nineteenth-Century German playwright, Friedrich Schiller, once claimed that all art is the product of a "play-urge." Children who dress up in adults' clothes to "play house" are exercising a creative play-urge to act out imagined roles. In later life this mimetic urge takes many forms, from role-playing in one's social environment to the actual adoption of acting as a profession. In some manner which we do not usually choose to admit, all of us—the conventional businessman, the militant general, the dissident student—are playing out the roles of our identity in the theater of the world.

But we know from experience that describing our own particular play as comedy, tragedy, melodrama, or farce is almost impossible. Ordinarily, we are not likely to admit or even to believe that it is exclusively any of these, or that we spend a lifetime playing the role of buffoon, villain, or hero. And we cannot readily think of our own lives as dramatic, since we are usually preoccupied with the impact of events as they occur. The fact that drama reproduces the experience of living in a heightened and esthetically satisfying form is probably one of the most compelling reasons for its existence.

That is, the dramatist performs for us what we cannot accomplish for ourselves. He permits us to see ourselves as others see us and to see others as we have known or suspected them to be. Much of what we see in real life, regardless of how it may be disguised by manners or convention, is conflict—conflict with parents, friends, enemies, neighbors, as well as conflict of emotions, ideas, and traditions. The substance of drama, as of all literature, is conflict taken from life and made recognizable by the skills of the dramatist, and ordered by him to stimulate our emotions and our thinking.

The basic conflict in drama is not always solemn or tragic or loud, however. It may be extremely funny; or it may be muted and subtle. In fact, some dramatists, with the support of the psychologists, contend that our quietest moments are our most crucial. To dramatize effectively these times in our lives when we may be quite alone—as Juliet is alone in Act IV, scene iii, of ROMEO AND JULIET, and as Romeo is alone in Act V, scene i—requires even greater skill than the moments reverberating with kettledrums and shouting.

Drama, then, derives from our profound urge to see our lives or the lives of others projected on the stage. It satisfies our need to stand back and look at our conflicts and those of others from a kind of vantage ground. As Hamlet says, the purpose of acting is "to hold as 'twere the mirror up to Nature." In so doing, the dramatist does more than show us pictures. By intensifying experience, he may help us better to interpret, better to understand our own experiences and those of our society.

A RAISIN

IN THE

SUN

by LORRAINE HANSBERRY

A RAISIN IN THE SUN Copyright © 1958, 1959, 1966 by Robert Nemiroff as Executor of the Estate of Lorraine Hansberry. Reprinted by permission of Random House, Inc.

Photos by Zodiac Photographers: New York, 1959.

In 1959, *A Raisin in the Sun* became the first play written by a black woman to be produced on Broadway and the first play by a black playwright to win the New York Drama Critics Circle Award.

Born in Chicago, in 1930, Miss Hansberry, the daughter of a well-to-do real estate broker, became interested in the theater during her high school days there. At that time, she wanted to be a painter, but after studying at Chicago's Art Institute and the University of Wisconsin, she decided that she had no talent for that art. In 1950 she moved to New York; three years later she married Robert Nemiroff, song writer and music publisher, and began writing plays.

During her brief lifetime, Miss Hansberry wrote several unfinished plays before completing *A Raisin in the Sun,* in 1958, and *The Sign in Sidney Brustein's Window,* her second and last play, produced on Broadway in 1964. On January 12, 1965, Lorraine Hansberry died of cancer at the age of thirty-four.

A Raisin in the Sun was written in reaction to plays in the American theater "about Negroes" rather than plays about human beings who incidentally happened to be black. The evening Miss Hansberry conceived *A Raisin in the Sun* she told her husband, "I'm going to write a social drama about Negroes that will be good art." * Her play achieves both of these goals.

A Raisin in the Sun, its title taken from "Harlem," a poem by Langston Hughes, is a play of social protest against the economic and social pressures that create the frustrations, disappointments, and hostilities of minority groups. Miss Hansberry's specific concerns, presented against the background of a Chicago Southside slum, are for ghetto living conditions and for the heartbreaking struggle to realize oneself in these surroundings. The Youngers (mother, son, daughter, daughter-in-law, and grandson) embody the hopes, dreams, failures, and frustrations of the economically depressed in a society where the American dream of success is held out to everyone. As Miss Hansberry says, "The family is typical—incapable of giving up about anything. All of them have a sense of the pursuit of life, and no wherewithal to bring it nearer." Her principal character, Walter Lee Younger, wages a losing battle with the American dream and the play is largely his story, for the climax hinges on his growing "into his manhood."

In writing about the Youngers' need for love, dignity, achievement, and continuity, Miss Hansberry makes her ghetto family relevant to families outside the black community and the Chicago slum. She presents a realistic appraisal of the financial and personal troubles of the Youngers and a plea for tolerance of economically depressed people everywhere.

* From an interview with Lorraine Hansberry by Nan Robertson entitled "Dramatist Against Odds," *The New York Times* (March 8, 1959), sect. 2, p. 3.

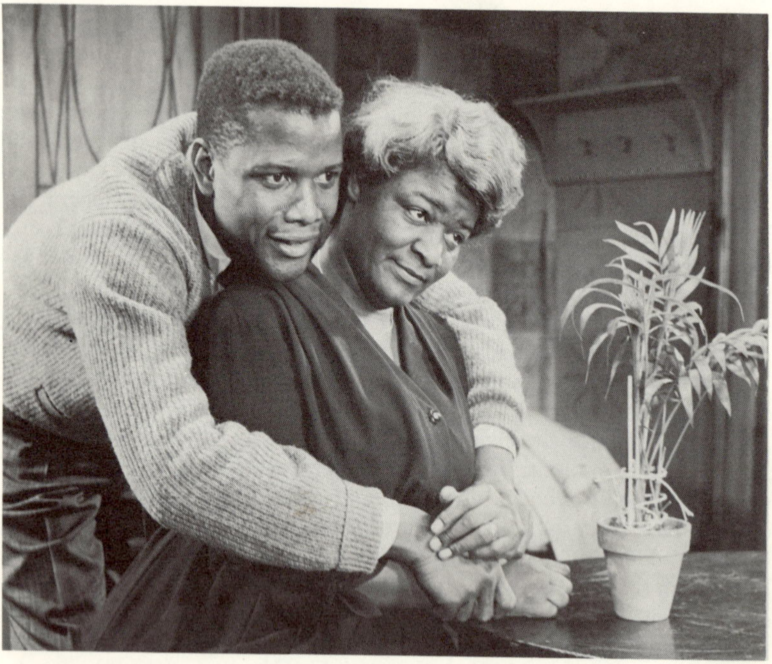

Characters

RUTH YOUNGER
TRAVIS YOUNGER
WALTER LEE YOUNGER (*Brother*)
BENEATHA YOUNGER
LENA YOUNGER (*Mama*)
JOSEPH ASAGAI
GEORGE MURCHISON
KARL LINDNER
BOBO
MOVING MEN

The action of the play is set in Chicago's Southside, sometime between World War II and the present.

ACT ONE

SCENE 1. *Friday morning*
SCENE 2. *The following morning*

ACT TWO

SCENE 1. *Later, the same day*
SCENE 2. *Friday night, a few weeks later*
SCENE 3. *Moving day, one week later*

ACT THREE

An hour later

To Mama: in gratitude for the dream

What happens to a dream deferred?
Does it dry up
Like a raisin in the sun?
Or fester like a sore—
And then run?
Does it stink like rotten meat?
Or crust and sugar over—
Like a syrupy sweet?

Maybe it just sags
Like a heavy load.

Or does it explode?

—LANGSTON HUGHES[*]

ACT ONE

SCENE I. *The* YOUNGER *living room would be a comfortable and well-ordered room if it were not for a number of indestructible contradictions to this state of being. Its furnishings are typical and undistinguished and their primary feature now is that they have clearly had to accommodate the living of too many people for too many years—and they are tired. Still, we can see that at some time, a time probably no longer remembered by the family (except perhaps for* MAMA*), the furnishings of this room were actually selected with care and love and even hope—and brought to this apartment and arranged with taste and pride.*

That was a long time ago. Now the once loved pattern of the couch upholstery has to fight to show itself from under acres of crocheted doilies and couch covers which have themselves finally come to be more important than the upholstery. And here a table or a chair has been moved to disguise the worn places in the carpet; but the carpet has fought back by showing its weariness, with depressing uniformity, elsewhere on its surface.

Weariness has, in fact, won in this room. Everything has been polished, washed, sat on, used, scrubbed too often. All pretenses but living itself have long since vanished from the very atmosphere of this room.

Moreover, a section of this room, for it is not really a room unto itself, though the landlord's lease would make it seem so, slopes backward to provide a small kitchen area, where the family prepares the meals that

---

[*] From "Dream Deferred." Copyright 1951 by Langston Hughes. Reprinted from *The Panther and the Lash* by Langston Hughes, by permission of Alfred A. Knopf, Inc.

are eaten in the living room proper, which must also serve as dining room. The single window that has been provided for these "two" rooms is located in this kitchen area. The sole natural light the family may enjoy in the course of a day is only that which fights its way through this little window.

At left, a door leads to a bedroom which is shared by MAMA and her daughter, BENEATHA. At right, opposite, is a second room (which in the beginning of the life of this apartment was probably a breakfast room), which serves as a bedroom for WALTER and his wife, RUTH.

Time: Sometime between World War II and the present.

Place: Chicago's Southside.

At Rise: It is morning dark in the living room. TRAVIS is asleep on the make-down bed at center. An alarm clock sounds from within the bedroom at right, and presently RUTH enters from that room and closes the door behind her. She crosses sleepily toward the window. As she passes her sleeping son she reaches down and shakes him a little. At the window she raises the shade and a dusky Southside morning light comes in feebly. She fills a pot with water and puts it on to boil. She calls to the boy, between yawns, in a slightly muffled voice.

RUTH is about thirty. We can see that she was a pretty girl, even exceptionally so, but now it is apparent that life has been little that she expected, and disappointment has already begun to hang in her face. In a few years, before thirty-five even, she will be known among her people as a "settled woman."

She crosses to her son and gives him a good, final, rousing shake.

RUTH. Come on now, boy, it's seven thirty! [*Her son sits up at last, in a stupor of sleepiness.*] I say hurry up, Travis! You ain't the only person in the world got to use a bathroom! [*The child, a sturdy, handsome little boy of ten or eleven, drags himself out of the bed and almost blindly takes his towels and "today's clothes" from drawers and a closet and goes out to the bathroom, which is in an outside hall and which is shared by another family or families on the same floor.* RUTH *crosses to the bedroom door at right and opens it and calls in to her husband.*] Walter Lee! . . . It's after seven thirty! Lemme see you do some waking up in there now! [*She waits.*] You better get up from there, man! It's after seven thirty I tell you. [*She waits again.*] All right, you just go ahead and lay there and next thing you know Travis be finished and Mr. Johnson'll be in there and you'll be fussing and cussing round here like a mad man! And be late too! [*She waits, at the end of patience.*] Walter Lee—it's time for you to get up!

[*She waits another second and then starts to go into the bedroom, but is apparently satisfied that her husband has begun to get up.*]

She stops, pulls the door to, and returns to the kitchen area. She wipes her face with a moist cloth and runs her fingers through her sleep-disheveled hair in a vain effort and ties an apron around her housecoat. The bedroom door at right opens and her husband stands in the doorway in his pajamas, which are rumpled and mismated. He is a lean, intense young man in his middle thirties, inclined to quick nervous movements and erratic speech habits—and always in his voice there is a quality of indictment.]

WALTER. Is he out yet?
RUTH. What you mean *out?* He ain't hardly got in there good yet.
WALTER [*wandering in, still more oriented to sleep than to a new day*]. Well, what was you doing all that yelling for if I can't even get in there yet? [*Stopping and thinking*] Check coming today?
RUTH. They *said* Saturday and this is just Friday and I hopes to God you ain't going to get up here first thing this morning and start talking to me 'bout no money—'cause I 'bout don't want to hear it.
WALTER. Something the matter with you this morning?
RUTH. No—I'm just sleepy as the devil. What kind of eggs you want?
WALTER. Not scrambled. [RUTH *starts to scramble eggs.*] Paper come? [RUTH *points impatiently to the rolled up* Tribune *on the table, and he gets it and spreads it out and vaguely reads the front page.*] Set off another bomb yesterday.
RUTH [*maximum indifference*]. Did they?
WALTER [*looking up*]. What's the matter with you?
RUTH. Ain't nothing the matter with me. And don't keep asking me that this morning.
WALTER. Ain't nobody bothering you. [*Reading the news of the day absently again*] Say Colonel McCormick is sick.
RUTH [*affecting tea-party interest*]. Is he now? Poor thing.
WALTER [*sighing and looking at his watch*]. Oh, me. [*He waits.*] Now what is that boy doing in that bathroom all this time? He just going to have to start getting up earlier. I can't be being late to work on account of him fooling around in there.
RUTH [*turning on him*]. Oh, no he ain't going to be getting up no earlier no such thing! It ain't his fault that he can't get to bed no earlier nights 'cause he got a bunch of crazy good-for-nothing clowns sitting up running their mouths in what is supposed to be his bedroom after ten o'clock at night. . . .
WALTER. That's what you mad about, ain't it? The things I want to talk about with my friends just couldn't be important in your mind, could they?

[*He rises and finds a cigarette in her handbag on the table and crosses to the little window and looks out, smoking and deeply enjoying this first one.*]

RUTH [*almost matter of factly, a complaint too automatic to deserve emphasis*]. Why you always got to smoke before you eat in the morning?

WALTER [*at the window*]. Just look at 'em down there. . . . Running and racing to work . . . [*he turns and faces his wife and watches her a moment at the stove, and then, suddenly*] You look young this morning, baby.

RUTH [*indifferently*]. Yeah?

WALTER. Just for a second—stirring them eggs. It's gone now—just for a second it was—you looked real young again. [*Then, drily*] It's gone now—you look like yourself again.

RUTH. Man, if you don't shut up and leave me alone.

WALTER [*looking out to the street again*]. First thing a man ought to learn in life is not to make love to no colored woman first thing in the morning. You all some evil people at eight o'clock in the morning.

[TRAVIS *appears in the hall doorway, almost fully dressed and quite wide awake now, his towels and pajamas across his shoulders. He opens the door and signals for his father to make the bathroom in a hurry.*]

TRAVIS [*watching the bathroom*]. Daddy, come on!

[WALTER *gets his bathroom utensils and flies out to the bathroom.*]

RUTH. Sit down and have your breakfast, Travis.

TRAVIS. Mama, this is Friday. [*Gleefully*] Check coming tomorrow, huh?

RUTH. You get your mind off money and eat your breakfast.

TRAVIS [*eating*]. This is the morning we supposed to bring the fifty cents to school.

RUTH. Well, I ain't got no fifty cents this morning.

TRAVIS. Teacher say we have to.

RUTH. I don't care what teacher say. I ain't got it. Eat your breakfast, Travis.

TRAVIS. I *am* eating.

RUTH. Hush up now and just eat!

[*The boy gives her an exasperated look for her lack of understanding, and eats grudgingly.*]

TRAVIS. You think Grandmama would have it?
RUTH. No! And I want you to stop asking your grandmother for money, you hear me?
TRAVIS [*outraged*]. Gaaaleee! I don't ask her, she just gimme it sometimes!
RUTH. Travis Willard Younger—I got too much on me this morning to be—
TRAVIS. Maybe Daddy—
RUTH. *Travis!*

[*The boy hushes abruptly. They are both quiet and tense for several seconds.*]

TRAVIS [*presently*]. Could I maybe go carry some groceries in front of the supermarket for a little while after school then?
RUTH. Just hush, I said. [TRAVIS *jabs his spoon into his cereal bowl viciously, and rests his head in anger upon his fists.*] If you through eating, you can get over there and make up your bed.

[*The boy obeys stiffly and crosses the room, almost mechanically, to the bed and more or less carefully folds the covering. He carries the bedding into his mother's room and returns with his books and cap.*]

TRAVIS [*sulking and standing apart from her unnaturally*]. I'm gone.
RUTH [*looking up from the stove to inspect him automatically*]. Come here. [*He crosses to her and she studies his head.*] If you don't take this comb and fix this here head, you better! [TRAVIS *puts down his books with a great sigh of oppression, and crosses to the mirror. His mother mutters under her breath about his "slubbornness."*] 'Bout to march out of here with that head looking just like chickens slept in it! I just don't know where you get your slubborn ways. . . . And get your jacket, too. Looks chilly out this morning.
TRAVIS [*with conspicuously brushed hair and jacket*]. I'm gone.
RUTH. Get carfare and milk money—[*waving one finger*]—and not a single penny for no caps, you hear me?
TRAVIS [*with sullen politeness*]. Yes'm.

[*He turns in outrage to leave. His mother watches after him as in his frustration he approaches the door almost comically. When she speaks to him, her voice has become a very gentle tease.*]

RUTH [*mocking; as she thinks he would say it*]. Oh, Mama makes me so mad sometimes, I don't know what to do! [*She waits and continues to his back as he stands stock-still in front of the door.*] I wouldn't kiss that woman good-bye for nothing in this world this morning! [*The boy finally turns around and rolls his eyes at her, knowing the mood has changed and he is vindicated; he does not, however, move toward her yet.*] Not for nothing in this world! [*She finally laughs aloud at him and holds out her arms to him and we see that it is a way between them, very old and practiced. He crosses to her and allows her to embrace him warmly but keeps his face fixed with masculine rigidity. She holds him back from her presently and looks at him and runs her fingers over the features of his face. With utter gentleness—*] Now—whose little old angry man are you?

TRAVIS [*the masculinity and gruffness start to fade at last*]. Aw gaalee—Mama . . .

RUTH [*mimicking*]. Aw—gaaaaalleeeee, Mama! [*She pushes him, with rough playfulness and finality, toward the door.*] Get on out of here or you going to be late.

TRAVIS [*in the face of love, new aggressiveness*]. Mama, could I *please* go carry groceries?

RUTH. Honey, it's starting to get so cold evenings.

WALTER [*coming in from the bathroom and drawing a make-believe gun from a make-believe holster and shooting at his son*]. What is it he wants to do?

RUTH. Go carry groceries after school at the supermarket.

WALTER. Well, let him go. . . .

TRAVIS [*quickly, to the ally*]. I *have* to—she won't gimme the fifty cents. . . .

WALTER [*to his wife only*]. Why not?

RUTH [*simply, and with flavor*]. 'Cause we don't have it.

WALTER [*to* RUTH *only*]. What you tell the boy things like that for? [*Reaching down into his pants with a rather important gesture*] Here, son—

[*He hands the boy the coin, but his eyes are directed to his wife's.* TRAVIS *takes the money happily.*]

TRAVIS. Thanks, Daddy.

[*He starts out.* RUTH *watches both of them with murder in her eyes.* WALTER *stands and stares back at her with defiance, and suddenly reaches into his pocket again on an afterthought.*]

WALTER [*without even looking at his son, still staring hard at his wife*]. In fact, here's another fifty cents. . . . Buy yourself some fruit today —or take a taxicab to school or something!

TRAVIS. Whoopee—

[*He leaps up and clasps his father around the middle with his legs, and they face each other in mutual appreciation; slowly* WALTER LEE *peeks around the boy to catch the violent rays from his wife's eyes and draws his head back as if shot.*]

WALTER. You better get down now—and get to school, man.

TRAVIS [*at the door*]. O.K. Good-bye. [*He exits.*]

WALTER [*after him, pointing with pride*]. That's *my* boy. [*She looks at him in disgust and turns back to her work.*] You know what I was thinking 'bout in the bathroom this morning?

RUTH. No.

WALTER. How come you always try to be so pleasant!

RUTH. What is there to be pleasant 'bout!

WALTER. You want to know what I was thinking 'bout in the bathroom or not!

RUTH. I know what you thinking 'bout.

WALTER [*ignoring her*]. 'Bout what me and Willy Harris was talking about last night.

RUTH [*immediately—a refrain*]. Willy Harris is a good-for-nothing loud mouth.

WALTER. Anybody who talks to me has got to be a good-for-nothing loud mouth, ain't he? And what you know about who is just a good-for-nothing loud mouth? Charlie Atkins was just a "good-for-nothing loud mouth" too, wasn't he! When he wanted me to go in the dry-cleaning business with him. And now—he's grossing a hundred thousand a year. A hundred thousand dollars a year! You still call *him* a loud mouth!

RUTH [*bitterly*]. Oh, Walter Lee. . . . [*She folds her head on her arms over the table.*]

WALTER [*rising and coming to her and standing over her*]. You tired, ain't you? Tired of everything. Me, the boy, the way we live—this beat-up hole—everything. Ain't you? [*She doesn't look up, doesn't answer.*] So tired—moaning and groaning all the time, but you wouldn't do nothing to help, would you? You couldn't be on my side that long for nothing, could you?

RUTH. Walter, please leave me alone.

WALTER. A man needs for a woman to back him up. . . .

RUTH. Walter—

WALTER. Mama would listen to you. You know she listen to you more than she do me and Bennie. She think more of you. All you have to do is just sit down with her when you drinking your coffee one morning and talking 'bout things like you do and—[*he sits down beside her and demonstrates graphically what he thinks her methods and tone should be*]—you just sip your coffee, see, and say easy like that you been thinking 'bout that deal Walter Lee is so interested in, 'bout the store and all, and sip some more coffee, like what you saying ain't really that important to you— And the next thing you know, she be listening good and asking you questions and when I come home—I can tell her the details. This ain't no fly-by-night proposition, baby. I mean we figured it out, me and Willy and Bobo.

RUTH [*with a frown*]. Bobo?

WALTER. Yeah. You see, this little liquor store we got in mind cost seventy-five thousand and we figured the initial investment on the place be 'bout thirty thousand, see. That be ten thousand each. Course, there's a couple of hundred you got to pay so's you don't spend your life just waiting for them clowns to let your license get approved—

RUTH. You mean graft?

WALTER [*frowning impatiently*]. Don't call it that. See there, that just goes to show you what women understand about the world. Baby, don't *nothing* happen for you in this world 'less you pay *somebody* off!

RUTH. Walter, leave me alone! [*She raises her head and stares at him vigorously—then says, more quietly*] Eat your eggs, they gonna be cold.

WALTER [*straightening up from her and looking off*]. That's it. There you are. Man say to his woman: I got me a dream. His woman say: Eat your eggs. [*Sadly, but gaining in power*] Man say: I got to take hold of this here world, baby! And a woman will say: Eat your eggs and go to work. [*Passionately now*] Man say: I got to change my life, I'm choking to death, baby! And his woman say—[*in utter anguish as he brings his fists down on his thighs*]—Your eggs is getting cold!

RUTH [*softly*]. Walter, that ain't none of our money.

WALTER [*not listening at all or even looking at her*]. This morning, I was lookin' in the mirror and thinking about it. . . . I'm thirty-five years old; I been married eleven years and I got a boy who sleeps in the living room—[*very, very quietly*]—and all I got to give him is stories about how rich white people live. . . .

RUTH. Eat your eggs, Walter.

WALTER. *Damn my eggs* . . . *damn all the eggs that ever was!*

RUTH. Then go to work.

WALTER [*looking up at her*]. See—I'm trying to talk to you 'bout myself—[*shaking his head with the repetition*]—and all you can say is eat them eggs and go to work.

RUTH [*wearily*]. Honey, you never say nothing new. I listen to you every day, every night and every morning, and you never say nothing new. [*Shrugging*] So you would rather *be* Mr. Arnold than be his chauffeur. So—I would *rather* be living in Buckingham Palace.

WALTER. That is just what is wrong with the colored woman in this world. . . . Don't understand about building their men up and making 'em feel like they somebody. Like they can do something.

RUTH [*drily, but to hurt*]. There *are* colored men who do things.

WALTER. No thanks to the colored woman.

RUTH. Well, being a colored woman, I guess I can't help myself none.

[*She rises and gets the ironing board and sets it up and attacks a huge pile of rough-dried clothes, sprinkling them in preparation for the ironing and then rolling them into tight fat balls.*]

WALTER [*mumbling*]. We one group of men tied to a race of women with small minds.

[*His sister* BENEATHA *enters. She is about twenty, as slim and intense as her brother. She is not as pretty as her sister-in-law, but her lean, almost intellectual face has a handsomeness of its own. She wears a bright-red flannel nightie, and her thick hair stands wildly about her head. Her speech is a mixture of many things; it is different from the rest of the family's insofar as education has permeated her sense of English—and perhaps the Midwest rather than the South has finally—at last—won out in her inflection; but not altogether, because over all of it is a soft slurring and transformed use of vowels which is the decided influence of the Southside. She passes through the room without looking at either* RUTH *or* WALTER *and goes to the outside door and looks, a little blindly, out to the bathroom. She sees that it has been lost to the Johnsons. She closes the door with a sleepy vengeance and crosses to the table and sits down a little defeated.*]

BENEATHA. I am going to start timing those people.

WALTER. You should get up earlier.

BENEATHA [*her face in her hands. She is still fighting the urge to go back to bed*]. Really—would you suggest dawn? Where's the paper?

WALTER [*pushing the paper across the table to her as he studies her almost clinically, as though he has never seen her before*]. You a horrible-looking chick at this hour.

BENEATHA [*drily*]. Good morning, everybody.

WALTER [*senselessly*]. How is school coming?

BENEATHA [*in the same spirit*]. Lovely. Lovely. And you know, biology is the greatest. [*Looking up at him*] I dissected something that looked just like you yesterday.

WALTER. I just wondered if you've made up your mind and everything.

BENEATHA [*gaining in sharpness and impatience*]. And what did I answer yesterday morning—and the day before that?
RUTH [*from the ironing board, like someone disinterested and old*]. Don't be so nasty, Bennie.
BENEATHA [*still to her brother*]. And the day before that and the day before that!
WALTER [*defensively*]. I'm interested in you. Something wrong with that? Ain't many girls who decide—
WALTER *and* BENEATHA [*in unison*]. —"to be a doctor."

[*Silence.*]

WALTER. Have we figured out yet just exactly how much medical school is going to cost?
RUTH. Walter Lee, why don't you leave that girl alone and get out of here to work?
BENEATHA [*exits to the bathroom and bangs on the door*]. Come on out of there, please! [*She comes back into the room.*]
WALTER [*looking at his sister intently*]. You know the check is coming tomorrow.
BENEATHA [*turning on him with a sharpness all her own*]. That money belongs to Mama, Walter, and it's for her to decide how she wants to use it. I don't care if she wants to buy a house or a rocket ship or just nail it up somewhere and look at it. It's hers. Not ours—*hers*.
WALTER [*bitterly*]. Now ain't that fine! You just got your mother's interest at heart, ain't you, girl? You such a nice girl—but if Mama got that money she can always take a few thousand and help you through school too—can't she?
BENEATHA. I have never asked anyone around here to do anything for me!
WALTER. No! And the line between asking and just accepting when the time comes is big and wide—ain't it!
BENEATHA [*with fury*]. What do you want from me, Brother—that I quit school or just drop dead, which!
WALTER. I don't want nothing but for you to stop acting holy 'round here. Me and Ruth done made some sacrifices for you—why can't you do something for the family?
RUTH. Walter, don't be dragging me in it.
WALTER. You are in it—Don't you get up and go work in somebody's kitchen for the last three years to help put clothes on her back?
RUTH. Oh, Walter—that's not fair. . . .
WALTER. It ain't that nobody expects you to get on your knees and say thank you, Brother; thank you, Ruth; thank you, Mama—and thank you, Travis, for wearing the same pair of shoes for two semesters—

BENEATHA [*dropping to her knees*]. Well—I *do*—all right?—thank everybody . . . and forgive me for ever wanting to be anything at all . . . forgive me, forgive me!

RUTH. Please stop it! Your mama'll hear you.

WALTER. Who the hell told you you had to be a doctor? If you so crazy 'bout messing 'round with sick people—then go be a nurse like other women—or just get married and be quiet. . . .

BENEATHA. Well—you finally got it said. . . . It took you three years but you finally got it said. Walter, give up; leave me alone—it's Mama's money.

WALTER. *He was my father, too!*

BENEATHA. So what? He was mine, too—and Travis' grandfather—but the insurance money belongs to Mama. Picking on me is not going to make her give it to you to invest in any liquor stores—[*under-breath, dropping into a chair*]—and I for one say, God bless Mama for that!

WALTER [*to* RUTH]. See—did you hear? Did you hear!

RUTH. Honey, please go to work.

WALTER. Nobody in this house is ever going to understand me.

BENEATHA. Because you're a nut.

WALTER. Who's a nut?

BENEATHA. You—you are a nut. Thee is mad, boy.

WALTER [*looking at his wife and his sister from the door, very sadly*]. The world's most backward race of people, and that's a fact.

BENEATHA [*turning slowly in her chair*]. And then there are all those prophets who would lead us out of the wilderness—[WALTER *slams out of the house.*]—into the swamps!

RUTH. Bennie, why you always gotta be pickin' on your brother? Can't you be a little sweeter sometimes? [*Door opens.* WALTER *walks in.*]

WALTER [*to* RUTH]. I need some money for carfare.

RUTH [*looks at him, then warms; teasing, but tenderly*]. Fifty cents? [*She goes to her bag and gets money.*] Here, take a taxi.

[WALTER *exits.* MAMA *enters. She is a woman in her early sixties, full-bodied and strong. She is one of those women of a certain grace and beauty who wear it so unobtrusively that it takes a while to notice. Her dark-brown face is surrounded by the total whiteness of her hair, and, being a woman who has adjusted to many things in life and overcome many more, her face is full of strength. She has, we can see, wit and faith of a kind that keep her eyes lit and full of interest and expectancy. She is, in a word, a beautiful woman. Her bearing is perhaps most like the noble bearing of the women of the Hereros of Southwest Africa—rather as if she imagines that as she walks she still bears a basket or a vessel upon her head. Her speech, on the other hand, is as careless as her carriage is precise—she is inclined to slur everything—but her voice is perhaps not so much quiet as simply soft.*]

MAMA. Who that 'round here slamming doors at this hour?

[*She crosses through the room, goes to the window, opens it, and brings in a feeble little plant growing doggedly in a small pot on the window sill. She feels the dirt and puts it back out.*]

RUTH. That was Walter Lee. He and Bennie was at it again.
MAMA. My children and they tempers. Lord, if this little old plant don't get more sun than it's been getting it ain't never going to see spring again. [*She turns from the window.*] What's the matter with you this morning, Ruth? You looks right peaked. You aiming to iron all them things? Leave some for me. I'll get to 'em this afternoon. Bennie honey, it's too drafty for you to be sitting 'round half dressed. Where's your robe?
BENEATHA. In the cleaners.
MAMA. Well, go get mine and put it on.
BENEATHA. I'm not cold, Mama, honest.
MAMA. I know—but you so thin. . . .
BENEATHA [*irritably*]. Mama, I'm not cold.
MAMA [*seeing the make-down bed as* TRAVIS *has left it*]. Lord have mercy, look at that poor bed. Bless his heart—he tries, don't he? [*She moves to the bed* TRAVIS *has sloppily made up.*]
RUTH. No—he don't half try at all 'cause he knows you going to come along behind him and fix everything. That's just how come he don't know how to do nothing right now—you done spoiled that boy so.
MAMA. Well—he's a little boy. Ain't supposed to know 'bout housekeeping. My baby, that's what he is. What you fix for his breakfast this morning?
RUTH [*angrily*]. I feed my son, Lena!
MAMA. I ain't meddling—[*underbreath; busy-bodyish*] I just noticed all last week he had cold cereal, and when it starts getting this chilly in the fall a child ought to have some hot grits or something when he goes out in the cold—
RUTH [*furious*]. I gave him hot oats—is that all right!
MAMA. I ain't meddling. [*Pause.*] Put a lot of nice butter on it? [RUTH *shoots her an angry look and does not reply.*] He likes lots of butter.
RUTH [*exasperated*]. Lena—
MAMA [*to* BENEATHA. MAMA *is inclined to wander conversationally some-*

times]. What was you and your brother fussing 'bout this morning?
BENEATHA. It's not important, Mama.

[*She gets up and goes to look out at the bathroom, which is apparently free, and she picks up her towels and rushes out.*]

MAMA. What was they fighting about?
RUTH. Now you know as well as I do.
MAMA [*shaking her head*]. Brother still worrying his self sick about that money?
RUTH. You know he is.
MAMA. You had breakfast?
RUTH. Some coffee.
MAMA. Girl, you better start eating and looking after yourself better. You almost thin as Travis.
RUTH. Lena—
MAMA. Un-hunh?
RUTH. What are you going to do with it?
MAMA. Now don't you start, child. It's too early in the morning to be talking about money. It ain't Christian.
RUTH. It's just that he got his heart set on that store—
MAMA. You mean that liquor store that Willy Harris want him to invest in?
RUTH. Yes—
MAMA. We ain't no business people, Ruth. We just plain working folks.
RUTH. Ain't nobody business people till they go into business. Walter Lee say colored people ain't never going to start getting ahead till they start gambling on some different kinds of things in the world—investments and things.
MAMA. What done got into you, girl? Walter Lee done finally sold you on investing.
RUTH. No. Mama, something is happening between Walter and me. I don't know what it is—but he needs something—something I can't give him any more. He needs this chance, Lena.
MAMA [*frowning deeply*]. But liquor, honey—
RUTH. Well—like Walter say—I spec people going to always be drinking themselves some liquor.
MAMA. Well—whether they drinks it or not ain't none of my business. But whether I go into business selling it to 'em *is,* and I don't want that on my ledger this late in life. [*Stopping suddenly and studying her daughter-in-law*] Ruth Younger, what's the matter with you today? You look like you could fall over right there.
RUTH. I'm tired.

MAMA. Then you better stay home from work today.

RUTH. I can't stay home. She'd be calling up the agency and screaming at them, "My girl didn't come in today—send me somebody! My girl didn't come in!" Oh, she just have a fit. . . .

MAMA. Well, let her have it. I'll just call her up and say you got the flu—

RUTH [*laughing*]. Why the flu?

MAMA. 'Cause it sounds respectable to 'em. Something white people get, too. They know 'bout the flu. Otherwise they think you been cut up or something when you tell 'em you sick.

RUTH. I got to go in. We need the money.

MAMA. Somebody would of thought my children done all but starved to death the way they talk about money here late. Child, we got a great big old check coming tomorrow.

RUTH [*sincerely, but also self-righteously*]. Now that's your money. It ain't got nothing to do with me. We all feel like that—Walter and Bennie and me—even Travis.

MAMA [*thoughtfully, and suddenly very far away*]. Ten thousand dollars—

RUTH. Sure is wonderful.

MAMA. Ten thousand dollars.

RUTH. You know what you should do, Miss Lena? You should take yourself a trip somewhere. To Europe or South America or someplace—

MAMA [*throwing up her hands at the thought*]. Oh, child!

RUTH. I'm serious. Just pack up and leave! Go on away and enjoy yourself some. Forget about the family and have yourself a ball for once in your life—

MAMA [*drily*]. You sound like I'm just about ready to die. Who'd go with me? What I look like wandering 'round Europe by myself?

RUTH. Shoot—these here rich white women do it all the time. They don't think nothing of packing up they suitcases and piling on one of them big steamships and—swoosh!—they gone, child.

MAMA. Something always told me I wasn't no rich white woman.

RUTH. Well—what are you going to do with it then?

MAMA. I ain't rightly decided. [*Thinking. She speaks now with emphasis.*] Some of it got to be put away for Beneatha and her schoolin'—and ain't nothing going to touch that part of it. Nothing. [*She waits several seconds, trying to make up her mind about something, and looks at* RUTH *a little tentatively before going on.*] Been thinking that we maybe could meet the notes on a little old two-story somewhere, with a yard where Travis could play in the summertime, if we use part of the insurance for a down payment and everybody kind of pitch in. I could maybe take on a little day work again, few days a week—

RUTH [*studying her mother-in-law furtively and concentrating on her ironing, anxious to encourage without seeming to*]. Well, Lord knows, we've put enough rent into this here rat trap to pay for four houses by now. . . .

MAMA [*looking up at the words "rat trap" and then looking around and leaning back and sighing—in a suddenly reflective mood—*]. "Rat trap"—yes, that's all it is. [*Smiling*] I remember just as well the day me and Big Walter moved in here. Hadn't been married but two weeks and wasn't planning on living here no more than a year. [*She shakes her head at the dissolved dream.*] We was going to set away, little by little, don't you know, and buy a little place out in Morgan Park. We had even picked out the house. [*Chuckling a little*] Looks right dumpy today. But Lord, child, you should know all the dreams I had 'bout buying that house and fixing it up and making me a little garden in the back—[*She waits and stops smiling.*] And didn't none of it happen. [*Dropping her hands in a futile gesture*]

RUTH [*keeps her head down, ironing*]. Yes, life can be a barrel of disappointments, sometimes.

MAMA. Honey, Big Walter would come in here some nights back then and slump down on that couch there and just look at the rug, and look at me and look at the rug and then back at me—and I'd know he was down then . . . really down. [*After a second very long and thoughtful pause; she is seeing back to times that only she can see.*] And then, Lord, when I lost that baby—little Claude—I almost thought I was going to lose Big Walter too. Oh, that man grieved hisself! He was one man to love his children.

RUTH. Ain't nothin' can tear at you like losin' your baby.

MAMA. I guess that's how come that man finally worked hisself to death like he done. Like he was fighting his own war with this here world that took his baby from him.

RUTH. He sure was a fine man, all right. I always liked Mr. Younger.

MAMA. Crazy 'bout his children! God knows there was plenty wrong with Walter Younger—hard-headed, mean, kind of wild with women—plenty wrong with him. But he sure loved his children. Always wanted them to have something—be something. That's where Brother gets all these notions, I reckon. Big Walter used to say, he'd get right wet in the eyes sometimes, lean his head back with the water standing in his eyes and say, "Seem like God didn't see fit to give the black man nothing but dreams—but He did give us children to make them dreams seem worth while." [*She smiles.*] He could talk like that, don't you know.

RUTH. Yes, he sure could. He was a good man, Mr. Younger.
MAMA. Yes, a fine man—just couldn't never catch up with his dreams, that's all.

[BENEATHA *comes in, brushing her hair and looking up to the ceiling, where the sound of a vacuum cleaner has started up.*]

BENEATHA. What could be so dirty on that woman's rugs that she has to vacuum them every single day?
RUTH. I wish certain young women 'round here who I could name would take inspiration about certain rugs in a certain apartment I could also mention.
BENEATHA [*shrugging*]. How much cleaning can a house need, for Christ's sakes.
MAMA [*not liking the Lord's name used thus*]. Bennie!
RUTH. Just listen to her—just listen!
BENEATHA. Oh, God!
MAMA. If you use the Lord's name just one more time—
BENEATHA [*a bit of a whine*]. Oh, Mama—
RUTH. Fresh—just fresh as salt, this girl!
BENEATHA [*drily*]. Well—if the salt loses its savor—
MAMA. Now that will do. I just ain't going to have you 'round here reciting the scriptures in vain—you hear me?
BENEATHA. How did I manage to get on everybody's wrong side by just walking into a room?
RUTH. If you weren't so fresh—
BENEATHA. Ruth, I'm twenty years old.
MAMA. What time you be home from school today?
BENEATHA. Kind of late. [*With enthusiasm*] Madeline is going to start my guitar lessons today.

[MAMA *and* RUTH *look up with the same expression.*]

MAMA. Your *what* kind of lessons?
BENEATHA. Guitar.
RUTH. Oh, Father!
MAMA. How come you done taken it in your mind to learn to play the guitar?
BENEATHA. I just want to, that's all.
MAMA [*smiling*]. Lord, child, don't you know what to do with yourself? How long it going to be before you get tired of this now—like you got tired of that little play-acting group you joined last year? [*Looking at* RUTH] And what was it the year before that?
RUTH. The horseback-riding club for which she bought that fifty-five-dollar riding habit that's been hanging in the closet ever since!

MAMA [*to* BENEATHA]. Why you got to flit so from one thing to another, baby?
BENEATHA [*sharply*]. I just want to learn to play the guitar. Is there anything wrong with that?
MAMA. Ain't nobody trying to stop you. I just wonders sometimes why you has to flit so from one thing to another all the time. You ain't never done nothing with all that camera equipment you brought home—
BENEATHA. I don't flit! I—I experiment with different forms of expression—
RUTH. Like riding a horse?
BENEATHA. —People have to express themselves one way or another.
MAMA. What is it you want to express?
BENEATHA [*angrily*]. Me! [MAMA *and* RUTH *look at each other and burst into raucous laughter.*] Don't worry—I don't expect you to understand.
MAMA [*to change the subject*]. Who you going out with tomorrow night?
BENEATHA [*with displeasure*]. George Murchison again.
MAMA [*pleased*]. Oh—you getting a little sweet on him?
RUTH. You ask me, this child ain't sweet on nobody but herself— [*Underbreath*] Express herself!

[*They laugh.*]

BENEATHA. Oh—I like George all right, Mama. I mean I like him enough to go out with him and stuff, but—
RUTH [*for devilment*]. What does *and stuff* mean?
BENEATHA. Mind your own business.
MAMA. Stop picking at her now, Ruth. [*A thoughtful pause, and then a suspicious sudden look at her daughter as she turns in her chair for emphasis*] What *does* it mean?
BENEATHA [*wearily*]. Oh, I just mean I couldn't ever really be serious about George. He's—he's so shallow.
RUTH. Shallow—what do you mean he's shallow? He's *rich!*
MAMA. Hush, Ruth.
BENEATHA. I know he's rich. He knows he's rich, too.
RUTH. Well—what other qualities a man got to have to satisfy you, little girl?
BENEATHA. You wouldn't even begin to understand. Anybody who married Walter could not possibly understand.
MAMA [*outraged*]. What kind of way is that to talk about your brother?
BENEATHA. Brother is a flip—let's face it.
MAMA [*to* RUTH, *helplessly*]. What's a flip?

RUTH [*glad to add kindling*]. She's saying he's crazy.
BENEATHA. Not crazy. Brother isn't really crazy yet—he—he's an elaborate neurotic.
MAMA. Hush your mouth!
BENEATHA. As for George. Well. George looks good—he's got a beautiful car and he takes me to nice places and, as my sister-in-law says, he is probably the richest boy I will ever get to know and I even like him sometimes—but if the Youngers are sitting around waiting to see if their little Bennie is going to tie up the family with the Murchisons, they are wasting their time.
RUTH. You mean you wouldn't marry George Murchison if he asked you someday? That pretty, rich thing? Honey, I knew you was odd—
BENEATHA. No I would not marry him if all I felt for him was what I feel now. Besides, George's family wouldn't really like it.
MAMA. Why not?
BENEATHA. Oh, Mama—The Murchisons are honest-to-God-real-*live*-rich colored people, and the only people in the world who are more snobbish than rich white people are rich colored people. I thought everybody knew that. I've met Mrs. Murchison. She's a scene!
MAMA. You must not dislike people 'cause they well off, honey.
BENEATHA. Why not? It makes just as much sense as disliking people 'cause they are poor, and lots of people do that.
RUTH [*a wisdom-of-the-ages manner. To* MAMA]. Well, she'll get over some of this—
BENEATHA. Get over it? What are you talking about, Ruth? Listen, I'm going to be a doctor. I'm not worried about who I'm going to marry yet—if I ever get married.
MAMA *and* RUTH. *If!*
MAMA. Now, Bennie—
BENEATHA. Oh, I probably will . . . but first I'm going to be a doctor, and George, for one, still thinks that's pretty funny. I couldn't be bothered with that, I am going to be a doctor and everybody around here better understand that!
MAMA [*kindly*]. 'Course you going to be a doctor, honey, God willing.
BENEATHA [*drily*]. God hasn't got a thing to do with it.
MAMA. Beneatha—that just wasn't necessary.
BENEATHA. Well—neither is God. I get sick of hearing about God.
MAMA. Beneatha!
BENEATHA. I mean it! I'm just tired of hearing about God all the time. What has He got to do with anything? Does he pay tuition?
MAMA. You 'bout to get your fresh little jaw slapped!
RUTH. That's just what she needs, all right!

BENEATHA. Why? Why can't I say what I want to around here, like everybody else?
MAMA. It don't sound nice for a young girl to say things like that—you wasn't brought up that way. Me and your father went to trouble to get you and Brother to church every Sunday.
BENEATHA. Mama, you don't understand. It's all a matter of ideas, and God is just one idea I don't accept. It's not important. I am not going out and be immoral or commit crimes because I don't believe in God. I don't even think about it. It's just that I get tired of Him getting credit for all the things the human race achieves through its own stubborn effort. There simply is no blasted God—there is only man and it is he who makes miracles!

[MAMA *absorbs this speech, studies her daughter and rises slowly and crosses to* BENEATHA *and slaps her powerfully across the face. After, there is only silence and the daughter drops her eyes from her mother's face, and* MAMA *is very tall before her.*]

MAMA. Now—you say after me, in my mother's house there is still God. [*There is a long pause and* BENEATHA *stares at the floor wordlessly.* MAMA *repeats the phrase with precision and cool emotion.*] In my mother's house there is still God.
BENEATHA. In my mother's house there is still God.

[*A long pause*]

MAMA [*walking away from* BENEATHA, *too disturbed for triumphant posture. Stopping and turning back to her daughter*]. There are some ideas we ain't going to have in this house. Not long as I am at the head of this family.
BENEATHA. Yes, ma'am.

[MAMA *walks out of the room.*]

RUTH [*almost gently, with profound understanding*]. You think you a woman, Bennie—but you still a little girl. What you did was childish—so you got treated like a child.
BENEATHA. I see. [*Quietly*] I also see that everybody thinks it's all right for Mama to be a tyrant. But all the tyranny in the world will never put a God in the heavens! [*She picks up her books and goes out.*]
RUTH [*goes to* MAMA's *door*]. She said she was sorry.
MAMA [*coming out, going to her plant*]. They frightens me, Ruth. My children.
RUTH. You got good children, Lena. They just a little off sometimes—but they're good.
MAMA. No—there's something come down between me and them that

don't let us understand each other and I don't know what it is. One done almost lost his mind thinking 'bout money all the time and the other done commence to talk about things I can't seem to understand in no form or fashion. What is it that's changing, Ruth?

RUTH [*soothingly, older than her years*]. Now . . . you taking it all too seriously. You just got strong-willed children and it takes a strong woman like you to keep 'em in hand.

MAMA [*looking at her plant and sprinkling a little water on it*]. They spirited all right, my children. Got to admit they got spirit—Bennie and Walter. Like this little old plant that ain't never had enough sunshine or nothing—and look at it. . . .

[*She has her back to* RUTH, *who has had to stop ironing and lean against something and put the back of her hand to her forehead.*]

RUTH [*trying to keep* MAMA *from noticing*]. You . . . sure . . . loves that little old thing, don't you? . . .

MAMA. Well, I always wanted me a garden like I used to see sometimes at the back of the houses down home. This plant is close as I ever got to having one. [*She looks out of the window as she replaces the plant.*] Lord, ain't nothing as dreary as the view from this window on a dreary day, is there? Why ain't you singing this morning, Ruth? Sing that "No Ways Tired." That song always lifts me up so— [*She turns at last to see that* RUTH *has slipped quietly into a chair, in a state of semiconsciousness.*] Ruth! Ruth honey—what's the matter with you . . . Ruth!

CURTAIN

SCENE 2. *It is the following morning; a Saturday morning, and house cleaning is in progress at the* YOUNGERS. *Furniture has been shoved hither and yon and* MAMA *is giving the kitchen-area walls a washing down.* BENEATHA, *in dungarees, with a handkerchief tied around her face, is spraying insecticide into the cracks in the walls. As they work, the radio is on and a Southside disc-jockey program is inappropriately filling the house with a rather exotic saxophone blues.* TRAVIS, *the sole idle one, is leaning on his arms, looking out of the window.*

TRAVIS. Grandmama, that stuff Bennie is using smells awful. Can I go downstairs, please?

MAMA. Did you get all them chores done already? I ain't seen you doing much.

TRAVIS. Yes'm—finished early. Where did Mama go this morning?

MAMA [*looking at* BENEATHA]. She had to go on a little errand.

TRAVIS. Where?
MAMA. To tend to her business.
TRAVIS. Can I go outside then?
MAMA. Oh, I guess so. You better stay right in front of the house, though . . . and keep a good lookout for the postman.
TRAVIS. Yes'm. [*He starts out and decides to give his* AUNT BENEATHA *a good swat on the legs as he passes her.*] Leave them poor little old cockroaches alone, they ain't bothering you none.

[*He runs as she swings the spray gun at him both viciously and playfully.* WALTER *enters from the bedroom and goes to the phone.*]

MAMA. Look out there, girl, before you be spilling some of that stuff on that child!
TRAVIS [*teasing*]. That's right—look out now! [*He exits.*]
BENEATHA [*drily*]. I can't imagine that it would hurt him—it has never hurt the roaches.
MAMA. Well, little boys' hides ain't as tough as Southside roaches.
WALTER [*into phone*]. Hello—Let me talk to Willy Harris.
MAMA. You better get over there behind the bureau. I seen one marching out of there like Napoleon yesterday.
WALTER. Hello, Willy? It ain't come yet. It'll be here in a few minutes. Did the lawyer give you the papers?
BENEATHA. There's really only one way to get rid of them, Mama—
MAMA. How?
BENEATHA. Set fire to this building.
WALTER. Good. Good. I'll be right over.
BENEATHA. Where did Ruth go, Walter?
WALTER. I don't know. [*He exits abruptly.*]
BENEATHA. Mama, where did Ruth go?
MAMA [*looking at her with meaning*]. To the doctor, I think.
BENEATHA. The doctor? What's the matter? [*They exchange glances.*] You don't think—
MAMA [*with her sense of drama*]. Now I ain't saying what I think. But I ain't never been wrong 'bout a woman neither.

[*The phone rings.*]

BENEATHA [*at the phone*]. Hay-lo . . . [*Pause, and a moment of recognition*] Well—when did you get back! . . . And how was it? . . . Of course I've missed you—in my way. . . . This morning? No . . . house cleaning and all that and Mama hates it if I let people come over when the house is like this. . . . You *have?* Well, that's different. . . . What is it— Oh, what the hell, come on over. . . . Right, see you then. [*She hangs up.*]

MAMA [*who has listened vigorously, as is her habit*]. Who is that you inviting over here with this house looking like this? You ain't got the pride you was born with!

BENEATHA. Asagai doesn't care how houses look, Mama—he's an intellectual.

MAMA. *Who?*

BENEATHA. Asagai—Joseph Asagai. He's an African boy I met on campus. He's been studying in Canada all summer.

MAMA. What's his name?

BENEATHA. Asagai, Joseph. Ah-sah-guy . . . He's from Nigeria.

MAMA. Oh, that's the little country that was founded by slaves way back. . . .

BENEATHA. No, Mama—that's Liberia.

MAMA. I don't think I never met no African before.

BENEATHA. Well, do me a favor and don't ask him a whole lot of ignorant questions about Africans. I mean, do they wear clothes and all that—

MAMA. Well, now, I guess if you think we so ignorant 'round here maybe you shouldn't bring your friends here—

BENEATHA. It's just that people ask such crazy things. All anyone seems to know about when it comes to Africa is Tarzan—

MAMA [*indignantly*]. Why should I know anything about Africa?

BENEATHA. Why do you give money at church for the missionary work?

MAMA. Well, that's to help save people.

BENEATHA. You mean save them from *heathenism*—

MAMA [*innocently*]. Yes.

BENEATHA. I'm afraid they need more salvation from the British and the French.

[RUTH *comes in forlornly and pulls off her coat with dejection. They both turn to look at her.*]

RUTH [*dispiritedly*]. Well, I guess from all the happy faces—everybody knows.

BENEATHA. You pregnant?

MAMA. Lord have mercy, I sure hope it's a little old girl. Travis ought to have a sister.

[BENEATHA *and* RUTH *give her a hopeless look for this grandmotherly enthusiasm.*]

BENEATHA. How far along are you?

RUTH. Two months.

BENEATHA. Did you mean to? I mean did you plan it or was it an accident?

MAMA. What do you know about planning or not planning?
BENEATHA. Oh, Mama.
RUTH [*wearily*]. She's twenty years old, Lena.
BENEATHA. Did you plan it, Ruth?
RUTH. Mind your own business.
BENEATHA. It is my business—where is he going to live, on the *roof?* [*There is silence following the remark as the three women react to the sense of it.*] Gee—I didn't mean that, Ruth, honest. Gee, I don't feel like that at all. I—I think it is wonderful.
RUTH [*dully*]. Wonderful.
BENEATHA. Yes—really.
MAMA [*looking at* RUTH, *worried*]. Doctor say everything going to be all right?
RUTH [*far away*]. Yes—she says everything is going to be fine. . . .
MAMA [*immediately suspicious*]. "She"—What doctor you went to?

[RUTH *folds over, near hysteria.*]

MAMA [*worriedly hovering over* RUTH]. Ruth honey—what's the matter with you—you sick?

[RUTH *has her fists clenched on her thighs and is fighting hard to suppress a scream that seems to be rising in her.*]

BENEATHA. What's the matter with her, Mama?
MAMA [*working her fingers in* RUTH's *shoulder to relax her*]. She be all right. Women gets right depressed sometimes when they get her way. [*Speaking softly, expertly, rapidly*] Now you just relax. That's right . . . just lean back, don't think 'bout nothing at all . . . nothing at all—
RUTH. I'm all right. . . .

[*The glassy-eyed look melts and then she collapses into a fit of heavy sobbing. The bell rings.*]

BENEATHA. Oh, my God—that must be Asagai.
MAMA [*to* RUTH]. Come on now, honey. You need to lie down and rest awhile . . . then have some nice hot food.

[*They exit,* RUTH's *weight on her mother-in-law.* BENEATHA, *herself profoundly disturbed, opens the door to admit a rather dramatic-looking young man with a large package.*]

ASAGAI. Hello, Alaiyo—
BENEATHA [*holding the door open and regarding him with pleasure*]. Hello . . . [*Long pause*] Well—come in. And please excuse every-

thing. My mother was very upset about my letting anyone come here with the place like this.

ASAGAI [*coming into the room*]. You look disturbed too. . . . Is something wrong?

BENEATHA [*still at the door, absently*]. Yes . . . we've all got acute ghetto-itus. [*She smiles and comes toward him, finding a cigarette and sitting.*] So—sit down! How was Canada?

ASAGAI [*a sophisticate*]. Canadian.

BENEATHA [*looking at him*]. I'm very glad you are back.

ASAGAI [*looking back at her in turn*]. Are you really?

BENEATHA. Yes—very.

ASAGAI. Why—you were quite glad when I went away. What happened?

BENEATHA. You went away.

ASAGAI. Ahhhhhhhh.

BENEATHA. Before—you wanted to be so serious before there was time.

ASAGAI. How much time must there be before one knows what one feels?

BENEATHA [*stalling this particular conversation. Her hands pressed together, in a deliberately childish gesture*]. What did you bring me?

ASAGAI [*handing her the package*]. Open it and see.

BENEATHA [*eagerly opening the package and drawing out some records and the colorful robes of a Nigerian woman*]. Oh, Asagai! . . . You got them for me! . . . How beautiful . . . and the records too! [*She lifts out the robes and runs to the mirror with them and holds the drapery up in front of herself.*]

ASAGAI [*coming to her at the mirror*]. I shall have to teach you how to drape it properly. [*He flings the material about her for the moment and stands back to look at her.*] Ah—*Oh-pay-gay-day, oh-gbah-mushay.* [*A Yoruba exclamation for admiration*] You wear it well . . . very well . . . mutilated hair and all.

BENEATHA [*turning suddenly*]. My hair—what's wrong with my hair?

ASAGAI [*shrugging*]. Were you born with it like that?

BENEATHA [*reaching up to touch it*]. No . . . of course not. [*She looks back to the mirror, disturbed.*]

ASAGAI [*smiling*]. How then?

BENEATHA. You know perfectly well how . . . as crinkly as yours . . . that's how.

ASAGAI. And it is ugly to you that way?

BENEATHA [*quickly*]. Oh, no—not ugly . . . [*More slowly, apologetically*] But it's so hard to manage when it's, well—raw.

ASAGAI. And so to accommodate that—you mutilate it every week?

BENEATHA. It's not mutilation!
ASAGAI [*laughing aloud at her seriousness*]. Oh . . . please! I am only teasing you because you are so very serious about these things. [*He stands back from her and folds his arms across his chest as he watches her pulling at her hair and frowning in the mirror.*] Do you remember the first time you met me at school? . . . [*He laughs.*] You came up to me and you said—and I thought you were the most serious little thing I had ever seen—you said: [*He imitates her.*] "Mr. Asagai—I want very much to talk with you. About Africa. You see, Mr. Agasai, I am looking for my *identity!*" [*He laughs.*]
BENEATHA [*turning to him, not laughing*]. Yes—[*Her face is quizzical, profoundly disturbed.*]
ASAGAI [*still teasing and reaching out and taking her face in his hands and turning her profile to him*]. Well . . . it is true that this is not so much a profile of a Hollywood queen as perhaps a queen of the Nile—[*A mock dismissal of the importance of the question*] But what does it matter? Assimilationism is so popular in your country.
BENEATHA [*wheeling, passionately, sharply*]. I am not an assimilationist!
ASAGAI [*the protest hangs in the room for a moment and* ASAGAI *studies her, his laughter fading*]. Such a serious one. [*There is a pause.*] So—you like the robes? You must take excellent care of them—they are from my sister's personal wardrobe.
BENEATHA [*with incredulity*]. You—you sent all the way home—for me?
ASAGAI [*with charm*]. For you—I would do much more. . . . Well, that is what I came for. I must go.
BENEATHA. Will you call me Monday?
ASAGAI. Yes . . . We have a great deal to talk about. I mean about identity and time and all that.
BENEATHA. Time?
ASAGAI. Yes. About how much time one needs to know what one feels.
BENEATHA. You never understood that there is more than one kind of feeling which can exist between a man and a woman—or, at least, there should be.
ASAGAI [*shaking his head negatively but gently*]. No. Between a man and a woman there need be only one kind of feeling. I have that for you. . . . Now even . . . right this moment. . . .
BENEATHA. I know—and by itself—it won't do. I can find that anywhere.
ASAGAI. For a woman it should be enough.
BENEATHA. I know—because that's what it says in all the novels that men write. But it isn't. Go ahead and laugh—but I'm not interested

in being someone's little episode in America or—[*with feminine vengeance*]—one of them! [ASAGAI *has burst into laughter again.*] That's funny as hell, huh!

ASAGAI. It's just that every American girl I have known has said that to me. White—black—in this you are all the same. And the same speech, too!

BENEATHA [*angrily*]. Yuk, yuk, yuk!

ASAGAI. It's how you can be sure that the world's most liberated women are not liberated at all. You all talk about it too much!

[MAMA *enters and is immediately all social charm because of the presence of a guest.*]

BENEATHA. Oh—Mama—this is Mr. Asagai.

MAMA. How do you do?

ASAGAI [*total politeness to an elder*]. How do you do, Mrs. Younger. Please forgive me for coming at such an outrageous hour on a Saturday.

MAMA. Well, you are quite welcome. I just hope you understand that our house don't always look like this. [*Chatterish*] You must come again. I would love to hear all about—[*not sure of the name*]—your country. I think it's so sad the way our American Negroes don't know nothing about Africa 'cept Tarzan and all that. And all that money they pour into these churches when they ought to be helping you people over there drive out them French and Englishmen done taken away your land.

[*The mother flashes a slightly superior look at her daughter upon completion of the recitation.*]

ASAGAI [*taken aback by this sudden and acutely unrelated expression of sympathy*]. Yes . . . yes . . . .

MAMA [*smiling at him suddenly and relaxing and looking him over*]. How many miles is it from here to where you come from?

ASAGAI. Many thousands.

MAMA [*looking at him as she would* WALTER]. I bet you don't half look after yourself, being away from your mama either. I spec you better come 'round here from time to time and get yourself some decent home-cooked meals . . . .

ASAGAI [*moved*]. Thank you. Thank you very much. [*They are all quiet, then*—] Well . . . I must go. I will call you Monday, Alaiyo.

MAMA. What's that he call you?

ASAGAI. Oh—"Alaiyo." I hope you don't mind. It is what you would call a nickname, I think. It is a Yoruba word. I am a Yoruba.

MAMA [*looking at* BENEATHA]. I—I thought he was from—

ASAGAI [*understanding*]. Nigeria is my country. Yoruba is my tribal origin—
BENEATHA. You didn't tell us what Alaiyo means . . . for all I know, you might be calling me Little Idiot or something . . . .
ASAGAI. Well . . . let me see . . . I do not know how just to explain it. . . . The sense of a thing can be so different when it changes languages.
BENEATHA. You're evading.
ASAGAI. No—really it is difficult. . . . [*Thinking*] It means . . . it means One for Whom Bread—Food—Is Not Enough. [*He looks at her.*] Is that all right?
BENEATHA [*understanding, softly*]. Thank you.
MAMA [*looking from one to the other and not understanding any of it*]. Well . . . that's nice. . . . You must come see us again—Mr.—
ASAGAI. Ah-sah-guy . . .
MAMA. Yes . . . Do come again.
ASAGAI. Good-bye. [*He exits.*]
MAMA [*after him*]. Lord, that's a pretty thing just went out here! [*Insinuatingly, to her daughter*] Yes, I guess I see why we done commence to get so interested in Africa 'round here. Missionaries my aunt Jenny! [*She exits.*]
BENEATHA. Oh, Mama! . . .

[*She picks up the Nigerian dress and holds it up to her in front of the mirror again. She sets the headdress on haphazardly and then notices her hair again and clutches at it and then replaces the headdress and frowns at herself. Then she starts to wriggle in front of the mirror as she thinks a Nigerian woman might.* TRAVIS *enters and regards her.*]

TRAVIS. You cracking up?
BENEATHA. Shut up.

[*She pulls the headdress off and looks at herself in the mirror and clutches at her hair again and squinches her eyes as if trying to imagine something. Then, suddenly, she gets her raincoat and kerchief and hurriedly prepares for going out.*]

MAMA [*coming back into the room*]. She's resting now. Travis, baby, run next door and ask Miss Johnson to please let me have a little kitchen cleanser. This here can is empty as Jacob's kettle.
TRAVIS. I just come in.
MAMA. Do as you told. [*He exits and she looks at her daughter.*] Where you going?
BENEATHA [*halting at the door*]. To become a queen of the Nile!

[*She exits in a breathless blaze of glory.* RUTH *appears in the bedroom doorway.*]

MAMA. Who told you to get up?
RUTH. Ain't nothing wrong with me to be lying in no bed for. Where did Bennie go?
MAMA [*drumming her fingers*]. Far as I could make out—to Egypt. [RUTH *just looks at her.*] What time is it getting to?
RUTH. Ten twenty. And the mailman going to ring that bell this morning just like he done every morning for the last umpteen years.

[TRAVIS *comes in with the cleanser can.*]

TRAVIS. She say to tell you that she don't have much.
MAMA [*angrily*]. Lord, some people I could name sure is tight-fisted! [*Directing her grandson*] Mark two cans of cleanser down on the list there. If she that hard up for kitchen cleanser, I sure don't want to forget to get her none!
RUTH. Lena—maybe the woman is just short on cleanser—
MAMA [*not listening*]. —Much baking powder as she done borrowed from me all these years, she could of done gone into the baking business!

[*The bell sounds suddenly and sharply and all three are stunned—serious and silent—mid-speech. In spite of all the other conversations and distractions of the morning, this is what they have been waiting for, even* TRAVIS, *who looks helplessly from his mother to his grandmother.* RUTH *is the first to come to life again.*]

RUTH [*to* TRAVIS]. Get down them steps, boy!

[TRAVIS *snaps to life and flies out to get the mail.*]

MAMA [*her eyes wide, her hand to her breast*]. You mean it done really come?
RUTH [*excitedly*]. Oh, Miss Lena!
MAMA [*collecting herself*]. Well . . . I don't know what we all so excited about 'round here for. We known it was coming for months.
RUTH. That's a whole lot different from having it come and being able to hold it in your hands . . . a piece of paper worth ten thousand dollars. . . . [TRAVIS *bursts back into the room. He holds the envelope high above his head, like a little dancer, his face is radiant and he is breathless. He moves to his grandmother with sudden slow ceremony and puts the envelope into her hands. She accepts it, and then merely holds it and looks at it.*] Come on! Open it . . . Lord have mercy, I wish Walter Lee was here!

TRAVIS. Open it, Grandmama!
MAMA [*staring at it*]. Now you all be quiet. It's just a check.
RUTH. *Open it.* . . .
MAMA [*still staring at it*]. Now don't act silly. . . . We ain't never been no people to act silly 'bout no money—
RUTH [*swiftly*]. We ain't never had none before—*open it!*

[MAMA *finally makes a good strong tear and pulls out the thin blue slice of paper and inspects it closely. The boy and his mother study it raptly over* MAMA's *shoulders.*]

MAMA. *Travis!* [*She is counting off with doubt.*] Is that the right number of zeros.
TRAVIS. Yes'm . . . ten thousand dollars. Gaalee, Grandmama, you rich.
MAMA [*She holds the check away from her, still looking at it. Slowly her face sobers into a mask of unhappiness*]. Ten thousand dollars. [*She hands it to* RUTH.] Put it away somewhere, Ruth. [*She does not look at* RUTH; *her eyes seem to be seeing something somewhere very far off.*] Ten thousand dollars they give you. Ten thousand dollars.
TRAVIS [*to his mother, sincerely*]. What's the matter with Grandmama —don't she want to be rich?
RUTH [*distractedly*]. You go on out and play now, baby. [TRAVIS *exits.* MAMA *starts wiping dishes absently, humming intently to herself.* RUTH *turns to her, with kind exasperation.*] You're gone and got yourself upset.
MAMA [*not looking at her*]. I spec if it wasn't for you all . . . I would just put that money away or give it to the church or something.
RUTH. Now what kind of talk is that. Mr. Younger would just be plain mad if he could hear you talking foolish like that.
MAMA [*stopping and staring off*]. Yes . . . he sure would. [*Sighing*] We got enough to do with that money, all right. [*She halts then, and turns and looks at her daughter-in-law hard;* RUTH *avoids her eyes and* MAMA *wipes her hands with finality and starts to speak firmly to* RUTH.] Where did you go today, girl?
RUTH. To the doctor.
MAMA [*impatiently*]. Now, Ruth . . . you know better than that. Old Doctor Jones is strange enough in his way but there ain't nothing 'bout him make somebody slip and call him "she"—like you done this morning.
RUTH. Well, that's what happened—my tongue slipped.
MAMA. You went to see that woman, didn't you?
RUTH. [*defensively, giving herself away*]. What woman you talking about?
MAMA [*angrily*]. That woman who—

[WALTER *enters in great excitement.*]

WALTER. Did it come?

MAMA [*quietly*]. Can't you give people a Christian greeting before you start asking about money?

WALTER [*to* RUTH]. Did it come? [RUTH *unfolds the check and lays it quietly before him, watching him intently with thoughts of her own.* WALTER *sits down and grasps it close and counts off the zeros.*] Ten thousand dollars— [*He turns suddenly, frantically to his mother and draws some papers out of his breast pocket.*] Mama—look. Old Willy Harris put everything on paper—

MAMA. Son—I think you ought to talk to your wife. . . . I'll go on out and leave you alone if you want—

WALTER. I can talk to her later— Mama, look—

MAMA. Son—

WALTER. WILL SOMEBODY PLEASE LISTEN TO ME TODAY!

MAMA [*quietly*]. I don't 'low no yellin' in this house, Walter Lee, and you know it— [WALTER *stares at them in frustration and starts to speak several times.*] And there ain't going to be no investing in no liquor stores. I don't aim to have to speak on that again.

[*A long pause*]

WALTER. Oh—so you don't aim to have to speak on that again? So *you* have decided. . . . [*Crumpling his papers*] Well, *you* tell that to my boy tonight when you put him to sleep on the living-room couch. . . . [*Turning to* MAMA *and speaking directly to her*] Yeah—and tell it to my wife, Mama, tomorrow when she has to go out of here to look after somebody else's kids. And tell it to *me,* Mama, every time we need a new pair of curtains and I have to watch *you* go out and work in somebody's kitchen. Yeah, you tell me then!

[WALTER *starts out.*]

RUTH. Where you going?

WALTER. I'm going out!

RUTH. Where?

WALTER. Just out of this house somewhere—

RUTH [*getting her coat*]. I'll come too.

WALTER. I don't want you to come!

RUTH. I got something to talk to you about, Walter.

WALTER. That's too bad.

MAMA [*still quietly*]. Walter Lee— [*She waits and he finally turns and looks at her.*] Sit down.

WALTER. I'm a grown man, Mama.

MAMA. Ain't nobody said you wasn't grown. But you still in my house and my presence. And as long as you are—you'll talk to your wife civil. Now sit down.
RUTH [*suddenly*]. Oh, let him go on out and drink himself to death! He makes me sick to my stomach! [*She flings her coat against him.*]
WALTER [*violently*]. And you turn mine too, baby! [RUTH *goes into their bedroom and slams the door behind her.*] That was my greatest mistake—
MAMA [*still quietly*]. Walter, what is the matter with you?
WALTER. Matter with me? Ain't nothing the matter with *me!*
MAMA. Yes there is. Something eating you up like a crazy man. Something more than me not giving you this money. The past few years I been watching it happen to you. You get all nervous acting and kind of wild in the eyes— [WALTER *jumps up impatiently at her words.*] I said sit there now, I'm talking to you!
WALTER. Mama—I don't need no nagging at me today.
MAMA. Seem like you getting to a place where you always tied up in some kind of knot about something. But if anybody ask you 'bout it you just yell at 'em and bust out the house and go out and drink somewheres. Walter Lee, people can't live with that. Ruth's a good, patient girl in her way—but you getting to be too much. Boy, don't make the mistake of driving that girl away from you.
WALTER. Why—what she do for me?
MAMA. She loves you.
WALTER. Mama—I'm going out. I want to go off somewhere and be by myself for a while.
MAMA. I'm sorry 'bout your liquor store, son. It just wasn't the thing for us to do. That's what I want to tell you about—
WALTER. I got to go out, Mama— [*He rises.*]
MAMA. It's dangerous, son.
WALTER. What's dangerous?
MAMA. When a man goes outside his home to look for peace.
WALTER [*beseechingly*]. Then why can't there never be no peace in this house then?
MAMA. You done found it in some other house?
WALTER. No—there ain't no woman! Why do women always think there's a woman somewhere when a man gets restless. [*Coming to her*] Mama—Mama—I want so many things . . . .
MAMA. Yes, son—
WALTER. I want so many things that they are driving me kind of crazy. . . . Mama—look at me.
MAMA. I'm looking at you. You a good-looking boy. You got a job, a nice wife, a fine boy and—

WALTER. A job. [*Looks at her*] Mama, a job? I open and close car doors all day long. I drive a man around in his limousine and I say, "Yes, sir; no, sir; very good, sir; shall I take the Drive, sir?" Mama, that ain't no kind of job . . . that ain't nothing at all. [*Very quietly*] Mama, I don't know if I can make you understand.

MAMA. Understand what, baby?

WALTER [*quietly*]. Sometimes it's like I can see the future stretched out in front of me—just plain as day. The future, Mama. Hanging over there at the edge of my days. Just waiting for me—a big, looming blank space—full of *nothing*. Just waiting for *me*. [*Pause*] Mama—sometimes when I'm downtown and I pass them cool, quiet-looking restaurants where them white boys are sitting back and talking 'bout things . . . sitting there turning deals worth millions of dollars . . . sometimes I see guys don't look much older than me—

MAMA. Son—how come you talk so much 'bout money?

WALTER [*with immense passion*]. Because it is life, Mama!

MAMA [*quietly*]. Oh— [*Very quietly*] So now it's life. Money is life. Once upon a time freedom used to be life—now it's money. I guess the world really do change . . . .

WALTER. No—it was always money, Mama. We just didn't know about it.

MAMA. No . . . something has changed. [*She looks at him.*] You something new, boy. In my time we was worried about not being lynched and getting to the North if we could and how to stay alive and still have a pinch of dignity too. . . . Now here come you and Beneatha—talking 'bout things we ain't never even thought about hardly, me and your daddy. You ain't satisfied or proud of nothing we done. I mean that you had a home; that we kept you out of trouble till you was grown; that you don't have to ride to work on the back of nobody's streetcar—You my children—but how different we done become.

WALTER. You just don't understand, Mama, you just don't understand.

MAMA. Son—do you know your wife is expecting another baby? [WALTER *stands, stunned, and absorbs what his mother has said.*] That's what she wanted to talk to you about. [WALTER *sinks down into a chair.*] This ain't for me to be telling—but you ought to know. [*She waits.*] I think Ruth is thinking 'bout getting rid of that child.

WALTER [*slowly understanding*]. No—no—Ruth wouldn't do that.

MAMA. When the world gets ugly enough—a woman will do anything for her family. *The part that's already living.*

WALTER. You don't know Ruth, Mama, if you think she would do that.

[RUTH *opens the bedroom door and stands there a little limp.*]

RUTH [*beaten*]. Yes I would too, Walter. [*Pause*] I gave her a five-dollar down payment.

[*There is total silence as the man stares at his wife and the mother stares at her son.*]

MAMA [*presently*]. Well— [*Tightly*] Well—son, I'm waiting to hear you say something. . . . I'm waiting to hear how you be your father's son. Be the man he was. . . . [*Pause*] Your wife say she going to destroy your child. And I'm waiting to hear you talk like him and say we a people who give children life, not who destroys them— [*She rises.*] I'm waiting to see you stand up and look like your daddy and say we done give up one baby to poverty and that we ain't going to give up nary another one. . . . I'm waiting.

WALTER. Ruth—

MAMA. If you a son of mine, tell her! [WALTER *turns, looks at her and can say nothing. She continues, bitterly.*] You . . . you are a disgrace to your father's memory. Somebody get me my hat.

CURTAIN

ACT TWO

SCENE I. *Time: Later the same day.*
At rise: RUTH *is ironing again. She has the radio going. Presently* BENEATHA's *bedroom door opens and* RUTH's *mouth falls and she puts down the iron in fascination.*

RUTH. What have we got on tonight!

BENEATHA [*emerging grandly from the doorway so that we can see her thoroughly robed in the costume* ASAGAI *brought*]. You are looking at what a well-dressed Nigerian woman wears— [*She parades for* RUTH, *her hair completely hidden by the headdress; she is coquettishly fanning herself with an ornate oriental fan, mistakenly more like Butterfly than any Nigerian that ever was.*] Isn't it beautiful? [*She promenades to the radio and, with an arrogant flourish, turns off the good loud blues that is playing.*] Enough of this assimilationist junk! [RUTH *follows her with her eyes as she goes to the phonograph and puts on a record and turns and waits ceremoniously for the music to come up. Then, with a shout—*] OCOMOGOSIAY!

[RUTH *jumps. The music comes up, a lovely Nigerian melody.* BENEATHA *listens, enraptured, her eyes far away—"back to the past." She begins to dance.* RUTH *is dumfounded.*]

RUTH. What kind of dance is that?
BENEATHA. A folk dance.
RUTH [*Pearl Bailey*]. What kind of folks do that, honey?
BENEATHA. It's from Nigeria. It's a dance of welcome.
RUTH. Who you welcoming?
BENEATHA. The men back to the village.
RUTH. Where they been?
BENEATHA. How should I know—out hunting or something. Anyway, they are coming back now. . . .
RUTH. Well, that's good.
BENEATHA [*with the record*].
   Alundi, alundi
   Alundi alunya
   Jop pu a jeepua
   Ang gu sooooooooooo

   Ai yai yae . . .
   Ayehaye—alundi . . .

[WALTER *comes in during this performance; he has obviously been drinking. He leans against the door heavily and watches his sister, at first with distaste. Then his eyes look off—"back to the past"— as he lifts both his fists to the roof, screaming.*]

WALTER. YEAH . . . AND ETHIOPIA STRETCH FORTH HER HANDS AGAIN! . . .
RUTH [*drily, looking at him*]. Yes—and Africa sure is claiming her own tonight. [*She gives them both up and starts ironing again.*]
WALTER [*all in a drunken, dramatic shout*]. Shut up! . . . I'm digging them drums . . . them drums move me! . . . [*He makes his weaving way to his wife's face and leans in close to her.*] In my *heart of hearts*—[*he thumps his chest*]—I am much warrior!
RUTH [*without even looking up*]. In your heart of hearts you are much drunkard.
WALTER [*coming away from her and starting to wander around the room, shouting*]. Me and Jomo . . . [*Intently, in his sister's face. She has stopped dancing to watch him in this unknown mood.*] That's my man, Kenyatta. [*Shouting and thumping his chest*] FLAMING SPEAR! HOT DAMN! [*He is suddenly in possession of an imaginary spear and actively spearing enemies all over the room.*] OCOMOGOSIAY . . . THE LION IS WAKING . . . OWIMOWEH! [*He pulls his shirt open and leaps up on a table and gestures with his spear. The bell rings.* RUTH *goes to answer.*]

BENEATHA [*to encourage* WALTER, *thoroughly caught up with this side of him*]. *OCOMOGOSIAY*, FLAMING SPEAR!
WALTER [*on the table, very far gone, his eyes pure glass sheets. He sees what we cannot, that he is a leader of his people, a great chief, a descendant of Chaka, and that the hour to march has come.*] Listen, my black brothers—
BENEATHA. OCOMOGOSIAY!
WALTER. —Do you hear the waters rushing against the shores of the coastlands—
BENEATHA. OCOMOGOSIAY!
WALTER. —Do you hear the screeching of the cocks in yonder hills beyond where the chiefs meet in council for the coming of the mighty war—
BENEATHA. OCOMOGOSIAY!
WALTER. —Do you hear the beating of the wings of the birds flying low over the mountains and the low places of our land—

[RUTH *opens the door*. GEORGE MURCHISON *enters.*]

BENEATHA. OCOMOGOSIAY!
WALTER. —Do you hear the singing of the women, singing the war songs of our fathers to the babies in the great houses . . . singing the sweet war songs? OH, DO YOU HEAR, MY BLACK BROTHERS!
BENEATHA [*completely gone*]. We hear you, Flaming Spear—
WALTER. Telling us to prepare for the greatness of the time— [*To* GEORGE] Black Brother! [*He extends his hand for the fraternal clasp.*]
GEORGE. Black Brother, hell!
RUTH [*having had enough, and embarrassed for the family*]. Beneatha, you got company—what's the matter with you? Walter Lee Younger, get down off that table and stop acting like a fool . . . .

[WALTER *comes down off the table suddenly and makes a quick exit to the bathroom.*]

RUTH. He's had a little to drink. . . . I don't know what her excuse is.
GEORGE [*to* BENEATHA]. Look honey, we're going *to* the theater—we're not going to be *in* it . . . so go change, huh?
RUTH. You expect this boy to go out with you looking like that?
BENEATHA [*looking at* GEORGE]. That's up to George. If he's ashamed of his heritage—
GEORGE. Oh, don't be so proud of yourself, Bennie—just because you look eccentric.
BENEATHA. How can something that's natural be eccentric?
GEORGE. That's what being eccentric means—being natural. Get dressed.

BENEATHA. I don't like that, George.
RUTH. Why must you and your brother make an argument out of everything people say?
BENEATHA. Because I hate assimilationist Negroes!
RUTH. Will somebody please tell me what assimila-whoever means!
GEORGE. Oh, it's just a college girl's way of calling people Uncle Toms —but that isn't what it means at all.
RUTH. Well, what does it mean?
BENEATHA [*cutting* GEORGE *off and staring at him as she replies to* RUTH]. It means someone who is willing to give up his own culture and submerge himself completely in the dominant, and in this case, *oppressive* culture!
GEORGE. Oh, dear, dear, dear! Here we go! A lecture on the African past! On our Great West African Heritage! In one second we will hear all about the great Ashanti empires; the great Songhay civilizations; and the great sculpture of Bénin—and then some poetry in the Bantu— and the whole monologue will end with the word *heritage!* [*Nastily*] Let's face it, baby, your heritage is nothing but a bunch of raggedy-assed spirituals and some grass huts!
BENEATHA. *Grass huts!* [RUTH *crosses to her and forcibly pushes her toward the bedroom.*] See there . . . you are standing there in your splendid ignorance talking about people who were the first to smelt iron on the face of the earth! [RUTH *is pushing her through the door.*] The Ashanti were performing surgical operations when the English—[RUTH *pulls the door to, with* BENEATHA *on the other side, and smiles graciously at* GEORGE. BENEATHA *opens the door and shouts the end of the sentence defiantly at* GEORGE]—were still tatooing themselves with blue dragons. . . . [*She goes back inside.*]
RUTH. Have a seat, George. [*They both sit.* RUTH *folds her hands rather primly on her lap, determined to demonstrate the civilization of the family.*] Warm, ain't it? I mean for September. [*Pause*] Just like they always say about Chicago weather: If it's too hot or cold for you, just wait a minute and it'll change. [*She smiles happily at this cliché of clichés.*] Everybody say it's got to do with them bombs and things they keep setting off. [*Pause*] Would you like a nice cold beer?
GEORGE. No, thank you. I don't care for beer. [*He looks at his watch.*] I hope she hurries up.
RUTH. What time is the show?
GEORGE. It's an eight-thirty curtain. That's just Chicago, though. In New York standard curtain time is eight forty. [*He is rather proud of this knowledge.*]
RUTH [*properly appreciating it*]. You get to New York a lot?

GEORGE [*offhand*]. Few times a year.
RUTH. Oh—that's nice. I've never been to New York.

[WALTER *enters. We feel he has relieved himself, but the edge of unreality is still with him.*]

WALTER. New York ain't got nothing Chicago ain't. Just a bunch of hustling people all squeezed up together—being "Eastern." [*He turns his face into a screw of displeasure.*]
GEORGE. Oh—you've been?
WALTER. Plenty of times.
RUTH [*shocked at the lie*]. Walter Lee Younger!
WALTER [*staring her down*]. Plenty! [*Pause*] What we got to drink in this house? Why don't you offer this man some refreshment. [*To* GEORGE] They don't know how to entertain people in this house, man.
GEORGE. Thank you—I don't really care for anything.
WALTER [*feeling his head; sobriety coming*]. Where's Mama?
RUTH. She ain't come back yet.
WALTER [*looking* MURCHISON *over from head to toe, scrutinizing his carefully casual tweed sports jacket over cashmere V-neck sweater over soft eyelet shirt and tie, and soft slacks, finished off with white buckskin shoes*]. Why all you college boys wear them fairyish-looking white shoes?
RUTH. Walter Lee!

[GEORGE MURCHISON *ignores the remark.*]

WALTER [*to* RUTH]. Well, they look crazy as hell—white shoes, cold as it is.
RUTH [*crushed*]. You have to excuse him—
WALTER. No he don't! Excuse me for what? What you always excusing me for! I'll excuse myself when I needs to be excused! [*A pause*] They look as funny as them black knee socks Beneatha wears out of here all the time.
RUTH. It's the college *style*, Walter.
WALTER. Style, hell. She looks like she got burnt legs or something!
RUTH. Oh, Walter—
WALTER [*an irritable mimic*]. Oh, Walter! Oh, Walter! [*To* MURCHISON] How's your old man making out? I understand you all going to buy that big hotel on the Drive? [*He finds a beer in the refrigerator, wanders over to* MURCHISON, *sipping and wiping his lips with the back of his hand, and straddling a chair backwards to talk to the other man.*] Shrewd move. Your old man is all right, man. [*Tapping his head and half winking for emphasis*] I mean he knows how to

operate. I mean he thinks *big*, you know what I mean, I mean for a *home*, you know? But I think he's kind of running out of ideas now. I'd like to talk to him. Listen, man, I got some plans that could turn this city upside down. I mean I think like he does. *Big.* Invest big, gamble big, hell, lose *big* if you have to, you know what I mean. It's hard to find a man on this whole Southside who understands my kind of thinking—you dig? [*He scrutinizes* MURCHISON *again, drinks his beer, squints his eyes and leans in close, confidential, man to man.*] Me and you ought to sit down and talk sometimes, man. Man, I got me some ideas . . . .

MURCHISON [*with boredom*]. Yeah—sometimes we'll have to do that, Walter.

WALTER [*understanding the indifference, and offended*]. Yeah—well, when you get the time, man. I know you a busy little boy.

RUTH. Walter, please—

WALTER [*bitterly, hurt*]. I know ain't nothing in this world as busy as you colored college boys with your fraternity pins and white shoes . . . .

RUTH [*covering her face with humiliation*]. Oh, Walter Lee—

WALTER. I see you all all the time—with the books tucked under your arms—going to your [*British A—a mimic*] "clahsses." And for what! What the hell you learning over there? Filling up your heads— [*counting off on his fingers*]—with the sociology and the psychology—but they teaching you how to be a man? How to take over and run the world? They teaching you how to run a rubber plantation or a steel mill? Naw—just to talk proper and read books and wear white shoes . . . .

GEORGE [*looking at him with distaste, a little above it all*]. You're all wacked up with bitterness, man.

WALTER [*intently, almost quietly, between the teeth, glaring at the boy*]. And you—ain't you bitter, man? Ain't you just about had it yet? Don't you see no stars gleaming that you can't reach out and grab? You happy?—You contented son-of-a-bitch—you happy? You got it made? Bitter? Man, I'm a volcano. Bitter? Here I am a giant—surrounded by ants! Ants who can't even understand what it is the giant is talking about.

RUTH [*passionately and suddenly*]. Oh, Walter—ain't you with nobody!

WALTER [*violently*]. No! 'Cause ain't nobody with me! Not even my own mother!

RUTH. Walter, that's a terrible thing to say!

[BENEATHA *enters, dressed for the evening in a cocktail dress and earrings.*]

GEORGE. Well—hey, you look great.
BENEATHA. Let's go, George. See you all later.
RUTH. Have a nice time.
GEORGE. Thanks. Good night. [*To* WALTER, *sarcastically*] Good night, Prometheus. [BENEATHA *and* GEORGE *exit.*]
WALTER [*to* RUTH]. Who is Prometheus?
RUTH. I don't know. Don't worry about it.
WALTER [*in fury, pointing after* GEORGE]. See there—they get to a point where they can't insult you man to man—they got to go talk about something ain't nobody never heard of!
RUTH. How do you know it was an insult? [*To humor him*] Maybe Prometheus is a nice fellow.
WALTER. Prometheus! I bet there ain't even no such thing! I bet that simple-minded clown—
RUTH. Walter— [*She stops what she is doing and looks at him.*]
WALTER [*yelling*]. Don't start!
RUTH. Start what?
WALTER. Your nagging! Where was I? Who was I with? How much money did I spend?
RUTH [*plaintively*]. Walter Lee—why don't we just try to talk about it. . . .
WALTER [*not listening*]. I been out talking with people who understand me. People who care about the things I got on my mind.
RUTH [*wearily*]. I guess that means people like Willy Harris.
WALTER. Yes, people like Willy Harris.
RUTH [*with a sudden flash of impatience*]. Why don't you all just hurry up and go into the banking business and stop talking about it!
WALTER. Why? You want to know why? 'Cause we all tied up in a race of people that don't know how to do nothing but moan, pray and have babies!

[*The line is too bitter even for him and he looks at her and sits down.*]

RUTH. Oh, Walter . . . [*Softly*] Honey, why can't you stop fighting me?
WALTER [*without thinking*]. Who's fighting you? Who even cares about you?

[*This line begins the retardation of his mood.*]

RUTH. Well— [*She waits a long time, and then with resignation starts to put away her things.*] I guess I might as well go on to bed. . . . [*More or less to herself*] I don't know where we lost it . . . but we have. . . . [*Then, to him*] I—I'm sorry about this new baby, Walter.

I guess maybe I better go on and do what I started ... I guess I just didn't realize how bad things was with us ... I guess I just didn't really realize— [*She starts out to the bedroom and stops.*] You want some hot milk?

WALTER. Hot milk?

RUTH. Yes—hot milk.

WALTER. Why hot milk?

RUTH. 'Cause after all that liquor you come home with you ought to have something hot in your stomach.

WALTER. I don't want no milk.

RUTH. You want some coffee then?

WALTER. No, I don't want no coffee. I don't want nothing hot to drink. [*Almost plaintively*] Why you always trying to give me something to eat?

RUTH [*standing and looking at him helplessly*]. What else can I give you, Walter Lee Younger?

[*She stands and looks at him and presently turns to go out again. He lifts his head and watches her going away from him in a new mood which began to emerge when he asked her "Who cares about you?"*]

WALTER. It's been rough, ain't it, baby? [*She hears and stops but does not turn around and he continues to her back.*] I guess between two people there ain't never as much understood as folks generally thinks there is. I mean like between me and you— [*She turns to face him.*] How we gets to the place where we scared to talk softness to each other. [*He waits, thinking hard himself.*] Why you think it got to be like that? [*He is thoughtful, almost as a child would be.*] Ruth, what is it gets into people ought to be close?

RUTH. I don't know, honey. I think about it a lot.

WALTER. On account of you and me, you mean? The way things are with us. The way something done come down between us.

RUTH. There ain't so much between us, Walter. . . . Not when you come to me and try to talk to me. Try to be with me . . . a little even.

WALTER [*total honesty*]. Sometimes . . . sometimes . . . I don't even know how to try.

RUTH. Walter—

WALTER. Yes?

RUTH [*coming to him, gently and with misgiving, but coming to him*]. Honey . . . life don't have to be like this. I mean sometimes people can do things so that things are better. . . . You remember how we used to talk when Travis was born . . . about the way we were going to live . . . the kind of house . . . [*She is stroking his head.*] Well, it's all starting to slip away from us. . . .

[MAMA *enters, and* WALTER *jumps up and shouts at her.*]

WALTER. Mama, where have you been?
MAMA. My—them steps is longer than they used to be. Whew! [*She sits down and ignores him.*] How you feeling this evening, Ruth?

[RUTH *shrugs, disturbed some at having been prematurely interrupted and watching her husband knowingly.*]

WALTER. Mama, where have you been all day?
MAMA [*still ignoring him and leaning on the table and changing to more comfortable shoes*]. Where's Travis?
RUTH. I let him go out earlier and he ain't come back yet. Boy, is he going to get it!
WALTER. Mama!
MAMA [*as if she has heard him for the first time*]. Yes, son?
WALTER. Where did you go this afternoon?
MAMA. I went downtown to tend to some business that I had to tend to.
WALTER. What kind of business?
MAMA. You know better than to question me like a child, Brother.
WALTER [*rising and bending over the table*]. Where were you, Mama? [*Bringing his fists down and shouting*] Mama, you didn't go do something with that insurance money, something crazy?

[*The front door opens slowly, interrupting him, and* TRAVIS *peeks his head in, less than hopefully.*]

TRAVIS [*to his mother*]. Mama, I—
RUTH. "Mama I" nothing! You're going to get it, boy! Get on in that bedroom and get yourself ready!
TRAVIS. But I—
MAMA. Why don't you all never let the child explain hisself.
RUTH. Keep out of it now, Lena.

[MAMA *clamps her lips together, and* RUTH *advances toward her son menacingly.*]

RUTH. A thousand times I have told you not to go off like that—
MAMA [*holding out her arms to her grandson*]. Well—at least let me tell him something. I want him to be the first one to hear. . . . Come here, Travis. [*The boy obeys, gladly.*] Travis—[*she takes him by the shoulder and looks into his face*]—you know that money we got in the mail this morning?

TRAVIS. Yes'm—

MAMA. Well—what you think your grandmama gone and done with that money?

TRAVIS. I don't know, Grandmama.

MAMA [*putting her finger on his nose for emphasis*]. She went out and she bought you a house! [*The explosion comes from* WALTER *at the end of the revelation and he jumps up and turns away from all of them in a fury.* MAMA *continues, to* TRAVIS] You glad about the house? It's going to be yours when you get to be a man.

TRAVIS. Yeah—I always wanted to live in a house.

MAMA. All right, gimme some sugar then—[TRAVIS *puts his arms around her neck as she watches her son over the boy's shoulder. Then, to* TRAVIS, *after the embrace*] Now when you say your prayers tonight, you thank God and your grandfather—'cause it was him who give you the house—in his way.

RUTH [*taking the boy from* MAMA *and pushing him toward the bedroom*]. Now you get out of here and get ready for your beating.

TRAVIS. Aw, Mama—

RUTH. Get on in there—[*Closing the door behind him and turning radiantly to her mother-in-law*] So you went and did it!

MAMA [*quietly, looking at her son with pain*]. Yes, I did.

RUTH [*raising both arms classically*]. Praise God! [*Looks at* WALTER *a moment, who says nothing. She crosses rapidly to her husband.*] Please, honey—let me be glad . . . you be glad too. [*She has laid her hands on his shoulders, but he shakes himself free of her roughly, without turning to face her.*] Oh, Walter . . . a home . . . *a home*. [*She comes back to* MAMA.] Well—where is it? How big is it? How much it going to cost?

MAMA. Well—

RUTH. When we moving?

MAMA [*smiling at her*]. First of the month.

RUTH [*throwing back her head with jubilance*]. Praise God!

MAMA [*tentatively, still looking at her son's back turned against her and* RUTH]. It's—it's a nice house too. . . . [*She cannot help speaking directly to him. An imploring quality in her voice, her manner, makes her almost like a girl now.*] Three bedrooms—nice big one for you and Ruth. . . . Me and Beneatha still have to share our room, but Travis have one of his own—and [*with difficulty*] I figure if the—new baby—is a boy, we could get one of them double-decker outfits. . . . And there's a yard with a little patch of dirt where I could maybe get to grow me a few flowers. . . . And a nice big basement. . . .

RUTH. Walter honey, be glad—

MAMA [*still to his back, fingering things on the table*]. 'Course I don't want to make it sound fancier than it is. . . . It's just a plain little old house—but it's made good and solid—and it will be *ours*. Walter Lee—it makes a difference in a man when he can walk on floors that belong to *him*. . . .
RUTH. Where is it?
MAMA [*frightened at this telling*]. Well—well—it's out there in Clybourne Park—

[RUTH's *radiance fades abruptly, and* WALTER *finally turns slowly to face his mother with incredulity and hostility.*]

RUTH. Where?
MAMA [*matter-of-factly*]. Four o six Clybourne Street, Clybourne Park.
RUTH. Clybourne Park? Mama, there ain't no colored people living in Clybourne Park.
MAMA [*almost idiotically*]. Well, I guess there's going to be some now.
WALTER [*bitterly*]. So that's the peace and comfort you went out and bought for us today!
MAMA [*raising her eyes to meet his finally*]. Son—I just tried to find the nicest place for the least amount of money for my family.
RUTH [*trying to recover from the shock*]. Well—well—'course I ain't one never been 'fraid of no crackers, mind you—but—well, wasn't there no other houses nowhere?
MAMA. Them houses they put up for colored in them areas way out all seem to cost twice as much as other houses. I did the best I could.
RUTH [*struck senseless with the news, in its various degrees of goodness and trouble, she sits a moment, her fists propping her chin in thought, and then she starts to rise, bringing her fists down with vigor, the radiance spreading from cheek to cheek again*]. Well—well!—All I can say is—if this is my time in life—*my time*—to say good-bye—[*and she builds with momentum as she starts to circle the room with an exuberant, almost tearfully happy release*]—to these Goddamned cracking walls!—[*she pounds the walls*]—and these marching roaches!—[*she wipes at an imaginary army of marching roaches*]—and this cramped little closet which ain't now or never was no kitchen! . . . then I say it loud and good, *Hallelujah! and good-bye misery.* . . . *I don't never want to see your ugly face again!* [*She laughs joyously, having practically destroyed the apartment, and flings her arms up and lets them come down happily, slowly, reflectively, over her abdomen, aware for the first time perhaps that the life therein pulses with happiness and not despair.*] Lena?
MAMA [*moved, watching her happiness*]. Yes, honey?
RUTH [*looking off*]. Is there—is there a whole lot of sunlight?

MAMA [*understanding*]. Yes, child, there's a whole lot of sunlight.

[*Long pause*]

RUTH [*collecting herself and going to the door of the room* TRAVIS *is in*]. Well—I guess I better see 'bout Travis. [*To* MAMA] Lord, I sure don't feel like whipping nobody today! [*She exits.*]

MAMA [*the mother and son are left alone now and the mother waits a long time, considering deeply, before she speaks*]. Son—you—you understand what I done, don't you? [WALTER *is silent and sullen.*] I—I just seen my family falling apart today . . . just falling to pieces in front of my eyes. . . . We couldn't of gone on like we was today. We was going backwards 'stead of forwards—talking 'bout killing babies and wishing each other was dead. . . . When it gets like that in life—you just got to do something different, push on out and do something bigger. . . . [*She waits.*] I wish you say something, son . . . I wish you'd say how deep inside you you think I done the right thing—

WALTER [*crossing slowly to his bedroom door and finally turning there and speaking measuredly*]. What you need me to say you done right for? *You* the head of this family. You run our lives like you want to. It was your money and you did what you wanted with it. So what you need for me to say it was all right for? [*Bitterly, to hurt her as deeply as he knows is possible*] So you butchered up a dream of mine —you—who always talking 'bout your children's dreams. . . .

MAMA. Walter Lee—

[*He just closes the door behind him.* MAMA *sits alone, thinking heavily.*]

CURTAIN

SCENE 2. *Time: Friday night. A few weeks later.*
At rise: Packing crates mark the intention of the family to move.
BENEATHA *and* GEORGE *come in, presumably from an evening out again.*

GEORGE. O.K. . . . O.K., whatever you say . . . [*They both sit on the couch. He tries to kiss her. She moves away.*] Look, we've had a nice evening; let's not spoil it, huh? . . .

[*He again turns her head and tries to nuzzle in and she turns away from him, not with distaste but with momentary lack of interest; in a mood to pursue what they were talking about.*]

BENEATHA. I'm *trying* to talk to you.

GEORGE. We always talk.
BENEATHA. Yes—and I love to talk.
GEORGE [*exasperated; rising*]. I know it and I don't mind it sometimes . . . I want you to cut it out, see—The moody stuff, I mean. I don't like it. You're a nice-looking girl . . . all over. That's all you need, honey, forget the atmosphere. Guys aren't going to go for the atmosphere—they're going to go for what they see. Be glad for that. Drop the Garbo routine. It doesn't go with you. As for myself, I want a nice—[*groping*]—simple [*thoughtfully*]—sophisticated girl . . . not a poet—O.K.?

[*She rebuffs him again and he starts to leave.*]

BENEATHA. Why are you angry?
GEORGE. Because this is stupid! I don't go out with you to discuss the nature of "quiet desperation" or to hear all about your thoughts—because the world will go on thinking what it thinks regardless—
BENEATHA. Then why read books? Why go to school?
GEORGE [*with artificial patience, counting on his fingers*]. It's simple. You read books—to learn facts—to get grades—to pass the course—to get a degree. That's all—it has nothing to do with thoughts.

[*A long pause*]

BENEATHA. I see. [*A longer pause as she looks at him*] Good night, George.

[GEORGE *looks at her a little oddly, and starts to exit. He meets* MAMA *coming in.*]

GEORGE. Oh—hello, Mrs. Younger.
MAMA. Hello, George, how you feeling?
GEORGE. Fine—fine, how are you?
MAMA. Oh, a little tired. You know them steps can get you after a day's work. You all have a nice time tonight?
GEORGE. Yes—a fine time. Well, good night.
MAMA. Good night. [*He exits.* MAMA *closes the door behind her.*] Hello, honey. What you sitting like that for?
BENEATHA. I'm just sitting.
MAMA. Didn't you have a nice time?
BENEATHA. No.
MAMA. No? What's the matter?
BENEATHA. Mama, George is a fool—honest. [*She rises.*]
MAMA [*hustling around unloading the packages she has entered with. She stops*]. Is he, baby?
BENEATHA. Yes.

[BENEATHA *makes up* TRAVIS' *bed as she talks.*]

MAMA. You sure?
BENEATHA. Yes.
MAMA. Well—I guess you better not waste your time with no fools.

[BENEATHA *looks up at her mother, watching her put groceries in the refrigerator. Finally she gathers up her things and starts into the bedroom. At the door she stops and looks back at her mother.*]

BENEATHA. Mama—
MAMA. Yes, baby—
BENEATHA. Thank you.
MAMA. For what?
BENEATHA. For understanding me this time.

[*She exits quickly and the mother stands, smiling a little, looking at the place where* BENEATHA *just stood.* RUTH *enters.*]

RUTH. Now don't you fool with any of this stuff, Lena—
MAMA. Oh, I just thought I'd sort a few things out.

[*The phone rings.* RUTH *answers.*]

RUTH [*at the phone*]. Hello—Just a minute. [*Goes to door*] Walter, it's Mrs. Arnold. [*Waits. Goes back to the phone. Tense*] Hello. Yes, this is his wife speaking . . . He's lying down now. Yes . . . well, he'll be in tomorrow. He's been very sick. Yes—I know we should have called, but we were so sure he'd be able to come in today. Yes—yes, I'm very sorry. Yes . . . Thank you very much. [*She hangs up.* WALTER *is standing in the doorway of the bedroom behind her.*] That was Mrs. Arnold.
WALTER [*indifferently*]. Was it?
RUTH. She said if you don't come in tomorrow that they are getting a new man. . . .
WALTER. Ain't that sad—ain't that crying sad.
RUTH. She said Mr. Arnold has had to take a cab for three days. . . . Walter, you ain't been to work for three days! [*This is a revelation to her.*] Where you been, Walter Lee Younger? [WALTER *looks at her and starts to laugh.*] You're going to lose your job.
WALTER. That's right . . .
RUTH. Oh, Walter, and with your mother working like a dog every day—
WALTER. That's sad too—Everything is sad.
MAMA. What you been doing for these three days, son?
WALTER. Mama—you don't know all the things a man what got leisure

can find to do in this city. . . . What's this—Friday night? Well—Wednesday I borrowed Willy Harris' car and I went for a drive . . . just me and myself and I drove and drove . . . Way out . . . way past South Chicago, and I parked the car and I sat and looked at the steel mills all day long. I just sat in the car and looked at them big black chimneys for hours. Then I drove back and I went to the Green Hat. [*Pause*] And Thursday—Thursday I borrowed the car again and I got in it and I pointed it the other way and I drove the other way—for hours—way, way up to Wisconsin, and I looked at the farms. I just drove and looked at the farms. Then I drove back and I went to the Green Hat. [*Pause*] And today—today I didn't get the car. Today I just walked. All over the South side. And I looked at the Negroes and they looked at me and finally I just sat down on the curb at Thirty-ninth and South Parkway and I just sat there and watched the Negroes go by. And then I went to the Green Hat. You all sad? You all depressed? And you know where I am going right now—

[RUTH *goes out quietly.*]

MAMA. Oh, Big Walter, is this the harvest of our days?

WALTER. You know what I like about the Green Hat? [*He turns the radio on and a steamy, deep blues pours into the room.*] I like this little cat they got there who blows a sax. . . . He blows. He talks to me. He ain't but 'bout five feet tall and he's got a conked head and his eyes is always closed and he's all music—

MAMA [*rising and getting some papers out of her handbag*]. Walter—

WALTER. And there's this other guy who plays the piano . . . and they got a sound. I mean they can work on some music. . . . They got the best little combo in the world in the Green Hat. . . . You can just sit there and drink and listen to them three men play and you realize that don't nothing matter worth a damn, but just being there—

MAMA. I've helped do it to you, haven't I, son? Walter, I been wrong.

WALTER. Naw—you ain't never been wrong about nothing, Mama.

MAMA. Listen to me, now. I say I been wrong, son. That I been doing to you what the rest of the world been doing to you. [*She stops and he looks up slowly at her and she meets his eyes pleadingly.*] Walter —what you ain't never understood is that I ain't got nothing, don't own nothing, ain't never really wanted nothing that wasn't for you. There ain't nothing as precious to me. . . . There ain't nothing worth holding on to, money, dreams, nothing else—if it means—if it means it's going to destroy my boy. [*She puts her papers in front of him and he watches her without speaking or moving.*] I paid the man thirty-five hundred dollars down on the house. That leaves sixty-five hundred dollars. Monday morning I want you to take this money and take three thousand dollars and put it in a savings account for Beneatha's medical schooling. The rest you put in a checking account—with your name on it. And from now on any penny that come out of it or that go in it is for you to look after. For you to decide. [*She drops her hands a little helplessly.*] It ain't much, but it's all I got in the world and I'm putting it in your hands. I'm telling you to be the head of this family from now on like you supposed to be.

WALTER [*stares at the money*]. You trust me like that, Mama?

MAMA. I ain't never stop trusting you. Like I ain't never stop loving you.

[*She goes out, and* WALTER *sits looking at the money on the table as the music continues in its idiom, pulsing in the room. Finally, in a decisive gesture, he gets up, and, in mingled joy and desperation, picks up the money. At the same moment,* TRAVIS *enters for bed.*]

TRAVIS. What's the matter, Daddy? You drunk?

WALTER [*sweetly, more sweetly than we have ever known him*]. No, Daddy ain't drunk. Daddy ain't going to never be drunk again. . . .

TRAVIS. Well, good night, Daddy.

[*The* FATHER *has come from behind the couch and leans over, embracing his son.*]

WALTER. Son, I feel like talking to you tonight.

TRAVIS. About what?

WALTER. Oh, about a lot of things. About you and what kind of man you going to be when you grow up. . . . Son—son, what do you want to be when you grow up?

TRAVIS. A bus driver.

WALTER [*laughing a little*]. A what? Man, that ain't nothing to want to be!

TRAVIS. Why not?

WALTER. 'Cause, man—it ain't big enough—you know what I mean.

TRAVIS. I don't know then. I can't make up my mind. Sometimes Mama asks me that too. And sometimes when I tell you I just want to be like you—she says she don't want me to be like that and sometimes she says she does. . . .

WALTER [*gathering him up in his arms*]. You know what, Travis? In seven years you going to be seventeen years old. And things is going to be very different with us in seven years, Travis. . . . One day when you are seventeen I'll come home—home from my office downtown somewhere—

TRAVIS. You don't work in no office, Daddy.
WALTER. No—but after tonight. After what your daddy gonna do tonight, there's going to be offices—a whole lot of offices. . . .
TRAVIS. What you gonna do tonight, Daddy?
WALTER. You wouldn't understand yet, son, but your daddy's gonna make a transaction . . . a business transaction that's going to change our lives. . . . That's how come one day when you 'bout seventeen years old I'll come home and I'll be pretty tired, you know what I mean, after a day of conferences and secretaries getting things wrong the way they do . . . 'cause an executive's life is hell, man— [*The more he talks, the farther away he gets.*] And I'll pull the car up on the driveway . . . just a plain black Chrysler, I think, with white walls—no—black tires. More elegant. Rich people don't have to be flashy . . . though I'll have to get something a little sportier for Ruth—maybe a Cadillac convertible to do her shopping in. . . . And I'll come up the steps to the house and the gardener will be clipping away at the hedges and he'll say, "Good evening, Mr. Younger." And I'll say, "Hello, Jefferson, how are you this evening?" And I'll go inside and Ruth will come downstairs and meet me at the door and we'll kiss each other and she'll take my arm and we'll go up to your room to see you sitting on the floor with the catalogues of all the great schools in America around you. . . . All the great schools in the world! And—and I'll say, all right son—it's your seventeenth birthday, what is it you've decided? . . . Just tell me where you want to go to school and you'll *go*. Just tell me, what it is you want to be— and you'll *be* it. . . . Whatever you want to be—Yessir! [*He holds his arms open for* TRAVIS.] You just name it, son . . . [TRAVIS *leaps into them.*] and I hand you the world!

[WALTER's *voice has risen in pitch and hysterical promise and on the last line he lifts* TRAVIS *high.*]

BLACKOUT

SCENE 3. *Time: Saturday, moving day, one week later.*
Before the curtain rises, RUTH's *voice, a strident, dramatic church alto, cuts through the silence.*
It is, in the darkness, a triumphant surge, a penetrating statement of expectation: "Oh, Lord, I don't feel no ways tired! Children, oh, glory hallelujah!"
As the curtain rises we see that RUTH *is alone in the living room, finishing up the family's packing. It is moving day. She is nailing crates and tying cartons.* BENEATHA *enters, carrying a guitar case, and watches her exuberant sister-in-law.*

RUTH. Hey!
BENEATHA [*putting away the case*]. Hi.
RUTH [*pointing at a package*]. Honey—look in that package there and see what I found on sale this morning at the South Center. [RUTH *gets up and moves to the package and draws out some curtains.*] Look-ahere—hand-turned hems!
BENEATHA. How do you know the window size out there?
RUTH [*who hadn't thought of that*]. Oh—Well, they bound to fit something in the whole house. Anyhow, they was too good a bargain to pass up. [RUTH *slaps her head, suddenly remembering something.*] Oh, Bennie—I meant to put a special note on that carton over there. That's your mama's good china and she wants 'em to be very careful with it.
BENEATHA. I'll do it.

[BENEATHA *finds a piece of paper and starts to draw large letters on it.*]

RUTH. You know what I'm going to do soon as I get in that new house?
BENEATHA. What?
RUTH. Honey—I'm going to run me a tub of water up to here.... [*With her fingers practically up to her nostrils*] And I'm going to get in it—and I am going to sit ... and sit ... and sit in that hot water and the first person who knocks to tell *me* to hurry up and come out—
BENEATHA. Gets shot at sunrise.
RUTH [*laughing happily*]. You said it, sister! [*Noticing how large* BENEATHA *is absent-mindedly making the note*] Honey, they ain't going to read that from no airplane.
BENEATHA [*laughing herself*]. I guess I always think things have more emphasis if they are big, somehow.
RUTH [*looking up at her and smiling*]. You and your brother seem to have that as a philosophy of life. Lord, that man—done changed so 'round here. You know—you know what we did last night? Me and Walter Lee?
BENEATHA. What?
RUTH [*smiling to herself*]. We went to the movies. [*Looking at* BENEATHA *to see if she understands*] We went to the movies. You know the last time me and Walter went to the movies together?
BENEATHA. No.
RUTH. Me neither. That's how long it been. [*Smiling again*] But we went last night. The picture wasn't much good, but that didn't seem to matter. We went—and we held hands.

BENEATHA. Oh, Lord!
RUTH. We held hands—and you know what?
BENEATHA. What?
RUTH. When we come out of the show it was late and dark and all the stores and things was closed up . . . and it was kind of chilly and there wasn't many people on the streets . . . and we was still holding hands, me and Walter.
BENEATHA. You're killing me.

[WALTER *enters with a large package. His happiness is deep in him; he cannot keep still with his new-found exuberance. He is singing and wiggling and snapping his fingers. He puts his package in a corner and puts a phonograph record, which he has brought in with him, on the record player. As the music comes up he dances over to* RUTH *and tries to get her to dance with him. She gives in at last to his raunchiness and in a fit of giggling allows herself to be drawn into his mood and together they deliberately burlesque an old social dance of their youth.*]

BENEATHA [*regarding them a long time as they dance, then drawing in her breath for a deeply exaggerated comment which she does not particularly mean*]. Talk about—olddddddddddd-fashionedddddddd—Negroes!
WALTER [*stopping momentarily*]. What kind of Negroes?

[*He says this in fun. He is not angry with her today, nor with anyone. He starts to dance with his wife again.*]

BENEATHA. Old-fashioned.
WALTER [*as he dances with* RUTH]. You know, when these *New Negroes* have their convention—[*pointing at his sister*]—that is going to be the chairman of the Committee on Unending Agitation. [*He goes on dancing, then stops.*] Race, race, race! . . . Girl, I do believe you are the first person in the history of the entire human race to successfully brainwash yourself. [BENEATHA *breaks up and he goes on dancing. He stops again, enjoying his tease.*] Damn, even the N double A C P takes a holiday sometimes! [BENEATHA *and* RUTH *laugh. He dances with* RUTH *some more and starts to laugh and stops and pantomimes someone over an operating table.*] I can just see that chick someday looking down at some poor cat on an operating table before she starts to slice him, saying . . . [*pulling his sleeves back maliciously*] "By the way, what are your views on civil rights down there? . . ."

[*He laughs at her again and starts to dance happily. The bell sounds.*]

BENEATHA. Sticks and stones may break my bones but . . . words will never hurt me!

[BENEATHA *goes to the door and opens it as* WALTER *and* RUTH *go on with the clowning.* BENEATHA *is somewhat surprised to see a quiet-looking middle-aged white man in a business suit holding his hat and a briefcase in his hand and consulting a small piece of paper.*]

MAN. Uh—how do you do, miss. I am looking for a Mrs.—[*he looks at the slip of paper*] Mrs. Lena Younger?

BENEATHA [*smoothing her hair with slight embarrassment*]. Oh—yes, that's my mother. Excuse me. [*She closes the door and turns to quiet the other two.*] Ruth! Brother! Somebody's here. [*Then she opens the door. The man casts a curious quick glance at all of them.*] Uh—come in please.

MAN [*coming in*]. Thank you.

BENEATHA. My mother isn't here just now. Is it business?

MAN. Yes . . . well, of a sort.

WALTER [*freely, the Man of the House*]. Have a seat. I'm Mrs. Younger's son. I look after most of her business matters.

[RUTH *and* BENEATHA *exchange amused glances.*]

MAN [*regarding* WALTER, *and sitting*]. Well—My name is Karl Lindner . . .

WALTER [*stretching out his hand*]. Walter Younger. This is my wife—[RUTH *nods politely*]—and my sister.

LINDNER. How do you do.

WALTER [*amiably, as he sits himself easily on a chair, leaning with interest forward on his knees and looking expectantly into the newcomer's face*]. What can we do for you, Mr. Lindner!

LINDNER [*some minor shuffling of the hat and briefcase on his knees*]. Well—I am a representative of the Clybourne Park Improvement Association—

WALTER [*pointing*]. Why don't you sit your things on the floor?

LINDNER. Oh—yes. Thank you. [*He slides the briefcase and hat under the chair.*] And as I was saying—I am from the Clybourne Park Improvement Association and we have had it brought to our attention at the last meeting that you people—or at least your mother—has bought a piece of residential property at—[*he digs for the slip of paper again*]—four o six Clybourne Street . . . .

WALTER. That's right. Care for something to drink? Ruth, get Mr. Lindner a beer.

LINDNER [*upset for some reason*]. Oh—no, really. I mean thank you very much, but no thank you.

RUTH [*innocently*]. Some coffee?

LINDNER. Thank you, nothing at all.

[BENEATHA *is watching the man carefully.*]

LINDNER. Well, I don't know how much you folks know about our organization. [*He is a gentle man; thoughtful and somewhat labored in his manner.*] It is one of those community organizations set up to look after—oh, you know, things like block upkeep and special projects and we also have what we call our New Neighbors Orientation Committee. . . .

BENEATHA [*drily*]. Yes—and what do they do?

LINDNER. [*turning a little to her and then returning the main force to* WALTER]. Well—it's what you might call a sort of welcoming committee, I guess. I mean they, we, I'm the chairman of the committee—go around and see the new people who move into the neighborhood and sort of give them the lowdown on the way we do things out in Clybourne Park.

BENEATHA [*with appreciation of the two meanings, which escape* RUTH *and* WALTER]. Un-huh.

LINDNER. And we also have the category of what the association calls—[*he looks elsewhere*]—uh—special community problems. . . .

BENEATHA. Yes—and what are some of those?

WALTER. Girl, let the man talk.

LINDNER [*with understated relief*]. Thank you. I would sort of like to explain this thing in my own way. I mean I want to explain to you in a certain way.

WALTER. Go ahead.

LINDNER. Yes. Well. I'm going to try to get right to the point. I'm sure we'll all appreciate that in the long run.

BENEATHA. Yes.

LINDNER. Well—

WALTER. Be still now!

LINDNER. Well—

RUTH [*still innocently*]. Would you like another chair—you don't look comfortable.

LINDNER [*more frustrated than annoyed*]. No, thank you very much. Please. Well—to get right to the point I—[*a great breath, and he is off at last*] I am sure you people must be aware of some of the incidents which have happened in various parts of the city when colored people have moved into certain areas—[BENEATHA *exhales heavily and starts tossing a piece of fruit up and down in the air.*] Well—because we have what I think is going to be a unique type of organization in American community life—not only do we deplore that kind of thing—but we are trying to do something about it. [BENEATHA *stops tossing and turns with a new and quizzical interest to the man.*] We feel—[*gaining confidence in his mission because of the interest in the faces of the people he is talking to*]—we feel that most of the trouble in this world, when you come right down to it—[*he hits his knee for emphasis*]—most of the trouble exists because people just don't sit down and talk to each other.

RUTH [*nodding as she might in church, pleased with the remark*]. You can say that again, mister.

LINDNER [*more encouraged by such affirmation*]. That we don't try hard enough in this world to understand the other fellow's problem. The other guy's point of view.

RUTH. Now that's right.

[BENEATHA *and* WALTER *merely watch and listen with genuine interest.*]

LINDNER. Yes—that's the way we feel out in Clybourne Park. And that's why I was elected to come here this afternoon and talk to you people. Friendly like, you know, the way people should talk to each other and see if we couldn't find some way to work this thing out. As I say, the whole business is a matter of *caring* about the other fellow. Anybody can see that you are a nice family of folks, hard-working and honest I'm sure. [BENEATHA *frowns slightly, quizzically, her head tilted regarding him.*] Today everybody knows what it means to be on the outside of *something*. And of course, there is always somebody who is out to take the advantage of people who don't always understand.

WALTER. What do you mean?

LINDNER. Well—you see our community is made up of people who've worked hard as the dickens for years to build up that little community. They're not rich and fancy people; just hard-working, honest people who don't really have much but those little homes and a dream of the kind of community they want to raise their children in. Now, I don't say we are perfect and there is a lot wrong in some of the things they want. But you've got to admit that a man, right or wrong, has the right to want to have the neighborhood he lives in in a certain kind of way. And at the moment the overwhelming majority of our people out there feel that people get along better, take more of a common interest in the life of the community, when they share a common background. I want you to believe me when I tell you that race prejudice simply doesn't enter into it. It is a matter of the people of Clybourne Park believing, rightly or wrongly, as I say, that for the happiness of all concerned that our Negro families are happier when they live in their *own* communities.

BENEATHA [*with a grand and bitter gesture*]. This, friends, is the Welcoming Committee!

WALTER [*dumfounded, looking at* LINDNER]. Is this what you came marching all the way over her to tell us?

LINDNER. Well, now we've been having a fine conversation. I hope you'll hear me all the way through.

WALTER [*tightly*]. Go ahead, man.

LINDNER. You see—in the face of all things I have said, we are prepared to make your family a very generous offer. . . .

BENEATHA. Thirty pieces and not a coin less!

WALTER. Yeah?

LINDNER [*putting on his glasses and drawing a form out of the briefcase*]. Our association is prepared, through the collective effort of our people, to buy the house from you at a financial gain to your family.

RUTH. Lord have mercy, ain't this the living gall!

WALTER. All right, you through?

LINDNER. Well, I want to give you the exact terms of the financial arrangement—

WALTER. We don't want to hear no exact terms of no arrangements. I want to know if you got any more to tell us 'bout getting together?

LINDNER [*taking off his glasses*]. Well—I don't suppose that you feel. . . .

WALTER. Never mind how I feel—you got any more to say 'bout how people ought to sit down and talk to each other? . . . Get out of my house, man. [*He turns his back and walks to the door.*]

LINDNER [*looking around at the hostile faces and reaching and assembling his hat and briefcase*]. Well—I don't understand why you people are reacting this way. What do you think you are going to gain by moving into a neighborhood where you just aren't wanted and where some elements—well—people can get awful worked up when they feel that their whole way of life and everything they've ever worked for is threatened.

WALTER. Get out.

LINDNER [*at the door, holding a small card*]. Well—I'm sorry it went like this.

WALTER. Get out.

LINDNER [*almost sadly, regarding* WALTER]. You just can't force people to change their hearts, son.

[*He turns and put his card on a table and exits.* WALTER *pushes the door to with stinging hatred, and stands looking at it.* RUTH *just sits and* BENEATHA *just stands. They say nothing.* MAMA *and* TRAVIS *enter.*]

MAMA. Well—this all the packing got done since I left out of here this morning. I testify before God that my children got all the energy of the dead. What time the moving men due?
BENEATHA. Four o'clock. You had a caller, Mama. [*She is smiling, teasingly.*]
MAMA. Sure enough—who?
BENEATHA [*her arms folded saucily*]. The Welcoming Committee.

[WALTER *and* RUTH *giggle.*]

MAMA [*innocently*]. Who?
BENEATHA. The Welcoming Committee. They said they're sure going to be glad to see you when you get there.
WALTER [*devilishly*]. Yeah, they said they can't hardly wait to see your face.

[*Laughter.*]

MAMA [*sensing their facetiousness*]. What's the matter with you all?
WALTER. Ain't nothing the matter with us. We just telling you 'bout the gentleman who came to see you this afternoon. From the Clybourne Park Improvement Association.
MAMA. What he want?
RUTH [*in the same mood as* BENEATHA *and* WALTER]. To welcome you, honey.
WALTER. He said they can't hardly wait. He said the one thing they don't have, that they just *dying* to have out there is a fine family of colored people! [*To* RUTH *and* BENEATHA] Ain't that right!
RUTH *and* BENEATHA [*mockingly*]. Yeah! He left his card in case—

[*They indicate the card, and* MAMA *picks it up and throws it on the floor—understanding and looking off as she draws her chair up to the table on which she has put her plant and some sticks and some cord.*]

MAMA. Father, give us strength. [*Knowingly—and without fun*] Did he threaten us?
BENEATHA. Oh—Mama—they don't do it like that any more. He talked Brotherhood. He said everybody ought to learn how to sit down and hate each other with good Christian fellowship.

[*She and* WALTER *shake hands to ridicule the remark.*]

MAMA [*Sadly*]. Lord, protect us . . . .
RUTH. You should hear the money those folks raised to buy the house from us. All we paid and then some.
BENEATHA. What they think we going to do—eat 'em?
RUTH. No, honey, marry 'em.
MAMA [*shaking her head*]. Lord, Lord, Lord. . . .
RUTH. Well—that's the way the crackers crumble. Joke.
BENEATHA [*laughingly noticing what her mother is doing*]. Mama, what are you doing?
MAMA. Fixing my plant so it won't get hurt none on the way. . . .
BENEATHA. Mama, you going to take *that* to the new house?
MAMA. Un-huh—
BENEATHA. That raggedy-looking old thing?
MAMA [*stopping and looking at her*]. It expresses *me*.
RUTH [*with delight, to* BENEATHA]. So there, Miss Thing!

[WALTER *comes to* MAMA *suddenly and bends down behind her and squeezes her in his arms with all his strength. She is overwhelmed by the suddenness of it and, though delighted, her manner is like that of* RUTH *with* TRAVIS.]

MAMA. Look out now, boy! You make me mess up my thing here!
WALTER [*his face lit, he slips down on his knees beside her, his arms still about her*]. Mama . . . you know what it means to climb up in the chariot?
MAMA [*gruffly, very happy*]. Get on away from me now. . . .
RUTH [*near the gift-wrapped package, trying to catch* WALTER'*s eye*]. Psst—
WALTER. What the old song say, Mama. . . .
RUTH. Walter— Now? [*She is pointing at the package.*]
WALTER [*speaking the lines, sweetly, playfully, in his mother's face*].
   I got wings . . . you got wings . . .
   All God's Children got wings . . .
MAMA. Boy—get out of my face and do some work. . . .
WALTER.
   When I get to heaven gonna put on my wings,
   Gonna fly all over God's heaven . . .
BENEATHA [*teasingly, from across the room*]. Everybody talking 'bout heaven ain't going there!
WALTER [*to* RUTH, *who is carrying the box across to them*]. I don't know, you think we ought to give her that. . . . Seems to me she ain't been very appreciative around here.

MAMA [*eying the box, which is obviously a gift*]. What is that?
WALTER [*taking it from* RUTH *and putting it on the table in front of* MAMA]. Well—what you all think? Should we give it to her?
RUTH. Oh—she was pretty good today.
MAMA. I'll good you— [*She turns her eyes to the box again.*]
BENEATHA. Open it, Mama.

[*She stands up, looks at it, turns and looks at all of them, and then presses her hands together and does not open the package.*]

WALTER [*sweetly*]. Open it, Mama. It's for you. [MAMA *looks in his eyes. It is the first present in her life without its being Christmas. Slowly she opens her package and lifts out, one by one, a brand-new sparkling set of gardening tools.* WALTER *continues, prodding*] Ruth made up the note—read it . . .
MAMA [*picking up the card and adjusting her glasses*]. "To our own Mrs. Miniver—Love from Brother, Ruth and Beneatha." Ain't that lovely . . . .
TRAVIS [*tugging at his father's sleeve*]. Daddy, can I give her mine now?
WALTER. All right, son. [TRAVIS *flies to get his gift.*] Travis didn't want to go in with the rest of us, Mama. He got his own. [*Somewhat amused*] We don't know what it is . . . .
TRAVIS [*racing back in the room with a large hatbox and putting it in front of his grandmother*]. Here!
MAMA. Lord have mercy, baby. You done gone and bought your grandmother a hat?
TRAVIS [*very proud*]. Open it!

[*She does and lifts out an elaborate, but very elaborate, wide gardening hat, and all the adults break up at the sight of it.*]

RUTH. Travis, honey, what is that?
TRAVIS [*who thinks it is beautiful and appropriate*]. It's a gardening hat! Like the ladies always have on in the magazines when they work in their gardens.
BENEATHA [*giggling fiercely*]. Travis—we were trying to make Mama Mrs. Miniver—not Scarlett O'Hara!
MAMA [*indignantly*]. What's the matter with you all! This here is a beautiful hat! [*Absurdly*] I always wanted me one just like it!

[*She pops it on her head to prove it to her grandson, and the hat is ludicrous and considerably oversized.*]

RUTH. Hot dog! Go, Mama!

WALTER [*doubled over with laughter*]. I'm sorry, Mama—but you look like you ready to go out and chop you some cotton sure enough!

[*They all laugh except* MAMA, *out of deference to* TRAVIS' *feelings.*]

MAMA [*gathering the boy up to her*]. Bless your heart—this is the prettiest hat I ever owned— [WALTER, RUTH, *and* BENEATHA *chime in noisily, festively and insincerely congratulating* TRAVIS *on his gift.*] What are we all standing around here for? We ain't finished packin' yet. Bennie, you ain't packed one book.

[*The bell rings.*]

BENEATHA. That couldn't be the movers . . . it's not hardly two good yet—

[BENEATHA *goes into her room.* MAMA *starts for door.*]

WALTER [*turning, stiffening*]. Wait—wait—I'll get it. [*He stands and looks at the door.*]

MAMA. You expecting company, son?

WALTER [*just looking at the door*]. Yeah—yeah . . . .

[MAMA *looks at* RUTH, *and they exchange innocent and unfrightened glances.*]

MAMA [*not understanding*]. Well, let them in, son.

BENEATHA [*from her room*]. We need some more string.

MAMA. Travis—you run to the hardware and get me some string cord.

[MAMA *goes out and* WALTER *turns and looks at* RUTH. TRAVIS *goes to a dish for money.*]

RUTH. Why don't you answer the door, man?

WALTER [*suddenly bounding across the floor to her*]. 'Cause sometimes it hard to let the future begin! [*Stooping down in her face*]

I got wings! You got wings!
All God's children got wings!

[*He crosses to the door and throws it open. Standing there is a very slight little man in a not too prosperous business suit and with haunted frightened eyes and a hat pulled down tightly, brim up, around his forehead.* TRAVIS *passes between the men and exits.* WALTER *leans deep in the man's face, still in his jubilance.*]

When I get to heaven gonna put on my wings,
Gonna fly all over God's heaven . . .

[*The little man just stares at him.*]

Heaven—

[*Suddenly he stops and looks past the little man into the empty hallway.*] Where's Willy, man?

BOBO. He ain't with me.

WALTER [*not disturbed*]. Oh—come on in. You know my wife.

BOBO [*dumbly, taking off his hat*]. Yes—h'you, Miss Ruth.

RUTH [*quietly, a mood apart from her husband already, seeing* BOBO]. Hello, Bobo.

WALTER. You right on time today. . . . Right on time. That's the way! [*He slaps* BOBO *on his back.*] Sit down . . . lemme hear.

[RUTH *stands stiffly and quietly in back of them, as though somehow she senses death, her eyes fixed on her husband.*]

BOBO [*his frightened eyes on the floor, his hat in his hands*]. Could I please get a drink of water, before I tell you about it, Walter Lee?

[WALTER *does not take his eyes off the man.* RUTH *goes blindly to the tap and gets a glass of water and brings it to* BOBO.]

WALTER. There ain't nothing wrong, is there?

BOBO. Lemme tell you—

WALTER. Man—didn't nothing go wrong?

BOBO. Lemme tell you—Walter Lee. [*Looking at* RUTH *and talking to her more than to* WALTER] You know how it was. I got to tell you how it was. I mean first I got to tell you how it was all the way . . . I mean about the money I put in, Walter Lee . . . .

WALTER [*with taut agitation now*]. What about the money you put in?

BOBO. Well—it wasn't much as we told you—me and Willy—[*He stops.*] I'm sorry, Walter. I got a bad feeling about it. I got a real bad feeling about it . . . .

WALTER. Man, what you telling me about all this for? . . . Tell me what happened in Springfield . . . .

BOBO. Springfield.

RUTH [*like a dead woman*]. What was supposed to happen in Springfield?

BOBO [*to her*]. This deal that me and Walter went into with Willy— Me and Willy was going to go down to Springfield and spread some money 'round so's we wouldn't have to wait so long for the liquor license. . . . That's what we were going to do. Everybody said that was the way you had to do, you understand, Miss Ruth?

WALTER. Man—what happened down there?

BOBO [*a pitiful man, near tears*]. I'm trying to tell you, Walter.

WALTER [*screaming at him suddenly*]. THEN TELL ME, GODDAMMIT . . . WHAT'S THE MATTER WITH YOU?
BOBO. Man . . . I didn't go to no Springfield, yesterday.
WALTER [*halted, life hanging in the moment*]. Why not?
BOBO [*the long way, the hard way to tell*]. 'Cause I didn't have no reasons to . . . .
WALTER. Man, what are you talking about!
BOBO. I'm talking about the fact that when I got to the train station yesterday morning—eight o'clock like we planned . . . Man—*Willy didn't never show up.*
WALTER. Why . . . where was he . . . where is he?
BOBO. That's what I'm trying to tell you . . . I don't know . . . I waited six hours . . . I called his house . . . and I waited . . . six hours . . . I waited in that train station six hours . . . [*Breaking into tears*] That was all the extra money I had in the world . . . . [*Looking up at* WALTER *with the tears running down his face*] Man, *Willy is gone.*
WALTER. Gone, what you mean Willy is gone? Gone where? You mean he went by himself. You mean he went off to Springfield by himself —to take care of getting the license—[*Turns and looks anxiously at* RUTH] You mean maybe he didn't want too many people in on the business down there? [*Looks to* RUTH *again, as before*] You know Willy got his own ways. [*Looks back to* BOBO] Maybe you was late yesterday and he just went on down there without you. Maybe— maybe—he's been callin' you at home tryin' to tell you what happened or something. Maybe—maybe—he just got sick. He's somewhere—he's got to be somewhere. We just got to find him—me and you got to find him. [*Grabs* BOBO *senselessly by the collar and starts to shake him*] We got to!
BOBO [*in sudden angry, frightened agony*]. What's the matter with you, Walter! *When a cat take off with your money he don't leave you no maps!*
WALTER [*turning madly, as though he is looking for* WILLY *in the very room*]. Willy! . . . Willy . . . don't do it. . . . Please don't do it. . . . Man, not with that money . . . Man, please, not with that money . . . Oh, God . . . Don't let it be true . . . . [*He is wandering around, crying out for* WILLY *and looking for him or perhaps for help from God.*] Man . . . I trusted you . . . Man, I put my life in your hands. . . . [*He starts to crumple down on the floor as* RUTH *just covers her face in horror.* MAMA *opens the door and comes into the room, with* BENEATHA *behind her.*] Man . . . [*He starts to pound the floor with his fists, sobbing wildly.*] *That money is made out of my father's flesh* . . . .

BOBO [*standing over him helplessly*]. I'm sorry, Walter. . . . [*Only* WALTER's *sobs reply.* BOBO *puts on his hat.*] I had my life staked on this deal, too. . . . [*He exits.*]

MAMA [*to* WALTER]. Son—[*She goes to him, bends down to him, talks to his bent head.*] Son . . . Is it gone? Son, I gave you sixty-five hundred dollars. Is it gone? All of it? Beneatha's money too?

WALTER [*lifting his head slowly*]. Mama . . . I never . . . went to the bank at all. . . .

MAMA [*not wanting to believe him*]. You mean . . . your sister's school money . . . you used that too . . . Walter? . . .

WALTER. Yessss! . . . All of it. . . . It's all gone. . . .

[*There is total silence.* RUTH *stands with her face covered with her hands;* BENEATHA *leans forlornly against a wall, fingering a piece of red ribbon from the mother's gift.* MAMA *stops and looks at her son without recognition and then, quite without thinking about it, starts to beat him senselessly in the face.* BENEATHA *goes to them and stops it.*]

BENEATHA. Mama!

[MAMA *stops and looks at both of her children and rises slowly and wanders vaguely, aimlessly away from them.*]

MAMA. I seen . . . him . . . night after night . . . come in . . . and look at that rug . . . and then look at me . . . the red showing in his eyes . . . the veins moving in his head. . . . I seen him grow thin and old before he was forty . . . working and working and working like somebody's old horse . . . killing himself . . . and you—you give it all away in a day. . . .

BENEATHA. Mama—

MAMA. Oh, God . . . [*She looks up to Him.*] Look down here—and show me the strength.

BENEATHA. Mama—

MAMA [*folding over*]. Strength . . .

BENEATHA [*plaintively*]. Mama . . .

MAMA. Strength!

CURTAIN

ACT THREE

An hour later.

At curtain, there is a sullen light of gloom in the living room, gray light not unlike that which began the first scene of Act One. At left we can see WALTER *within his room, alone with himself. He is stretched out on the bed, his shirt out and open, his arms under his head. He does not smoke, he does not cry out, he merely lies there, looking up at the ceiling, much as if he were alone in the world.*

In the living room BENEATHA *sits at the table, still surrounded by the now almost ominous packing crates. She sits looking off. We feel that this is a mood struck perhaps an hour before, and it lingers now, full of the empty sound of profound disappointment. We see on a line from her brother's bedroom the sameness of their attitudes. Presently the bell rings and* BENEATHA *rises without ambition or interest in answering. It is* ASAGAI, *smiling broadly, striding into the room with energy and happy expectation and conversation.*

ASAGAI. I came over . . . I had some free time. I thought I might help with the packing. Ah, I like the look of packing crates! A household in preparation for a journey! It depresses some people . . . but for me . . . it is another feeling. Something full of the flow of life, do you understand? Movement, progress . . . . It makes me think of Africa.

BENEATHA. Africa!

ASAGAI. What kind of a mood is this? Have I told you how deeply you move me?

BENEATHA. He gave away the money, Asagai . . . .

ASAGAI. Who gave away what money?

BENEATHA. The insurance money. My brother gave it away.

ASAGAI. Gave it away?

BENEATHA. He made an investment! With a man even Travis wouldn't have trusted.

ASAGAI. And it's gone?

BENEATHA. Gone!

ASAGAI. I'm very sorry. . . . And you, now?

BENEATHA. Me? . . . Me? . . . Me I'm nothing. . . . Me. When I was very small . . . we used to take our sleds out in the wintertime and the only hills we had were the ice-covered stone steps of some houses down the street. And we used to fill them in with snow and make them smooth and slide down them all day . . . and it was very dangerous you know . . . far too steep . . . and sure enough one

day a kid named Rufus came down too fast and hit the sidewalk
. . . and we saw his face just split open right there in front of us.
. . . And I remember standing there looking at his bloody open face
thinking that was the end of Rufus. But the ambulance came and
they took him to the hospital and they fixed the broken bones and
they sewed it all up . . . and the next time I saw Rufus he just had
a little line down the middle of his face. . . . I never got over
that . . . .

[WALTER *sits up, listening on the bed. Throughout this scene it is important that we feel his reaction at all times, that he visibly respond to the words of his sister and* ASAGAI.]

ASAGAI. What?

BENEATHA. That that was what one person could do for another, fix him up—sew up the problem, make him all right again. That was the most marvelous thing in the world. . . . I wanted to do that. I always thought it was the one concrete thing in the world that a human being could do. Fix up the sick, you know—and make them whole again. This was truly being God . . . .

ASAGAI. You wanted to be God?

BENEATHA. No—I wanted to cure. It used to be so important to me. I wanted to cure. It used to matter. I used to care. I mean about people and how their bodies hurt . . . .

ASAGAI. And you've stopped caring?

BENEATHA. Yes—I think so.

ASAGAI. Why?

[WALTER *rises, goes to the door of his room and is about to open it, then stops and stands listening, leaning on the door jamb.*]

BENEATHA. Because it doesn't seem deep enough, close enough to what ails mankind—I mean this thing of sewing up bodies or administering drugs. Don't you understand? It was a child's reaction to the world. I thought that doctors had the secret to all the hurts. . . . That's the way a child sees things—or an idealist.

ASAGAI. Children see things very well sometimes—and idealists even better.

BENEATHA. I know that's what you think. Because you are still where I left off—you still care. This is what you see for the world, for Africa. You with the dreams of the future will patch up all Africa—you are going to cure the Great Sore of colonialism with Independence—

ASAGAI. Yes!

BENEATHA. Yes—and you think that one word is the penicillin of the human spirit: "Independence!" But then what?
ASAGAI. That will be the problem for another time. First we must get there.
BENEATHA. And where does it end?
ASAGAI. End? Who even spoke of an end? To life? To living?
BENEATHA. An end to misery!
ASAGAI [*smiling*]. You sound like a French intellectual.
BENEATHA. No! I sound like a human being who just had her future taken right out of her hands! While I was sleeping in my bed in there, things were happening in this world that directly concerned me—and nobody asked me, consulted me—they just went out and did things—and changed my life. Don't you see there isn't any real progress, Asagai, there is only one large circle that we march in, around and around, each of us with our own little picture—in front of us—our own little mirage that we think is the future.
ASAGAI. That is the mistake.
BENEATHA. What?
ASAGAI. What you just said—about the circle. It isn't a circle—it is simply a long line—as in geometry, you know, one that reaches into infinity. And because we cannot see the end—we also cannot see how it changes. And it is very odd but those who see the changes are called "idealists"—and those who cannot, or refuse to think, they are the "realists." It is very strange, and amusing too, I think.
BENEATHA. You—you are almost religious.
ASAGAI. Yes . . . I think I have the religion of doing what is necessary in the world—and of worshipping man—because he is so marvelous, you see.
BENEATHA. Man is foul! And the human race deserves its misery!
ASAGAI. You see: *you* have become the religious one in the old sense. Already, and after such a small defeat, you are worshipping despair.
BENEATHA. From now on, I worship the truth—and the truth is that people are puny, small and selfish. . . .
ASAGAI. Truth? Why is it that you despairing ones always think that only you have the truth? I never thought to see *you* like that. You! Your brother made a stupid, childish mistake—and you are grateful to him. So that now you can give up the ailing human race on account of it. You talk about what good is struggle; what good is anything? Where are we all going? And why are we bothering?
BENEATHA. *And you cannot answer it!* All your talk and dreams about Africa and Independence. Independence and then what? What about all the crooks and petty thieves and just plain idiots who will come into power to steal and plunder the same as before—only now they

will be black and do it in the name of the new Independence— You cannot answer that.

ASAGAI [*shouting over her*]. *I live the answer!* [*Pause.*] In my village at home it is the exceptional man who can even read a newspaper . . . or who ever *sees* a book at all. I will go home and much of what I will have to say will seem strange to the people of my village. . . . But I will teach and work and things will happen, slowly and swiftly. At times it will seem that nothing changes at all . . . and then again . . . the sudden dramatic events which make history leap into the future. And then quiet again. Retrogression even. Guns, murder, revolution. And I even will have moments when I wonder if the quiet was not better than all that death and hatred. But I will look about my village at the illiteracy and disease and ignorance and I will not wonder long. And perhaps . . . perhaps I will be a great man. . . . I mean perhaps I will hold on to the substance of truth and find my way always with the right course . . . and perhaps for it I will be butchered in my bed some night by the servants of empire. . . .

BENEATHA. *The martyr!*

ASAGAI. . . . or perhaps I shall live to be a very old man, respected and esteemed in my new nation. . . . And perhaps I shall hold office and this is what I'm trying to tell you, Alaiyo; perhaps the things I believe now for my country will be wrong and outmoded, and I will not understand and do terrible things to have things my way or merely to keep my power. Don't you see that there will be young men and women, not British soldiers then, but my own black countrymen . . . to step out of the shadows some evening and slit my then useless throat? Don't you see they have always been there . . . that they always will be. And that such a thing as my own death will be an advance? They who might kill me even . . . actually replenish me!

BENEATHA. Oh, Asagai, I know all that.

ASAGAI. Good! Then stop moaning and groaning and tell me what you plan to do.

BENEATHA. Do?

ASAGAI. I have a bit of a suggestion.

BENEATHA. What?

ASAGAI [*rather quietly for him*]. That when it is all over—that you come home with me—

BENEATHA [*slapping herself on the forehead with exasperation born of misunderstanding*]. Oh—Asagai—at this moment you decide to be romantic!

ASAGAI [*quickly understanding the misunderstanding*]. My dear, young creature of the New World—I do not mean across the city—I mean across the ocean; home—to Africa.

BENEATHA [*slowly understanding and turning to him with murmured amazement*]. To—to Nigeria?
ASAGAI. Yes! . . . [*Smiling and lifting his arms playfully*] Three hundred years later the African Prince rose up out of the seas and swept the maiden back across the middle passage over which her ancestors had come—
BENEATHA [*unable to play*]. Nigeria?
ASAGAI. Nigeria. Home. [*Coming to her with genuine romantic flippancy*] I will show you our mountains and our stars; and give you cool drinks from gourds and teach you the old songs and the ways of our people—and, in time, we will pretend that—[*very softly*]—you have only been away for a day—

[*She turns her back to him, thinking. He swings her around and takes her full in his arms in a long embrace which proceeds to passion.*]

BENEATHA [*pulling away*]. You're getting me all mixed up—
ASAGAI. Why?
BENEATHA. Too many things—too many things have happened today. I must sit down and think. I don't know what I feel about anything right this minute. [*She promptly sits down and props her chin on her fist.*]
ASAGAI [*charmed*]. All right, I shall leave you. No—don't get up. [*Touching her, gently, sweetly*] Just sit awhile and think. . . . Never be afraid to sit awhile and think. [*He goes to door and looks at her.*] How often I have looked at you and said, "Ah—so this is what the New World hath finally wrought. . . ."

[*He exits.* BENEATHA *sits on alone. Presently* WALTER *enters from his room and starts to rummage through things, feverishly looking for something. She looks up and turns in her seat.*]

BENEATHA [*hissingly*]. Yes—just look at what the New World hath wrought! . . . Just look! [*She gestures with bitter disgust.*] There he is! *Monsieur le petit bourgeois noir*—himself! There he is—Symbol of a Rising Class! Entrepreneur! Titan of the system! [WALTER *ignores her completely and continues frantically and destructively looking for something and hurling things to floor and tearing things out of their place in his search.* BENEATHA *ignores the eccentricity of his actions and goes on with the monologue of insult.*] Did you dream of yachts on Lake Michigan, Brother? Did you see yourself on that Great Day sitting down at the Conference Table, surrounded by all the mighty bald-headed men in America? All halted, waiting, breathless, waiting for your pronouncements on industry? Waiting for you—Chairman of the Board? [WALTER *finds what he is looking for—a small piece of white paper—and pushes it in his pocket and puts on his coat and rushes out without ever having looked at her. She shouts after him.*] I look at you and I see the final triumph of stupidity in the world!

[*The door slams and she returns to just sitting again.* RUTH *comes quickly out of* MAMA's *room.*]

RUTH. Who was that?
BENEATHA. Your husband.
RUTH. Where did he go?
BENEATHA. Who knows—maybe he has an appointment at U.S. Steel.
RUTH [*anxiously, with frightened eyes*]. You didn't say nothing bad to him, did you?
BENEATHA. Bad? Say anything bad to him? No—I told him he was a sweet boy and full of dreams and everything is strictly peachy keen, as the ofay kids say!

[MAMA *enters from her bedroom. She is lost, vague, trying to catch hold, to make some sense of her former command of the world, but it still eludes her. A sense of waste overwhelms her gait; a measure of apology rides on her shoulders. She goes to her plant, which has remained on the table, looks at it, picks it up and takes it to the window sill and sits it outside, and she stands and looks at it a long moment. Then she closes the window, straightens her body with effort and turns around to her children.*]

MAMA. Well—ain't it a mess in here, though? [*A false cheerfulness, a beginning of something*] I guess we all better stop moping around and get some work done. All this unpacking and everything we got to do. [RUTH *raises her head slowly in response to the sense of the line; and* BENEATHA *in similar manner turns very slowly to look at her mother.*] One of you all better call the moving people and tell 'em not to come.
RUTH. Tell 'em not to come?
MAMA. Of course, baby. Ain't no need in 'em coming all the way here and having to go back. They charges for that too. [*She sits down, fingers to her brow, thinking.*] Lord, ever since I was a little girl, I always remembers people saying, "Lena—Lena Eggleston, you aims too high all the time. You needs to slow down and see life a little more like it is. Just slow down some." That's what they always used to say down home—"Lord, that Lena Eggleston is a high-minded thing. She'll get her due one day!"
RUTH. No, Lena . . . .

MAMA. Me and Big Walter just didn't never learn right.
RUTH. Lena, no! We gotta go. Bennie—tell her . . . . [*She rises and crosses to* BENEATHA *with her arms outstretched.* BENEATHA *doesn't respond.*] Tell her we can still move . . . the notes ain't but a hundred and twenty-five a month. We got four grown people in this house—we can work . . . .
MAMA [*to herself*]. Just aimed too high all the time—
RUTH [*turning and going to* MAMA *fast—the words pouring out with urgency and desperation*]. Lena—I'll work. . . . I'll work twenty hours a day in all the kitchens in Chicago. . . . I'll strap my baby on my back if I have to and scrub all the floors in America and wash all the sheets in America if I have to—but we got to move. . . . We got to get out of here . . . .

[MAMA *reaches out absently and pats* RUTH's *hand.*]

MAMA. No—I sees things differently now. Been thinking 'bout some of the things we could do to fix this place up some. I seen a second-hand bureau over on Maxwell Street just the other day that could fit right there. [*She points to where the new furniture might go.* RUTH *wanders away from her.*] Would need some new handles on it and then a little varnish and then it look like something brand-new. And—we can put up them new curtains in the kitchen. . . . Why this place be looking fine. Cheer us all up so that we forget trouble ever came. . . . [*To* RUTH] And you could get some nice screens to put up in your room round the baby's bassinet. . . . [*She looks at both of them, pleadingly.*] Sometimes you just got to know when to give up some things . . . and hold on to what you got.

[WALTER *enters from the outside, looking spent and leaning against the door, his coat hanging from him.*]

MAMA. Where you been, son?
WALTER [*breathing hard*]. Made a call.
MAMA. To who, son?
WALTER. To The Man.
MAMA. What man, baby?
WALTER. The Man, Mama. Don't you know who The Man is?
RUTH. Walter Lee?
WALTER. *The Man.* Like the guys in the streets say—The Man. Captain Boss—Mistuh Charley . . . Old Captain Please Mr. Bossman . . .
BENEATHA [*suddenly*]. Lindner!
WALTER. That's right! That's good. I told him to come right over.
BENEATHA [*fiercely, understanding*]. For what? What do you want to see him for!

WALTER [*looking at his sister*]. We going to do business with him.
MAMA. What you talking 'bout, son?
WALTER. Talking 'bout life, Mama. You all always telling me to see life like it is. Well—I laid in there on my back today . . . and I figured it out. Life just like it is. Who gets and who don't get. [*He sits down with his coat on and laughs.*] Mama, you know it's all divided up. Life is. Sure enough. Between the takers and the "tooken." [*He laughs.*] I've figured it out finally. [*He looks around at them.*] Yeah. Some of us always getting "tooken." [*He laughs.*] People like Willy Harris, they don't never get "tooken." And you know why the rest of us do? 'Cause we all mixed up. Mixed up bad. We get to looking 'round for the right and the wrong; and we worry about it and cry about it and stay up nights trying to figure out 'bout the wrong and the right of things all the time. . . . And all the time, man, them takers is out there operating, just taking and taking. Willy Harris? Shoot—Willy Harris don't even count. He don't even count in the big scheme of things. But I'll say one thing for old Willy Harris . . . he's taught me something. He's taught me to keep my eye on what counts in this world. Yeah—[*shouting out a little*] Thanks, Willy!
RUTH. What did you call that man for, Walter Lee?
WALTER. Called him to tell him to come on over to the show. Gonna put on a show for the man. Just what he wants to see. You see, Mama, the man came here today and he told us that them people out there where you want us to move—well they so upset they willing to pay us not to move out there. [*He laughs again.*] And—and oh, Mama—you would of been proud of the way me and Ruth and Bennie acted. We told him to get out . . . Lord have mercy! We told the man to get out. Oh, we was some proud folks this afternoon, yeah. [*He lights a cigarette.*] We were still full of that old-time stuff. . . .
RUTH [*coming toward him slowly*]. You talking 'bout taking them people's money to keep us from moving in that house?
WALTER. I ain't just talking 'bout it, baby—I'm telling you that's what's going to happen.
BENEATHA. Oh, God! Where is the bottom! Where is the real honest-to-God bottom so he can't go any farther!
WALTER. See—that's old stuff. You and that boy that was here today. You all want everybody to carry a flag and a spear and sing some marching songs, huh? You wanna spend your life looking into things and trying to find the right and the wrong part, huh? Yeah. You know what's going to happen to that boy someday—he'll find himself sitting in a dungeon, locked in forever—and the takers will have

the key! Forget it, baby! There ain't no causes—there ain't nothing but taking in this world, and he who takes most is smartest—and it don't make a damn bit of difference *how*.

MAMA. You making something inside me cry, son. Some awful pain inside me.

WALTER. Don't cry, Mama. Understand. That white man is going to walk in that door able to write checks for more money than we ever had. It's important to him and I'm going to help him . . . I'm going to put on the show, Mama.

MAMA. Son—I come from five generations of people who was slaves and sharecroppers—but ain't nobody in my family never let nobody pay 'em no money that was a way of telling us we wasn't fit to walk the earth. We ain't never been that poor. [*Raising her eyes and looking at him*] We ain't never been that dead inside.

BENEATHA. Well—we are dead now. All the talk about dreams and sunlight that goes on in this house. All dead.

WALTER. What's the matter with you all! I didn't make this world! It was give to me this way! Hell, yes, I want me some yachts someday! Yes, I want to hang some real pearls 'round my wife's neck. Ain't she supposed to wear no pearls? Somebody tell me—tell me, who decides which women is suppose to wear pearls in this world. I tell you I am a *man*—and I think my wife should wear some pearls in this world!

[*This last line hangs a good while and* WALTER *begins to move about the room. The word "Man" has penetrated his consciousness; he mumbles it to himself repeatedly between strange agitated pauses as he moves about.*]

MAMA. Baby, how you going to feel on the inside?

WALTER. Fine! . . . Going to feel fine . . . a man . . . .

MAMA. You won't have nothing left then, Walter Lee.

WALTER [*coming to her*]. I'm going to feel fine, Mama. I'm going to look that son-of-a-bitch in the eyes and say—[*he falters*]—and say, "All right, Mr. Lindner—[*he falters even more*]—that's your neighborhood out there. You got the right to keep it like you want. You got the right to have it like you want. Just write the check and—the house is yours." And, and I am going to say— [*His voice almost breaks.*] And you—you people just put the money in my hand and you won't have to live next to this bunch of stinking niggers! . . . [*He straightens up and moves away from his mother, walking around the room.*] Maybe—maybe I'll just get down on my black knees . . . . [*He does so;* RUTH *and* BENNIE *and* MAMA *watch him in frozen horror.*] Captain, Mistuh, Bossman. [*He starts crying.*] A-hee-hee-

hee! [*Wringing his hands in profoundly anguished imitation*] Yasssssuh! Great White Father, just gi' ussen de money, fo' God's sake, and we's ain't gwine come out deh and dirty up yo' white folks neighborhood. . . .

[*He breaks down completely, then gets up and goes into the bedroom.*]

BENEATHA. That is not a man. That is nothing but a toothless rat.

MAMA. Yes—death done come in this here house. [*She is nodding, slowly, reflectively.*] Done come walking in my house. On the lips of my children. You what supposed to be my beginning again. You—what supposed to be my harvest. [*To* BENEATHA] You—you mourning your brother?

BENEATHA. He's no brother of mine.

MAMA. What you say?

BENEATHA. I said that that individual in that room is no brother of mine.

MAMA. That's what I thought you said. You feeling like you better than he is today? [BENEATHA *does not answer.*] Yes? What you tell him a minute ago? That he wasn't a man? Yes? You give him up for me? You done wrote his epitaph too—like the rest of the world? Well, who give you the privilege?

BENEATHA. Be on my side for once! You saw what he just did, Mama! You saw him—down on his knees. Wasn't it you who taught me—to despise any man who would do that. Do what he's going to do.

MAMA. Yes—I taught you that. Me and your daddy. But I thought I taught you something else too . . . I thought I taught you to love him.

BENEATHA. Love him? There is nothing left to love.

MAMA. There is always something left to love. And if you ain't learned that, you ain't learned nothing. [*Looking at her*] Have you cried for that boy today? I don't mean for yourself and for the family 'cause we lost the money. I mean for him; what he been through and what it done to him. Child, when do you think is the time to love somebody the most; when they done good and made things easy for everybody? Well then, you ain't through learning—because that ain't the time at all. It's when he's at his lowest and can't believe in hisself 'cause the world done whipped him so. When you starts measuring somebody, measure him right, child, measure him right. Make sure you done taken into account what hills and valleys he come through before he got to wherever he is.

[TRAVIS *bursts into the room at the end of the speech, leaving the door open.*]

TRAVIS. Grandmama—the moving men are downstairs! The truck just pulled up.

MAMA [*turning and looking at him*]. Are they, baby? They downstairs?

[*She sighs and sits.* LINDNER *appears in the doorway. He peers in and knocks lightly, to gain attention, and comes in. All turn to look at him.*]

LINDNER [*hat and briefcase in hand*]. Uh—hello . . .

[RUTH *crosses mechanically to the bedroom door and opens it and lets it swing open freely and slowly as the lights come up on* WALTER *within, still in his coat, sitting at the far corner of the room. He looks up and out through the room to* LINDNER.]

RUTH. He's here.

[*A long minute passes and* WALTER *slowly gets up.*]

LINDNER [*coming to the table with efficiency, putting his briefcase on the table and starting to unfold papers and unscrew fountain pens*]. Well, I certainly was glad to hear from you people. [WALTER *has begun the trek out of the room, slowly and awkwardly, rather like a small boy, passing the back of his sleeve across his mouth from time to time.*] Life can really be so much simpler than people let it be most of the time. Well—with whom do I negotiate? You, Mrs. Younger, or your son here? [MAMA *sits with her hands folded on her lap and her eyes closed as* WALTER *advances.* TRAVIS *goes close to* LINDNER *and looks at the papers curiously.*] Just some official papers, sonny.

RUTH. Travis, you go downstairs.

MAMA [*opening her eyes and looking into* WALTER's]. No. Travis, you stay right here. And you make him understand what you doing, Walter Lee. You teach him good. Like Willy Harris taught you. You show where our five generations done come to. Go ahead, son—

WALTER [*looks down into his boy's eyes.* TRAVIS *grins at him merrily and* WALTER *draws him beside him with his arm lightly around his shoulders*]. Well, Mr. Lindner. [BENEATHA *turns away.*] We called you—[*there is a profound, simple groping quality in his speech*]—because, well, me and my family—[*He looks around and shifts from one foot to the other.*] Well—we are very plain people . . . .

LINDNER. Yes—

WALTER. I mean—I have worked as a chauffeur most of my life—and my wife here, she does domestic work in people's kitchens. So does my mother. I mean—we are plain people . . . .

LINDNER. Yes, Mr. Younger—
WALTER [*really like a small boy, looking down at his shoes and then up at the man*]. And—uh—well, my father, well, he was a laborer most of his life.
LINDNER [*absolutely confused*]. Uh, yes—
WALTER [*looking down at his toes once again*]. My father almost beat a man to death once because this man called him a bad name or something, you know what I mean?
LINDNER. No, I'm afraid I don't.
WALTER [*finally straightening up*]. Well, what I mean is that we come from people who had a lot of pride. I mean—we are very proud people. And that's my sister over there and she's going to be a doctor —and we are very proud—
LINDNER. Well—I am sure that is very nice, but—
WALTER [*starting to cry and facing the man eye to eye*]. What I am telling you is that we called you over here to tell you that we are very proud and that this is—this is my son, who makes the sixth generation of our family in this country, and that we have all thought about your offer and we have decided to move into our house because my father—my father—he earned it. [MAMA *has her eyes closed and is rocking back and forth as though she were in church, with her head nodding the amen yes.*] We don't want to make no trouble for nobody or fight no causes—but we will try to be good neighbors. That's all we got to say. [*He looks the man absolutely in the eyes.*] We don't want your money. [*He turns and walks away from the man.*]
LINDNER [*looking around at all of them*]. I take it then that you have decided to occupy.
BENEATHA. That's what the man said.
LINDNER [*to* MAMA *in her reverie*]. Then I would like to appeal to you, Mrs. Younger. You are older and wiser and understand things better I am sure . . . .
MAMA [*rising*]. I am afraid you don't understand. My son said we was going to move and there ain't nothing left for me to say. [*Shaking her head with double meaning*] You know how these young folks is nowadays, mister. Can't do a thing with 'em. Goodbye.
LINDNER [*folding up his materials*]. Well—if you are that final about it . . . . There is nothing left for me to say. [*He finishes. He is almost ignored by the family, who are concentrating on* WALTER LEE. *At the door* LINDNER *halts and looks around.*] I sure hope you people know what you're doing. [*He shakes his head and exits.*]
RUTH [*looking around and coming to life*]. Well, for God's sake—if

the moving men are here—LET'S GET THE HELL OUT OF HERE!

MAMA [*into action*]. Ain't it the truth! Look at all this here mess. Ruth, put Travis' good jacket on him. . . . Walter Lee, fix your tie and tuck your shirt in, you look just like somebody's hoodlum. Lord have mercy, where is my plant? [*She flies to get it amid the general bustling of the family, who are deliberately trying to ignore the nobility of the past moment.*] You all start on down. . . . Travis child, don't go empty-handed. . . . Ruth, where did I put that box with my skillets in it? I want to be in charge of it myself. . . . I'm going to make us the biggest dinner we ever ate tonight. . . . Beneatha, what's the matter with them stockings? Pull them things up, girl . . . .

[*The family starts to file out as two moving men appear and begin to carry out the heavier pieces of furniture, bumping into the family as they move about.*]

BENEATHA. Mama, Asagai—asked me to marry him today and go to Africa—
MAMA [*in the middle of her getting-ready activity*]. He did? You ain't old enough to marry nobody—[*Seeing the moving men lifting one of her chairs precariously*] Darling, that ain't no bale of cotton, please handle it so we can sit in it again. I had that chair twenty-five years . . . .

[*The movers sigh with exasperation and go on with their work.*]

BENEATHA [*girlishly and unreasonably trying to pursue the conversation*]. To go to Africa, Mama—be a doctor in Africa . . . .
MAMA [*distracted*]. Yes, baby—
WALTER. Africa! What he want you to go to Africa for?
BENEATHA. To practice there . . . .
WALTER. Girl, if you don't get all them silly ideas out your head! You better marry yourself a man with some loot . . . .
BENEATHA [*angrily, precisely as in the first scene of the play*]. What have you got to do with who I marry!
WALTER. Plenty. Now I think George Murchison—

[*He and* BENEATHA *go out yelling at each other vigorously;* BENEATHA *is heard saying that she would not marry* GEORGE MURCHISON *if he were Adam and she were Eve, etc. The anger is loud and real till their voices diminish.* RUTH *stands at the door and turns to* MAMA *and smiles knowingly.*]

MAMA [*fixing her hat at last*]. Yeah—they something all right, my children . . . .
RUTH. Yeah—they're something. Let's go, Lena.
MAMA [*stalling, starting to look around at the house*]. Yes—I'm coming. Ruth—
RUTH. Yes?
MAMA [*quietly, woman to woman*]. He finally come into his manhood today, didn't he? Kind of like a rainbow after the rain . . . .
RUTH [*biting her lip lest her own pride explode in front of* MAMA]. Yes, Lena.

[WALTER's *voice calls for them raucously.*]

MAMA [*waving* RUTH *out vaguely*]. All right, honey—go on down. I be down directly.

> [RUTH *hesitates, then exits.* MAMA *stands, at last alone in the living room, her plant on the table before her as the lights start to come down. She looks around at all the walls and ceilings and suddenly, despite herself, while the children call below, a great heaving thing rises in her and she puts her fist to her mouth, takes a final desperate look, pulls her coat about her, pats her hat and goes out. The lights dim down. The door opens and she comes back in, grabs her plant, and goes out for the last time.*]

CURTAIN

ALL MY SONS

by ARTHUR MILLER

ALL MY SONS From *Arthur Miller's Collected Plays.* Copyright ©
1947 by Arthur Miller. Reprinted by permission of The Viking Press, Inc.

CAUTION: This play in its printed form is designed for the reading public only.
All dramatic rights in it are fully protected by copyright, and no public or
private performance—professional or amateur—may be given without the
written permission of the author and the payment of royalty. As the courts have
also ruled that the public reading of a play constitutes a public performance,
no such reading may be given except under the conditions stated above.
Communication should be addressed to the author's representative, International
Famous Agency, Inc., 1301 Avenue of the Americas, New York, N.Y. 10019.

Photos by Jim McDonald: Resident professional company, McCarter Theatre of
Princeton University, 1970 production.

Arthur Miller ranks with Eugene O'Neill, Thornton Wilder, Tennessee Williams, and Edward Albee among the most important American playwrights of the twentieth century. *All My Sons* was Miller's first successful Broadway play, and with it he won the New York Drama Critics Circle Award. Since 1947, when it was first performed, Miller has added *Death of a Salesman, The Crucible, A View from the Bridge, After the Fall, Incident at Vichy,* and *The Price* to a growing list of major American plays.

The action of *All My Sons* turns on the meaning of antisocial acts for the individual and for society at large. The time is three and one-half years after the crime of the story was committed, but the entrance of Chris Keller and his fiancée, whose father was Chris's father's former business partner, precipitates the crisis and catastrophe of the play. The sixty-one-year-old Joe Keller has no sense of the chainlike connection between his family, his business, and the rest of the world. His past acts, dictated by his "Look out for number one!" philosophy, have planted the seeds of consequences which begin to germinate as the play opens. And the play's action, set in motion by his son's conscience, develops Miller's theme: the interrelatedness of our acts and their consequences—the past and the present. The method Miller has chosen to dramatize his theme places the play squarely within the generational conflict. Until his son Chris discovers the enormity of his father's crime, Joe believes his act has been redeemed by his parental motive. "For you," he repeats to Chris, "I did it all for you."

One of the play's more remarkable qualities is that within an atmosphere of suburban normality with characters as recognizable as the next-door neighbors, Arthur Miller explores some of the profound social questions that have emerged in the twentieth century, especially during the last two decades. In *All My Sons* he holds up to scrutiny the relationship of the individual to society and examines the belief that man's conscience will inevitably create order out of chaos, civilization out of the jungle of human ideas and acts.

Characters

JOE KELLER
KATE KELLER (MOTHER), *his wife*
CHRIS KELLER, *his son*
ANN DEEVER
GEORGE DEEVER
DR. JIM BAYLISS
SUE BAYLISS, *his wife*
FRANK LUBEY
LYDIA LUBEY, *his wife*
BERT, *a boy*

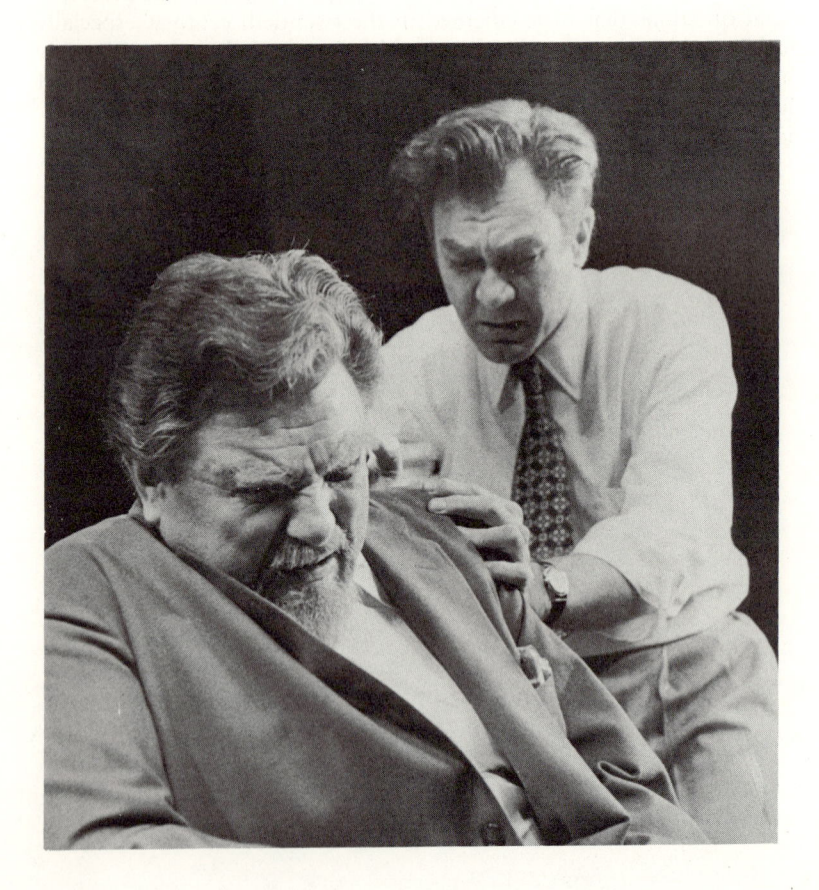

ACT ONE

The back yard of the Keller home in the outskirts of an American town. August of our era.

The stage is hedged on right and left by tall, closely planted poplars which lend the yard a secluded atmosphere. Upstage is filled with the back of the house and its open, unroofed porch which extends into the yard some six feet. The house is two stories high and has seven rooms. It would have cost perhaps fifteen thousand in the early twenties when it was built. Now it is nicely painted, looks tight and comfortable, and the yard is green with sod, here and there plants whose season is gone. At the right, beside the house, the entrance of the driveway can be seen, but the poplars cut off view of its continuation downstage. In the left corner, downstage, stands the four-foot-high stump of a slender apple tree whose upper trunk and branches lie toppled beside it, fruit still clinging to its branches.

Downstage right is a small, trellised arbor, shaped like a sea shell, with a decorative bulb hanging from its forward-curving roof. Garden chairs and a table are scattered about. A garbage pail on the ground next to the porch steps, a wire leaf-burner near it.

On the rise: It is early Sunday morning. JOE KELLER *is sitting in the sun reading the want ads of the Sunday paper, the other sections of which lie neatly on the ground beside him. Behind his back, inside the arbor,* DOCTOR JIM BAYLISS *is reading part of the paper at the table.*

KELLER *is nearing sixty. A heavy man of stolid mind and build, a business man these many years, but with the imprint of the machine-shop worker and boss still upon him. When he reads, when he speaks, when he listens, it is with the terrible concentration of the uneducated man for whom there is still wonder in many commonly known things, a man whose judgments must be dredged out of experience and a peasant-like common sense. A man among men.*

DOCTOR BAYLISS *is nearly forty. A wry self-controlled man, an easy talker, but with a wisp of sadness that clings even to his self-effacing humor.*

At curtain, JIM *is standing at left, staring at the broken tree. He taps a pipe on it, blows through the pipe, feels in his pockets for tobacco, then speaks.*

JIM. Where's your tobacco?
KELLER. I think I left it on the table. [JIM *goes slowly to table on the arbor, finds a pouch, and sits there on the bench, filling his pipe.*] Gonna rain tonight.
JIM. Paper says so?

KELLER. Yeah, right here.
JIM. Then it can't rain.

> [FRANK LUBEY *enters, through a small space between the poplars.* FRANK *is thirty-two but balding. A pleasant, opinionated man, uncertain of himself, with a tendency toward peevishness when crossed, but always wanting it pleasant and neighborly. He rather saunters in, leisurely, nothing to do. He does not notice* JIM *in the arbor. On his greeting,* JIM *does not bother looking up.*]

FRANK. Hya.
KELLER. Hello, Frank. What's doin'?
FRANK. Nothin'. Walking off my breakfast. [*Looks up at the sky*] That beautiful? Not a cloud.
KELLER [*looking up*]. Yeah, nice.
FRANK. Every Sunday ought to be like this.
KELLER [*indicating the sections beside him*]. Want the paper?
FRANK. What's the difference, it's all bad news. What's today's calamity?
KELLER. I don't know, I don't read the news part any more. It's more interesting in the want ads.
FRANK. Why, you trying to buy something?
KELLER. No, I'm just interested. To see what people want, y'know? For instance, here's a guy is lookin' for two Newfoundland dogs. Now what's he want with two Newfoundland dogs?
FRANK. That is funny.
KELLER. Here's another one. Wanted—old dictionaries. High prices paid. Now what's a man going to do with an old dictionary?
FRANK. Why not? Probably a book collector.
KELLER. You mean he'll make a living out of that?
FRANK. Sure, there's a lot of them.
KELLER [*shaking his head*]. All the kind of business goin' on. In my day, either you were a lawyer, or a doctor, or you worked in a shop. Now—
FRANK. Well, I was going to be a forester once.
KELLER. Well, that shows you; in my day, there was no such thing. [*Scanning the page, sweeping it with his hand*] You look at a page like this you realize how ignorant you are. [*Softly, with wonder, as he scans page*] Psss!
FRANK [*noticing tree*]. Hey, what happened to your tree?
KELLER. Ain't that awful? The wind must've got it last night. You heard the wind, didn't you?
FRANK. Yeah, I got a mess in my yard, too. [*Goes to tree*] What a pity. [*Turning to* KELLER] What'd Kate say?

KELLER. They're all asleep yet. I'm just waiting for her to see it.
FRANK [*struck*]. You know?—it's funny.
KELLER. What?
FRANK. Larry was born in August. He'd been twenty-seven this month. And his tree blows down.
KELLER [*touched*]. I'm surprised you remember his birthday, Frank. That's nice.
FRANK. Well, I'm working on his horoscope.
KELLER. How can you make him a horoscope? That's for the future, ain't it?
FRANK. Well, what I'm doing is this, see. Larry was reported missing on November twenty-fifth, right?
KELLER. Yeah?
FRANK. Well, then, we assume that if he was killed it was on November twenty-fifth. Now, what Kate wants—
KELLER. Oh, Kate asked you to make a horoscope?
FRANK. Yeah, what she wants to find out is whether November twenty-fifth was a favorable day for Larry.
KELLER. What is that, favorable day?
FRANK. Well, a favorable day for a person is a fortunate day, according to his stars. In other words it would be practically impossible for him to have died on his favorable day.
KELLER. Well, was that his favorable day?—November twenty-fifth?
FRANK. That's what I'm working on to find out. It takes time! See, the point is, if November twenty-fifth was his favorable day, then it's completely possible he's alive somewhere, because—I mean it's possible. [*He notices* JIM *now.* JIM *is looking at him as though at an idiot. To* JIM—*with an uncertain laugh*] I didn't even see you.
KELLER [*to* JIM]. Is he talkin' sense?
JIM. Him? He's all right. He's just completley out of his mind, that's all.
FRANK [*peeved*]. The trouble with you is, you don't *believe* in anything.
JIM. And your trouble is that you believe in *anything*. *You* didn't see my kid this morning, did you?
FRANK. No.
KELLER. Imagine? He walked off with his thermometer. Right out of his bag.
JIM [*getting up*]. What a problem. One look at a girl and he takes her temperature. [*Goes to driveway, looks upstage toward street*]
FRANK. That boy's going to be a real doctor; he's smart.
JIM. Over my dead body he'll be a doctor. A good beginning, too.
FRANK. Why? It's an honorable profession.

JIM [*looking at him tiredly*]. Frank, will you stop talking like a civics book? [KELLER *laughs.*]
FRANK. Why, I saw a movie a couple of weeks ago, reminded me of you. There was a doctor in that picture—
KELLER. Don Ameche!
FRANK. I think it was, yeah. And he worked in his basement discovering things. That's what you ought to do; you could help humanity, instead of—
JIM. I would love to help humanity on a Warner Brothers salary.
KELLER [*pointing at him, laughing*]. That's very good, Jim.
JIM [*looking toward house*]. Well, where's the beautiful girl was supposed to be here?
FRANK [*excited*]. Annie came?
KELLER. Sure, sleepin' upstairs. We picked her up on the one o'clock train last night. Wonderful thing. Girl leaves here, a scrawny kid. Couple of years go by, she's a regular woman. Hardly recognized her, and she was running in and out of this yard all her life. That was a very happy family used to live in your house, Jim.
JIM. Like to meet her. The block can use a pretty girl. In the whole neighborhood there's not a damned thing to look at. [SUE, JIM's *wife, enters. She is rounding forty, an overweight woman who fears it. On seeing her* JIM *wryly adds*] Except my wife, of course.
SUE [*in same spirit*]. Mrs. Adams is on the phone, you dog.
JIM [*to* KELLER]. Such is the condition which prevails—[*going to his wife*] my love, my light.
SUE. Don't sniff around me. [*Pointing to their house*] And give her a nasty answer. I can smell her perfume over the phone.
JIM. What's the matter with her now?
SUE. I don't know, dear. She sounds like she's in terrible pain—unless her mouth is full of candy.
JIM. Why don't you just tell her to lay down?
SUE. She enjoys it more when you tell her to lay down. And when are you going to see Mr. Hubbard?
JIM. My dear; Mr. Hubbard is not sick, and I have better things to do than to sit there and hold his hand.
SUE. It seems to me that for ten dollars you could hold his hand.
JIM [*to* KELLER]. If your son wants to play golf tell him I'm ready. Or if he'd like to take a trip around the world for about thirty years. [*He exits.*]
KELLER. Why do you needle him? He's a doctor, women are supposed to call him up.
SUE. All I said was Mrs. Adams is on the phone. Can I have some of your parsley?

KELLER. Yeah, sure. [*She goes to parsley box and pulls some parsley.*] You were a nurse too long, Susie. You're too . . . too . . . realistic.
SUE [*laughing, pointing at him*]. Now you said it!

[LYDIA LUBEY *enters. She is a robust, laughing girl of twenty-seven.*]

LYDIA. Frank, the toaster—[*Sees the others*] Hya.
KELLER. Hello!
LYDIA [*to* FRANK]. The toaster is off again.
FRANK. Well, plug it in, I just fixed it.
LYDIA [*kindly, but insistently*]. Please, dear, fix it back like it was before.
FRANK. I don't know why you can't learn to turn on a simple thing like a toaster! [*He exits.*]
SUE [*laughing*]. Thomas Edison.
LYDIA [*apologetically*]. He's really very handy. [*She sees broken tree.*] Oh, did the wind get your tree?
KELLER. Yeah, last night.
LYDIA. Oh, what a pity. Annie get in?
KELLER. She'll be down soon. Wait'll you meet her, Sue, she's a knockout.
SUE. I should've been a man. People are always introducing me to beautiful women. [*To* JOE] Tell her to come over later: I imagine she'd like to see what we did with her house. And thanks. [*She exits.*]
LYDIA. Is she still unhappy, Joe?
KELLER. Annie? I don't suppose she goes around dancing on her toes, but she seems to be over it.
LYDIA. She going to get married? Is there anybody—?
KELLER. I suppose—say, it's a couple years already. She can't mourn a boy forever.
LYDIA. It's so strange—Annie's here and not even married. And I've got three babies. I always thought it'd be the other way around.
KELLER. Well, that's what a war does. I had two sons, now I got one. It changed all the tallies. In my day when you had sons it was an honor. Today a doctor could make a million dollars if he could figure out a way to bring a boy into the world without a trigger finger.
LYDIA. You know, I was just reading—

[*Enter* CHRIS KELLER *from house, stands in doorway.*]

LYDIA. Hya, Chris.

[FRANK *shouts from offstage.*]

FRANK. Lydia, come in here! If you want the toaster to work don't plug in the malted mixer.
LYDIA [*embarrassed, laughing*]. Did I?
FRANK. And the next time I fix something don't tell me I'm crazy! Now come in here!
LYDIA [*to* KELLER]. I'll never hear the end of this one.
KELLER [*calling to* FRANK]. So what's the difference? Instead of toast have a malted!
LYDIA. Sh! sh! [*She exits, laughing.*]

[CHRIS *watches her off. He is thirty-two; like his father, solidly built, a listener. A man capable of immense affection and loyalty. He has a cup of coffee in one hand, part of a doughnut in the other.*]

KELLER. You want the paper?
CHRIS. That's all right, just the book section. [*He bends down and pulls out part of paper on porch floor.*]
KELLER. You're always reading the book section and you never buy a book.
CHRIS [*coming down to settee*]. I like to keep abreast of my ignorance. [*He sits on settee.*]
KELLER. What is that, every week a new book comes out?
CHRIS. Lot of new books.
KELLER. All different.
CHRIS. All different.

[KELLER *shakes his head, puts knife down on bench, takes oilstone up to the cabinet.*]

KELLER. Pss! Annie up yet?
CHRIS. Mother's giving her breakfast in the dining room.
KELLER [*looking at broken tree*]. See what happened to the tree?
CHRIS [*without looking up*]. Yeah.
KELLER. What's Mother going to say?

[BERT *runs on from driveway. He is about eight. He jumps on stool, then on* KELLER'S *back.*]

BERT. You're finally up.
KELLER [*swinging him around and putting him down*]. Ha! Bert's here! Where's Tommy? He's got his father's thermometer again.
BERT. He's taking a reading.
CHRIS. What!
BERT. But it's only oral.

KELLER. Oh, well, there's no harm in oral. So what's new this morning, Bert?
BERT. Nothin'. [*He goes to broken tree, walks around it.*]
KELLER. Then you couldn't 've made a complete inspection of the block. In the beginning, when I first made you a policeman you used to come in every morning with something new. Now, nothin's ever new.
BERT. Except some kids from Thirtieth Street. They started kicking a can down the block, and I made them go away because you were sleeping.
KELLER. Now you're talkin', Bert. Now you're on the ball. First thing you know I'm liable to make you a detective.
BERT [*pulling him down by the lapel and whispering in his ear*]. Can I see the jail now?
KELLER. Seein' the jail ain't allowed, Bert. You know that.
BERT. Aw, I betcha there isn't even a jail. I don't see any bars on the cellar windows.
KELLER. Bert, on my word of honor there's a jail in the basement. I showed you my gun, didn't I?
BERT. But that's a hunting gun.
KELLER. That's an arresting gun!
BERT. Then why don't you ever arrest anybody? Tommy said another dirty word to Doris yesterday, and you didn't even demote him.

[KELLER *chuckles and winks at* CHRIS, *who is enjoying all this.*]

KELLER. Yeah, that's a dangerous character, that Tommy. [*Beckons him closer*] What word does he say?
BERT [*backing away quickly in great embarrassment*]. Oh, I can't say that.
KELLER [*grabbing him by the shirt and pulling him back*]. Well, gimme an idea.
BERT. I can't. It's not a nice word.
KELLER. Just whisper it in my ear. I'll close my eyes. Maybe I won't even hear it.

[BERT, *on tiptoe, puts his lips to* KELLER's *ear, then in unbearable embarrassment steps back.*]

BERT. I can't, Mr. Keller.
CHRIS [*laughing*]. Don't make him do that.
KELLER. Okay, Bert. I take your word. Now go out, and keep both eyes peeled.
BERT [*interested*]. For what?

KELLER. For what! Bert, the whole neighborhood is depending on you. A policeman don't ask questions. Now peel them eyes!
BERT [*mystified, but willing*]. Okay. [*He runs off stage back of arbor.*]
KELLER [*calling after him*]. And mum's the word, Bert.

[BERT *stops and sticks his head through the arbor.*]

BERT. About what?
KELLER. Just in general. Be v-e-r-y careful.
BERT [*nodding in bewilderment*]. Okay. [*He exits.*]
KELLER [*laughing*]. I got all the kids crazy!
CHRIS. One of these days, they'll all come in here and beat your brains out.
KELLER. What's she going to say? Maybe we ought to tell her before she sees it.
CHRIS. She saw it.
KELLER. How could she see it? I was the first one up. She was still in bed.
CHRIS. She was out here when it broke.
KELLER. When?
CHRIS. About four this morning. [*Indicating window above them*] I heard it cracking and I woke up and looked out. She was standing right here when it cracked.
KELLER. What was she doing out here four in the morning?
CHRIS. I don't know. When it cracked she ran back into the house and cried in the kitchen.
KELLER. Did you talk to her?
CHRIS. No, I—I figured the best thing was to leave her alone.

[*Pause*]

KELLER [*deeply touched*]. She cried hard?
CHRIS. I could hear her right through the floor of my room.
KELLER [*after slight pause*]. What was she doing out here at that hour? [CHRIS *silent. With an undertone of anger showing*] She's dreaming about him again. She's walking around at night.
CHRIS. I guess she is.
KELLER. She's getting just like after he died. [*Slight pause*] What's the meaning of that?
CHRIS. I don't know the meaning of it. [*Slight pause*] But I know one thing, Dad. We've made a terrible mistake with Mother.
KELLER. What?
CHRIS. Being dishonest with her. That kind of thing always pays off, and now it's paying off.

KELLER. What do you mean, dishonest?
CHRIS. You know Larry's not coming back and I know it. Why do we allow her to go on thinking that we believe with her?
KELLER. What do you want to do, argue with her?
CHRIS. I don't want to argue with her, but it's time she realized that nobody believes Larry is alive any more. [KELLER *simply moves away, thinking, looking at the ground.*] Why shouldn't she dream of him, walk the nights waiting for him? Do we contradict her? Do we say straight out that we have no hope any more? That we haven't had any hope for years now?
KELLER [*frightened at the thought*]. You can't say that to her.
CHRIS. We've got to say it to her.
KELLER. How're you going to prove it? Can you prove it?
CHRIS. For God's sake, three years! Nobody comes back after three years. It's insane.
KELLER. To you it is, and to me. But not to her. You can talk yourself blue in the face, but there's no body and there's no grave, so where are you?
CHRIS. Sit down, Dad. I want to talk to you.

[KELLER *looks at him searchingly a moment.*]

KELLER. The trouble is the Goddam newspapers. Every month some boy turns up from nowhere, so the next one is going to be Larry, so—
CHRIS. All right, all right, listen to me. [*Slight pause.* KELLER *sits on settee.*] You know why I asked Annie here, don't you?
KELLER [*he knows, but—*]. Why?
CHRIS. You know.
KELLER. Well, I got an idea, but— What's the story?
CHRIS. I'm going to ask her to marry me. [*Slight pause*]

[KELLER *nods.*]

KELLER. Well, that's only your business, Chris.
CHRIS. You know it's not only my business.
KELLER. What do you want me to do? You're old enough to know your own mind.
CHRIS [*asking, annoyed*]. Then it's all right, I'll go ahead with it?
KELLER. Well, you want to be sure Mother isn't going to—
CHRIS. Then it isn't just my business.
KELLER. I'm just sayin'—
CHRIS. Sometimes you infuriate me, you know that? Isn't it your business, too, if I tell this to Mother and she throws a fit about it? You have such a talent for ignoring things.

KELLER. I ignore what I gotta ignore. The girl is Larry's girl.
CHRIS. She's not Larry's girl.
KELLER. From Mother's point of view he is not dead and you have no right to take his girl. [*Slight pause*] Now you can go on from there if you know where to go, but I'm tellin' you I don't know where to go. See? I don't know. Now what can I do for you?
CHRIS. I don't know why it is, but every time I reach out for something I want, I have to pull back because other people will suffer. My whole bloody life, time after time after time.
KELLER. You're a considerate fella, there's nothing wrong in that.
CHRIS. To hell with that.
KELLER. Did you ask Annie yet?
CHRIS. I wanted to get this settled first.
KELLER. How do you know she'll marry you? Maybe she feels the same way Mother does?
CHRIS. Well, if she does, then that's the end of it. From her letters I think she's forgotten him. I'll find out. And then we'll thrash it out with Mother? Right? Dad, don't avoid me.
KELLER. The trouble is, you don't see enough women. You never did.
CHRIS. So what? I'm not fast with women.
KELLER. I don't see why it has to be Annie.
CHRIS. Because it is.
KELLER. That's a good answer, but it don't answer anything. You haven't seen her since you went to war. It's five years.
CHRIS. I can't help it. I know her best. I was brought up next door to her. These years when I think of someone for my wife, I think of Annie. What do you want, a diagram?
KELLER. I don't want a diagram . . . I—I'm— She thinks he's coming back, Chris. You marry that girl and you're pronouncing him dead. Now what's going to happen to Mother? Do you know? I don't! [*Pause*]
CHRIS. All right, then, Dad.
KELLER [*thinking* CHRIS *has retreated*]. Give it some thought.
CHRIS. I've given it three years of thought. I'd hoped that if I waited, Mother would forget Larry and then we'd have a regular wedding and everything happy. But if that can't happen here, then I'll have to get out.
KELLER. What the hell is *this*?
CHRIS. I'll get out. I'll get married and live some place else. Maybe in New York.
KELLER. Are you crazy?
CHRIS. I've been a good son too long, a good sucker. I'm through with it.
KELLER. You've got a business here, what the hell is this?

CHRIS. The business! The business doesn't inspire me.
KELLER. Must you be inspired?
CHRIS. Yes. I like it an hour a day. If I have to grub for money all day long at least at evening I want it beautiful. I want a family, I want some kids, I want to build something I can give myself to. Annie is in the middle of that. Now . . . where do I find it?
KELLER. You mean— [*Goes to him*] Tell me something, you mean you'd leave the business?
CHRIS. Yes. On this I would.
KELLER [*after a pause*]. Well . . . you don't want to think like that.
CHRIS. Then help me stay here.
KELLER. All right, but—but don't think like that. Because what the hell did I work for? That's only for you, Chris, the whole shootin' match is for you!
CHRIS. I know that, Dad. Just you help me stay here.
KELLER [*putting a fist up to* CHRIS'*s jaw*]. But don't think that way, you hear me?
CHRIS. I am thinking that way.
KELLER [*lowering his hand*]. I don't understand you, do I?
CHRIS. No, you don't. I'm a pretty tough guy.
KELLER. Yeah. I can see that.

[MOTHER *appears on porch. She is in her early fifties, a woman of uncontrolled inspirations and an overwhelming capacity for love.*]

MOTHER. Joe?
CHRIS [*going toward porch*]. Hello, Mom.
MOTHER [*indicating house behind her; to* KELLER]. Did you take a bag from under the sink?
KELLER. Yeah, I put it in the pail.
MOTHER. Well, get it out of the pail. That's my potatoes.
 [CHRIS *bursts out laughing—goes up into alley.*]
KELLER [*laughing*]. I thought it was garbage.
MOTHER. Will you do me a favor, Joe? Don't be helpful.
KELLER. I can afford another bag of potatoes.
MOTHER. Minnie scoured that pail in boiling water last night. It's cleaner than your teeth.
KELLER. And I don't understand why, after I worked forty years and I got a maid, why I have to take out the garbage.
MOTHER. If you would make up your mind that every bag in the kitchen isn't full of garbage you wouldn't be throwing out my vegetables. Last time it was the onions.

[CHRIS *comes on, hands her bag.*]

KELLER. I don't like garbage in the house.
MOTHER. Then don't eat. [*She goes into the kitchen with bag.*]
CHRIS. That settles you for today.
KELLER. Yeah, I'm in last place again. I don't know, once upon a time I used to think that when I got money again I would have a maid and my wife would take it easy. Now I got money, and I got a maid, and my wife is workin' for the maid. [*He sits in one of the chairs.*]

[MOTHER *comes out on last line. She carries a pot of string beans.*]

MOTHER. It's her day off, what are you crabbing about?
CHRIS [*to* MOTHER]. Isn't Annie finished eating?
MOTHER [*looking around preoccupiedly at yard*]. She'll be right out. [*Moves*] That wind did some job on this place. [*Of the tree*] So much for that, thank God.
KELLER [*indicating chair beside him*]. Sit down, take it easy.
MOTHER [*pressing her hand to top of her head*]. I've got such a funny pain on the top of my head.
CHRIS. Can I get you an aspirin?

[MOTHER *picks a few petals off ground, stands there smelling them in her hand, then sprinkles them over plants.*]

MOTHER. No more roses. It's so funny . . . everything decides to happen at the same time. This month is his birthday; his tree blows down, Annie comes. Everything that happened seems to be coming back. I was just down the cellar, and what do I stumble over? His baseball glove. I haven't seen it in a century.
CHRIS. Don't you think Annie looks well?
MOTHER. Fine. There's no question about it. She's a beauty . . . . I still don't know what brought her here. Not that I'm not glad to see her, but—
CHRIS. I just thought we'd all like to see each other again. [MOTHER *just looks at him, nodding ever so slightly—almost as though admitting something.*] And I wanted to see her myself.
MOTHER [*as her nods halt, to* KELLER]. The only thing is I think her nose got longer. But I'll always love that girl. She's one that didn't jump into bed with somebody else as soon as it happened with her fella.
KELLER [*as though that were impossible for* ANNIE]. Oh, what're you—?
MOTHER. Never mind. Most of them didn't wait till the telegrams were opened. I'm just glad she came, so you can see I'm not *completely* out of my mind. [*Sits, and rapidly breaks string beans in the pot.*]
CHRIS. Just because she isn't married doesn't mean she's been mourning Larry.

MOTHER [*with an undercurrent of observation*]. Why then isn't she?
CHRIS [*a little flustered*]. Well . . . it could've been any number of things.
MOTHER [*directly at him*]. Like what, for instance?
CHRIS [*embarrassed, but standing his ground*]. I don't know. Whatever it is. Can I get you an aspirin?

[MOTHER *puts her hand to her head. She gets up and goes aimlessly toward the trees on rising.*]

MOTHER. It's not like a headache.
KELLER. You don't sleep, that's why. She's wearing out more bedroom slippers than shoes.
MOTHER. I had a terrible night. [*She stops moving.*] I never had a night like that.
CHRIS [*looking at* KELLER]. What was it, Mom? Did you dream?
MOTHER. More, more than a dream.
CHRIS [*hesitantly*]. About Larry?
MOTHER. I was fast asleep, and— [*Raising her arm over the audience*] Remember the way he used to fly low past the house when he was in training? When we used to see his face in the cockpit going by? That's the way I saw him. Only high up. Way, way up, where the clouds are. He was so real I could reach out and touch him. And suddenly he started to fall. And crying, crying to me . . . Mom, Mom! I could hear him like he was in the room. Mom! . . . it was his voice! If I could touch him I knew I could stop him, if I could only— [*Breaks off, allowing her outstretched hand to fall*] I woke up and it was so funny— The wind . . . it was like the roaring of his engine. I came out here . . . I must've still been half asleep. I could hear that roaring like he was going by. The tree snapped right in front of me—and I like—came awake. [*She is looking at tree. She suddenly realizes something, turns with a reprimanding finger shaking slightly at* KELLER.] See? We should never have planted that tree. I said so in the first place; it was too soon to plant a tree for him.
CHRIS [*alarmed*]. Too soon!
MOTHER [*angering*]. We rushed into it. Everybody was in such a hurry to bury him. I *said* not to plant it yet. [*To* KELLER] I *told* you to—!
CHRIS. Mother, Mother! [*She looks into his face.*] The wind blew it down. What significance has that got? What are you talking about? Mother, please. . . . Don't go through it all again, will you? It's no good, it doesn't accomplish anything. I've been thinking, y'know?— maybe we ought to put our minds to forgetting him?
MOTHER. That's the third time you've said that this week.
CHRIS. Because it's not right; we never took up our lives again. We're

like at a railroad station waiting for a train that never comes in.

MOTHER [*pressing top of her head*]. Get me an aspirin, heh?

CHRIS. Sure, and let's break out of this, heh, Mom? I thought the four of us might go out to dinner a couple of nights, maybe go dancing out at the shore.

MOTHER. Fine. [*To* KELLER] We can do it tonight.

KELLER. Swell with me!

CHRIS. Sure, let's have some fun. [*To* MOTHER] You'll start with this aspirin. [*He goes up and into house with new spirit. Her smile vanishes.*]

MOTHER [*with an accusing undertone*]. Why did he invite her here?

KELLER. Why does that bother you?

MOTHER. She's been in New York three and a half years, why all of a sudden—?

KELLER. Well, maybe—maybe he just wanted to see her.

MOTHER. Nobody comes seven hundred miles "just to see."

KELLER. What do you mean? He lived next door to the girl all his life, why shouldn't he want to see her again? [MOTHER *looks at him critically.*] Don't look at me like that, he didn't tell me any more than he told you.

MOTHER [*a warning and a question*]. He's not going to marry her.

KELLER. How do you know he's even thinking of it?

MOTHER. It's got that about it.

KELLER [*sharply watching her reaction*]. Well? So what?

MOTHER [*alarmed*]. What's going on here, Joe?

KELLER. Now listen, kid—

MOTHER [*avoiding contact with him*]. She's not his girl, Joe; she knows she's not.

KELLER. You can't read her mind.

MOTHER. Then why is she still single? New York is full of men, why isn't she married? [*Pause*] Probably a hundred people told her she's foolish, but she's waited.

KELLER. How do you know why she waited?

MOTHER. She knows what I know, that's why. She's faithful as a rock. In my worst moments, I think of her waiting, and I know again that I'm right.

KELLER. Look, it's a nice day. What are we arguing for?

MOTHER [*warningly*]. Nobody in this house dast take her faith away, Joe. Strangers might. But not his father, not his brother.

KELLER [*exasperated*]. What do you want me to do? What do you want?

MOTHER. I want you to act like he's coming back. Both of you. Don't think I haven't noticed you since Chris invited her. I won't stand for any nonsense.

KELLER. But, Kate—

MOTHER. Because if he's not coming back, then I'll kill myself! Laugh. Laugh at me. [*She points to tree.*] But why did that happen the very night she came back? Laugh, but there are meanings in such things. She goes to sleep in his room and his memorial breaks in pieces. Look at it; look. [*She sits on bench.*] Joe—

KELLER. Calm yourself.

MOTHER. Believe with me, Joe. I can't stand all alone.

KELLER. Calm yourself.

MOTHER. Only last week a man turned up in Detroit, missing longer than Larry. You read it yourself.

KELLER. All right, all right, calm yourself.

MOTHER. You above all have got to believe, you—

KELLER [*rising*]. Why me above all?

MOTHER. Just don't stop believing.

KELLER. What does that mean, me above all?

[BERT *comes rushing on.*]

BERT. Mr. Keller! Say, Mr. Keller . . . [*Pointing up driveway*] Tommy just said it again!

KELLER [*not remembering any of it*]. Said what? Who?

BERT. The dirty word.

KELLER. Oh. Well—

BERT. Gee, aren't you going to arrest him? I warned him.

MOTHER [*with suddenness*]. Stop that, Bert. Go home. [BERT *backs up, as she advances.*] There's no jail here.

KELLER [*as though to say, "Oh-what-the-hell-let-him-believe-there-is"*]. Kate—

MOTHER [*turning on* KELLER *furiously*]. There's no jail here! I want you to stop that jail business! [*He turns, shamed, but peeved.*]

BERT [*past her to* KELLER]. He's right across the street.

MOTHER. Go home, Bert. [BERT *turns around and goes up driveway. She is shaken. Her speech is bitten off, extremely urgent.*] I want you to stop that, Joe. That whole jail business!

KELLER [*alarmed, therefore angered*]. Look at you, look at you shaking.

MOTHER [*trying to control herself, moving about clasping her hands*]. I can't help it.

KELLER. What have I got to hide? What the hell is the matter with you, Kate?

MOTHER. I didn't say you had anything to hide, I'm just telling you to stop it! Now stop it! [*As* ANN *and* CHRIS *appear on porch.* ANN *is twenty-six, gentle but despite herself capable of holding fast to what she knows.* CHRIS *opens door for her.*]

ANN. Hya, Joe! [*She leads off a general laugh that is not self-conscious because they know one another too well.*]

CHRIS [*bringing* ANN *down, with an outstretched, chivalric arm*]. Take a breath of that air, kid. You never get air like that in New York.

MOTHER [*genuinely overcome with it*]. Annie, where did you get that dress!

ANN. I couldn't resist. I'm taking it right off before I ruin it. [*Swings around*] How's that for three weeks' salary?

MOTHER [*to* KELLER]. Isn't she the most—? [*To* ANN] It's gorgeous, simply gor—

CHRIS [*to* MOTHER]. No kidding, now, isn't she the prettiest gal you ever saw?

MOTHER [*caught short by his obvious admiration, she finds herself reaching out for a glass of water and aspirin in his hand, and—*]. You gained a little weight, didn't you, darling? [*She gulps pill and drinks.*]

ANN. It comes and goes.

KELLER. Look how nice her legs turned out!

ANN [*as she runs to fence*]. Boy, the poplars got thick, didn't they?

[KELLER *moves to settee and sits.*]

KELLER. Well, it's three years, Annie. We're gettin' old, kid.

MOTHER. How does Mom like New York? [ANN *keeps looking through trees.*]

ANN [*a little hurt*]. Why'd they take our hammock away?

KELLER. Oh, no, it broke. Couple of years ago.

MOTHER. What broke? He had one of his light lunches and flopped into it.

ANN [*laughs and turns back toward* JIM's *yard*]. Oh, excuse me!

[JIM *has come to fence and is looking over it. He is smoking a cigar. As she cries out, he comes on around on stage.*]

JIM. How do you do. [*To* CHRIS] She looks very intelligent!

CHRIS. Ann, this is Jim—Doctor Bayliss.

ANN [*shaking* JIM's *hand*]. Oh, sure, he writes a lot about you.

JIM. Don't you believe it. He likes everybody. In the battalion he was known as Mother McKeller.

ANN. I can believe it. You know—? [*To* MOTHER] It's so strange seeing him out of that yard. [*To* CHRIS] I guess I never grew up. It almost seems that Mom and Pop are in there now. And you and my brother doing algebra, and Larry trying to copy my homework. Gosh, those dear dead days beyond recall.

JIM. Well, I hope that doesn't mean you want me to move out?

SUE [*calling from offstage*]. Jim, come in here! Mr. Hubbard is on the phone!

JIM. I told you I don't want—

SUE [*commandingly sweet*]. Please, dear! Please!

JIM [*resigned*]. All right, Susie. [*Trailing off*] All right, all right . . . [*To* ANN] I've only met you, Ann, but if I may offer you a piece of advice—When you marry, never—even in your mind—never count your husband's money.

SUE [*from offstage*]. Jim?

JIM. At once! [*Turns and goes off*] At once. [*He exits.*]

MOTHER [ANN *is looking at her. She speaks meaningfully*]. I told her to take up the guitar. It'd be a common interest for them. [*They laugh.*] Well, he loves the guitar!

[ANN, *as though to overcome* MOTHER, *becomes suddenly lively, crosses to* KELLER *on settee, sits on his lap.*]

ANN. Let's eat at the shore tonight! Raise some hell around here, like we used to before Larry went!

MOTHER [*emotionally*]. You think of him! You see? [*Triumphantly*] She thinks of him!

ANN [*with an uncomprehending smile*]. What do you mean, Kate?

MOTHER. Nothing. Just that you—remember him, he's in your thoughts.

ANN. That's a funny thing to say; how could I help remembering him?

MOTHER [*It is drawing to a head the wrong way for her; she starts anew. She rises and comes to* ANN]. Did you hang up your things?

ANN. Yeah . . . [*To* CHRIS] Say, you've sure gone in for clothes. I could hardly find room in the closet.

MOTHER. No, don't you remember? That's Larry's room.

ANN. You mean . . . they're Larry's?

MOTHER. Didn't you recognize them?

ANN [*slowly rising, a little embarrassed*]. Well, it never occurred to me that you'd—I mean the shoes are all shined.

MOTHER. Yes, dear. [*Slight pause.* ANN *can't stop staring at her.* MOTHER *breaks it by speaking with the relish of gossip, putting her arm around* ANN *and walking with her.*] For so long I've been aching for a nice conversation with you, Annie. Tell me something.

ANN. What?

MOTHER. I don't know. Something nice.

CHRIS [*wryly*]. She means do you go out much?
MOTHER. Oh, shut up.
KELLER. And are any of them serious?
MOTHER [*laughing, sits in her chair*]. Why don't you both choke?
KELLER. Annie, you can't go into a restaurant with that woman any more. In five minutes thirty-nine strange people are sitting at the table telling her their life story.
MOTHER. If I can't ask Annie a personal question—
KELLER. Askin' is all right, but don't beat her over the head. You're beatin' her, you're beatin' her. [*They are laughing.*]

[ANN *takes pan of beans off stool, puts them on floor under chair and sits.*]

ANN [*to* MOTHER]. Don't let them bulldoze you. Ask me anything you like. What do you want to know, Kate? Come on, let's gossip.
MOTHER [*to* CHRIS *and* KELLER]. She's the only one is got any sense. [*To* ANN] Your mother—she's not getting a divorce, heh?
ANN. No, she's calmed down about it now. I think when he gets out they'll probably live together. In New York, of course.
MOTHER. That's fine. Because your father is still—I mean he's a decent man after all is said and done.
ANN. I don't care. She can take him back if she likes.
MOTHER. And you? You—[*shakes her head negatively*]—go out much? [*Slight pause*]
ANN [*delicately*]. You mean am I still waiting for him?
MOTHER. Well, no. I don't expect you to wait for him but—
ANN [*kindly*]. But that's what you mean, isn't it?
MOTHER. Well . . . yes.
ANN. Well, I'm not, Kate.
MOTHER [*faintly*]. You're not?
ANN. Isn't it ridiculous? You don't really imagine he's—?
MOTHER. I know, dear, but don't say it's ridiculous, because the papers were full of it; I don't know about New York, but there was half a page about a man missing even longer than Larry, and he turned up from Burma.
CHRIS [*coming to* ANN]. He couldn't have wanted to come home very badly, Mom.
MOTHER. Don't be so smart.
CHRIS. You can have a helluva time in Burma.
ANN [*rises and swings around in back of* CHRIS]. So I've heard.
CHRIS. Mother, I'll bet you money that you're the only woman in the country who after three years is still—
MOTHER. You're sure?

CHRIS. Yes, I am.
MOTHER. Well, if you're sure then you're sure. [*She turns her head away an instant.*] They don't say it on the radio but I'm sure that in the dark at night they're still waiting for their sons.
CHRIS. Mother, you're absolutely—
MOTHER [*waving him off*]. Don't be so damned smart! Now stop it! [*Slight pause*] There are just a few things you *don't* know. All of you. And I'll tell you one of them, Annie. Deep, deep in your heart you've always been waiting for him.
ANN [*resolutely*]. No, Kate.
MOTHER [*with increasing demand*]. But deep in your heart, Annie!
CHRIS. She ought to know, shouldn't she?
MOTHER. Don't let them tell you what to think. Listen to your heart. Only your heart.
ANN. Why does your heart tell you he's alive?
MOTHER. Because he has to be.
ANN. But why, Kate?
MOTHER [*going to her*]. Because certain things have to be, and certain things can never be. Like the sun has to rise, it has to be. That's why there's God. Otherwise anything could happen. But there's God, so certain things can never happen. I would know, Annie—just like I knew the day he—[*indicates* CHRIS]—went into that terrible battle. Did he write me? Was it in the papers? No, but that morning I couldn't raise my head off the pillow. Ask Joe. Suddenly, I knew. I knew! And he was nearly killed that day. Ann, you *know* I'm right!

[ANN *stands there in silence, then turns trembling, going upstage.*]

ANN. No, Kate.
MOTHER. I have to have some tea.

[FRANK *appears, carrying ladder.*]

FRANK. Annie! [*Coming down*] How are you, gee whiz!
ANN [*taking his hand*]. Why, Frank, you're losing your hair.
KELLER. He's got responsibility.
FRANK. Gee whiz!
KELLER. Without Frank the stars wouldn't know when to come out.
FRANK [*laughs, to* ANN]. You look more womanly. You've matured. You—
KELLER. Take it easy, Frank, you're a married man.
ANN [*as they laugh*]. You still haberdashering?
FRANK. Why not? Maybe I too can get to be president. How's your brother? Got his degree, I hear.

ANN. Oh, George has his own office now!
FRANK. Don't say! [*Funereally*] And your dad? Is he—?
ANN [*abruptly*]. Fine. I'll be in to see Lydia.
FRANK [*sympathetically*]. How about it, does Dad expect a parole soon?
ANN [*with growing ill-ease*]. I really don't know, I—
FRANK [*staunchly defending her father for her sake*]. I mean because I feel, y'know, that if an intelligent man like your father is put in prison, there ought to be a law that says either you execute him, or let him go after a year.
CHRIS [*interrupting*]. Want a hand with that ladder, Frank?
FRANK [*taking cue*]. That's all right, I'll— [*Picks up ladder*] I'll finish the horoscope tonight, Kate. [*Embarrassed*] See you later, Ann, you look wonderful. [*He exits. They look at* ANN.]
ANN [*to* CHRIS, *as she sits slowly on stool*]. Haven't they stopped talking about Dad?
CHRIS [*comes down and sits on arm of chair*]. Nobody talks about him any more.
KELLER [*rises and comes to her*]. Gone and forgotten, kid.
ANN. Tell me. Because I don't want to meet anybody on the block if they're going to—
CHRIS. I don't want you to worry about it.
ANN [*to* KELLER]. Do they still remember the case, Joe? Do they talk about you?
KELLER. The only one still talks about it is my wife.
MOTHER. That's because you keep on playing policeman with the kids. All their parents hear out of you is jail, jail, jail.
KELLER. Actually what happened was that when I got home from the penitentiary the kids got very interested in me. You know kids. I was—[*laughs*]—like the expert on the jail situation. And as time passed they got it confused and . . . I ended up a detective. [*Laughs*]
MOTHER. Except that *they* didn't get it confused. [*To* ANN] He hands out police badges from the Post Toasties boxes. [*They laugh.*]

[ANN *rises and comes to* KELLER, *putting her arm around his shoulder.*]

ANN [*wondrously at them, happy*]. Gosh, it's wonderful to hear you laughing about it.
CHRIS. Why, what'd you expect?
ANN. The last thing I remember on this block was one word—"Murderers!" Remember that, Kate?—Mrs. Hammond standing in front of our house and yelling that word? She's still around, I suppose?

MOTHER. They're all still around.
KELLER. Don't listen to her. Every Saturday night the whole gang is playin' poker in this arbor. All the ones who yelled murderer takin' my money now.
MOTHER. Don't, Joe; she's a sensitive girl, don't fool her. [*To* ANN] They still remember about Dad. It's different with him. [*Indicates* JOE] He was exonerated, your father's still there. That's why I wasn't so enthusiastic about your coming. Honestly, I know how sensitive you are, and I told Chris, I said—
KELLER. Listen, you do like I did and you'll be all right. The day I come home, I got out of my car—but not in front of the house . . . on the corner. You should've been here, Annie, and you too, Chris; you'd-a seen something. Everybody knew I was getting out that day; the porches were loaded. Picture it now; none of them believed I was innocent. The story was, I pulled a fast one getting myself exonerated. So I get out of my car, and I walk down the street. But very slow. And with a smile. The beast! I was the beast; the guy who sold cracked cylinder heads to the Army Air Force; the guy who made twenty-one P-40s crash in Australia. Kid, walkin' down the street that day I was guilty as hell. Except I wasn't, and there was a court paper in my pocket to prove I wasn't, and I walked . . . past . . . the porches. Result? Fourteen months later I had one of the best shops in the state again, a respected man again; bigger than ever.
CHRIS [*with admiration*]. Joe McGuts.
KELLER [*now with great force*]. That's the only way you lick 'em is guts! [*To* ANN] The worst thing you did was to move away from here. You made it tough for your father when he gets out. That's why I tell you, I like to see him move back right on this block.
MOTHER [*pained*]. How could they move back?
KELLER. It ain't gonna end *till* they move back! [*To* ANN] Till people play cards with him again, and talk with him, and smile with him—you play cards with a man you know he can't be a murderer. And the next time you write him I like you to tell him just what I said. [ANN *simply stares at him.*] You hear me?
ANN [*surprised*]. Don't you hold anything against him?
KELLER. Annie, I never believed in crucifying people.
ANN [*mystified*]. But he was your partner, he dragged you through the mud.
KELLER. Well, he ain't my sweetheart, but you gotta forgive, don't you?
ANN. You, either, Kate? Don't you feel any—?
KELLER [*to* ANN]. The next time you write Dad—
ANN. I don't write him.

KELLER [*struck*]. Well, every now and then you—
ANN [*a little shamed, but determined*]. No, I've *never* written to him. Neither has my brother. [*To* CHRIS] Say, do you feel this way, too?
CHRIS. He murdered twenty-one pilots.
KELLER. What the hell kinda talk is that?
MOTHER. That's not a thing to say about a man.
ANN. What else can you say? When they took him away I followed him, went to him every visiting day. I was crying all the time. Until the news came about Larry. Then I realized. It's wrong to pity a man like that. Father or no father, there's only one way to look at him. He knowingly shipped out parts that would crash an airplane. And how do you know Larry wasn't one of them?
MOTHER. I was waiting for that. [*Going to her*] As long as you're here, Annie, I want to ask you never to say that again.
ANN. You surprise me. I thought you'd be mad at him.
MOTHER. What your father did had nothing to do with Larry. Nothing.
ANN. But we can't know that.
MOTHER [*striving for control*]. As long as you're here!
ANN [*perplexed*]. But, Kate—
MOTHER. Put that out of your head!
KELLER. Because—
MOTHER [*quickly to* KELLER]. That's all, that's enough. [*Places her hand on her head*] Come inside now, and have some tea with me. [*She turns and goes up steps.*]
KELLER [*to* ANN]. The one thing you—
MOTHER [*sharply*]. He's not dead, so there's no argument! Now come!
KELLER [*angrily*]. In a minute! [MOTHER *turns and goes into house.*] Now look, Annie—
CHRIS. All right, Dad, forget it.
KELLER. No, she dasn't feel that way. Annie—
CHRIS. I'm sick of the whole subject, now cut it out.
KELLER. You want her to go on like this? [*To* ANN] Those cylinder heads went into P-40s only. What's the matter with you? You know Larry never flew a P-40.
CHRIS. So who flew those P-40s, pigs?
KELLER. The man was a fool, but don't make a murderer out of him. You got no sense? Look what it does to her! [*To* ANN] Listen, you gotta appreciate what was doin' in that shop in the war. The both of you! It was a madhouse. Every half hour the Major callin' for cylinder heads, they were whippin' us with the telephone. The trucks were hauling them away hot, damn near. I mean just try to see it human, see it human. All of a sudden a batch comes out with a

crack. That happens, that's the business. A fine, hairline crack. All right, so—so he's a little man, your father, always scared of loud voices. What'll the Major say?—Half a day's production shot. . . . What'll I say? You know what I mean? Human. [*He pauses.*] So he takes out his tools and he—covers over the cracks. All right—that's bad, it's wrong, but that's what a little man does. If I could have gone in that day I'd a told him—junk 'em, Steve, we can afford it. But alone he was afraid. But I know he meant no harm. He believed they'd hold up a hundred percent. That's a mistake, but it ain't murder. You mustn't feel that way about him. You understand me? It ain't right.

ANN [*she regards him a moment*]. Joe, let's forget it.

KELLER. Annie, the day the news came about Larry he was in the next cell to mine—Dad. And he cried, Annie—he cried half the night.

ANN [*touched*]. He shoulda cried all night. [*Slight pause*]

KELLER [*almost angered*]. Annie, I do not understand why you—!

CHRIS [*breaking in—with nervous urgency*]. Are you going to stop it?

ANN. Don't yell at him. He just wants everybody happy.

KELLER [*clasps her around waist, smiling*]. That's my sentiments. Can you stand steak?

CHRIS. And champagne!

KELLER. Now you're operatin'! I'll call Swanson's for a table! Big time tonight, Annie!

ANN. Can't scare me.

KELLER [*to* CHRIS, *pointing at* ANN]. I like that girl. Wrap her up. [*They laugh. Goes up porch*] You got nice legs, Annie! . . . I want to see everybody drunk tonight. [*Pointing to* CHRIS] Look at him, he's blushin'! [*He exits, laughing, into house.*]

CHRIS [*calling after him*]. Drink your tea, Casanova. [*He turns to* ANN.] Isn't he a great guy?

ANN. You're the only one I know who loves his parents.

CHRIS. I know. It went out of style, didn't it?

ANN [*with a sudden touch of sadness*]. It's all right. It's a good thing. [*She looks about.*] You know? It's lovely here. The air is sweet.

CHRIS [*hopefully*]. You're not sorry you came?

ANN. Not sorry, no. But I'm—not going to stay.

CHRIS. Why?

ANN. In the first place, your mother as much as told me to go.

CHRIS. Well—

ANN. You saw that—and then you—you've been kind of—

CHRIS. What?

ANN. Well . . . kind of embarrassed ever since I got here.

CHRIS. The trouble is I planned on kind of sneaking up on you over a period of a week or so. But they take it for granted that we're all set.

ANN. I knew they would. Your mother anyway.
CHRIS. How did you know?
ANN. From *her* point of view, why else would I come?
CHRIS. Well . . . would you want to? [ANN *still studies him.*] I guess you know this is why I asked you to come.
ANN. I guess this is why I came.
CHRIS. Ann, I love you. I love you a great deal. [*Finally*] I love you. [*Pause. She waits.*] I have no imagination . . . that's all I know to tell you. [ANN *is waiting, ready.*] I'm embarrassing you. I didn't want to tell it to you here. I wanted some place we'd never been; a place where we'd be brand new to each other. . . . You feel it's wrong here, don't you? This yard, this chair? I want you to be ready for me. I don't want to win you away from anything.
ANN [*putting her arms around him*]. Oh, Chris, I've been ready a long, long time!
CHRIS. Then he's gone forever. You're sure.
ANN. I almost got married two years ago.
CHRIS. Why didn't you?
ANN. You started to write to me— [*Slight pause*]
CHRIS. You felt something that far back?
ANN. Every day since!
CHRIS. Ann, why didn't you let me know?
ANN. I was waiting for you, Chris. Till then you never wrote. And when you did, what did you say? You sure can be ambiguous, you know.
CHRIS [*looks toward house, then at her, trembling*]. Give me a kiss, Ann. Give me a— [*They kiss.*] God, I kissed you, Annie, I kissed Annie. How long, how long I've been waiting to kiss you!
ANN. I'll never forgive you. Why did you wait all these years? All I've done is sit and wonder if I was crazy for thinking of you.
CHRIS. Annie, we're going to live now! I'm going to make you so happy. [*He kisses her, but without their bodies touching.*]
ANN [*a little embarrassed*]. Not like that you're not.
CHRIS. I kissed you . . . .
ANN. Like Larry's brother. Do it like you, Chris. [*He breaks away from her abruptly.*] What is it, Chris?
CHRIS. Let's drive some place . . . I want to be alone with you.
ANN. No . . . what is it, Chris, your mother?
CHRIS. No—nothing like that.
ANN. Then what's wrong? Even in your letters, there was something ashamed.

CHRIS. Yes. I suppose I have been. But it's going from me.
ANN. You've got to tell me—
CHRIS. I don't know how to start. [*He takes her hand.*]
ANN. It wouldn't work this way. [*Slight pause*]
CHRIS [*speaks quietly, factually at first*]. It's all mixed up with so many other things. . . . You remember, overseas, I was in command of a company?
ANN. Yeah, sure.
CHRIS. Well, I lost them.
ANN. How many?
CHRIS. Just about all.
ANN. Oh, gee!
CHRIS. It takes a little time to toss that off. Because they weren't just men. For instance, one time it'd been raining several days and this kid came to me, and gave me his last pair of dry socks. Put them in my pocket. That's only a little thing—but . . . that's the kind of guys I had. They didn't die; they killed themselves for each other. I mean that exactly; a little more selfish and they'd 've been here today. And I got an idea—watching them go down. Everything was being destroyed, see, but it seemed to me that one new thing was made. A kind of—responsibility. Man for man. You understand me? —To show that, to bring that onto the earth again like some kind of a monument and everyone would feel it standing there, behind him, and it would make a difference to him. [*Pause*] And then I came home and it was incredible. I—there was no meaning in it here; the whole thing to them was a kind of a—bus accident. I went to work with Dad, and that rat race again. I felt—what you said— ashamed somehow. Because nobody was changed at all. It seemed to make suckers out of a lot of guys. I felt wrong to be alive, to open the bankbook, to drive the new car, to see the new refrigerator. I mean you can take those things out of a war, but when you drive that car you've got to know that it came out of the love a man can have for a man, you've got to be a little better because of that. Otherwise what you have is really loot, and there's blood on it. I didn't want to take any of it. And I guess that included you.
ANN. And you still feel that way?
CHRIS. I want you now, Annie.
ANN. Because you mustn't feel that way any more. Because you have a right to whatever you have. Everything, Chris, understand that? To me, too. . . . And the money, there's nothing wrong in your money. Your father put hundreds of planes in the air, you should be proud. A man should be paid for that . . . .
CHRIS. Oh Annie, Annie . . . I'm going to make a fortune for you!

KELLER [*offstage*]. Hello . . . Yes. Sure.
ANN [*laughing softly*]. What'll I do with a fortune?

[*They kiss.* KELLER *enters from house.*]

KELLER [*thumbing toward house*]. Hey, Ann, your brother—[*They step apart shyly.* KELLER *comes down, and wryly*] What is this, Labor Day?
CHRIS [*waving him away, knowing the kidding will be endless*]. All right, all right.
ANN. You shouldn't burst out like that.
KELLER. Well, nobody told me it was Labor Day. [*Looks around*] Where's the hot dogs?
CHRIS [*loving it*]. All right. You said it once.
KELLER. Well, as long as I know it's Labor Day from now on, I'll wear a bell around my neck.
ANN [*affectionately*]. He's so subtle!
CHRIS. George Bernard Shaw as an elephant.
KELLER. George!—hey, you kissed it out of my head—your brother's on the phone.
ANN [*surprised*]. My brother?
KELLER. Yeah, George. Long distance.
ANN. What's the matter, is anything wrong?
KELLER. I don't know, Kate's talking to him. Hurry up, she'll cost him five dollars.
ANN [*takes a step upstage, then comes down toward* CHRIS]. I wonder if we ought to tell your mother yet? I mean I'm not very good in an argument.
CHRIS. We'll wait till tonight. After dinner. Now don't get tense, just leave it to me.
KELLER. What're you telling her?
CHRIS. Go ahead, Ann. [*With misgivings,* ANN *goes up and into house.*] We're getting married, Dad. [KELLER *nods indecisively.*] Well, don't you say anything?
KELLER [*distracted*]. I'm glad, Chris, I'm just—George is calling from Columbus.
CHRIS. Columbus!
KELLER. Did Annie tell you he was going to see his father today?
CHRIS. No, I don't think she knew anything about it.
KELLER [*asking uncomfortably*]. Chris! You—you think you know her pretty good?
CHRIS [*hurt and apprehensive*]. What kind of a question?
KELLER. I'm just wondering. All these years George don't go to see his father. Suddenly he goes . . . and she comes here.

CHRIS. Well, what about it?
KELLER. It's crazy, but it comes to my mind. She don't hold nothin' against me, does she?
CHRIS [*angry*]. I don't know what you're talking about.
KELLER [*a little more combatively*]. I'm just talkin'. To his last day in court the man blamed it all on me; and this is his daughter. I mean if she was sent here to find out something?
CHRIS [*angered*]. Why? What is there to find out?
ANN [*on phone, offstage*]. Why are you so excited, George? What happened there?
KELLER. I mean if they want to open up the case again, for the nuisance value, to hurt us?
CHRIS. Dad . . . how could you think that of her?
ANN [*simultaneously, still on phone*]. But what did he say to you, for God's sake?
KELLER. It couldn't be, heh. You know.
CHRIS. Dad, you amaze me . . . .
KELLER [*breaking in*]. All right, forget it, forget it. [*With great force, moving about*] I want a clean start for you, Chris. I want a new sign over the plant—Christopher Keller, Incorporated.
CHRIS [*a little uneasily*]. J. O. Keller is good enough.
KELLER. We'll talk about it. I'm going to build you a house, stone, with a driveway from the road. I want you to spread out, Chris, I want you to use what I made for you. [*He is close to him now.*] I mean, with joy, Chris, without shame . . . with joy.
CHRIS [*touched*]. I will, Dad.
KELLER [*with deep emotion*]. Say it to me.
CHRIS. Why?
KELLER. Because sometimes I think you're . . . ashamed of the money.
CHRIS. No, don't feel that.
KELLER. Because it's good money, there's nothing wrong with that money.
CHRIS [*a little frightened*]. Dad, you don't have to tell me this.
KELLER [*with overriding affection and self-confidence now. He grips* CHRIS *by the back of the neck, and with laughter between his determined jaws*]. Look, Chris, I'll go to work on Mother for you. We'll get her so drunk tonight we'll all get married! [*Steps away, with a wide gesture of his arm*] There's gonna be a wedding, kid, like there never was seen! Champagne, tuxedos—!

[*He breaks off as* ANN's *voice comes out loud from the house where she is still talking on phone.*]

ANN. Simply because when you get excited you don't control yourself.... [MOTHER *comes out of house.*] Well, what did he tell you for God's sake? [*Pause*] All right, come then. [*Pause*] Yes, they'll all be here. Nobody's running away from you. And try to get hold of yourself, will you? [*Pause*] All right, all right. Good-bye.

[*There is a brief pause as* ANN *hangs up receiver, then comes out of kitchen.*]

CHRIS. Something happen?

KELLER. He's coming here?

ANN. On the seven o'clock. He's in Columbus. [*To* MOTHER] I told him it would be all right.

KELLER. Sure, fine! Your father took sick?

ANN [*mystified*]. No, George didn't say he was sick. I— [*Shaking it off*] I don't know, I suppose it's something stupid, you know my brother— [*She comes to* CHRIS.] Let's go for a drive, or something . . .

CHRIS. Sure. Give me the keys, Dad.

MOTHER. Drive through the park. It's beautiful now.

CHRIS. Come on, Ann. [*To them*] Be back right away.

ANN [*as she and* CHRIS *exit up driveway*]. See you.

[MOTHER *comes down toward* KELLER, *her eyes fixed on him.*]

KELLER. Take your time. [*To* MOTHER] What does George want?

MOTHER. He's been in Columbus since this morning with Steve. He's gotta see Annie right away, he says.

KELLER. What for?

MOTHER. I don't know. [*She speaks with warning.*] He's a lawyer now, Joe. George is a lawyer. All these years he never even sent a postcard to Steve. Since he got back from the war, not a postcard.

KELLER. So what?

MOTHER [*her tension breaking out*]. Suddenly he takes an airplane from New York to see him. An airplane!

KELLER. Well? So?

MOTHER [*trembling*]. Why?

KELLER. I don't read minds. Do you?

MOTHER. Why, Joe? What has Steve suddenly got to tell him that he takes an airplane to see him?

KELLER. What do I care what Steve's got to tell him?

MOTHER. You're sure, Joe?

KELLER [*frightened, but angry*]. Yes, I'm sure.

MOTHER [*sits stiffly in a chair*]. Be smart now, Joe. The boy is coming. Be smart.

KELLER [*desperately*]. Once and for all, did you hear what I said? I said I'm sure!
MOTHER [*nods weakly*]. All right, Joe. [*He straightens up.*] Just . . . be smart.
[KELLER, *in hopeless fury, looks at her, turns around, goes up to porch and into house, slamming screen door violently behind him.* MOTHER *sits in chair downstage, stiffly, staring, seeing.*]

CURTAIN

ACT TWO

As twilight falls, that evening.
On the rise, CHRIS *is discovered sawing the broken-off tree, leaving stump standing alone. He is dressed in good pants, white shoes, but without a shirt. He disappears with tree up the alley when* MOTHER *appears on porch. She comes down and stands watching him. She has on a dressing gown, carries a tray of grape-juice drink in a pitcher, and glasses with sprigs of mint in them.*

MOTHER [*calling up alley*]. Did you have to put on good pants to do that? [*She comes downstage and puts tray on table in the arbor. Then looks around uneasily, then feels pitcher for coolness.* CHRIS *enters from alley brushing off his hands.*] You notice there's more light with that thing gone?
CHRIS. Why aren't you dressing?
MOTHER. It's suffocating upstairs. I made a grape drink for Georgie. He always liked grape. Come and have some.
CHRIS [*impatiently*]. Well, come on, get dressed. And what's Dad sleeping so much for? [*He goes to table and pours a glass of juice.*]
MOTHER. He's worried. When he's worried he sleeps. [*Pauses. Looks into his eyes*] We're dumb, Chris. Dad and I are stupid people. We don't know anything. You've got to protect us.
CHRIS. You're silly; what's there to be afraid of?
MOTHER. To his last day in court Steve never gave up the idea that Dad made him do it. If they're going to open the case again I won't live through it.
CHRIS. George is just a damn fool, Mother. How can you take him seriously?
MOTHER. That family hates us. Maybe even Annie—

CHRIS. Oh, now, Mother . . . .
MOTHER. You think just because you like everybody, they like you!
CHRIS. All right, stop working yourself up. Just leave everything to me.
MOTHER. When George goes home tell her to go with him.
CHRIS [*noncommittally*]. Don't worry about Annie.
MOTHER. Steve is her father, too.
CHRIS. Are you going to cut it out? Now, come.
MOTHER [*going upstage with him*]. You don't realize how people can hate, Chris, they can hate so much they'll tear the world to pieces.

[ANN, *dressed up, appears on porch.*]

CHRIS. Look! She's dressed already. [*As he and* MOTHER *mount porch*] I've just got to put on a shirt.
ANN [*in a preoccupied way*]. Are you feeling well, Kate?
MOTHER. What's the difference, dear. There are certain people, y'know, the sicker they get, the longer they live. [*She goes into house.*]
CHRIS. You look nice.
ANN. We're going to tell her tonight.
CHRIS. Absolutely, don't worry about it.
ANN. I wish we could tell her now. I can't stand scheming. My stomach gets hard.
CHRIS. It's not scheming, we'll just get her in a better mood.
MOTHER [*offstage, in the house*]. Joe, are you going to sleep all day!
ANN [*laughing*]. The only one who's relaxed is your father. He's fast asleep.
CHRIS. I'm relaxed.
ANN. Are you?
CHRIS. Look. [*He holds out his hand and makes it shake.*] Let me know when George gets here.

[*He goes into the house.* ANN *moves aimlessly, and then is drawn toward tree stump. She goes to it, hesitantly touches broken top in the hush of her thoughts. Offstage* LYDIA *calls,* "Johnny! Come get your supper!" SUE *enters, and halts, seeing* ANN.]

SUE. Is my husband—?
ANN [*turns, startled*]. Oh!
SUE. I'm terribly sorry.
ANN. It's all right, I—I'm a little silly about the dark.
SUE [*looks about*]. It is getting dark.
ANN. Are you looking for your husband?
SUE. As usual. [*Laughs tiredly*] He spends so much time here, they'll be charging him rent.

ANN. Nobody was dressed so he drove over to the depot to pick up my brother.
SUE. Oh, your brother's in?
ANN. Yeah, they ought to be here any minute now. Will you have a cold drink?
SUE. I will, thanks. [ANN *goes to table and pours.*] My husband. Too hot to drive me to beach. Men are like little boys; for the neighbors they'll always cut the grass.
ANN. People like to do things for the Kellers. Been that way since I can remember.
SUE. It's amazing. I guess your brother's coming to give you away, heh?
ANN [*giving her drink*]. I don't know. I suppose.
SUE. You must be all nerved up.
ANN. It's always a problem getting yourself married, isn't it?
SUE. That depends on your shape, of course. I don't see why you should have had a problem.
ANN. I've had chances—
SUE. I'll bet. It's romantic . . . it's very unusual to me, marrying the brother of your sweetheart.
ANN. I don't know. I think it's mostly that whenever I need somebody to tell me the truth I've always thought of Chris. When he tells you something you know it's so. He relaxes me.
SUE. And he's got money. That's important, you know.
ANN. It wouldn't matter to me.
SUE. You'd be surprised. It makes all the difference. I married an intern. On my salary. And that was bad, because as soon as a woman supports a man he owes her something. You can never owe somebody without resenting them. [ANN *laughs.*] That's true, you know.
ANN. Underneath, I think the doctor is very devoted.
SUE. Oh, certainly. But it's bad when a man always sees the bars in front of him. Jim thinks he's in jail all the time.
ANN. Oh . . .
SUE. That's why I've been intending to ask you a small favor, Ann. It's something very important to me.
ANN. Certainly, if I can do it.
SUE. You can. When you take up housekeeping, try to find a place away from here.
ANN. Are you fooling?
SUE. I'm very serious. My husband is unhappy with Chris around.
ANN. How is that?
SUE. Jim's a successful doctor. But he's got an idea he'd like to do medical research. Discover things. You see?

ANN. Well, isn't that good?
SUE. Research pays twenty-five dollars a week minus laundering the hair shirt. You've got to give up your life to go into it.
ANN. How does Chris—
SUE [*with growing feeling*]. Chris makes people want to be better than it's possible to be. He does that to people.
ANN. Is that bad?
SUE. My husband has a family, dear. Every time he has a session with Chris he feels as though he's compromising by not giving up everything for research. As though Chris or anybody else isn't compromising. It happens with Jim every couple of years. He meets a man and makes a statue out of him.
ANN. Maybe he's right. I don't mean that Chris is a statue, but—
SUE. Now darling, you know he's not right.
ANN. I don't agree with you. Chris—
SUE. Let's face it, dear. Chris is working with his father, isn't he? He's taking money out of that business every week in the year.
ANN. What of it?
SUE. You ask me what of it?
ANN. I certainly do. [*She seems about to burst out.*] You oughtn't cast aspersions like that, I'm surprised at you.
SUE. You're surprised at me!
ANN. He'd never take five cents out of that plant if there was anything wrong with it.
SUE. You know that.
ANN. I know it. I resent everything you've said.
SUE [*moving toward her*]. You know what I resent, dear?
ANN. Please, I don't want to argue.
SUE. I resent living next door to the Holy Family. It makes me look like a bum, you understand?
ANN. I can't do anything about that.
SUE. Who is he to ruin a man's life? Everybody knows Joe pulled a fast one to get out of jail.
ANN. That's not true!
SUE. Then why don't you go out and talk to people? Go on, talk to them. There's not a person on the block who doesn't know the truth.
ANN. That's a lie. People come here all the time for cards and—
SUE. So what? They give him credit for being smart. I do, too, I've got nothing against Joe. But if Chris wants people to put on the hair shirt let him take off his broadcloth. He's driving my husband crazy with that phony idealism of his, and I'm at the end of my rope on it! [CHRIS *enters on porch, wearing shirt and tie now. She turns quickly, hearing. With a smile*] Hello, darling. How's Mother?

CHRIS. I thought George came.
SUE. No, it was just us.
CHRIS [*coming down to them*]. Susie, do me a favor, heh? Go up to Mother and see if you can calm her. She's all worked up.
SUE. She still doesn't know about you two?
CHRIS [*laughs a little*]. Well, she senses it, I guess. You know my mother.
SUE [*going up to porch*]. Oh, yeah, she's psychic.
CHRIS. Maybe there's something in the medicine chest.
SUE. I'll give her one of everything. [*On porch*] Don't worry about Kate; couple of drinks, dance her around a little. . . . She'll love Ann. [*To* ANN] Because you're the female version of him. [CHRIS *laughs.*] Don't be alarmed, I said version. [*She goes into house.*]
CHRIS. Interesting woman, isn't she?
ANN. Yeah, she's very interesting.
CHRIS: She's a great nurse, you know, she—
ANN [*in tension, but trying to control it*]. Are you still doing that?
CHRIS [*sensing something wrong, but still smiling*]. Doing what?
ANN. As soon as you get to know somebody you find a distinction for them. How do you know she's a great nurse?
CHRIS. What's the matter, Ann?
ANN. The woman hates you. She despises you!
CHRIS. Hey . . . What's hit you?
ANN. Gee, Chris—
CHRIS. What happened here?
ANN. You never— Why didn't you tell me?
CHRIS. Tell you what?
ANN. She says they think Joe is guilty.
CHRIS. What difference does it make what they think?
ANN. I don't care what they think, I just don't understand why you took the trouble to deny it. You said it was all forgotten.
CHRIS. I didn't want you to feel there was anything wrong in you coming here, that's all. I know a lot of people think my father was guilty, and I assumed there might be some question in your mind.
ANN. But I never once said I suspected him.
CHRIS. Nobody says it.
ANN. Chris, I know how much you love him, but it could never—
CHRIS. Do you think I could forgive him if he'd done that thing?
ANN. I'm not here out of a blue sky, Chris. I turned my back on my father, if there's anything wrong here now—
CHRIS. I know that, Ann.
ANN. George is coming from Dad, and I don't think it's with a blessing.

CHRIS. He's welcome here. You've got nothing to fear from George.
ANN. Tell me that. . . . Just tell me that.
CHRIS. The man is innocent, Ann. Remember he was falsely accused once and it put him through hell. How would you behave if you were faced with the same thing again? Annie, believe me, there's nothing wrong for you here, believe me, kid.
ANN. All right, Chris, all right. [*They embrace as* KELLER *appears quietly on porch.* ANN *simply studies him.*]
KELLER. Every time I come out here it looks like Playland! [*They break and laugh in embarrassment.*]
CHRIS. I thought you were going to shave?
KELLER [*sitting on bench*]. In a minute. I just woke up, I can't see nothin'.
ANN. You look shaved.
KELLER. Oh, no. [*Massages his jaw*] Gotta be extra special tonight. Big night, Annie. So how's it feel to be a married woman?
ANN [*laughs*]. I don't know, yet.
KELLER [*to* CHRIS]. What's the matter, you slippin'? [*He takes a little box of apples from under the bench as they talk.*]
CHRIS. The great roué!
KELLER. What is that, roué?
CHRIS. It's French.
KELLER. Don't talk dirty. [*They laugh.*]
CHRIS [*to* ANN]. You ever meet a bigger ignoramus?
KELLER. Well, somebody's got to make a living.
ANN [*as they laugh*]. That's telling him.
KELLER. I don't know, everybody's gettin' so Goddam educated in this country there'll be nobody to take away the garbage. [*They laugh.*] It's gettin' so the only dumb ones left are the bosses.
ANN. You're not so dumb, Joe.
KELLER. I know, but you go into our plant, for instance. I got so many lieutenants, majors and colonels that I'm ashamed to ask somebody to sweep the floor. I gotta be careful I'll insult somebody. No kiddin'. It's a tragedy: you stand on the street today and spit, you're gonna hit a college man.
CHRIS. Well, don't spit.
KELLER [*breaks apple in half, passing it to* ANN *and* CHRIS]. I mean to say, it's comin' to a pass. [*He takes a breath.*] I been thinkin', Annie . . . your brother, George. I been thinkin' about your brother George. When he comes I like you to *brooch* something to him.
CHRIS. Broach.
KELLER. What's the matter with brooch?

CHRIS [*smiling*]. It's not English.
KELLER. When I went to night school it was brooch.
ANN [*laughing*]. Well, in day school it's broach.
KELLER. Don't surround me, will you? Seriously, Ann . . . You say he's not well. George, I been thinkin', why should he knock himself out in New York with that cut-throat competition, when I got so many friends here; I'm very friendly with some big lawyers in town. I could set George up here.
ANN. That's awfully nice of you, Joe.
KELLER. No, kid, it ain't nice of me. I want you to understand me. I'm thinking of Chris. [*Slight pause*] See . . . this is what I mean. You get older, you want to feel that you—accomplished something. My only accomplishment is my son. I ain't brainy. That's all I accomplished. Now, a year, eighteen months, your father'll be a free man. Who is he going to come to, Annie? His baby. You. He'll come, old, mad, into your house.
ANN. That can't matter any more, Joe.
KELLER. I don't want that to come between us. [*Gestures between* CHRIS *and himself*]
ANN. I can only tell you that that could never happen.
KELLER. You're in love now, Annie, but believe me, I'm older than you and I know—a daughter is a daughter, and a father is a father. And it could happen. [*He pauses.*] I like you and George to go to him in prison and tell him . . . "Dad, Joe wants to bring you into the business when you get out."
ANN [*surprised, even shocked*]. You'd have him as a partner?
KELLER. No, no partner. A good job. [*Pause. He sees she is shocked, a little mystified. He gets up, speaks more nervously.*] I want him to know, Annie . . . while he's sitting there I want him to know that when he gets out he's got a place waitin' for him. It'll take his bitterness away. To know you got a place . . . it sweetens you.
ANN. Joe, you owe him nothing.
KELLER. I owe him a good kick in the teeth, but he's your father.
CHRIS. Then kick him in the teeth! I don't want him in the plant, so that's that! You understand? And besides, don't talk about him like that. People misunderstand you!
KELLER. And I don't understand why she has to crucify the man.
CHRIS. Well, it's her father, if she feels—
KELLER. No, no.
CHRIS [*almost angrily*]. What's it to you? Why—?
KELLER [*a commanding outburst in high nervousness*]. A father is a father! [*As though the outburst had revealed him, he looks about,*

wanting to retract it. His hand goes to his cheek.] I better—I better shave. [*He turns and a smile is on his face. To* ANN] I didn't mean to yell at you, Annie.

ANN. Let's forget the whole thing, Joe.

KELLER. Right. [*To* CHRIS] She's likeable.

CHRIS [*a little peeved at the man's stupidity*]. Shave, will you?

KELLER. Right again.

[*As he turns to porch* LYDIA *comes hurrying from her house.*]

LYDIA. I forgot all about it. [*Seeing* CHRIS *and* ANN] Hya. [*To* JOE] I promised to fix Kate's hair for tonight. Did she comb it yet?

KELLER. Always a smile, hey, Lydia?

LYDIA. Sure, why not?

KELLER [*going up on porch*]. Come on up and comb my Katie's hair. [LYDIA *goes up on porch.*] She's got a big night, make her beautiful.

LYDIA. I will.

KELLER [*holds door open for her and she goes into kitchen. To* CHRIS *and* ANN]. Hey, that could be a song. [*He sings softly.*]
  "Come on up and comb my Katie's hair . . .
  Oh, come on up, 'cause she's my lady fair—"
[*To* ANN] How's that for one year of night school? [*He continues singing as he goes into kitchen.*]
  "Oh, come on up, come on up, and comb my lady's hair—"

[JIM BAYLISS *rounds corner of driveway, walking rapidly.* JIM *crosses to* CHRIS, *motions him and pulls him down excitedly.* KELLER *stands just inside kitchen door, watching them.*]

CHRIS. What's the matter? Where is he?

JIM. Where's your mother?

CHRIS. Upstairs, dressing.

ANN [*crossing to them rapidly*]. What happened to George?

JIM. I asked him to wait in the car. Listen to me now. Can you take some advice? [*They wait.*] Don't bring him in here.

ANN. Why?

JIM. Kate is in bad shape, you can't explode this in front of her.

ANN. Explode what?

JIM. You know why he's here, don't try to kid it away. There's blood in his eye; drive him somewhere and talk to him alone.

[ANN *turns to go up drive, takes a couple of steps, sees* KELLER, *and stops. He goes quietly on into house.*]

CHRIS [*shaken, and therefore angered*]. Don't be an old lady.

JIM. He's come to take her home. What does that mean? [*To* ANN

You know what that means. Fight it out with him someplace else.
ANN [*comes back down toward* CHRIS]. I'll drive . . . him somewhere.
CHRIS. [*goes to her*]. No.
JIM. Will you stop being an idiot?
CHRIS. Nobody's afraid of him here. Cut that out!

[*He starts for driveway, but is brought up short by* GEORGE, *who enters there.* GEORGE *is* CHRIS's *age, but a paler man, now on the edge of his self-restraint. He speaks quietly, as though afraid to find himself screaming. An instant's hesitation and* CHRIS *steps up to him, hand extended, smiling.*]

CHRIS. Helluva way to do; what're you sitting out there for?
GEORGE. Doctor said your mother isn't well, I—
CHRIS. So what? She'd want to see you, wouldn't she? We've been waiting for you all afternoon. [*He put his hand on* GEORGE's *arm, but* GEORGE *pulls away, coming across toward* ANN.]
ANN [*touching his collar*]. This is filthy, didn't you bring another shirt?

[GEORGE *breaks away from her, and moves down, examining the yard. Door opens, and he turns rapidly, thinking it is* KATE, *but it's* SUE. *She looks at him; he turns away and moves to fence. He looks over it at his former home.* SUE *comes downstage.*]

SUE [*annoyed*]. How about the beach, Jim?
JIM. Oh, it's too hot to drive.
SUE. How'd you get to the station—Zeppelin?
CHRIS. This is Mrs. Bayliss, George. [*Calling, as* GEORGE *pays no attention, staring at house*] George! [GEORGE *turns.*] Mrs. Bayliss.
SUE. How do you do.
GEORGE [*removing his hat*]. You're the people who bought our house, aren't you?
SUE. That's right. Come and see what we did with it before you leave.
GEORGE [*walks down and away from her*]. I liked it the way it was.
SUE [*after a brief pause*]. He's frank, isn't he?
JIM [*pulling her off*]. See you later. . . . Take it easy, fella. [*They exit.*]
CHRIS [*calling after them*]. Thanks for driving him! [*Turning to* GEORGE] How about some grape juice? Mother made it especially for you.
GEORGE [*with forced appreciation*]. Good old Kate, remembered my grape juice.
CHRIS. You drank enough of it in this house. How've you been, George—Sit down.

GEORGE [*keeps moving*]. It takes me a minute. [*Looking around*] It seems impossible.
CHRIS. What?
GEORGE. I'm back here.
CHRIS. Say, you've gotten a little nervous, haven't you?
GEORGE. Yeah, toward the end of the day. What're you, big executive now?
CHRIS. Just kind of medium. How's the law?
GEORGE. I don't know. When I was studying in the hospital it seemed sensible, but outside there doesn't seem to be much of a law. The trees got thick, didn't they? [*Points to stump*] What's that?
CHRIS. Blew down last night. We had it there for Larry. You know.
GEORGE. Why, afraid you'll forget him?
CHRIS [*starts for* GEORGE]. Kind of a remark is that?
ANN [*breaking in, putting a restraining hand on* CHRIS]. When did you start wearing a hat?
GEORGE [*discovers hat in his hand*]. Today. From now on I decided to look like a lawyer, anyway. [*He holds it up to her.*] Don't you recognize it?
ANN. Why? Where—?
GEORGE. Your father's—He asked me to wear it.
ANN. How is he?
GEORGE. He got smaller.
ANN. Smaller?
GEORGE. Yeah, little. [*Holds out his hand to measure*] He's a little man. That's what happens to suckers, you know. It's good I went to him in time—another year there'd be nothing left but his smell.
CHRIS. What's the matter, George, what's the trouble?
GEORGE. The trouble? The trouble is when you make suckers out of people once, you shouldn't try to do it twice.
CHRIS. What does that mean?
GEORGE [*to* ANN]. You're not married yet, are you?
ANN. George, will you sit down and stop—?
GEORGE. Are you married yet?
ANN. No, I'm not married yet.
GEORGE. You're not going to marry him.
ANN. Why am I not going to marry him?
GEORGE. Because his father destroyed your family.
CHRIS. Now look, George . . .
GEORGE. Cut it short, Chris. Tell her to come home with me. Let's not argue, you know what I've got to say.
CHRIS. George, you don't want to be the voice of God, do you?
GEORGE. I'm—

CHRIS. That's been your trouble all your life, George, you dive into things. What kind of a statement is that to make? You're a big boy now.

GEORGE. I'm a big boy now.

CHRIS. Don't come bulling in here. If you've got something to say, be civilized about it.

GEORGE. Don't civilize me!

ANN. Shhh!

CHRIS [*ready to hit him*]. Are you going to talk like a grown man or aren't you?

ANN [*quickly, to forestall an outburst*]. Sit down, dear. Don't be angry, what's the matter? [*He allows her to seat him, looking at her.*] Now what happened? You kissed me when I left, now you—

GEORGE [*breathlessly*]. My life turned upside down since then. I couldn't go back to work when you left. I wanted to go to Dad and tell him you were going to be married. It seemed impossible not to tell him. He loved you so much. [*He pauses.*] Annie—we did a terrible thing. We can never be forgiven. Not even to send him a card at Christmas. I didn't see him once since I got home from the war! Annie, you don't know what was done to that man. You don't know what happened.

ANN [*afraid*]. Of course I know.

GEORGE. You can't know, you wouldn't be here. Dad came to work that day. The night foreman came to him and showed him the cylinder heads . . . they were coming out of the process with defects. There was something wrong with the process. So Dad went directly to the phone and called here and told Joe to come down right away. But the morning passed. No sign of Joe. So Dad called again. By this time he had over a hundred defectives. The Army was screaming for stuff and Dad didn't have anything to ship. So Joe told him . . . on the phone he told him to weld, cover up the cracks in any way he could, and ship them out.

CHRIS. Are you through now?

GEORGE [*surging up at him*]. I'm not through now! [*Back to* ANN] Dad was afraid. He wanted Joe there if he was going to do it. But Joe can't come down. . . . He's sick. Sick! He suddenly gets the flu! Suddenly! But he promised to take responsibility. Do you understand what I'm saying? On the telephone you can't have responsibility! In a court you can always deny a phone call and that's exactly what he did. They knew he was a liar the first time, but in the appeal they believed that rotten lie and now Joe is a big shot and your father is the patsy. [*He gets up.*] Now what're you going to do? Eat his food, sleep in his bed? Answer me; what're you going to do?

CHRIS. What're you going to do, George?
GEORGE. He's too smart for me, I can't prove a phone call.
CHRIS. Then how dare you come in here with that rot?
ANN. George, the court—
GEORGE. The court didn't know your father! But you know him. You know in your heart Joe did it.
CHRIS [*whirling him around*]. Lower your voice or I'll throw you out of here!
GEORGE. She knows. She knows.
CHRIS [*to* ANN]. Get him out of here, Ann. Get him out of here.
ANN. George, I know everything you've said. Dad told that whole thing in court, and they—
GEORGE [*almost a scream*]. The court did not know him, Annie!
ANN. Shhh!—But he'll say anything, George. You know how quick he can lie.
GEORGE [*turning to* CHRIS, *with deliberation*]. I'll ask you something, and look me in the eye when you answer me.
CHRIS. I'll look you in the eye.
GEORGE. You know your father—
CHRIS. I know him well.
GEORGE. And that's the same Joe Keller who never left his shop without cylinder heads be repaired and shipped out of his shop without even knowing about it?
CHRIS. He's that kind of boss.
GEORGE. And that's the same Joe Keller who never left his shop without first going around to see that all the lights were out.
CHRIS [*with growing anger*]. The same Joe Keller.
GEORGE. The same man who knows how many minutes a day his workers spend in the toilet.
CHRIS. The same man.
GEORGE. And my father, that frightened mouse who'd never buy a shirt without somebody along—that man would dare do such a thing on his own?
CHRIS. On his own. And because he's a frightened mouse this is another thing he'd do—throw the blame on somebody else because he's not man enough to take it himself. He tried it in court but it didn't work, but with a fool like you it works!
GEORGE. Oh, Chris, you're a liar to yourself!
ANN [*deeply shaken*]. Don't talk like that!
CHRIS [*sits facing* GEORGE]. Tell me, George. What happened? The court record was good enough for you all these years, why isn't it good now? Why did you believe it all these years?
GEORGE [*after a slight pause*]. Because you believed it. . . . That's the

truth, Chris. I believed everything, because I thought you did. But today I heard it from his mouth. From his mouth it's altogether different than the record. Anyone who knows him, and knows your father, will believe it from his mouth. Your Dad took everything we have. I can't beat that. But she's one item he's not going to grab. [*He turns to* ANN.] Get your things. Everything they have is covered with blood. You're not the kind of a girl who can live with that. Get your things.

CHRIS. Ann . . . you're not going to believe that, are you?

ANN [*goes to him*]. You know it's not true, don't you?

GEORGE. How can he tell you? It's his father. [*To* CHRIS] None of these things ever even cross your mind?

CHRIS. Yes, they crossed my mind. Anything can cross your mind!

GEORGE. *He knows,* Annie. He knows!

CHRIS. The voice of God!

GEORGE. Then why isn't your name on the business? Explain that to her!

CHRIS. What the hell has that got to do with—?

GEORGE. Annie, why isn't his name on it?

CHRIS. Even when I don't own it!

GEORGE. Who're you kidding? Who gets it when he dies? [*To* ANN] Open your eyes, you know the both of them, isn't that the first thing they'd do, the way they love each other?—J. O. Keller and Son? [*Pause.* ANN *looks from him to* CHRIS.] I'll settle it. Do you want to settle it, or are you afraid to?

CHRIS. What do you mean?

GEORGE. Let me go up and talk to your father. In ten minutes you'll have the answer. Or are you afraid of the answer?

CHRIS. I'm not afraid of the answer. I know the answer. But my mother isn't well and I don't want a fight here now.

GEORGE. Let me go to him.

CHRIS. You're not going to start a fight here now.

GEORGE [*to* ANN]. What more do you want! [*There is a sound of footsteps in the house.*]

ANN [*turns her head suddenly toward house*]. Someone's coming.

CHRIS [*to* GEORGE, *quietly*]. You won't say anything now.

ANN. You'll go soon. I'll call a cab.

GEORGE. You're coming with me.

ANN. And don't mention marriage, because we haven't told her yet.

GEORGE. You're coming with me.

ANN. You understand? Don't—George, you're not going to start anything now! [*She hears footsteps.*] Shsh!

[MOTHER *enters on porch. She is dressed almost formally; her hair is fixed. They are all turned toward her. On seeing* GEORGE *she raises both hands, comes down toward him.*]

MOTHER. Georgie, Georgie.
GEORGE [*he has always liked her*]. Hello, Kate.
MOTHER [*cups his face in her hands*]. They made an old man out of you. [*Touches his hair*] Look, you're gray.
GEORGE [*her pity, open and unabashed, reaches into him, and he smiles sadly*]. I know, I—
MOTHER. I told you when you went away, don't try for medals.
GEORGE [*laughs, tiredly*]. I didn't try, Kate. They made it very easy for me.
MOTHER [*actually angry*]. Go on. You're all alike. [*To* ANN] Look at him, why did you say he's fine? He looks like a ghost.
GEORGE [*relishing her solicitude*]. I feel all right.
MOTHER. I'm sick to look at you. What's the matter with your mother, why don't she feed you?
ANN. He just hasn't any appetite.
MOTHER. If he ate in my house he'd have an appetite. [*To* ANN] I pity your husband! [*To* GEORGE] Sit down. I'll make you a sandwich.
GEORGE [*sits with an embarrassed laugh*]. I'm really not hungry.
MOTHER. Honest to God, it breaks my heart to see what happened to all the children. How we worked and planned for you, and you end up no better than us.
GEORGE [*with deep feeling for her*]. You . . . you haven't changed at all, you know that, Kate?
MOTHER. None of us changed, Georgie. We all love you. Joe was just talking about the day you were born and the water got shut off. People were carrying basins from a block away—a stranger would have thought the whole neighborhood was on fire! [*They laugh. She sees the juice. To* ANN] Why didn't you give him some juice!
ANN [*defensively*]. I offered it to him.
MOTHER [*scoffingly*]. You offered it to him! [*Thrusting glass into* GEORGE'*s hand*] Give it to him! [*To* GEORGE, *who is laughing*] And now you're going to sit here and drink some juice . . . and look like something!
GEORGE [*sitting*]. Kate, I feel hungry already.
CHRIS [*proudly*]. She could turn Mahatma Gandhi into a heavyweight!
MOTHER [*to* CHRIS, *with great energy*]. Listen, to hell with the restaurant! I got a ham in the icebox, and frozen strawberries, and avocados, and—
ANN. Swell, I'll help you!

GEORGE. The train leaves at eight-thirty, Ann.
MOTHER [*to* ANN]. You're leaving?
CHRIS. No, Mother, she's not—
ANN [*breaking through it, going to* GEORGE]. You hardly got here; give yourself a chance to get acquainted again.
CHRIS. Sure, you don't even know us any more.
MOTHER. Well, Chris, if they can't stay, don't—
CHRIS. No, it's just a question of George, Mother, he planned on—
GEORGE [*gets up politely, nicely, for* KATE'*s sake*]. Now wait a minute, Chris . . . .
CHRIS [*smiling and full of command, cutting him off*]. If you want to go, I'll drive you to the station now, but if you're staying, no arguments while you're here.
MOTHER [*at last confessing the tension*]. Why should he argue? [*She goes to him. With desperation and compassion, stroking his hair*] Georgie and us have no argument. How could we have an argument, Georgie? We all got hit by the same lightning, how can you—? Did you see what happened to Larry's tree, Georgie? [*She has taken his arm, and unwillingly he moves across stage with her.*] Imagine? While I was dreaming of him in the middle of the night, the wind came along and—

[LYDIA *enters on porch. As soon as she sees him:*]

LYDIA. Hey, Georgie! Georgie! Georgie! Georgie! Georgie! [*She comes down to him eagerly. She has a flowered hat in her hand, which* KATE *takes from her as she goes to* GEORGE.]
GEORGE [*as they shake hands eagerly, warmly*]. Hello, Laughy. What'd you do, grow?
LYDIA. I'm a big girl now.
MOTHER. Look what she can do to a hat!
ANN [*to* LYDIA, *admiring the hat*]. Did you make that?
MOTHER. In ten minutes! [*She puts it on.*]
LYDIA [*fixing it on her head*]. I only rearranged it.
GEORGE. You still make your own clothes?
CHRIS [*of* MOTHER]. Ain't she classy! All she needs now is a Russian wolfhound.
MOTHER [*moving her head*]. It feels like somebody is sitting on my head.
ANN. No, it's beautiful, Kate.
MOTHER [*kisses* LYDIA. *To* GEORGE]. She's a genius! You should've married her. [*They laugh.*] This one can feed you!
LYDIA [*strangely embarrassed*]. Oh, stop that, Kate.
GEORGE [*to* LYDIA]. Didn't I hear you had a baby?

MOTHER. You don't hear so good. She's got three babies.
GEORGE [*a little hurt by it—to* LYDIA]. No kidding, three?
LYDIA. Yeah, it was one, two, three— You've been away a long time, Georgie.
GEORGE. I'm beginning to realize.
MOTHER [*to* CHRIS *and* GEORGE]. The trouble with you kids is you *think* too much.
LYDIA. Well, we think, too.
MOTHER. Yes, but not all the time.
GEORGE [*with almost obvious envy*]. They never took Frank, heh?
LYDIA [*a little apologetically*]. No, he was always one year ahead of the draft.
MOTHER. It's amazing. When they were calling boys twenty-seven Frank was just twenty-eight, when they made it twenty-eight he was just twenty-nine. That's why he took up astrology. It's all in when you were born, it just goes to show.
CHRIS. What does it go to show?
MOTHER [*to* CHRIS]. Don't be so intelligent. Some superstitions are very nice! [*To* LYDIA] Did he finish Larry's horoscope?
LYDIA. I'll ask him now, I'm going in. [*To* GEORGE, *a little sadly, almost embarrassed*] Would you like to see my babies? Come on.
GEORGE. I don't think so, Lydia.
LYDIA [*understanding*]. All right. Good luck to you, George.
GEORGE. Thanks. And to you . . . And Frank. [*She smiles at him, turns, and goes off to her house.* GEORGE *stands staring after her.*]
LYDIA [*as she runs off*]. Oh, Frank!
MOTHER [*reading his thoughts*]. She got pretty, heh?
GEORGE [*sadly*]. Very pretty.
MOTHER [*as a reprimand*]. She's beautiful, you damned fool!
GEORGE [*looks around longingly; and softly, with a catch in his throat*]. She makes it seem so nice around here.
MOTHER [*shaking her finger at him*]. Look what happened to you because you wouldn't listen to me! I told you to marry that girl and stay out of the war!
GEORGE [*laughs at himself*]. She used to laugh too much.
MOTHER. And you didn't laugh enough. While you were getting mad about Fascism Frank was getting into her bed.
GEORGE [*to* CHRIS]. He won the war, Frank.
CHRIS. All the battles.
MOTHER [*in pursuit of this mood*]. The day they started the draft, Georgie, I told you you loved that girl.
CHRIS [*laughs*]. And truer love hath no man!
MOTHER. I'm smarter than any of you.

GEORGE [*laughing*]. She's wonderful!
MOTHER. And now you're going to listen to me, George. You had big principles, Eagle Scouts the three of you; so now I got a tree, and this one—[*indicating* CHRIS]—when the weather gets bad he can't stand on his feet; and that big dope—[*pointing to* LYDIA's *house*]—next door who never reads anything but Andy Gump has three children and his house paid off. Stop being a philosopher, and look after yourself. Like Joe was just saying—you move back here, he'll help you get set, and I'll find you a girl and put a smile on your face.
GEORGE. Joe? Joe wants me here?
ANN [*eagerly*]. He asked me to tell you, and I think it's a good idea.
MOTHER. Certainly. Why must you make believe you hate us? Is that another principle?—that you have to hate us? You don't hate us, George, I know you, you can't fool me, I diapered you. [*Suddenly, to* ANN] You remember Mr. Marcy's daughter?
ANN [*laughing, to* GEORGE]. She's got you hooked already! [GEORGE *laughs, is excited.*]
MOTHER. You look her over, George; you'll see she's the most beautiful—
CHRIS. She's got warts, George.
MOTHER [*to* CHRIS]. She hasn't got warts! [*To* GEORGE] So the girl has a little beauty mark on her chin—
CHRIS. And two on her nose.
MOTHER. You remember. Her father's the retired police inspector.
CHRIS. Sergeant, George.
MOTHER. He's a very kind man!
CHRIS. He looks like a gorilla.
MOTHER [*to* GEORGE]. He never shot anybody.

[*They all burst out laughing, as* KELLER *appears in doorway.* GEORGE *rises abruptly and stares at* KELLER, *who comes rapidly down to him.*]

KELLER [*the laughter stops. With strained joviality*]. Well! Look who's here! [*Extending his hand*] Georgie, good to see ya.
GEORGE [*shaking hands—somberly*]. How're you, Joe?
KELLER. So-so. Gettin' old. You comin' out to dinner with us?
GEORGE. No, got to be back in New York.
ANN. I'll call a cab for you. [*She goes up into the house.*]
KELLER. Too bad you can't stay, George. Sit down. [*To* MOTHER] He looks fine.
MOTHER. He looks terrible.
KELLER. That's what I said, you look terrible, George. [*They laugh.*] I wear the pants and she beats me with the belt.

GEORGE. I saw your factory on the way from the station. It looks like General Motors.
KELLER. I wish it was General Motors, but it ain't. Sit down, George. Sit down. [*Takes cigar out of his pocket*] So you finally went to see your father, I hear?
GEORGE. Yes, this morning. What kind of stuff do you make now?
KELLER. Oh, little of everything. Pressure cookers, an assembly for washing machines. Got a nice, flexible plant now. So how'd you find Dad? Feel all right?
GEORGE [*searching* KELLER, *speaking indecisively*]. No, he's not well, Joe.
KELLER [*lighting his cigar*]. Not his heart again, is it?
GEORGE. It's everything, Joe. It's his soul.
KELLER [*blowing out smoke*]. Uh huh—
CHRIS. How about seeing what they did with your house?
KELLER. Leave him be.
GEORGE [*to* CHRIS, *indicating* KELLER]. I'd like to talk to him.
KELLER. Sure, he just got here. That's the way they do, George. A little man makes a mistake and they hang him by the thumbs; the big ones become ambassadors. I wish you'd-a told me you were going to see Dad.
GEORGE [*studying him*]. I didn't know you were interested.
KELLER. In a way, I am. I would like him to know, George, that as far as I'm concerned, any time he wants, he's got a place with me. I would like him to know that.
GEORGE. He hates your guts, Joe. Don't you know that?
KELLER. I imagined it. But that can change, too.
MOTHER. Steve was never like that.
GEORGE. He's like that now. He'd like to take every man who made money in the war and put him up against a wall.
CHRIS. He'll need a lot of bullets.
GEORGE. And he'd better not get any.
KELLER. That's a sad thing to hear.
GEORGE [*with bitterness dominant*]. Why? What'd you expect him to think of you?
KELLER [*the force of his nature rising, but under control*]. I'm sad to see he hasn't changed. As long as I know him, twenty-five years, the man never learned how to take the blame. You know that, George.
GEORGE [*he does*]. Well, I—
KELLER. But you do know it. Because the way you come in here you don't look like you remember it. I mean like in nineteen thirty-seven when we had the shop on Flood Street. And he damn near blew us all up with that heater he left burning for two days without water.

He wouldn't admit that was his fault, either. I had to fire a mechanic to save his face. You remember that.

GEORGE. Yes, but—

KELLER. I'm just mentioning it, George. Because this is just another one of a lot of things. Like when he gave Frank that money to invest in oil stock.

GEORGE [*distressed*]. I know that, I—

KELLER [*driving in, but restrained*]. But it's good to remember those things, kid. The way he cursed Frank because the stock went down. Was that Frank's fault? To listen to him Frank was a swindler. And all the man did was give him a bad tip.

GEORGE [*gets up, moves away*]. I know those things. . . .

KELLER. Then remember them, remember them. [ANN *comes out of house.*] There are certain men in the world who rather see everybody hung before they'll take blame. You understand me, George?

[*They stand facing each other,* GEORGE *trying to judge him.*]

ANN [*coming downstage*]. The cab's on its way. Would you like to wash?

MOTHER [*with the thrust of hope*]. Why must he go? Make the midnight, George.

KELLER. Sure, you'll have dinner with us!

ANN. How about it? Why not? We're eating at the lake, we could have a swell time.

[*A long pause, as* GEORGE *looks at* ANN, CHRIS, KELLER, *then back to her.*]

GEORGE. All right.

MOTHER. Now you're talking.

CHRIS. I've got a shirt that'll go right with that suit.

MOTHER. Size fifteen and a half, right, George?

GEORGE. Is Lydia—? I mean—Frank and Lydia coming?

MOTHER. I'll get you a date that'll make her look like a— [*She starts upstage.*]

GEORGE [*laughing*]. No, I don't want a date.

CHRIS. I know somebody just for you! Charlotte Tanner! [*He starts for the house.*]

KELLER. Call Charlotte, that's right.

MOTHER. Sure, call her up. [CHRIS *goes into house.*]

ANN. You go up and pick out a shirt and tie.

GEORGE [*stops, looks around at them and the place*]. I never felt at home anywhere but here. I feel so— [*He nearly laughs, and turns away from them.*] Kate, you look so young, you know? You didn't change

at all. It . . . rings an old bell. [*Turns to* KELLER] You too, Joe you're amazingly the same. The whole atmosphere is.
KELLER. Say, I ain't got time to get sick.
MOTHER. He hasn't been laid up in fifteen years.
KELLER. Except my flu during the war.
MOTHER. Huhh?
KELLER. My flu, when I was sick during . . . the war.
MOTHER. Well, sure . . . [*To* GEORGE] I mean except for that flu. [GEORGE *stands perfectly still.*] Well, it slipped my mind, don't look at me that way. He wanted to go to the shop but he couldn't lift himself off the bed. I thought he had pneumonia.
GEORGE. Why did you say he's never—?
KELLER. I know how you feel, kid, I'll never forgive myself. If I could've gone in that day I'd never allow Dad to touch those heads.
GEORGE. She said you've never been sick.
MOTHER. I said he was sick, George.
GEORGE [*going to* ANN]. Ann, didn't you hear her say—?
MOTHER. Do you remember every time you were sick?
GEORGE. I'd remember pneumonia. Especially if I got it just the day my partner was going to patch up cylinder heads. . . . What happened that day, Joe?

[FRANK *enters briskly from driveway, holding* LARRY'*s horoscope in his hand. He comes to* KATE.]

FRANK. Kate! Kate!
MOTHER. Frank, did you see George?
FRANK [*extending his hand*]. Lydia told me, I'm glad to . . . you'll have to pardon me. [*Pulling* MOTHER *over*] I've got something amazing for you, Kate, I finished Larry's horoscope.
MOTHER. You'd be interested in this, George. It's wonderful the way he can understand the—
CHRIS [*entering from house*]. George, the girl's on the phone—
MOTHER [*desperately*]. He finished Larry's horoscope!
CHRIS. Frank, can't you pick a better time than this?
FRANK. The greatest men who ever lived believed in the stars!
CHRIS. Stop filling her head with that junk!
FRANK. Is it junk to feel that there's a greater power than ourselves? I've studied the stars of his life! I won't argue with you, I'm telling you. Somewhere in this world your brother is alive!
MOTHER [*instantly to* CHRIS]. Why isn't it possible?
CHRIS. Because it's insane.
FRANK. Just a minute now. I'll tell you something and you can do as you please. Just let me say it. He was supposed to have died on

November twenty-fifth. But November twenty-fifth was his favorable day.

CHRIS. Mother!

MOTHER. Listen to him!

FRANK. It was a day when everything good was shining on him, the kind of day he should've married on. You can laugh at a lot of it, I can understand you laughing. But the odds are a million to one that a man won't die on his favorable day. That's known, that's known, Chris!

MOTHER. Why isn't it possible, why isn't it possible, Chris!

GEORGE [*to* ANN]. Don't you understand what she's saying? She just told you to go. What are you waiting for now?

CHRIS. Nobody can tell her to go. [*A car horn is heard.*]

MOTHER [*to* FRANK]. Thank you, darling, for your trouble. Will you tell him to wait, Frank?

FRANK [*as he goes*]. Sure thing.

MOTHER [*calling out*]. They'll be right out, driver!

CHRIS. She's not leaving, Mother.

GEORGE. You heard her say it, he's never been sick!

MOTHER. He misunderstood me, Chris! [CHRIS *looks at her, struck.*]

GEORGE [*to* ANN]. He simply told your father to kill pilots, and covered himself in bed!

CHRIS. You'd better answer him, Annie. Answer him.

MOTHER. I packed your bag, darling.

CHRIS. What?

MOTHER. I packed your bag. All you've got to do is close it.

ANN. I'm not closing anything. He asked me here and I'm staying till he tells me to go. [*To* GEORGE] Till Chris tells me!

CHRIS. That's all! Now get out of here, George!

MOTHER [*to* CHRIS]. But if that's how he feels—

CHRIS. That's all, nothing more till Christ comes, about the case or Larry as long as I'm here! [*To* GEORGE] Now get out of here, George!

GEORGE [*to* ANN]. You tell me. I want to hear you tell me.

ANN. Go, George!

[*They disappear up the driveway,* ANN *saying, "Don't take it that way, Georgie! Please don't take it that way."*]

CHRIS [*turning to his mother*]. What do you mean, you packed her bag? How dare you pack her bag?

MOTHER. Chris—

CHRIS. How dare you pack her bag?

MOTHER. She doesn't belong here.

CHRIS. Then I don't belong here.

MOTHER. She's Larry's girl.
CHRIS. And I'm his brother and he's dead, and I'm marrying his girl.
MOTHER. Never, never in this world!
KELLER. You lost your mind?
MOTHER. You have nothing to say!
KELLER [*cruelly*]. I got plenty to say. Three and a half years you been talking like a maniac—

[MOTHER *smashes him across the face.*]

MOTHER. Nothing. You have nothing to say. Now I say. He's coming back, and everybody has got to wait.
CHRIS. Mother, Mother—
MOTHER. Wait, wait—
CHRIS. How long? How long?
MOTHER [*rolling out of her*]. Till he comes; forever and ever till he comes!
CHRIS [*as an ultimatum*]. Mother, I'm going ahead with it.
MOTHER. Chris, I've never said no to you in my life, now I say no!
CHRIS. You'll never let him go till I do it.
MOTHER. I'll never let him go and you'll never let him go!
CHRIS. I've let him go. I've let him go a long—
MOTHER [*with no less force, but turning from him*]. Then let your father go. [*Pause.* CHRIS *stands transfixed.*]
KELLER. She's out of her mind.
MOTHER. Altogether! [*To* CHRIS, *but not facing them*] Your brother's alive, darling, because if he's dead, your father killed him. Do you understand me now? As long as you live, that boy is alive. God does not let a son be killed by his father. Now you see, don't you? Now you see. [*Beyond control, she hurries up and into house.*]
KELLER [CHRIS *has not moved. He speaks insinuatingly, questioningly.*] She's out of her mind.
CHRIS [*in a broken whisper*]. Then . . . you did it?
KELLER [*with the beginning of plea in his voice*]. He never flew a P-40—
CHRIS [*struck; deadly*]. But the others.
KELLER [*insistently*]. She's out of her mind. [*He takes a step toward* CHRIS, *pleadingly.*]
CHRIS [*unyielding*]. Dad . . . you did it?
KELLER. He never flew a P-40, what's the matter with you?
CHRIS [*still asking, and saying*]. Then you did it. To the others.

[*Both hold their voices down.*]

KELLER [*afraid of him, his deadly insistence*]. What's the matter with you? What the hell is the matter with you?
CHRIS [*quietly, incredibly*]. How could you do that? How?
KELLER. What's the matter with you!
CHRIS. Dad . . . Dad, you killed twenty-one men!
KELLER. What, killed?
CHRIS. You killed them, you murdered them.
KELLER [*as though throwing his whole nature open before* CHRIS]. How could I kill anybody?
CHRIS. Dad! Dad!
KELLER [*trying to hush him*]. I didn't kill anybody!
CHRIS. Then explain it to me. What did you do? Explain it to me or I'll tear you to pieces!
KELLER [*horrified at his overwhelming fury*]. Don't, Chris, don't—
CHRIS. I want to know what you did, now what did you do? You had a hundred and twenty cracked engine-heads, now what did you do?
KELLER. If you're going to hang me then I—
CHRIS. I'm listening. God Almighty, I'm listening!
KELLER [*Their movements now are those of subtle pursuit and escape.* KELLER *keeps a step out of* CHRIS's *range as he talks*]. You're a boy, what could I do! I'm in business, a man is in business; a hundred and twenty cracked, you're out of business; you got a process, the process don't work you're out of business; you don't know how to operate, your stuff is no good; they close you up, they tear up your contracts, what the hell's it to them? You lay forty years into a business and they knock you out in five minutes, what could I do, let them take forty years, let them take my life away? [*His voice cracking.*] I never thought they'd install them. I swear to God. I thought they'd stop 'em before anybody took off.
CHRIS. Then why'd you ship them out?
KELLER. By the time they could spot them I thought I'd have the process going again, and I could show them they needed me and they'd let it go by. But weeks passed and I got no kickback, so I was going to tell them.
CHRIS. Then why didn't you tell them?
KELLER. It was too late. The paper, it was all over the front page, twenty-one went down, it was too late. They came with handcuffs into the shop, what could I do? [*He sits on bench.*] Chris . . . Chris, I did it for you, it was a chance and I took it for you. I'm sixty-one years old, when would I have another chance to make something for you? Sixty-one years old you don't get another chance, do ya?
CHRIS. You even knew they wouldn't hold up in the air.

KELLER. I didn't say that.
CHRIS. But you were going to warn them not to use them—
KELLER. But that don't mean—
CHRIS. It means you knew they'd crash.
KELLER. It don't mean that.
CHRIS. Then you *thought* they'd crash.
KELLER. I was afraid maybe—
CHRIS. You were afraid maybe! God in heaven, what kind of a man are you? Kids were hanging in the air by those heads. You knew that!
KELLER. For you, a business for you!
CHRIS [*with burning fury*]. For me! Where do you live, where have you come from? For me!—I was dying every day and you were killing my boys and you did it for me? What the hell do you think I was thinking of, the Goddam business? Is that as far as your mind can see, the business? What is that, the world—the business? What the hell do you mean, you did it for me? Don't you have a country? Don't you live in the world? What the hell are you? You're not even an animal, no animal kills his own, what are you? What must I do to you? I ought to tear the tongue out of your mouth, what must I do? [*With his fist he pounds down upon his father's shoulder. He stumbles away, covering his face as he weeps.*] What must I do, Jesus God, what must I do?
KELLER. Chris . . . My Chris . . . .

CURTAIN

ACT THREE

Two o'clock the following morning, MOTHER *is discovered on the rise, rocking ceaselessly in a chair, staring at her thoughts. It is an intense, slight, sort of rocking. A light shows from upstairs bedroom, lower floor windows being dark. The moon is strong and casts its bluish light.*

Presently JIM, *dressed in jacket and hat, appears, and seeing her, goes up beside her.*

JIM. Any news?
MOTHER. No news.
JIM [*gently*]. You can't sit up all night, dear, why don't you go to bed?
MOTHER. I'm waiting for Chris. Don't worry about me, Jim, I'm perfectly all right.
JIM. But it's almost two o'clock.

MOTHER. I can't sleep. [*Slight pause*] You had an emergency?
JIM [*tiredly*]. Somebody had a headache and thought he was dying. [*Slight pause*] Half of my patients are quite mad. Nobody realizes how many people are walking around loose, and they're cracked as coconuts. Money. Money-money-money-money. You say it long enough it doesn't mean anything. [*She smiles, makes a silent laugh.*] Oh, how I'd love to be around when that happens!
MOTHER [*shaking her head*]. You're so childish, Jim! Sometimes you are.
JIM [*looks at her a moment*]. Kate. [*Pause*] What happened?
MOTHER. I told you. He had an argument with Joe. Then he got in the car and drove away.
JIM. What kind of an argument?
MOTHER. An argument, Joe. . . . He was crying like a child, before.
JIM. They argued about Ann?
MOTHER [*after slight hesitation*]. No, not Ann. Imagine? [*Indicates lighted window above*] She hasn't come out to that room since he left. All night in that room.
JIM [*looks at window, then at her*]. What'd Joe do, tell him?
MOTHER [*stops rocking*]. Tell him what?
JIM. Don't be afraid, Kate, I know. I've always known.
MOTHER. How?
JIM. It occurred to me a long time ago.
MOTHER. I always had the feeling that in the back of his head, Chris . . . almost knew. I didn't think it would be such a shock.
JIM [*gets up*]. Chris would never know how to live with a thing like that. It takes a certain talent—for lying. You have it, and I do. But not him.
MOTHER. What do you mean? . . . He's not coming back?
JIM. Oh, no, he'll come back. We all come back, Kate. These private little revolutions always die. The compromise is always made. In a peculiar way. Frank is right—every man does have a star. The star of one's honesty. And you spend your life groping for it, but once it's out it never lights again. I don't think he went very far. He probably just wanted to be alone to watch his star go out.
MOTHER. Just as long as he comes back.
JIM. I wish he wouldn't, Kate. One year I simply took off, went to New Orleans; for two months I lived on bananas and milk, and studied a certain disease. It was beautiful. And then she came, and she cried. And I went back home with her. And now I live in the usual darkness; I can't find myself; it's even hard sometimes to remember the kind of man I wanted to be. I'm a good husband; Chris is a good son—he'll come back.

[KELLER *comes out on porch in dressing gown and slippers. He goes upstage—to alley.* JIM *goes to him.*]

JIM. I have a feeling he's in the park. I'll look around for him. Put her to bed, Joe; this is no good for what she's got. [JIM *exits up driveway.*]

KELLER [*coming down*]. What does he want here?

MOTHER. His friend is not home.

KELLER [*comes down to her. His voice is husky*]. I don't like him mixing in so much.

MOTHER. It's too late, Joe. He knows.

KELLER [*apprehensively*]. How does he know?

MOTHER. He guessed a long time ago.

KELLER. I don't like that.

MOTHER [*laughs dangerously, quietly into the line*]. What you don't like.

KELLER. Yeah, what I don't like.

MOTHER. You can't bull yourself through this one, Joe, you better be smart now. This thing—this thing is not over yet.

KELLER [*indicating lighted window above*]. And what is she doing up there? She don't come out of the room.

MOTHER. I don't know, what is she doing? Sit down, stop being mad. You want to live? You better figure out your life.

KELLER. She don't know, does she?

MOTHER. She saw Chris storming out of here. It's one and one—she knows how to add.

KELLER. Maybe I ought to talk to her?

MOTHER. Don't ask me, Joe.

KELLER [*almost an outburst*]. Then who do I ask? But I don't think she'll do anything about it.

MOTHER. You're asking me again.

KELLER. I'm askin' you. What am I, a stranger? I thought I had a family here. What happened to my family?

MOTHER. You've got a family. I'm simply telling you that I have no strength to think any more.

KELLER. You have no strength. The minute there's trouble you have no strength.

MOTHER. Joe, you're doing the same thing again; all your life whenever there's trouble you yell at me and you think that settles it.

KELLER. Then what do I do? Tell me, talk to me, what do I do?

MOTHER. Joe . . . I've been thinking this way. If he comes back—

KELLER. What do you mean "if"? He's comin' back!

MOTHER. I think if you sit him down and you—explain yourself. I mean you ought to make it clear to him that you know you did a terrible thing. [*Not looking into his eyes*] I mean if he saw that you realize what you did. You see?

KELLER. What ice does that cut?

MOTHER [*a little fearfully*]. I mean if you told him that you want to pay for what you did.

KELLER [*sensing . . . quietly*]. How can I pay?

MOTHER. Tell him—you're willing to go to prison. [*Pause*]

KELLER [*struck, amazed*]. I'm willing to—?

MOTHER [*quickly*]. You wouldn't go, he wouldn't ask you to go. But if you told him you wanted to, if he could feel that you wanted to pay, maybe he would forgive you.

KELLER. He would forgive me! For what?

MOTHER. Joe, you know what I mean.

KELLER. I don't know what you mean! You wanted money, so I made money. What must I be forgiven? You wanted money, didn't you?

MOTHER. I didn't want it that way.

KELLER. I didn't want it that way, either! What difference is it what you want? I spoiled the both of you. I should've put him out when he was ten like I was put out, and make him earn his keep. Then he'd know how a buck is made in this world. Forgiven! I could live on a quarter a day myself, but I got a family so I—

MOTHER. Joe, Joe . . . It don't excuse it that you did it for the family.

KELLER. It's got to excuse it!

MOTHER. There's something bigger than the family to him.

KELLER. Nothin' is bigger!

MOTHER. There is to him.

KELLER. There's nothin' he could do that I wouldn't forgive. Because he's my son. Because I'm his father and he's my son.

MOTHER. Joe, I tell you—

KELLER. Nothin's bigger than that. And you're goin' to tell him, you understand? I'm his father and he's my son, and if there's something bigger than that I'll put a bullet in my head!

MOTHER. You stop that!

KELLER. You heard me. Now you know what to tell him. [*Pause. He moves from her—halts.*] But he wouldn't put me away though. . . . He wouldn't do that. . . . Would he?

MOTHER. He loved you, Joe, you broke his heart.

KELLER. But to put me away. . . .

MOTHER. I don't know. I'm beginning to think we don't really know him. They say in the war he was such a killer. Here he was always afraid of mice. I don't know him. I don't know what he'll do.

KELLER. Goddam, if Larry was alive he wouldn't act like this. He understood the way the world is made. He listened to me. To him the world had a forty-foot front, it ended at the building line. This one, everything bothers him. You make a deal, overcharge two cents, and his hair falls out. He don't understand money. Too easy, it came too easy. Yes, sir. Larry. That was a boy we lost. Larry. Larry. [*He slumps on chair in front of her.*] What am I gonna do, Kate?

MOTHER. Joe, Joe, please.... You'll be all right, nothing is going to happen.

KELLER [*desperately, lost*]. For you, Kate, for both of you, that's all I ever lived for....

MOTHER. I know, darling, I know. [ANN *enters from house. They say nothing, waiting for her to speak.*]

ANN. Why do you stay up? I'll tell you when he comes.

KELLER [*rises, goes to her*]. You didn't eat supper, did you? [*To* MOTHER] Why don't you make her something?

MOTHER. Sure, I'll—

ANN. Never mind, Kate, I'm all right. [*They are unable to speak to each other.*] There's something I want to tell you. [*She starts, then halts.*] I'm not going to do anything about it.

MOTHER. She's a good girl! [*To* KELLER] You see? She's a—

ANN. I'll do nothing about Joe, but you're going to do something for me. [*Directly to* MOTHER] You made Chris feel guilty with me. Whether you wanted to or not, you've crippled him in front of me. I'd like you to tell him that Larry is dead and that you know it. You understand me? I'm not going out of here alone. There's no life for me that way. I want you to set him free. And then I promise you, everything will end, and we'll go away, and that's all.

KELLER. You'll do that. You'll tell him.

ANN. I know what I'm asking, Kate. You had two sons. But you've only got one now.

KELLER. You'll tell him.

ANN. And you've got to say it to him so he knows you mean it.

MOTHER. My dear, if the boy was dead, it wouldn't depend on my words to make Chris know it.... The night he gets into your bed, his heart will dry up. Because he knows and you know. To his dying day he'll wait for his brother! No, my dear, no such thing. You're going in the morning, and you're going alone. That's your life, that's your lonely life. [*She goes to porch, and starts in.*]

ANN. Larry is dead, Kate.

MOTHER [*she stops*]. Don't speak to me.

ANN. I said he's dead. I know! He crashed off the coast of China

November twenty-fifth! His engine didn't fail him. But he died. I know . . . .
MOTHER. How did he die? You're lying to me. If you know, how did he die?
ANN. I loved him. You know I loved him. Would I have looked at anyone else if I wasn't sure? That's enough for you.
MOTHER [*moving on her*]. What's enough for me? What're you talking about? [*She grasps* ANN's *wrists.*]
ANN. You're hurting my wrists.
MOTHER. What are you talking about! [*Pause. She stares at* ANN *a moment, then turns and goes to* KELLER.]
ANN. Joe, go in the house.
KELLER. Why should I—
ANN. Please go.
KELLER. Lemme know when he comes. [KELLER *goes into house.*]
MOTHER [*as she sees* ANN *taking a letter from her pocket*]. What's that?
ANN. Sit down. [MOTHER *moves left to chair, but does not sit.*] First you've got to understand. When I came, I didn't have any idea that Joe—I had nothing against him or you. I came to get married. I hoped . . . So I didn't bring this to hurt you. I thought I'd show it to you only if there was no other way to settle Larry in your mind.
MOTHER. Larry? [*Snatches letter from* ANN's *hand*]
ANN. He wrote it to me just before he— [MOTHER *opens and begins to read letter.*] I'm not trying to hurt you, Kate. You're making me do this, now remember you're— Remember. I've been so lonely, Kate . . . I can't leave here alone again. [*A long, low moan comes from* MOTHER's *throat as she reads.*] You made me show it to you. You wouldn't believe me. I told you a hundred times, why wouldn't you believe me!
MOTHER. Oh, my God . . .
ANN [*with pity and fear*]. Kate, please, please. . . .
MOTHER. My God, my God. . . .
ANN. Kate, dear, I'm so sorry . . . I'm so sorry.

[CHRIS *enters from driveway. He seems exhausted.*]

CHRIS. What's the matter—?
ANN. Where were you? . . . You're all perspired. [MOTHER *doesn't move.*] Where were you?
CHRIS. Just drove around a little. I thought you'd be gone.
ANN. Where do I go? I have nowhere to go.
CHRIS [*to* MOTHER]. Where's Dad?
ANN. Inside lying down.

CHRIS. Sit down, both of you. I'll say what there is to say.
MOTHER. I didn't hear the car. . . .
CHRIS. I left it in the garage.
MOTHER. Jim is out looking for you.
CHRIS. Mother . . . I'm going away. There are a couple of firms in Cleveland, I think I can get a place. I mean, I'm going away for good. [*To* ANN *alone*] I know what you're thinking, Annie. It's true. I'm yellow. I was made yellow in this house because I suspected my father and I did nothing about it, but if I knew that night when I came home what I know now, he'd be in the district attorney's office by this time, and I'd have brought him there. Now if I look at him, all I'm able to do is cry.
MOTHER. What are you talking about? What else can you do?
CHRIS. I could jail him! I could jail him, if I were human any more. But I'm like everybody else now. I'm practical now. You made me practical.
MOTHER. But you have to be.
CHRIS. The cats in that alley are practical, the bums who ran away when we were fighting were practical. Only the dead ones weren't practical. But now I'm practical, and I spit on myself. I'm going away. I'm going now.
ANN [*going up to him*]. I'm coming with you.
CHRIS. No, Ann.
ANN. Chris, I don't ask you to do anything about Joe.
CHRIS. You do, you do.
ANN. I swear I never will.
CHRIS. In your heart you always will.
ANN. Then do what you have to do!
CHRIS. Do what? What is there to do? I've looked all night for a reason to make him suffer.
ANN. There's reason, there's reason!
CHRIS. What? Do I raise the dead when I put him behind bars? Then what'll I do it for? We used to shoot a man who acted like a dog, but honor was real there, you were protecting something. But here? This is the land of the great big dogs, you don't love a man here, you eat him! That's the principle; the only one we live by—it just happened to kill a few people this time, that's all. The world's that way, how can I take it out on him? What sense does that make? This is a zoo, a zoo!
ANN [*to* MOTHER]. You know what he's got to do! Tell him!
MOTHER. Let him go.
ANN. I won't let him go. You'll tell him what he's got to do. . . .
MOTHER. Annie!

ANN. Then I will!

[KELLER *enters from house.* CHRIS *sees him, goes down near arbor.*]

KELLER. What's the matter with you? I want to talk to you.

CHRIS. I've got nothing to say to you.

KELLER [*taking his arm*]. I want to talk to you!

CHRIS [*pulling violently away from him*]. Don't do that, Dad. I'm going to hurt you if you do that. There's nothing to say, so say it quick.

KELLER. Exactly what's the matter? What's the matter? You got too much money? Is that what bothers you?

CHRIS [*with an edge of sarcasm*]. It bothers me.

KELLER. If you can't get used to it, then throw it away. You hear me? Take every cent and give it to charity, throw it in the sewer. Does that settle it? In the sewer, that's all. You think I'm kidding? I'm tellin' you what to do, if it's dirty then burn it. It's your money, that's not my money. I'm a dead man, I'm an old dead man, nothing's mine. Well, talk to me! What do you want to do!

CHRIS. It's not what I want to do. It's what you want to do.

KELLER. What should I want to do? [CHRIS *is silent.*] Jail? You want me to go to jail? If you want me to go, say so! Is that where I belong? Then tell me so! [*Slight pause*] What's the matter, why can't you tell me? [*Furiously*] You say everything else to me, say that! [*Slight pause*] I'll tell you why you can't say it. Because you know I don't belong there. Because you know! [*With growing emphasis and passion, and a persistent tone of desperation*] Who worked for nothin' in that war? When they work for nothin', I'll work for nothin'. Did they ship a gun or a truck outa Detroit before they got their price? Is that clean? It's dollars and cents, nickels and dimes; war and peace, it's nickels and dimes, what's clean? Half the Goddam country is gotta go if I go! That's why you can't tell me.

CHRIS. That's exactly why.

KELLER. Then . . . why am *I* bad?

CHRIS. *I* know you're no worse than most men but I thought you were better. I never saw you as a man. I saw you as my father. [*Almost breaking*] I can't look at you this way, I can't look at myself!

[*He turns away, unable to face* KELLER. ANN *goes quickly to* MOTHER, *takes letter from her and starts for* CHRIS. MOTHER *instantly rushes to intercept her.*]

MOTHER. Give me that!

ANN. He's going to read it! [*She thrusts letter into* CHRIS'*s hand.*] Larry. He wrote it to me the day he died.

KELLER. Larry!

MOTHER. Chris, it's not for you. [*He starts to read.*] Joe . . . go away. . . .
KELLER [*mystified, frightened*]. Why'd she say, Larry, what—?
MOTHER [*desperately pushes him toward alley, glancing at* CHRIS]. Go to the street, Joe, go to the street! [*She comes down beside* KELLER.] Don't Chris . . . [*Pleading from her whole soul*] Don't tell him.
CHRIS [*quietly*]. Three and one half years . . . talking, talking. Now you tell me what you must do. . . . This is how he died, now tell me where you belong.
KELLER [*pleading*]. Chris, a man can't be a Jesus in this world!
CHRIS. I know all about the world. I know the whole crap story. Now listen to this, and tell me what a man's got to be! [*Reads*] "My dear Ann: . . ." You listening? He wrote this the day he died. Listen, don't cry. . . . Listen! "My dear Ann: It is impossible to put down the things I feel. But I've got to tell you something. Yesterday they flew in a load of papers from the States and I read about Dad and your father being convicted. I can't express myself. I can't tell you how I feel—I can't bear to live any more. Last night I circled the base for twenty minutes before I could bring myself in. How could he have done that? Every day three or four men never come back and he sits back there doing business. . . . I don't know how to tell you what I feel. . . . I can't face anybody. . . . I'm going out on a mission in a few minutes. They'll probably report me missing. If they do, I want you to know that you mustn't wait for me. I tell you, Ann, if I had him here now I could kill him—" [KELLER *grabs letter from* CHRIS's *hand and reads it. After a long pause*] Now blame the world. Do you understand that letter?
KELLER [*speaking almost inaudibly*]. I think I do. Get the car. I'll put on my jacket. [*He turns and starts slowly for the house.* MOTHER *rushes to intercept him.*]
MOTHER. Why are you going? You'll sleep, why are you going?
KELLER. I can't sleep here. I'll feel better if I go.
MOTHER. You're so foolish. Larry was your son too, wasn't he? You know he'd never tell you to do this.
KELLER [*looking at letter in his hand*]. Then what is this if it isn't telling me? Sure, he was my son. But I think to him they were all my sons. And I guess they were, I guess they were. I'll be right down. [*Exits into house*]
MOTHER [*to* CHRIS, *with determination*]. You're not going to take him!
CHRIS. I'm taking him.
MOTHER. It's up to you, if you tell him to stay he'll stay. Go and tell him!
CHRIS. Nobody could stop him now.

MOTHER. You'll stop him! How long will he live in prison? Are you trying to kill him?
CHRIS [*holding out letter*]. I thought you read this!
MOTHER [*of* LARRY, *the letter*]. The war is over! Didn't you hear? It's over!
CHRIS. Then what was Larry to you? A stone that fell into the water? It's not enough for him to be sorry. Larry didn't kill himself to make you and Dad sorry.
MOTHER. What more can we be!
CHRIS. You can be better! Once and for all you can know there's a universe of people outside and you're responsible to it, and unless you know that, you threw away your son because that's why he died.

[*A shot is heard in the house. They stand frozen for a brief second.* CHRIS *starts for porch, pauses at step, turns to* ANN.]

CHRIS. Find Jim! [*He goes on into the house and* ANN *runs up driveway.* MOTHER *stands alone, transfixed.*]
MOTHER [*softly, almost moaning*]. Joe . . . Joe . . . Joe . . . Joe . . . [CHRIS *comes out of house, down to* MOTHER's *arms.*]
CHRIS [*almost crying*]. Mother, I didn't mean to—
MOTHER. Don't dear. Don't take it on yourself. Forget now. Live. [CHRIS *stirs as if to answer.*] Shhh . . . [*She puts his arms down gently and moves toward porch.*] Shhh . . . [*As she reaches porch steps she begins sobbing.*]

CURTAIN

PICNIC

ON THE

BATTLEFIELD

by FERNANDO ARRABAL

TRANSLATED BY *Barbara Wright*

PICNIC ON THE BATTLEFIELD Reprinted by permission of Grove Press, Inc. Translation copyright © 1967 by Calder & Boyars, Ltd., London.

Photos by Allan Zola Kronzek: Old Post Office Theatre, East Hampton, Long Island; 1970 production, directed by Thomas Ewing.

𝓕ernando Arrabal, whose life reflects the violent events of modern European history, was born in Spain in 1932. As a child, he lived through the Spanish Civil War in which his father was sentenced to death by the followers of Franco and later mysteriously disappeared from prison. As a young man, he lived under a military dictatorship, experiencing the suppression of civil liberties and the general atmosphere of fear, humiliation, and poverty that followed the revolution. But, at the age of twenty-three, he went into voluntary exile in France where, writing in French, he launched his career as a playwright.

His early years have had a lasting influence on Arrabal's work. The themes of his autobiographical novel, *Baal Babylon*, and his plays, such as *Guernica, The Labyrinth, The Automobile Graveyard,* and *The Architect and the Emperor of Assyria,* are rooted in childhood memories as well as in his more recent responses to world events. His first play, *Picnic on the Battlefield*, which premiered on April 25, 1959, in Paris, places Arrabal in the theatrical tradition that Martin Esslin has described as the *theater of the absurd*. This theatrical movement has created one of the more exciting forms of playwriting in the modern theater and represents a sharp break in theme and technique with older theatrical traditions. Absurdist playwrights, such as Eugène Ionesco, Samuel Beckett, Jean Genet, and Fernando Arrabal, portray man in an absurd situation in which he longs for and expects truth, justice, and meaning but instead confronts a mechanical and indifferent universe. For the absurdists, man's situation, like that of the Tépans in *Picnic on the Battlefield*, is both ludicrous and terrifying. While the senselessness of the human condition is the whole cloth out of which the absurdist play is made, the plays impose their internal logic on a concrete, external situation, such as a picnic on a battlefield or a hotel in the middle of an automobile junkyard.

As an absurdist play, *Picnic on the Battlefield* dramatizes (1) the meaninglessness of war for the young men of both sides who are sent into battle, (2) the holiday mood of the parents for whom the realities of war are romanticized memories of cavalry charges and whose own hostility, barely kept beneath the surface in domestic quarrels and stories, is but a smaller reflection of the larger violence, (3) the omnipresent bureaucracy of the war machine that mechanically sends persons to death, and (4) the faceless corpsmen who seek out their quota of corpses on any given day of battle. The absurd situation of the Tépans bringing a picnic to the battlefield for their soldier-son and all that follows is, at once, ridiculous and frightening. But Arrabal's trenchant comment on human nature and the divided generations makes *Picnic on the Battlefield* a play with universal meaning.

Characters

ZAPO (*a soldier*)
M. TÉPAN (*the soldier's father*)
MME. TÉPAN (*the soldier's mother*)
ZÉPO (*an enemy soldier*)
FIRST STRETCHER BEARER
SECOND STRETCHER BEARER

A battlefield. The stage is covered with barbed wire and sandbags. The battle is at its height. Rifle shots, exploding bombs and machine guns can be heard.

ZAPO *is alone on the stage, flat on his stomach, hidden among the sandbags. He is very frightened. The sound of the fighting stops. Silence.*

ZAPO *takes a ball of wool and some needles out of a canvas workbag and starts knitting a pullover, which is already quite far advanced. The field telephone, which is by his side, suddenly starts ringing.*

ZAPO. Hallo, hallo . . . yes, Captain . . . yes, I'm the sentry of sector 47 . . . . Nothing new, Captain. . . . Excuse me, Captain, but when's the fighting going to start again? And what am I supposed to do with the hand-grenades? Do I chuck them in front of me or behind me? . . . Don't get me wrong, I didn't mean to annoy you . . . Captain, I really feel terribly lonely, couldn't you send me someone to keep me company? . . . Even if it's only a nanny-goat? [*The Captain is obviously severely reprimanding him.*] Whatever you say, Captain, whatever you say.

[ZAPO *hangs up. He mutters to himself. Silence. Enter* M. *and* MME. TÉPAN, *carrying baskets as if they are going to a picnic. They address their son, who has his back turned and doesn't see them come in.*]

M. TÉPAN [*ceremoniously*]. Stand up, my son, and kiss your mother on the brow. [ZAPO, *surprised, gets up and kisses his mother very respectfully on the forehead. He is about to speak, but his father doesn't give him a chance.*] And now, kiss me.
ZAPO. But, dear Father and dear Mother, how did you dare to come all this way, to such a dangerous place? You must leave at once.
M. TÉPAN. So you think you've got something to teach your father about war and danger, do you? All this is just a game to me. How many times—to take the first example that comes to mind—have I got off an underground train while it was still moving?
MME. TÉPAN. We thought you must be bored, so we came to pay you a little visit. This war must be a bit tedious, after all.
ZAPO. It all depends.
M. TÉPAN. I know exactly what happens. To start with you're attracted by the novelty of it all. It's fun to kill people, and throw hand-grenades about, and wear uniforms—you feel smart, but in the end you get bored stiff. You'd have found it much more interesting in my day. Wars were much more lively, much more highly colored. And

157

then, the best thing was that there were horses, plenty of horses. It was a real pleasure; if the Captain ordered us to attack, there we all were immediately, on horseback, in our red uniforms. It was a sight to be seen. And then there were the charges at the gallop, sword in hand, and suddenly you found yourself face to face with the enemy, and he was equal to the occasion too—with his horses—there were always horses, lots of horses, with their well-rounded rumps—in his highly polished boots, and his green uniform.

MME. TÉPAN. No no, the enemy uniform wasn't green. It was blue. I remember distinctly that it was blue.

M. TÉPAN. I tell you it was green.

MME. TÉPAN. When I was little, how many times did I go out on to the balcony to watch the battle and say to the neighbor's little boy: "I bet you a gumdrop the blues win." And the blues were our enemies.

M. TÉPAN. Oh well, you must be right, then.

MME. TÉPAN. I've always liked battles. As a child I always said that when I grew up I wanted to be a Colonel of dragoons. But my mother wouldn't hear of it, you know how she will stick to her principles at all costs.

M. TÉPAN. Your mother's just a half-wit.

ZAPO. I'm sorry, but you really must go. You can't come into a war unless you're a soldier.

M. TÉPAN. I don't give a damn, we came here to have a picnic with you in the country and to enjoy our Sunday.

MME. TÉPAN. And I've prepared an excellent meal, too. Sausage, hard-boiled eggs—you know how you like them!—ham sandwiches, red wine, salad, and cakes.

ZAPO. All right, let's have it your way. But if the Captain comes he'll be absolutely furious. Because he isn't at all keen on us having visits when we're at the front. He never stops telling us: "Discipline and hand-grenades are what's wanted in a war, not visits."

M. TÉPAN. Don't worry, I'll have a few words to say to your Captain.

ZAPO. And what if we have to start fighting again?

M. TÉPAN. You needn't think that'll frighten me, it won't be the first fighting I've seen. Now if only it was battles on horseback! Times have changed, you can't understand. [*Pause*] We came by motor bike. No one said a word to us.

ZAPO. They must have thought you were the referees.

M. TÉPAN. We had enough trouble getting through, though. What with all the tanks and jeeps.

MME. TÉPAN. And do you remember the bottleneck that cannon caused, just when we got here?

M. TÉPAN. You mustn't be surprised at anything in wartime, everyone knows that.
MME. TÉPAN. Good, let's start our meal.
M. TÉPAN. You're quite right, I feel as hungry as a hunter. It's the smell of gunpowder.
MME. TÉPAN. We'll sit on the rug while we're eating.
ZAPO. Can I bring my rifle with me?
MME. TÉPAN. You leave your rifle alone. It's not good manners to bring your rifle to table with you. [*Pause*] But you're absolutely filthy, my boy. How on earth did you get into such a state? Let's have a look at your hands.
ZAPO [*ashamed, holding out his hands*]. I had to crawl about on the ground during the manoeuvers.
MME. TÉPAN. And what about your ears?
ZAPO. I washed them this morning.
MME. TÉPAN. Well that's all right, then. And your teeth? [*He shows them.*] Very good. Who's going to give her little boy a great big kiss for cleaning his teeth so nicely? [*To her husband*] Well, go on, kiss your son for cleaning his teeth so nicely. [M. TÉPAN *kisses his son.*] Because, you know, there's one thing I *will* not have, and that's making fighting a war an excuse for not washing.
ZAPO. Yes, Mother.

[*They eat.*]

M. TÉPAN. Well, my boy, did you make a good score?
ZAPO. When?
M. TÉPAN. In the last few days, of course.
ZAPO. Where?
M. TÉPAN. At the moment, since you're fighting a war.
ZAPO. No, nothing much. I didn't make a good score. Hardly ever scored a bull.
M. TÉPAN. Which are you best at shooting, enemy horses or soldiers?
ZAPO. No, not horses, there aren't any horses any more.
M. TÉPAN. Well, soldiers then?
ZAPO. Could be.
M. TÉPAN. Could be? Aren't you sure?
ZAPO. Well you see . . . I shoot without taking aim [*pause*] and at the same time I say a Pater Noster for the chap I've shot.
M. TÉPAN. You must be braver than that. Like your father.
MME. TÉPAN. I'm going to put a record on.

[*She puts a record on the gramophone—a pasodoble. All three are sitting on the ground, listening.*]

M. TÉPAN. That really *is* music. Yes indeed, olé!

[*The music continues. Enter an enemy soldier:* ZÉPO. *He is dressed like* ZAPO. *The only difference is the color of their uniforms.* ZÉPO *is in green and* ZAPO *is in gray.* ZÉPO *listens to the music open-mouthed. He is behind the family so they can't see him. The record ends. As he gets up* ZAPO *discovers* ZÉPO. *Both put their hands up.* M. *and* MME. TÉPAN *look at them in surprise.*]

What's going on?

[ZAPO *reacts—he hesitates. Finally, looking as if he's made up his mind, he points his rifle at* ZÉPO.]

ZAPO. Hands up!

[ZÉPO *puts his hands up even higher, looking even more terrified.* ZAPO *doesn't know what to do. Suddenly he goes quickly over to* ZÉPO *and touches him gently on the shoulder, like a child playing a game of "tag."*]

Got you! [*To his father, very pleased*] There we are! A prisoner!
M. TÉPAN. Fine. And now what're you going to do with him?
ZAPO. I don't know, but, well, could be—they might make me a corporal.
M. TÉPAN. In the meantime you'd better tie him up.
ZAPO. Tie him up? Why?
M. TÉPAN. Prisoners always get tied up!
ZAPO. How?
M. TÉPAN. Tie up his hands.
MME. TÉPAN. Yes, there's no doubt about that, you must tie up his hands, I've always seen them do that.
ZAPO. Right. [*To the prisoner*] Put your hands together, if you please.
ZÉPO. Don't hurt me too much.
ZAPO. I won't.
ZÉPO. Ow! You're hurting me.
M. TÉPAN. Now now, don't maltreat your prisoner.
MME. TÉPAN. Is that the way I brought you up? How many times have I told you that we must be considerate to our fellowmen?
ZAPO. I didn't do it on purpose. [*To* ZÉPO] And like that, does it hurt?
ZÉPO. No, it's all right like that.
M. TÉPAN. Tell him straight out, say what you mean, don't mind us.
ZÉPO. It's all right like that.
M. TÉPAN. Now his feet.
ZAPO. His feet as well, whatever next?
M. TÉPAN. Didn't they teach you the rules?

ZAPO. Yes.
M. TÉPAN. Well then!
ZAPO [*very politely, to* ZÉPO]. Would you be good enough to sit on the ground, please?
ZÉPO. Yes, but don't hurt me.
MME. TÉPAN. You'll see, he'll take a dislike to you.
ZAPO. No he won't, no he won't. I'm not hurting you, am I?
ZÉPO. No, that's perfect.
ZAPO. Papa, why don't you take a photo of the prisoner on the ground and me with my foot on his stomach?
M. TÉPAN. Oh yes, that'd look good.
ZÉPO. Oh no, not that!
MME. TÉPAN. Say yes, don't be obstinate.
ZÉPO. No. I said no, and no it is.
MME. TÉPAN. But just a little teeny weeny photo, what harm could that do you? And we could put it in the dining room, next to the life-saving certificate my husband won thirteen years ago.
ZÉPO. No—you won't shift me.
ZAPO. But why won't you let us?
ZÉPO. I'm engaged. And if she sees the photo one day, she'll say I don't know how to fight a war properly.
ZAPO. No she won't, all you'll need to say is that it isn't you, it's a panther.
MME. TÉPAN. Come on, do say yes.
ZÉPO. All right then. But only to please you.
ZAPO. Lie down flat.

[ZÉPO *lies down.* ZAPO *puts a foot on his stomach and grabs his rifle with a martial air.*]

MME. TÉPAN. Stick your chest out a bit further.
ZAPO. Like this?
MME. TÉPAN. Yes, like that, and don't breathe.
M. TÉPAN. Try and look like a hero.
ZAPO. What d'you mean, like a hero?
M. TÉPAN. It's quite simple; try and look like the butcher does when he's boasting about his successes with the girls.
ZAPO. Like this?
M. TÉPAN. Yes, like that.
MME. TÉPAN. The most important thing is to puff your chest out and not breathe.
ZÉPO. Have you nearly finished?
M. TÉPAN. Just be patient a moment. One . . . two . . . three.
ZAPO. I hope I'll come out well.

MME. TÉPAN. Yes, you looked very martial.
M. TÉPAN. You were fine.
MME. TÉPAN. It makes me want to have my photo taken with you.
M. TÉPAN. Now there's a good idea.
ZAPO. Right. I'll take it if you like.
MME. TÉPAN. Give me your helmet to make me look like a soldier.
ZÉPO. I don't want any more photos. Even one's far too many.
ZAPO. Don't take it like that. After all, what harm can it do you?
ZÉPO. It's my last word.
M. TÉPAN [*to his wife*]. Don't press the point, prisoners are always very sensitive. If we go on he'll get cross and spoil our fun.
ZAPO. Right, what're we going to do with him, then?
MME. TÉPAN. We could invite him to lunch. What do you say?
M. TÉPAN. I don't see why not.
ZAPO [*to* ZÉPO]. Well, will you have lunch with us, then?
ZÉPO. Er . . .
M. TÉPAN. We brought a good bottle with us.
ZÉPO. Oh well, all right then.
MME. TÉPAN. Make yourself at home, don't be afraid to ask for anything you want.
ZÉPO. All right.
M. TÉPAN. And what about you, did you make a good score?
ZÉPO. When?
M. TÉPAN. In the last few days, of course.
ZÉPO. Where?
M. TÉPAN. At the moment, since you're fighting a war.
ZÉPO. No, nothing much. I didn't make a good score, hardly ever scored a bull.
M. TÉPAN. Which are you best at shooting? Enemy horses or soldiers?
ZÉPO. No, not horses, there aren't any horses any more.
M. TÉPAN. Well, soldiers then?
ZÉPO. Could be.
M. TÉPAN. Could be? Aren't you sure?
ZÉPO. Well you see . . . I shoot without taking aim [*pause*] and at the same time I say an Ave Maria for the chap I've shot.
ZAPO. An Ave Maria? I'd have thought you'd have said a Pater Noster.
ZÉPO. No, always an Ave Maria. [*Pause*] It's shorter.
M. TÉPAN. Come come, my dear fellow, you must be brave.
MME. TÉPAN [*to* ZÉPO]. We can untie you if you like.
ZÉPO. No, don't bother, it doesn't matter.
M. TÉPAN. Don't start getting stand-offish with us now. If you'd like us to untie you, say so.
MME. TÉPAN. Make yourself comfortable.

zépo. Well, if that's how you feel, you can untie my feet, but it's only to please you.

M. TÉPAN. Zapo, untie him.

[zapo *unties him.*]

MME. TÉPAN. Well, do you feel better?

zépo. Yes, of course. I really am putting you to a lot of inconvenience.

M. TÉPAN. Not at all, just make yourself at home. And if you'd like us to untie your hands you only have to say so.

zépo. No, not my hands, I don't want to impose upon you.

M. TÉPAN. No no, my dear chap, no no. I tell you, it's no trouble at all.

zépo. Right . . . Well then, untie my hands too. But only for lunch, eh? I don't want you to think that you give me an inch and I take an ell.

M. TÉPAN. Untie his hands, son.

MME. TÉPAN. Well, since our distinguished prisoner is so charming, we're going to have a marvelous day in the country.

zépo. Don't call me your distinguished prisoner, just call me your prisoner.

MME. TÉPAN. Won't that embarrass you?

zépo. No no, not at all.

M. TÉPAN. Well, I must say you're modest.

[*Noise of aeroplanes.*]

zapo. Aeroplanes. They're sure to be coming to bomb us.

[zapo *and* zépo *throw themselves on the sandbags and hide.*]

[*To his parents*] Take cover. The bombs will fall on you.

> [*The noise of the aeroplanes overpowers all the other noises. Bombs immediately start to fall. Shells explode very near the stage but not on it. A deafening noise.*
>
> zapo *and* zépo *are cowering down between the sandbags.* M. TÉPAN *goes on talking calmly to his wife, and she answers in the same unruffled way. We can't hear what they are saying because of the bombing.* MME. TÉPAN *goes over to one of the baskets and takes an umbrella out of it. She opens it.* M. *and* MME. TÉPAN *shelter under it as if it were raining. They are standing up. They shift rhythmically from one foot to the other and talk about their personal affairs.*
>
> *The bombing continues.*
>
> *Finally the aeroplanes go away. Silence.*

M. TÉPAN *stretches an arm outside the umbrella to make sure that nothing more is falling from the heavens.*]

M. TÉPAN [*to his wife*]. You can shut your umbrella.

[MME. TÉPAN *does so. They both go over to their son and tap him lightly on the behind with the umbrella.*]

Come on, out you come. The bombing's over.

[ZAPO *and* ZÉPO *come out of their hiding place.*]

ZAPO. Didn't you get hit?
M. TÉPAN. What d'you think could happen to your father? [*Proudly*] Little bombs like that! Don't make me laugh!

[*Enter, left, two* RED CROSS SOLDIERS. *They are carrying a stretcher.*]

FIRST STRETCHER BEARER. Any dead here?
ZAPO. No, no one around these parts.
FIRST STRETCHER BEARER. Are you sure you've looked properly?
ZAPO. Sure.
FIRST STRETCHER BEARER. And there isn't a single person dead?
ZAPO. I've already told you there isn't.
FIRST STRETCHER BEARER. No one wounded, even?
ZAPO. Not even that.
SECOND STRETCHER BEARER [*to the* FIRST STRETCHER BEARER]. Well, now we're in a mess! [*To* ZAPO *persuasively*] Just look again, search everywhere, and see if you can't find us a stiff.
FIRST STRETCHER BEARER. Don't keep on about it, they've told you quite quite clearly there aren't any.
SECOND STRETCHER BEARER. What a lousy trick!
ZAPO. I'm terribly sorry. I promise you I didn't do it on purpose.
SECOND STRETCHER BEARER. That's what they all say. That no one's dead and that they didn't do it on purpose.
FIRST STRETCHER BEARER. Oh, let the chap alone!
M. TÉPAN [*obligingly*]. We should be only too pleased to help you. At your service.
SECOND STRETCHER BEARER. Well, really, if things go on like this I don't know what the Captain will say to us.
M. TÉPAN. But what's it all about?
SECOND STRETCHER BEARER. Quite simply that the others' wrists are aching with carting so many corpses and wounded men about, and that we haven't found any yet. And it's not because we haven't looked!
M. TÉPAN. Well yes, that really is annoying. [*To* ZAPO] Are you quite sure no one's dead?

ZAPO. Obviously, Papa.
M. TÉPAN. Have you looked under all the sandbags?
ZAPO. Yes, Papa.
M. TÉPAN [*angrily*]. Well then, you might as well say straight out that you don't want to lift a finger to help these gentlemen, when they're so nice, too!
FIRST STRETCHER BEARER. Don't be angry with him. Let him be. We must just hope we'll have more luck in another trench and that all the lot'll be dead.
M. TÉPAN. I should be delighted.
MME. TÉPAN. Me too. There's nothing I like more than people who put their hearts into their work.
M. TÉPAN [*indignantly, addressing his remarks to the wings*]. Then is no one going to do anything for these gentlemen?
ZAPO. If it only rested with me, it'd already be done.
ZÉPO. I can say the same.
M. TÉPAN. But look here, is neither of you even wounded?
ZAPO [*ashamed*]. No, not me.
M. TÉPAN [*to* ZÉPO]. What about you?
ZÉPO [*ashamed*]. Me neither. I never have any luck.
MME. TÉPAN [*pleased*]. Now I remember! This morning, when I was peeling the onions, I cut my finger. Will that do you?
M. TÉPAN. Of course it will! [*Enthusiastically*] They'll take you off at once!
FIRST STRETCHER BEARER. No, that won't work. With ladies it doesn't work.
M. TÉPAN. We're no further advanced, then.
FIRST STRETCHER BEARER. Never mind.
SECOND STRETCHER BEARER. We may be able to make up for it in the other trenches.

[*They start to go off.*]

M. TÉPAN. Don't worry! If we find a dead man we'll keep him for you! No fear of us giving him to anyone else!
SECOND STRETCHER BEARER. Thank you very much, sir.
M. TÉPAN. Quite all right, old chap, think nothing of it.

[*The two* STRETCHER BEARERS *say good-bye. All four answer them. The* STRETCHER BEARERS *go out.*]

MME. TÉPAN. That's what's so pleasant about spending a Sunday in the country. You always meet such nice people. [*Pause*] But why are you enemies?
ZÉPO. I don't know, I'm not very well educated.

MME. TÉPAN. Was it by birth, or did you become enemies afterwards?
ZÉPO. I don't know, I don't know anything about it.
M. TÉPAN. Well then, how did you come to be in the war?
ZÉPO. One day, at home, I was just mending my mother's iron, a man came and asked me: "Are you Zépo?" "Yes." "Right, you must come to the war." And so I asked him: "But what war?" and he said: "Don't you read the papers then? You're just a peasant!" I told him I did read the papers but not the war bits. . . .
ZAPO. Just how it was with me—exactly how it was with me.
M. TÉPAN. Yes, they came to fetch you too.
MME. TÉPAN. No, it wasn't quite the same; that day you weren't mending an iron, you were mending the car.
M. TÉPAN. I was talking about the rest of it. [*To* ZÉPO] Go on, what happened then?
ZÉPO. Then I told him I had a fiancée and that if I didn't take her to the pictures on Sundays she wouldn't like it. He said that that wasn't the least bit important.
ZAPO. Just how it was with me—exactly how it was with me.
ZÉPO. And then my father came down and he said I couldn't go to war because I didn't have a horse.
ZAPO. Just what my father said.
ZÉPO. That man said you didn't need a horse any more, and I asked him if I could take my fiancée with me. He said no. Then I asked whether I could take my aunt with me so that she could make me one of her custards on Thursdays; I'm very fond of them.
MME. TÉPAN [*realizing that she'd forgotten it*]. Oh! The custard!
ZÉPO. He said no again.
ZAPO. Same as with me.
ZÉPO. And ever since then I've been alone in the trench nearly all the time.
MME. TÉPAN. I think you and your distinguished prisoner might play together this afternoon, as you're so close to each other and so bored.
ZAPO. Oh no, Mother, I'm too afraid, he's an enemy.
M. TÉPAN. Now now, you mustn't be afraid.
ZAPO. If you only knew what the General was saying about the enemy!
MME. TÉPAN. What did he say?
ZAPO. He said the enemy are very nasty people. When they take prisoners they put little stones in their shoes so that it hurts them to walk.
MME. TÉPAN. How awful! What barbarians!
M. TÉPAN [*indignantly, to* ZÉPO]. And aren't you ashamed to belong to an army of criminals?

ZÉPO. I haven't done anything. I don't do anybody any harm.
MME. TÉPAN. He was trying to take us in, pretending to be such a little saint!
M. TÉPAN. We oughtn't to have untied him. You never know, we only need to turn our backs and he'll be putting a stone in our shoes.
ZÉPO. Don't be so nasty to me.
M. TÉPAN. What d'you think we *should* be, then? I'm indignant. I know what I'll do. I'll go and find the Captain and ask him to let me fight in the war.
ZAPO. He won't let you, you're too old.
M. TÉPAN. Then I'll buy myself a horse and a sword and come and fight on my own account.
MME. TÉPAN. Bravo! If I were a man I'd do the same.
ZÉPO. Don't be like that with me, Madame. Anyway I'll tell you something—our General told us the same thing about you.
MME. TÉPAN. How could he dare tell such a lie!
ZAPO. No—but the same thing really?
ZÉPO. Yes, the same thing.
M. TÉPAN. Perhaps it was the same man who talked to you both?
MME. TÉPAN. Well if it was the same man he might at least have said something different. That's a fine thing—saying the same thing to everyone!
M. TÉPAN [*to* ZÉPO, *in a different tone of voice*]. Another little drink?
MME. TÉPAN. I hope you liked our lunch?
M. TÉPAN. In any case, it was better than last Sunday.
ZÉPO. What happened?
M. TÉPAN. Well, we went to the country and we put the food on the rug. While we'd got our backs turned a cow ate up all our lunch, and the napkins as well.
ZÉPO. What a greedy cow!
M. TÉPAN. Yes, but afterwards, to get our own back, we ate the cow.

[*They laugh.*]

ZAPO [*to* ZÉPO]. They couldn't have been very hungry after that!
M. TÉPAN. Cheers! [*They all drink.*]
MME. TÉPAN [*to* ZÉPO]. And what do you do to amuse yourself in the trench?
ZÉPO. I spend my time making flowers out of rags, to amuse myself. I get terribly bored.
MME. TÉPAN. And what do you do with the flowers?
ZÉPO. At the beginning I used to send them to my fiancée, but one day she told me that the greenhouse and the cellar were already full

of them and that she didn't know what to do with them any more, and she asked me, if I didn't mind, to send her something else.
MME. TÉPAN. And what did you do?
ZÉPO. I tried to learn to make something else, but I couldn't. So I go on making rag flowers to pass the time.
MME. TÉPAN. Do you throw them away afterwards, then?
ZÉPO. No, I've found a way to use them now. I give one flower for each pal who dies. That way I know that even if I make an awful lot there'll never be enough.
M. TÉPAN. That's a good solution you've hit on.
ZÉPO [*shyly*]. Yes.
ZAPO. Well, what I do is knit, so as not to get bored.
MME. TÉPAN. But tell me, are all the soldiers as bored as you?
ZÉPO. It all depends on what they do to amuse themselves.
ZAPO. It's the same on our side.
M. TÉPAN. Then let's stop the war.
ZÉPO. How?
M. TÉPAN. It's very simple. [*To* ZAPO] You just tell your pals that the enemy soldiers don't want to fight a war, and you [*to* ZÉPO] say the same to your comrades. And then everyone goes home.
ZAPO. Marvelous!
MME. TÉPAN. And then you'll be able to finish mending the iron.
ZAPO. How is it that no one thought of such a good idea before?
MME. TÉPAN. Your father is the only one who's capable of thinking up such ideas; don't forget he's a former student of the École Normale, *and* a philatelist.
ZÉPO. But what will the sergeant-majors and corporals do?
M. TÉPAN. We'll give them some guitars and castanets to keep them quiet!
ZÉPO. Very good idea.
M. TÉPAN. You see how easy it is. Everything's fixed.
ZÉPO. We shall have a tremendous success.
ZAPO. My pals will be terribly pleased.
MME. TÉPAN. What d'you say to putting on the pasodoble we were playing just now, to celebrate?
ZÉPO. Perfect.
ZAPO. Yes, put the record on, Mother.

[MME. TÉPAN *puts a record on. She turns the handle. She waits. Nothing can be heard.*]

M. TÉPAN. I can't hear a thing.
MME. TÉPAN. Oh, how silly of me! Instead of putting a record on I put on a beret.

[*She puts the record on. A gay pasodoble is heard.* ZAPO *dances with* ZÉPO, *and* MME. TÉPAN *with her husband. They are all very gay. The field telephone rings. None of the four hears it. They go on dancing busily. The telephone rings again. The dance continues.*

The battle starts up again with a terrific din of bombs, shots and bursts of machine-gun fire. None of the four has seen anything and they go on dancing merrily. A burst of machine-gun fire mows them all down. They fall to the ground, stone dead. A shot must have grazed the gramophone; the record keeps repeating the same thing, like a scratched record. The music of the scratched record can be heard till the end of the play.

The two STRETCHER BEARERS *enter left. They are carrying the empty stretcher.*]

SUDDEN CURTAIN

GHOSTS

by HENRIK IBSEN

NEWLY TRANSLATED FROM THE NORWEGIAN BY *Michael Meyer*

GHOSTS   From *Ghosts and Three Other Plays* by Henrik Ibsen, translated by Michael Meyer. Copyright © 1962 by Michael Meyer. Reprinted by permission of Doubleday & Company, Inc.

Photos by Zoë Dominic: The Royal Shakespeare Company, 1967 production at the Aldwych Theatre.

G*hosts* has been interpreted as a dramatization of the sins of the fathers being visited upon the children. When the play was first performed in England (March 13, 1891), it was shrilly attacked as subversive and indecent, a moral cancer unfit to be exposed before civilized Englishmen living in that outwardly most proper of historical periods, the Victorian age. That the play should have elicited such strident cries of outrage seems strange to us today until we remember that Victorian society was publicly dedicated to the total suppression of unpleasant private truths, and it was precisely those truths that Ibsen meant to convey when he chose the word "ghosts" for his title. Though Ibsen always maintained that he took no sides on moral issues but rather played the role of a reporter and interrogator, he obviously recognized that private truths were often suppressed or hidden by old-fashioned ideas, outworn conventions, the tyranny of duty, morality, and above all, "respectability."

Great tragedy must be subtle, for it is played in a world where truth is likely to be elusive and unpleasant. Ibsen spent many years in Norway and later in Italy and Germany developing the dramatic skills which are so evident in the plays of his maturity, such as *A Doll's House, The Master Builder, The Wild Duck,* and *An Enemy of the People.* But nothing he wrote displays greater intensity and sheer dramatic mastery than *Ghosts.*

Although the action of *Ghosts* concentrates on the fate of the young Oswald, the acts and nonacts are those of his mother Mrs. Alving. Mrs. Alving believes that by sending her young son to Paris where he has become an artist she has saved him from the knowledge of his dead father's dissolute character. As the play opens Oswald has returned, and his mother has prepared a new life for him. But Oswald has his own ideas about the conduct of his life. When in the pursuit of those ideas he discloses his attraction to Regina, Mrs. Alving decides she must disclose the entire truth to him.

Throughout the entire play each disclosure from the past has an immediate and uncontrollable effect on the events dramatized on the stage. By the time the final curtain comes down, Mrs. Alving's conflict with her parents and with Pastor Manders and Oswald's conflict with the ideas of the older generation—the ideas his mother has lived by and that Pastor Manders still believes—have led inexorably to tragedy. Everything Mrs. Alving believes she has accomplished in trying to protect her son and maintain "respectability" is undone. Everything she wanted to accomplish in overcoming the past has become forever impossible.

Ibsen has been quite correctly called a pioneer in dramatic realism. To dramatize the subtle conflicts of *Ghosts,* he has used effective symbols. Oswald's syphilis, derived from his father's dissipated life and at the time believed to be congenital, leading incurably to insanity, symbolizes the disease of society passed on to the younger generation. The orphanage, which Mrs. Alving has erected with the Alving fortune in order to purge and memorialize the family name, is burned to the ground, justly, according to the laws of tragedy. And the additional legacy Mrs. Alving has inherited from her husband, which she has assigned for support of the orphanage, ends up in the unscrupulous hands of Engstrand for the establishment of a brothel.

Perhaps the most effective symbols of all are the natural elements that surround the Alving home in the little provincial Norwegian town where the action takes place. Throughout the major portion of the play the house is shrouded in rain and fog while Mrs. Alving continues to try to shield Oswald from the truth about his father, and Oswald, newly arrived from a sunlit Paris, longs for clear weather.

Only at the final moments of Act Three, when Oswald, his brain aflame with the ravages of syphilis, calls upon his mother to give him the sun, do the clouds dissipate and the blinding rays shine through in truth and destruction.

Characters

    MRS. HELEN ALVING, *widow of Captain Alving, late Chamberlain to the King*
    OSWALD ALVING, *her son, a painter*
    PASTOR MANDERS
    ENGSTRAND, *a carpenter*
    REGINA ENGSTRAND, *Mrs. Alving's maid*

The action takes place on Mrs. Alving's country estate by a large fjord in Western Norway.

ACT ONE

A spacious garden-room, with a door in the left-hand wall and two doors in the right-hand wall. In the center of the room is a round table with chairs around it; on the table are books, magazines and newspapers. Downstage left is a window, in front of which is a small sofa with a sewing table by it. Backstage the room opens out into a slightly narrower conservatory, with walls of large panes of glass. In the right-hand wall of the conservatory is a door leading down to the garden. Through the glass wall a gloomy fjord landscape is discernible, veiled by steady rain.

ENGSTRAND, a carpenter, is standing at the garden door. His left leg is slightly crooked; under the sole of his boot is fixed a block of wood. REGINA, with an empty garden syringe in her hand, bars his entry.

REGINA [*keeping her voice low*]. What do you want? Stay where you are! You're dripping wet!

ENGSTRAND. It is God's blessed rain, my child.

REGINA. The Devil's bloody rain, more like.

ENGSTRAND. Why, Regina, the way you talk! [*Limps a few steps into the room*] What I wanted to say is—

REGINA. Here, you! Don't make such a noise with that foot. The young master's asleep upstairs.

ENGSTRAND. In bed—at this hour? Why, the day's half gone.

REGINA. That's none of your business.

ENGSTRAND. I was out drinking last night—

REGINA. I'm sure.

ENGSTRAND. We are but flesh and blood, my child—

REGINA [*drily*]. Quite.

ENGSTRAND. And the temptations of this world are manifold. But God is my witness; I was at my bench by half past five this morning.

REGINA. Yes, yes. Come on now, clear off. I don't want to be caught having a rendezvous with you.

ENGSTRAND. You don't what?

REGINA. I don't want anyone to see you here. Come on, go away, get out.

ENGSTRAND [*comes a few steps nearer*]. Not before I've had a word with you. This afternoon I'll be through with the job down at the school house, and tonight I'm catching the steamer back to town.

REGINA [*mutters*]. Happy journey.

ENGSTRAND. Thank you, my child. They're dedicating the new Orphanage here tomorrow, and there'll be celebrations, with intoxicating liquor. And no one shall say of Jacob Engstrand that he can't turn his back on temptation. [REGINA *laughs scornfully.*] Yes, well, there'll be a lot of tip-top people coming here tomorrow. Pastor Manders is expected from town.

REGINA. He's arriving today.

ENGSTRAND. Well, there you are. And I'm not bloody well going to risk getting into his bad books.

REGINA. Oh, so that's it.

ENGSTRAND. What do you mean?

REGINA [*looks knowingly at him*]. What are you trying to fool the Pastor into this time?

ENGSTRAND. Hush! Are you mad? Me try to fool Pastor Manders? Oh no, Pastor Manders is much too good a friend to me for that. Now what I wanted to talk to you about is this. I'm going back home tonight.

REGINA. The sooner you go the better.

ENGSTRAND. Yes, but I want to take you with me, Regina.

REGINA [*her jaw drops*]. You want to take *me*—? What are you talking about?

ENGSTRAND. I want to take you with me, I say.

REGINA [*scornfully*]. Home with you? Not likely I won't!

ENGSTRAND. Oh, we'll see, we'll see.

REGINA. You bet your life we'll see. You expect me to go back and live with you? In that house? After Mrs. Alving's brought me up in her own home, treats me as though I was one of the family? Get out!

ENGSTRAND. What the hell's this? Are you setting yourself up against your father, my girl?

REGINA [*mutters without looking at him*]. You've said often enough that I'm no concern of yours.

ENGSTRAND. Oh—you don't want to take any notice of that—

REGINA. What about all the times you've sworn at me and called me a—oh, *mon dieu!*

ENGSTRAND. May God strike me dead if I ever used such a vile word!

REGINA. Oh, I know what word you used.

ENGSTRAND. Yes, but that was only when I wasn't myself. Hm. The temptations of this world are manifold, Regina.

REGINA. Ugh!

ENGSTRAND. And when your mother was being difficult. I had to think up some way to nark her. She was always acting the fine lady. [*Mimics*] "Let me go, Engstrand! Stop it! I've been in service for three years with Chamberlain Alving at Rosenvold, and don't you forget it!" [*Laughs*] She never could forget the Captain had been made a Chamberlain when she was working for him.

REGINA. Poor mother! You killed her soon enough with your bullying.

ENGSTRAND [*uncomfortably*]. That's right, blame me for everything.
REGINA [*turns away and mutters beneath her breath*]. Ugh! And that leg!
ENGSTRAND. What's that you said, my child?
REGINA. *Pied de mouton!*
ENGSTRAND. What's that, English?
REGINA. Yes.
ENGSTRAND. Ah, well. They've made a scholar of you out here anyway, and that'll come in handy now, Regina.
REGINA [*after a short silence*]. And—what was it you wanted me for in town?
ENGSTRAND. Fancy asking such a question! What should a father want from his only child? Aren't I a lonely, forsaken widower?
REGINA. Oh, don't try to fool me with that rubbish. What do you want me up there for?
ENGSTRAND. Well, it's like this. I'm thinking of starting out on something new.
REGINA [*sniffs*]. You've tried that often enough. And you've always made a mess of it.
ENGSTRAND. Yes, but this time, you'll see, Regina! God rot me if I don't—!
REGINA [*stamps her foot*]. Stop swearing!
ENGSTRAND. Ssh, ssh! How right you are, my child! Now what I wanted to say was this. I've put quite a bit of money aside out of the work I've been doing at this new Orphanage.
REGINA. Have you? Good for you.
ENGSTRAND. Well, there ain't much for a man to spend his money on out here in the country, is there?
REGINA. Well? Go on.
ENGSTRAND. Yes, well you see, so I thought I'd put the money into something that might bring me in a bit. A kind of hostelry for sailors—
REGINA [*disgusted*]. Oh, my God!
ENGSTRAND. A real smart place, you understand—not one of those low waterfront joints. No, damn it, this is going to be for captains and officers and—tip-top people, you understand.
REGINA. And I'm to—?
ENGSTRAND. You're going to help me. Just for appearance's sake, of course. You won't have to work hard, my child. You can fix your own hours.
REGINA. I see!
ENGSTRAND. Well, we've got to have a bit of skirt on show, I mean that's obvious. Got to give them a little fun in the evenings—dancing and singing and so forth. You must remember these men are wandering

mariners lost on the ocean of life. [*Comes closer*] Now don't be stupid and make things difficult for yourself, Regina. What can you make of yourself out here? What good is it going to do you, all this fine education Mrs. Alving's given you? I hear you're going to look after the orphans down the road. Is that what you want to do? Are you so anxious to ruin your health for those filthy brats?

REGINA. No, if things work out the way I—Ah well, they might. They might.

ENGSTRAND. What are you talking about?

REGINA. Never you mind. This money you've managed to save out here—is it a lot?

ENGSTRAND. All told I'd say it comes to between seven and eight hundred crowns.

REGINA. Not bad.

ENGSTRAND. Enough to make a start with, my child.

REGINA. Aren't you going to give me any of it?

ENGSTRAND. Not damn likely I'm not.

REGINA. Aren't you even going to send me a new dress?

ENGSTRAND. You just come back to town and set up with me, and you'll get dresses enough.

REGINA [*laughs scornfully*]. I could do *that* on my own, if I wanted to.

ENGSTRAND. No, Regina, you need a father's hand to guide you. There's a nice house I can get in Little Harbour Street. They don't want much cash on the nail; and we could turn it into a sort of—well—sailors' mission.

REGINA. But I don't want to live with *you!* I don't want anything to do with you. Come on, get out.

ENGSTRAND. You wouldn't need to stay with me for long, my child. More's the pity. If you play your cards properly. The way you've blossomed out these last few years, you—

REGINA. Yes?

ENGSTRAND. You wouldn't have to wait long before some nice officer—perhaps even a captain—

REGINA. I don't want to marry any of them. Sailors haven't any *savoir vivre*.

ENGSTRAND. Haven't any what?

REGINA. I know sailors. There's no future in marrying them.

ENGSTRAND. All right then, don't marry them. You can do just as well without. [*Lowers his voice*] The Englishman—him with the yacht —fifty pounds he paid out—and she wasn't any prettier than you.

REGINA [*goes toward him*]. Get out!

ENGSTRAND [*shrinks*]. Now, now, you wouldn't hit your own father!

REGINA. Wouldn't I? You say another word about mother, and you'll

see! Get out. I tell you! [*Pushes him toward the garden door*] And don't slam the door. Young Mr. Alving's—
ENGSTRAND. Yes, I know. He's asleep. Why do you fuss so much about him? [*More quietly*] Ah-ha! You wouldn't be thinking of *him*, would you?
REGINA. Out, and be quick about it! You're out of your mind. No, not that way. Here's Pastor Manders. Go out through the kitchen.
ENGSTRAND [*goes right*]. All right, I'll go. But you ask *him*—his Reverence. He'll tell you what a child's duty is to its father. I am your father, you know, whatever you say. I can prove it from the parish register.

[*He goes out through the second door, which* REGINA *has opened and closes behind him. She looks quickly at herself in the mirror, dusts herself with her handkerchief, and straightens her collar; then she begins to water the flowers.* PASTOR MANDERS, *in an overcoat and carrying an umbrella, and with a small traveling bag on a strap from his shoulder, enters through the garden door into the conservatory.*]

MANDERS. Good morning, Miss Engstrand.
REGINA [*turns in surprise and delight*]. Why, Pastor Manders! Has the boat come already?
MANDERS. It arrived a few minutes ago. [*Enters the garden room*] Very tiresome this rain we're having.
REGINA [*follows him*]. A blessing for the farmers, though, sir.
MANDERS. Yes, you are right. We city people tend to forget that. [*Begins to take off his overcoat*]
REGINA. Oh, please let me help you! There. Oh, it's soaking! I'll hang it up in the hall. Oh, and the umbrella! I'll open it out to let it dry.

[*She takes the coat and umbrella out through the other door, right.* MANDERS *takes his bag from his shoulder and puts it and his hat on a chair. Meanwhile* REGINA *comes back.*]

MANDERS. Ah, it's good to be under a dry roof again. Well, I trust all is well here?
REGINA. Yes, thank you, sir.
MANDERS. Everyone very busy, I suppose, getting ready for tomorrow?
REGINA. Oh, yes, there are one or two things to be done.
MANDERS. Mrs. Alving is at home, I hope?
REGINA. Oh, dear me, yes, she's just gone upstairs to make a cup of chocolate for the young master.
MANDERS. Ah, yes. I heard when I got off the boat that Oswald had returned.

REGINA. Yes, he arrived the day before yesterday. We hadn't expected him until today.

MANDERS. In good health and spirits, I trust?

REGINA. Oh yes, thank you, I think so. He felt dreadfully tired after his journey, though. He came all the way from Paris in one go—*par rapide.* I think he's having a little sleep just now, so we'd better talk just a tiny bit quietly.

MANDERS. Ssh! We'll be like mice!

REGINA [*moves an armchair near the table*]. Now sit down and make yourself comfortable, sir. [*He sits. She puts a footstool under his feet.*] There now. Are you quite comfortable?

MANDERS. Thank you, thank you; yes, very comfortable. [*Looks at her*] Do you know, Miss Engstrand, I really believe you've grown since I last saw you.

REGINA. Do you think so? Madam says I've rounded out a bit too.

MANDERS. Rounded out? Well, yes, a little perhaps. Not too much.

[*Short pause*]

REGINA. Shall I tell Madam you've come?

MANDERS. Thank you, there's no hurry, my dear child. Er—tell me now, Regina, how is your father getting on out here?

REGINA. Thank you, Pastor, he's doing very well.

MANDERS. He came to see me when he was last in town.

REGINA. No, did he really? He's always so happy when he gets a chance to speak to you, sir.

MANDERS. And you go down and see him quite often?

REGINA. I? Oh yes, of course—whenever I get the chance—

MANDERS. Your father hasn't a very strong character, Miss Engstrand. He badly needs a hand to guide him.

REGINA. Oh—yes, I dare say you're right there.

MANDERS. He needs to have someone near him whom he is fond of, and whose judgment he respects. He admitted it quite openly the last time he visited me.

REGINA. Yes, he said something of the sort to me too. But I don't know whether Mrs. Alving will want to lose me, especially now we've the new Orphanage to look after. Besides, I'd hate to leave Mrs. Alving. She's always been so kind to me.

MANDERS. But my dear girl, a daughter's duty! Naturally we would have to obtain your mistress's permission first.

REGINA. But I don't know that it'd be right and proper for me to keep house for an unmarried man at my age.

MANDERS. What! But my dear Miss Engstrand, this is your own father we're talking about!

REGINA. Yes—but all the same—Oh yes, if it was a nice house, with a real gentleman—
MANDERS. But my dear Regina—!
REGINA. Someone I could feel affection for and look up to as a father—
MANDERS. But my dear good child—!
REGINA. Oh, I'd so love to go and live in the city. Out here it's so dreadfully lonely—and you know, don't you, sir, what it means to be all alone in the world? And I'm quick and willing—I think I can say that. Oh, Pastor Manders, don't you know of a place I could go to?
MANDERS. I? No, I'm afraid I don't know of anyone at all.
REGINA. Oh, but do please think of me if ever you should, dear, dear Pastor Manders.
MANDERS [gets up]. Yes, yes, Miss Engstrand, I certainly will.
REGINA. You see, if only I—
MANDERS. Will you be so good as to fetch Mrs. Alving for me?
REGINA. Yes, sir. I'll fetch her at once.

[*She goes out left.* PASTOR MANDERS *walks up and down the room a couple of times, stands for a moment upstage with his hands behind his back and looks out into the garden. Then he comes back to the part of the room where the table is, picks up a book and glances at its title page, starts and looks at some of the others.*]

MANDERS. Hm! I see!

[MRS. ALVING *enters through the door left. She is followed by* REGINA, *who at once goes out through the door downstage right.*]

MRS. ALVING [*holds out her hand*]. Welcome to Rosenlund, Pastor.
MANDERS. Good morning, Mrs. Alving. Well, I've kept my promise.
MRS. ALVING. Punctual as always.
MANDERS. But you know it wasn't easy for me to get away. All these blessed boards and committees I sit on—
MRS. ALVING. All the kinder of you to arrive in such good time. Now we can get our business settled before lunch. But where's your luggage?
MANDERS [*quickly*]. My portmanteau is down at the village store. I shall be sleeping there.
MRS. ALVING [*represses a smile*]. I can't persuade you to spend a night in my house even now?
MANDERS. No, no, Mrs. Alving—it's very kind of you, but I'll sleep down there as usual. It's so convenient for when I go on board again.
MRS. ALVING. As you please. Though I really think two old people like you and me could—

MANDERS. Bless me, you're joking. But of course you must be very happy. The great day tomorrow—and you have Oswald home again.

MRS. ALVING. Yes, you can imagine how happy that makes me. It's over two years since he was home last. And now he's promised to stay with me the whole winter.

MANDERS. No, has he really? Well, that's nice of him. He knows his filial duty. I fancy life in Paris and Rome must offer altogether different attractions.

MRS. ALVING. Yes, but his home is here; and his mother. Ah, my dear boy; he loves his mother, God bless him.

MANDERS. It would be sad indeed if distance and dabbling in art and such things should blunt his natural affections.

MRS. ALVING. It certainly would. But luckily there's nothing wrong with him. I'll be amused to see whether you recognize him again. He'll be down later; he's upstairs now taking a little rest on the sofa. But please sit down, my dear Pastor.

MANDERS. Thank you. Er—you're sure this is a convenient moment—?

MRS. ALVING. Certainly.

[*She sits down at the table.*]

MANDERS. Good. Well, then—[*Goes over to the chair on which his bag is lying, takes out a sheaf of papers, sits down on the opposite side of the table and looks for a space to put down the papers*] Well, to begin with, here are the—[*Breaks off*] Tell me, Mrs. Alving, how do *these* books come to be here?

MRS. ALVING. Those books? I'm reading them.

MANDERS. You read writings of this kind?

MRS. ALVING. Certainly I do.

MANDERS. And does this kind of reading make you feel better or happier?

MRS. ALVING. I think they make me feel more secure.

MANDERS. How extraordinary! In what way?

MRS. ALVING. Well, they sort of explain and confirm many things that puzzle me. Yes, that's what's so strange, Pastor Manders—there isn't really anything new in these books—there's nothing in them that most people haven't already thought for themselves. It's only that most people either haven't fully realized it, or they won't admit it.

MANDERS. Well, dear God! Do you seriously believe that most people—?

MRS. ALVING. Yes, I do.

MANDERS. But surely not in this country? Not people like us?

MRS. ALVING. Oh, yes. People like us too.

MANDERS. Well, really! I must say—!

MRS. ALVING. But what do you object to in these books?

MANDERS. Object to? You surely don't imagine I spend my time studying such publications?
MRS. ALVING. In other words, you've no idea what you're condemning?
MANDERS. I've read quite enough about these writings to disapprove of them.
MRS. ALVING. Don't you think you ought to form your own opinion—?
MANDERS. My dear Mrs. Alving, there are many occasions in life when one must rely on the judgment of others. That is the way things are and it is good that it should be so. If it were not so, what would become of society?
MRS. ALVING. Yes, yes. You may be right.
MANDERS. Of course I don't deny there may be quite a lot that is attractive about these writings. And I cannot exactly blame you for wishing to keep informed of these intellectual movements in the great world outside about which one hears so much. After all, you have allowed your son to wander there for a number of years. But—
MRS. ALVING. But—?
MANDERS [*lowers his voice*]. But one does not have to talk about it, Mrs. Alving. One really does not need to account to all and sundry for what one reads and thinks within one's own four walls.
MRS. ALVING. No, of course not. I quite agree with you.
MANDERS. Remember the duty you owe to this Orphanage which you decided to found at a time when your attitude toward spiritual matters was quite different from what it is now—as far as *I* can judge.
MRS. ALVING. Yes, yes, that's perfectly true. But it was the Orphanage we were going to—
MANDERS. It was the Orphanage we were going to discuss, yes. But— be discreet, dear Mrs. Alving! And now let us turn to our business. [*Opens the packet and takes out some of the papers*] You see these?
MRS. ALVING. Are those the deeds?
MANDERS. All of them. Ready and completed. As you can imagine, it's been no easy task to get them all through in time. I really had to get out my whip. The authorities are almost painfully conscientious when you want a decision from them. But here we have them nevertheless. [*Leafs through them*] Here is the executed conveyance of the farmstead named Solvik in the Manor of Rosenvold, with its newly constructed buildings, schoolrooms, staff accommodation and chapel. And here is the settlement of the endowment and the trust deed of the institution. Look. [*Reads*] Deed of trust for the Captain Alving Memorial Home.
MRS. ALVING [*stares for a long while at the paper*]. So there it is.
MANDERS. I thought I'd say Captain rather than Chamberlain. Captain looks less ostentatious.

MRS. ALVING. Yes, yes, as you think best.

MANDERS. And here is the bankbook for the capital which has been placed on deposit to cover the running expenses of the Orphanage.

MRS. ALVING. Thank you; but I think it would be more convenient if you kept that, if you don't mind.

MANDERS. Certainly, certainly. I think we may as well leave the money on deposit to begin with. Admittedly the interest isn't very attractive—four percent with six months notice of withdrawal. If we could obtain a good mortgage later—of course it would have to be a first mortgage and of unimpeachable security—we might reconsider the matter.

MRS. ALVING. Yes, well, dear Pastor Manders, you know best about all that.

MANDERS. Anyway, I'll keep my eyes open. But now there's another matter I've several times been meaning to ask you about.

MRS. ALVING. And what is that?

MANDERS. Should the buildings of the Orphanage be insured or not?

MRS. ALVING. Yes, of course they must be insured.

MANDERS. Ah, but wait a minute, Mrs. Alving. Let us consider this question a little more closely.

MRS. ALVING. Everything I have is insured—buildings, furniture, crops, livestock.

MANDERS. Naturally. On your own estate. I do the same, of course. But you see, this is quite a different matter. The Orphanage is, so to speak, to be consecrated to a higher purpose.

MRS. ALVING. Yes, but—

MANDERS. As far as I personally am concerned, I see nothing offensive in securing ourselves against all eventualities—

MRS. ALVING. Well, I certainly don't.

MANDERS. But what is the feeling among the local people out here? You can judge that better than I can.

MRS. ALVING. The feeling?

MANDERS. Are there many people with a right to an opinion—I mean, people who really have the right to hold an opinion—who might take offense?

MRS. ALVING. Well, what do you mean by people who have the right to hold an opinion?

MANDERS. Oh, I am thinking chiefly of people sufficiently independent and influential to make it impossible for one to ignore their opinions altogether.

MRS. ALVING. There are quite a few people like that who I suppose might take offense—

MANDERS. You see! In town, we have a great many such people. Followers of other denominations. People might very easily come to the conclusion that neither you nor I have sufficient trust in the ordinance of a Higher Power.

MRS. ALVING. But my dear Pastor, as long as you yourself—

MANDERS. I know, I know—my conscience is clear, that is true. But all the same, we couldn't prevent a false and unfavorable interpretation being placed on our action. And that might well adversely influence the purpose for which the Orphanage has been dedicated.

MRS. ALVING. If that were so I—

MANDERS. And I can't altogether close my eyes to the difficult—I might even say deeply embarrassing—position in which I might find myself. Among influential circles in town there is a great interest in the cause of the Orphanage. After all, it is to serve the town as well, and it is hoped that it may considerably ease the burden of the ratepayers in respect to the poor. But since I have acted as your adviser and been in charge of the business side I must admit I fear certain overzealous persons might in the first place direct their attacks against me—

MRS. ALVING. Well, you mustn't lay yourself open to that.

MANDERS. Not to speak of the attacks which would undoubtedly be launched against me in certain newspapers and periodicals, and which—

MRS. ALVING. Enough, dear Pastor Manders. That settles it.

MANDERS. Then you do not wish the Orphanage to be insured?

MRS. ALVING. No. We will forget about it.

MANDERS [*leans back in his chair*]. But suppose an accident should occur—you never can tell—would you be able to make good the damage?

MRS. ALVING. No, quite frankly I couldn't.

MANDERS. Well, but you know, Mrs. Alving, this is really rather a serious responsibility we are taking on our shoulders.

MRS. ALVING. But do you think we have any alternative?

MANDERS. No, that's just it. I don't think there is any real alternative. We must not lay ourselves open to misinterpretation. And we have no right to antagonize public opinion.

MRS. ALVING. At any rate you, as a clergyman, must not.

MANDERS. And I really think we must believe that such an institution will have luck on its side—nay, that it stands under special protection.

MRS. ALVING. Let us hope so, Pastor Manders.

MANDERS. Shall we take the risk, then?

MRS. ALVING. Yes, let us.

MANDERS. Good. As you wish. [*Makes a note*] No insurance, then.

MRS. ALVING. It's strange you happened to mention this today—

MANDERS. I've often thought of raising the matter with you—

MRS. ALVING. Because yesterday we almost had a fire down there.

MANDERS. What!

MRS. ALVING. Well, it was nothing much really. Some shavings caught fire in the carpentry shop.

MANDERS. Where Engstrand works?

MRS. ALVING. Yes. They say he's very careless with matches.

MANDERS. He's got so many things to think about, poor man—so many temptations. Thank heaven I hear he has now resolved to lead a virtuous life.

MRS. ALVING. Oh? Who says so?

MANDERS. He has assured me so himself. And he's a good worker.

MRS. ALVING. Oh, yes—as long as he keeps sober—

MANDERS. Yes, that is a grievous weakness! But he is often compelled to yield to it because of his bad leg, he says. The last time he was in town I was quite touched. He came to see me and thanked me so sincerely because I had got him this job here, so that he could be near Regina.

MRS. ALVING. I don't think he sees her very often.

MANDERS. Oh yes, he told me himself. He talks to her every day.

MRS. ALVING. Oh, well. Possibly.

MANDERS. He is so conscious of his need to have someone who can restrain him when temptation presents itself. That is what is so lovable about Jacob Engstrand, that he comes to one like a child and accuses himself and admits his weakness. The last time he came up and talked to me—Tell me, Mrs. Alving, if it were absolutely vital for the poor man to have Regina back to live with him again—

MRS. ALVING [*rises swiftly*]. Regina!

MANDERS. You must not oppose it.

MRS. ALVING. I certainly shall. Anyway, Regina is going to work at the Orphanage.

MANDERS. But don't forget, he is her father—

MRS. ALVING. Oh, I know very well the kind of father he's been to her. No, I shall never consent to her going back to him.

MANDERS [*rises*]. But my dear Mrs. Alving, you mustn't get so emotional about it. You seem quite frightened. It's very sad the way you misjudge this man Engstrand.

MRS. ALVING [*more quietly*]. Never mind that. I have taken Regina into my house, and here she shall stay. [*Listens*] Hush now, dear Pastor Manders, let's not say anything more about it. [*Happily*] Listen!

There's Oswald coming downstairs. Now we will think of nothing but him.

[OSWALD ALVING, *in a light overcoat, with his hat in his hand and smoking a big meerschaum pipe, enters through the door left.*]

OSWALD [*stops in the doorway*]. Oh, I'm sorry—I thought you were in the study. [*Comes closer*] Good morning, Pastor.
MANDERS [*stares*]. Why—! Most extraordinary!
MRS. ALVING. Well, Pastor Manders, what do you think of him?
MANDERS. I think—I think—! But is this really—?
OSWALD. Yes, this is the Prodigal Son, Pastor.
MANDERS. Oh, but my dear young friend—!
OSWALD. Well, the son, anyway.
MRS. ALVING. Oswald is thinking of the time when you used to be so strongly opposed to his becoming a painter.
MANDERS. Many a step which to human eyes seems dubious often turns out—[*Shakes his hand*] Anyway, welcome, welcome! My dear Oswald—! I trust you will allow me to call you by your Christian name?
OSWALD. What else?
MANDERS. Excellent. Now, my dear Oswald, what I was going to say was this. You mustn't think I condemn the artistic profession out of hand. I presume there are many who succeed in keeping the inner man untarnished in that profession too.
OSWALD. Let us hope so.
MRS. ALVING [*happily*]. I know one person who has remained pure both inwardly and outwardly. Just look at him, Pastor Manders.
OSWALD [*wanders across the room*]. Yes, yes, mother dear, please.
MANDERS. Unquestionably—there's no denying that. Besides, you have begun to acquire a name now. The newspapers often speak of you, and in most flattering terms. Well—that is to say, I don't seem to have read about you quite so much lately.
OSWALD [*by the flowers upstage*]. I haven't done so much painting lately.
MRS. ALVING. Even painters have to rest now and then.
MANDERS. I suppose so. To prepare themselves and conserve their energies for some great work.
OSWALD. Yes. Mother, shall we be eating soon?
MRS. ALVING. In about half an hour. He still enjoys his food, thank heaven.
MANDERS. And his tobacco, I see.
OSWALD. I found father's pipe upstairs in the bedroom, so I—
MANDERS. Of course!

MRS. ALVING. What do you mean?

MANDERS. When Oswald appeared in that doorway with that pipe in his mouth, it was just as though I saw his father alive again.

OSWALD. Oh? Really?

MRS. ALVING. Oh, how can you say that? Oswald takes after me.

MANDERS. Yes; but there's an expression at the corner of his mouth, something about his lips, that reminds me so vividly of Alving—at any rate now when he's smoking.

MRS. ALVING. How can you say that? Oswald has much more the mouth of a clergyman, I think.

MANDERS. True, true. Some of my colleagues have a similar expression.

MRS. ALVING. But put away that pipe, my dear boy. I don't want any smoke in here.

OSWALD [obeys]. I'm sorry. I only wanted to try it. You see, I smoked it once when I was a child.

MRS. ALVING. What?

OSWALD. Yes. I was quite small at the time. I remember, I went upstairs to see father in his room one evening. He was so happy and cheerful.

MRS. ALVING. Oh, you don't remember anything from that time.

OSWALD. Oh, yes, I remember very clearly, he picked me up and sat me on his knee and let me smoke his pipe. "Puff away, boy," he said, "puff hard." And I puffed as hard as I could. I felt myself go pale and the sweat broke out on my forehead in great drops. And that made him roar with laughter—

MANDERS. How very strange.

MRS. ALVING. My dear, it's just something Oswald has dreamed.

OSWALD. No, mother, I didn't dream it. Surely you must remember— you came in and carried me back into the nursery. Then I was sick and I saw you crying. Did father often play jokes like that?

MANDERS. In his youth he was an extremely gay young man—

OSWALD. And yet he managed to achieve so much. So much that was good and useful; although he died so young.

MANDERS. Yes, you have inherited the name of an industrious and worthy man, my dear Oswald Alving. Well, I hope this will spur you on.

OSWALD. Yes, it ought to, oughtn't it?

MANDERS. In any case it was good of you to come home and join us in honoring him.

OSWALD. It was the least I could do for father.

MRS. ALVING. And the best thing of all is that I'm going to have him here for so long.

MANDERS. Yes, I hear you're staying the winter.

OSWALD. I am here for an indefinite period, Pastor. Oh, but it's good to be home!
MRS. ALVING [*warmly*]. Yes, Oswald. It is, isn't it?
MANDERS [*looks at him sympathetically*]. Yes, you went out into the world early, my dear Oswald.
OSWALD. I did. Sometimes I wonder if it wasn't too early.
MRS. ALVING. Oh, nonsense. It's good for a healthy lad; especially if he's an only child. It's bad for them to stay at home with their mother and father and be pampered.
MANDERS. That is a very debatable point, Mrs. Alving. When all is said and done, the parental home is where a child belongs.
OSWALD. I agree with you there, Pastor.
MANDERS. Take your own son. Well, it will do no harm to talk about it in his presence. What has been the consequence for him? Here he is, twenty-six or twenty-seven years old, and he's never had the opportunity to know what a real home is like.
OSWALD. I beg your pardon, sir, but there you're quite mistaken.
MANDERS. Oh? I thought you had spent practically all your time in artistic circles.
OSWALD. I have.
MANDERS. Mostly among young artists.
OSWALD. Yes.
MANDERS. But I thought most of those people lacked the means to support a family and make a home for themselves.
OSWALD. Some of them can't afford to get married, sir.
MANDERS. Yes, that's what I'm saying.
OSWALD. But that doesn't mean they can't have a home. Several of them have; and very good and comfortable homes at that.

[MRS. ALVING *listens intently and nods, but says nothing.*]

MANDERS. But I'm not speaking about bachelor establishments. By a home I mean a family establishment, where a man lives with his wife and children.
OSWALD. Quite. Or with his children and their mother.
MANDERS [*starts and claps his hands together*]. Merciful heavens! You don't—?
OSWALD. Yes?
MANDERS. Lives with—with the mother of his children?
OSWALD. Yes, would you rather he disowned the mother of his children?
MANDERS. So you are speaking of unlegalized relationships! These so-called free marriages!
OSWALD. I've never noticed anything particularly free about the way such people live.

MANDERS. But how is it possible that—that any reasonably well brought up man or young woman can bring themselves to live like that—openly, for everyone to see?

OSWALD. But what else can they do? A poor young artist—a poor young girl—It costs a lot of money to get married. What can they do?

MANDERS. What can they do? I'll tell you, Mr. Alving, what they can do. They should have kept away from each other in the first place—that's what they should have done.

OSWALD. That argument won't get you far with young people who are in love and have red blood in their veins.

MRS. ALVING. No, that won't get you very far.

MANDERS [*takes no notice*]. And to think that the authorities tolerate such behavior! That it is allowed to happen openly! [*Turns to* MRS. ALVING] Wasn't I right to be so concerned about your son? In circles where immorality is practiced openly and is, one might almost say, accepted—

OSWALD. Let me tell you something, sir, I have been a regular Sunday guest in one or two of these irregular households—

MANDERS. On Sundays!

OSWALD. Yes, that's the day when one's meant to enjoy oneself. But I have never heard an offensive word there, far less ever witnessed anything which could be called immoral. No; do you know when and where I have encountered immorality in artistic circles?

MANDERS. No, I don't, thank heaven.

OSWALD. Well, I shall tell you. I have encountered it when one or another of our model husbands and fathers came down there to look around a little on their own—and did the artists the honor of visiting then in their humble bistros. Then we learned a few things. Those gentlemen were able to tell us about places and things of which we had never dreamed.

MANDERS. What! Are you suggesting that honorable men from this country—!

OSWALD. Have you never, when these honorable men returned home, have you never heard them hold forth on the rampancy of immorality in foreign countries?

MANDERS. Yes, of course—

MRS. ALVING. I've heard that, too.

OSWALD. Well, you can take their word for it. Some of them are experts. [*Clasps his head*] Oh, that that beautiful and wonderful life of freedom should be soiled like this!

MRS. ALVING. You mustn't get overexcited, Oswald. It isn't good for you.

OSWALD. No you're right, mother. It isn't good for my health. It's that damned tiredness, you know. Well, I'll take a little walk before dinner. I'm sorry, Pastor. I know you can't see it from my point of view. But I had to say what I felt.

[*He goes out through the second door on the right.*]

MRS. ALVING. My poor boy—!
MANDERS. Yes, you may well say that. So it's come to this.

[MRS. ALVING *looks at him but remains silent.*]

MANDERS [*walks up and down*]. He called himself the prodigal son. Alas, alas!

[MRS. ALVING *still looks at him.*]

MANDERS. And what do you say to all this?
MRS. ALVING. I say that Oswald was right in every word he said.
MANDERS [*stops dead*]. Right? Right? In expressing those principles!
MRS. ALVING. Here in my loneliness I have come to think like him, Pastor Manders. But I have never dared to bring up the subject. Now my son shall speak for me.
MANDERS. I feel deeply sorry for you, Mrs. Alving. But now I will have to speak to you in earnest. I am not addressing you now as your business manager and adviser, nor as your and your late husband's old friend. I stand before you now as your priest, as I did at the moment when you had strayed so far.
MRS. ALVING. And what has the priest to say to me?
MANDERS. First I wish to refresh your memory, Mrs. Alving. The occasion is appropriate. Tomorrow will be the tenth anniversary of your husband's death. Tomorrow the memorial to him who is no longer with us is to be unveiled. Tomorrow I shall address the whole assembled flock. But today I wish to speak to you alone.
MRS. ALVING. Very well, Pastor. Speak.
MANDERS. Have you forgotten that after barely a year of marriage you stood on the very brink of the abyss? That you abandoned your house and home—that you deserted your husband—yes, Mrs. Alving, deserted, deserted—and refused to return to him, although he begged and entreated you to do so?
MRS. ALVING. Have you forgotten how desperately unhappy I was during that first year?
MANDERS. Yes, that is the sign of the rebellious spirit, to demand happiness from this earthly life. What right have we to happiness? No, Mrs. Alving, we must do our duty! And your duty was to remain with the man you had chosen, and to whom you were bound by a sacred bond.

MRS. ALVING. You know quite well the kind of life Alving led at that time; the depravities he indulged in.

MANDERS. I am only too aware of the rumors that were circulating about him; and I least of anyone approve his conduct during his youthful years, if those rumors contained the truth. But a wife is not appointed to be her husband's judge. It was your duty humbly to bear that cross which a higher will had seen fit to assign to you. But instead you rebelliously fling down that cross, abandon the erring soul you should have supported, hazard your good name, and very nearly ruin the reputations of others.

MRS. ALVING. Others? Another's, you mean?

MANDERS. It was extremely inconsiderate of you to seek refuge with me.

MRS. ALVING. With our priest? With an old friend?

MANDERS. Exactly. Well, you may thank God that I possessed the necessary firmness—that I was able to dissuade you from your frenzied intentions and that it was granted to me to lead you back on to the path of duty and home to your lawful husband.

MRS. ALVING. Yes, Pastor Manders, that was certainly your doing.

MANDERS. I was merely a humble tool in the hand of a higher purpose. And that I persuaded you to bow to the call of duty and obedience, has not that proved a blessing which will surely enrich the remainder of your days? Did I not foretell all this? Did not Alving turn from his aberrations, like a man? Did he not afterwards live a loving and blameless life with you for the remainder of his days? Did he not become a public benefactor, did he not inspire you so that in time you became his right hand in all his enterprises? And a very capable right hand—oh, yes, I know that, Mrs. Alving, I give you credit for that. But now I come to the next great error of your life.

MRS. ALVING. And what do you mean by that?

MANDERS. Once you disowned your duties as a wife. Since then, you have disowned your duties as a mother.

MRS. ALVING. Ah—!

MANDERS. All your days you have been ruled by a fatal spirit of willfulness. You have always longed for a life unconstrained by duties and principles. You have never been willing to suffer the curb of discipline. Everything that has been troublesome in your life you have cast off ruthlessly and callously, as if it were a burden which you had the right to reject. It was no longer convenient to you to be a wife, so you left your husband. You found it tiresome to be a mother, so you put your child out to live among strangers.

MRS. ALVING. Yes, that is true. I did.

MANDERS. And in consequence you have become a stranger to him.

MRS. ALVING. No, no! That's not true!
MANDERS. It is. It must be. And how have you got him back? Think well, Mrs. Alving! You have sinned greatly against your husband. You admit that by raising the monument to him down there. Confess too, now, how you have sinned against your son. There may still be time to bring him back from the paths of wantonness. Turn; and save what may still be saved in him. [*With raised forefinger*] For verily, Mrs. Alving, as a mother you carry a heavy burden of guilt. This I have regarded it as my duty to say to you.

[*Silence*]

MRS. ALVING [*slow and controlled*]. You have had your say, Pastor; and tomorrow you will speak publicly at my husband's ceremony. I shall not speak tomorrow. But now I shall say a few words to you, just as you have said a few words to me.
MANDERS. Of course. You wish to excuse your conduct—
MRS. ALVING. No. I simply want to tell you what happened.
MANDERS. Oh?
MRS. ALVING. Everything that you have just said about me and my husband and our life together after you, as you put it, had led me back on to the path of duty—all that is something of which you have no knowledge from your own observations. From that moment you, who used to visit us every day, never once set foot in our house.
MANDERS. You and your husband moved from town shortly afterwards.
MRS. ALVING. Yes. And you never came out here to see us while my husband was alive. It was only the business connected with the Orphanage that compelled you to visit me.
MANDERS [*quietly and uncertainly*]. Helen—if this is intended as a reproach, I must beg you to consider the—
MRS. ALVING. The duty you owed to your position, yes. And then I was a wife who had run away from her husband. One can never be too careful with such unprincipled women.
MANDERS. My dear . . . Mrs. Alving, you exaggerate grotesquely.
MRS. ALVING. Yes, yes, well, let us forget it. What I wanted to say was that when you judge my conduct as a wife, you are content to base your judgment on common opinion.
MANDERS. Yes, well; what of it?
MRS. ALVING. But now, Manders, now I shall tell the truth. I have sworn to myself that one day you should know it. Only you.
MANDERS. And what is the truth?
MRS. ALVING. The truth is that my husband died just as dissolute as he had always lived.
MANDERS [*gropes for a chair*]. What did you say?

MRS. ALVING. Just as dissolute, at any rate in his desires, after nineteen years of marriage, as he was before you wedded us.
MANDERS. You call these youthful escapades—these irregularities—excesses, if you like—evidence of a dissolute life!
MRS. ALVING. That is the expression our doctor used.
MANDERS. I don't understand you.
MRS. ALVING. It doesn't matter.
MANDERS. I cannot believe my ears. You mean your whole married life—all those years you shared with your husband—were nothing but a façade!
MRS. ALVING. Yes. Now you know.
MANDERS. But—but this I cannot accept! I don't understand—I cannot credit it! But how on earth is it possible—how could such a thing be kept secret?
MRS. ALVING. I had to fight, day after day, to keep it secret. After Oswald was born I thought things became a little better with Alving. But it didn't last long. And now I had to fight a double battle, fight with all my strength to prevent anyone knowing what kind of a man my child's father was. And you know what a winning personality Alving had. No one could believe anything but good of him. He was one of those people whose reputations remain untarnished by the way they live. But then, Manders—you must know this too—then came the most loathsome thing of all.
MANDERS. More loathsome than this!
MRS. ALVING. I had put up with him, although I knew well what went on secretly outside the house. But when he offended within our four walls—
MANDERS. What are you saying? Here!
MRS. ALVING. Yes, here in our own home. In there—[*points to the first door on the right*]—it was in the dining room I first found out about it. I had something to do in there and the door was standing ajar. Then I heard our maid come up from the garden to water the flowers in there.
MANDERS. Oh, yes?
MRS. ALVING. A few moments later I heard Alving enter the room. He said something to her. And then I heard—[*gives a short laugh*]—I still don't know whether to laugh or cry—I heard my own servant whisper: "Stop it, Mr. Alving! Let me go!"
MANDERS. What an unseemly frivolity! But it was nothing more than a frivolity, Mrs. Alving. Believe me.
MRS. ALVING. I soon found out what to believe. My husband had his way with the girl. And that relationship had consequences, Pastor Manders.

MANDERS [*petrified*]. And all this took place in this house! In this house!
MRS. ALVING. I had endured much in this house. To keep him at home in the evenings—and at night—I had to make myself his companion in his secret dissipations up in his room. There I had to sit alone with him, had to clink my glass with his and drink with him, listen to his obscene and senseless driveling, had to fight him with my fists to haul him into bed—
MANDERS [*shocked*]. I don't know how you managed to endure it.
MRS. ALVING. I had to, for my little son's sake. But when the final humiliation came—when my own servant—then I swore to myself: "This must stop!" And so I took over the reins of this house; both as regards him and everything else. For now, you see, I had a weapon against him; he dared not murmur. It was then that I sent Oswald away. He was nearly seven and was beginning to notice things and ask questions, the way children do. I couldn't bear that, Manders. I thought the child could not help but be poisoned merely by breathing in this tainted home. That was why I sent him away. And so now you know why he was never allowed to set foot in his home while his father was alive. No one knows what it cost me.
MANDERS. You have indeed been sorely tried.
MRS. ALVING. I could never have borne it if I had not had my work. Yes, for I think I can say that I have worked! All the additions to the estate, all the improvements, all the useful innovations for which Alving was praised—do you imagine he had the energy to initiate any of them? He, who spent the whole day lying on the sofa reading old court circulars? No; let me tell you this too; I drove him forward when he was in his happier moods; and I had to bear the whole burden when he started again on his dissipations or collapsed in sniveling helplessness.
MANDERS. And it is to this man that you raise a memorial.
MRS. ALVING. There you see the power of a guilty conscience.
MANDERS. A guilty—? What do you mean?
MRS. ALVING. I always believed that some time, inevitably, the truth would have to come out, and that it would be believed. The Orphanage would destroy all rumors and banish all doubt.
MANDERS. You certainly made no mistake there, Mrs. Alving.
MRS. ALVING. And then I had another motive. I wanted to make sure that my own son, Oswald, should not inherit anything whatever from his father.
MANDERS. You mean it was Alving's money that—?
MRS. ALVING. Yes. The annual donations that I have made to this Orphanage add up to the sum—I have calculated it carefully—the sum which made Lieutenant Alving, in his day, "a good match."

MANDERS. I understand—
MRS. ALVING. It was the sum with which he bought me. I do not wish that money to come into Oswald's hands. My son shall inherit everything from me.

[OSWALD ALVING *enters through the second door on the right; he has removed his hat and overcoat outside.*]

MRS. ALVING [*goes toward him*]. Are you back already? My dear, dear boy!
OSWALD. Yes; what's one to do outside in this eternal rain? But I hear we're about to have dinner. How splendid.
REGINA [*enters from the kitchen with a parcel*]. A parcel has just come for you, madam. [*Hands it to her*]
MRS. ALVING [*with a glance at* PASTOR MANDERS]. Copies of the songs for tomorrow's ceremony, I suppose.
MANDERS. Hm—
REGINA. Dinner is served, madam.
MRS. ALVING. Good. We'll come presently. I just want to—[*Begins to open the parcel*]
REGINA [*to* OSWALD]. Shall it be white port or red port, Mr. Oswald?
OSWALD. Both, Miss Engstrand.
REGINA. *Bien*—very good, Mr. Oswald.

[*She goes into the dining room.*]

OSWALD. I'd better help her open the bottles—[*Follows her into the dining room. The door swings half open behind him.*]
MRS. ALVING [*who has opened the parcel*]. Yes, that's right. It's the copies of the songs, Pastor Manders.
MANDERS [*with folded hands*]. How I am to make my address tomorrow with a clear conscience, I—!
MRS. ALVING. Oh, you'll find a way—
MANDERS [*quietly, so as not to be heard in the dining room*]. Yes, there mustn't be any scandal.
MRS. ALVING [*firmly, in a low voice*]. No. But now this long, loathsome comedy is over. From the day after tomorrow, it will be as if the dead had never lived in this house. There will be no one here but my boy and his mother.

[*From the dining room is heard the crash of a chair being knocked over. At the same time* REGINA *says sharply, but keeping her voice low.*]

REGINA. Oswald! Are you mad? Let me go!
MRS. ALVING [*starts in fear*]. Ah!

[*She stares distraught at the half-open door.* OSWALD *coughs and begins to hum. A bottle is uncorked.*]

MANDERS [*indignantly*]. What is going on, Mrs. Alving? What was that?
MRS. ALVING [*hoarsely*]. Ghosts. The couple in the conservatory—walk.
MANDERS. What are you saying! Regina—? Is she—?
MRS. ALVING. Yes. Come. Not a word.

[*She grips* PASTOR MANDER's *arm and walks falteringly toward the door of the dining room.*]

ACT TWO

The same room. The mist still lies heavily over the landscape. PASTOR MANDERS *and* MRS. ALVING *enter from the dining room.*

MRS. ALVING [*still in the doorway*]. I'm glad you enjoyed it, Pastor Manders. [*Speaks into the dining room*] Aren't you joining us, Oswald?
OSWALD [*offstage*]. No, thank you. I think I'll go out and take a walk.
MRS. ALVING. Yes, do. It's stopped raining now. [*Closes the door of the dining room, and goes over to the hall door and calls*] Regina!
REGINA [*offstage*]. Yes, madam.
MRS. ALVING. Go down to the wash-house and give them a hand with the garlands.
REGINA. Very good, madam.

[MRS. ALVING *makes sure that* REGINA *has gone, then closes the door.*]

MANDERS. He can't hear anything from in there, can he?
MRS. ALVING. Not when the door is shut. Anyway, he's going out.
MANDERS. I am still stunned. I don't understand how I managed to swallow a mouthful of that excellent meal.
MRS. ALVING [*restless but controlled, walks up and down*]. Neither do I. But what is to be done?
MANDERS. Yes, what is to be done? Upon my word, I don't know. I'm so sadly inexperienced in matters of this kind.
MRS. ALVING. I am convinced that no harm has been done yet.
MANDERS. No, heaven forbid! Nevertheless, it's a most improper situation.

MRS. ALVING. It's only a casual whim of Oswald's. You can be certain of that.
MANDERS. Well, as I said, I don't know about these things; but I'm sure—
MRS. ALVING. She must leave the house. And at once. That's obvious—
MANDERS. Yes, naturally.
MRS. ALVING. But where to? We can't just—
MANDERS. Where to? Home to her father, of course.
MRS. ALVING. To whom, did you say?
MANDERS. To her—oh, no, Engstrand isn't her—! But, dear God, Mrs. Alving, how can this be possible? Surely you must be mistaken.
MRS. ALVING. Unfortunately I know I'm not mistaken. In the end Johanna had to confess to me; and Alving couldn't deny it. So there was nothing to be done but hush the matter up.
MANDERS. Yes, I suppose that was the only thing to do.
MRS. ALVING. The girl left my service at once, and was given a considerable sum of money to keep her mouth shut for the time being. The remaining difficulties she solved for herself when she got to town. She renewed an old acquaintance with Engstrand, let it be known, I dare say, how much money she had, and spun him a story about some foreigner or other who'd been here with a yacht that summer. Then she and Engstrand got themselves married in a hurry. Well, you married them yourself.
MANDERS. But how can that be true? I remember clearly how Engstrand came to me to arrange the wedding. He was completely abject, and accused himself most bitterly of having indulged with his betrothed in a moment of weakness.
MRS. ALVING. Well, he had to take the blame on himself.
MANDERS. But to be so dishonest! And to me! I certainly would never have believed that of Jacob Engstrand. I'll speak to him seriously about this. He can be sure of that. And the immorality of it! For money! How much was it you gave the girl?
MRS. ALVING. Fifty pounds.
MANDERS. Just imagine! To go and marry a fallen woman for a paltry fifty pounds!
MRS. ALVING. What about me? I went and married a fallen man.
MANDERS. Good God Almighty, what are you saying? A fallen man!
MRS. ALVING. Do you think Alving was any purer when I accompanied him to the altar than Johanna was when Engstrand married her?
MANDERS. But the two things are utterly different—
MRS. ALVING. Not so different. Oh, yes, there was a big difference in the price. A paltry fifty pounds against an entire fortune.
MANDERS. But how can you compare two such different situations?

After all, you were obeying the counsels of your heart, and of your family.

MRS. ALVING [*does not look at him*]. I thought you understood the direction in which what you call my heart had strayed at that time.

MANDERS [*distantly*]. If I had understood anything of the kind, I should not have been a daily guest in your husband's house.

MRS. ALVING. Anyway, I didn't follow my own counsel. That is certain.

MANDERS. Well then, you obeyed your nearest relatives. Your mother and your two aunts. As was your duty.

MRS. ALVING. Yes, that is true. The three of them worked out a balance sheet for me. Oh, it's incredible how patly they proved that it would be utter madness for me to turn down such an offer. If my mother could look down now and see what all that promise of splendor has led to.

MANDERS. No one can be held responsible for the outcome. And this much at least is sure, that your marriage was celebrated in an orderly fashion and in full accordance with the law.

MRS. ALVING [*by the window*]. All this talk about law and order. I often think that is what causes all the unhappiness in the world.

MANDERS. Mrs. Alving, now you are being sinful.

MRS. ALVING. Yes, perhaps I am. But I can't stand being bound by all these obligations and petty considerations. I can't! I must find my own way to freedom.

MANDERS. What do you mean by that?

MRS. ALVING [*taps on the window frame*]. I should never have concealed the truth about Alving's life. But I dared not do otherwise—and it wasn't only for Oswald's sake. I was such a coward.

MANDERS. Coward?

MRS. ALVING. If people had known, they would have said: "Poor man, it isn't surprising he strays now and then. After all, his wife ran away from him."

MANDERS. Perhaps they would not have been altogether unjustified.

MRS. ALVING [*looks hard at him*]. If I were a real mother, I would take Oswald and say to him: "Listen, my boy. Your father was a degenerate—"

MANDERS. But great heavens above—!

MRS. ALVING. And I would tell him everything I have told you. The whole story.

MANDERS. You scandalize me, Mrs. Alving.

MRS. ALVING. Yes, I know. I know! I scandalize myself. [*Comes away from the window*] That's how cowardly I am.

MANDERS. You call it cowardice to do your simple duty! Have you forgotten that a child shall love and honor its father and mother?

MRS. ALVING. Let us not generalize so. Let us ask: "Shall Oswald love and honor Captain Alving?"
MANDERS. Is there not a voice in your mother's heart which forbids you to destroy your son's ideals?
MRS. ALVING. Yes, but what about the truth?
MANDERS. Yes, but what about the ideals?
MRS. ALVING. Oh, ideals, ideals! If only I weren't such a coward!
MANDERS. Don't despise our ideals, Mrs. Alving. Retribution will surely follow. Take Oswald in particular. He hasn't many ideals, I'm afraid. But this much I have discovered, that his father is to him an ideal.
MRS. ALVING. You are right there.
MANDERS. And you yourself have awakened and fostered these ideas of his, by your letters.
MRS. ALVING. Yes. I was bound by these obligations and considerations, so I lied to my son, year out and year in. Oh, what a coward, what a coward I have been!
MANDERS. You have established a happy illusion in your son, Mrs. Alving—and you should certainly not regard that as being of little value.
MRS. ALVING. Hm. I wonder. But I shan't allow him to have any relations with Regina. He is not going to make that poor girl unhappy.
MANDERS. Good heavens, no! That would be dreadful.
MRS. ALVING. If I knew that he meant it seriously, and that it would make him happy—
MANDERS. Yes? What then?
MRS. ALVING. But that's impossible. Unfortunately Regina isn't that type.
MANDERS. How do you mean?
MRS. ALVING. If only I weren't such an abject coward, I'd say to him: "Marry her, or make what arrangements you please. As long as you're honest and open about it—"
MANDERS. Merciful God! You mean a legal marriage! What a terrible idea! It's absolutely unheard-of—!
MRS. ALVING. Unheard-of, did you say? Put your hand on your heart, Pastor Manders, and tell me—do you really believe there aren't married couples like that to be found in this country—as closely related as these two?
MANDERS. I simply don't understand you.
MRS. ALVING. Oh, yes you do.
MANDERS. You're thinking that by chance possibly—? Yes, alas, family life is indeed not always as pure as it should be. But in the kind of case you mean, one can never be sure—at any rate, not absolutely—

But in this case—! That you, a mother, could want to allow your own—

MRS. ALVING. But I don't *want* to. I wouldn't allow it for any price in the world. That's just what I'm saying.

MANDERS. No, because you are a coward, as you put it. But if you weren't a coward—! Great God in heaven, what a shocking relationship!

MRS. ALVING. Well, we all stem from a relationship of that kind, so we are told. And who was it who arranged things like that in the world, Pastor Manders?

MANDERS. I shall not discuss such questions with you, Mrs. Alving. You are not in the right spiritual frame of mind for that. But that you dare to say that it is cowardly of you—!

MRS. ALVING. I shall tell you what I mean. I am frightened, because there is in me something ghostlike from which I can never free myself.

MANDERS. What did you call it?

MRS. ALVING. Ghostlike. When I heard Regina and Oswald in there, it was as if I saw ghosts. I almost think we are all ghosts—all of us, Pastor Manders. It isn't just what we have inherited from our father and mother that walks in us. It is all kinds of dead ideas and all sorts of old and obsolete beliefs. They are not alive in us; but they remain in us none the less, and we can never rid ourselves of them. I only have to take a newspaper and read it, and I see ghosts between the lines. There must be ghosts all over the country. They lie as thick as grains of sand. And we're all so horribly afraid of the light.

MANDERS. Aha—so there we have the fruits of your reading. Fine fruits indeed! Oh, these loathsome, rebellious, free-thinking books!

MRS. ALVING. You are wrong, my dear Pastor. It was you yourself who first spurred me to think; and I thank and bless you for it.

MANDERS. I?

MRS. ALVING. Yes, when you forced me into what you called duty; when you praised as right and proper what my whole spirit rebelled against as something abominable. It was then that I began to examine the seams of your learning. I only wanted to pick at a single knot; but when I had worked it loose, the whole fabric fell apart. And then I saw that it was machine-sewn.

MANDERS [*quiet, shaken*]. Is this the reward of my life's hardest struggle?

MRS. ALVING. Call it rather your life's most pitiful defeat.

MANDERS. It was my life's greatest victory, Helen. The victory over myself.

MRS. ALVING. It was a crime against us both.

MANDERS. That I besought you, saying: "Woman, go home to your lawful husband," when you came to me distraught and cried: "I am here! Take me!" Was that a crime?

MRS. ALVING. Yes, I think so.

MANDERS. We two do not understand each other.

MRS. ALVING. No; not any longer.

MANDERS. Never—never even in my most secret moments have I thought of you except as another man's wedded wife.

MRS. ALVING. Oh? I wonder.

MANDERS. Helen—

MRS. ALVING. One forgets so easily what one was like.

MANDERS. I do not. I am the same as I always was.

MRS. ALVING [*changes the subject*]. Well, well, well—let's not talk any more about the past. Now you're up to your ears in commissions and committees; and I sit here fighting with ghosts, both in me and around me.

MANDERS. I will help you to bring to heel the ghosts around you. After all the dreadful things you have told me today, my conscience will not permit me to allow a young and unprotected girl to remain in your house.

MRS. ALVING. Don't you think it would be best if we could get her taken care of? I mean—well, decently married.

MANDERS. Indubitably. I think it would be desirable for her in every respect. Regina is just now at the age when—well, I don't really understand these things, but—

MRS. ALVING. Regina matured early.

MANDERS. Yes, didn't she? I seem to remember that she was noticeably well developed from a physical point of view when I prepared her for confirmation. But for the present at any rate she must go home. To her father's care—no, but of course, Engstrand isn't—! That he—that *he* could conceal the truth from me like that!

[*There is a knock on the door leading to the hall.*]

MRS. ALVING. Who can that be? Come in.

ENGSTRAND [*appears in the doorway in his Sunday suit*]. Begging your pardon, madam, but—

MANDERS. Aha! Hm!

MRS. ALVING. Oh, is it you, Engstrand?

ENGSTRAND. There weren't any of the servants about, so I took the liberty of giving a little knock.

MRS. ALVING. Yes, yes. Well, come in. Do you want to speak to me about something?

ENGSTRAND [*enters*]. No, thank you, ma'am. It's the Pastor I really wanted to have a word with.

MANDERS [*walks up and down*]. Hm; really? You want to speak to me? Do you indeed?
ENGSTRAND. Yes, I'd be so terribly grateful if—
MANDERS [*stops in front of him*]. Well! May I ask what is the nature of your question?
ENGSTRAND. Well, it's like this, Pastor. We've been paid off down there now—a thousand thanks, Mrs. Alving—and now we're ready with everything—and so I thought it'd only be right and proper if we who have worked so well together all this time—I thought we might conclude with a few prayers this evening.
MANDERS. Prayers? Down at the Orphanage?
ENGSTRAND. Well, of course, sir, if you don't think it's the right thing to do—
MANDERS. Oh yes, yes, indeed I do, but—hm—
ENGSTRAND. I've been in the habit of holding a little service myself down there of an evening—
MANDERS. Have you?
ENGSTRAND. Yes, now and then. Just a little edification, as you might say. But I'm only a poor humble man and haven't the proper gifts, God forgive me—and so I thought, seeing as Pastor Manders happens to be out here—
MANDERS. Now look here, Engstrand, first I must ask you a question. Are you in the correct frame of mind for such a meeting? Do you feel your conscience is clear and free?
ENGSTRAND. Oh, God forgive us, let's not talk about conscience, Pastor.
MANDERS. Yes, that's just what we are going to talk about. Well? What is your answer?
ENGSTRAND. Well—a man's conscience can be a bit of a beggar now and then—
MANDERS. Well, at least you admit it. But now, will you tell me the truth! What's all this about Regina?
MRS. ALVING [*quickly*]. Pastor Manders!
MANDERS [*soothingly*]. Leave this to me—
ENGSTRAND. Regina? Good heavens, how you frighten me! [*Looks at* MRS. ALVING] Surely nothing's happened to Regina?
MANDERS. Let us hope not. But what I meant was, what's all this about you and Regina? You call yourself her father, don't you? Hm?
ENGSTRAND [*uncertainly*]. Well—hm—you know all about me and poor Johanna.
MANDERS. Now I want no more prevarication. Your late wife told the whole truth to Mrs. Alving before she left her service.
ENGSTRAND. Well, may the—! No, did she really?
MANDERS. So now you are unmasked, Engstrand.

ENGSTRAND. And she promised and swore on the Bible that she—
MANDERS. Swore on the Bible—!
ENGSTRAND. No, she only promised, but so sincerely.
MANDERS. And all these years you have concealed the truth from me. Concealed it from *me*, who trusted you so implicitly.
ENGSTRAND. Yes, I'm afraid I have, I suppose.
MANDERS. Have I deserved this from you, Engstrand? Haven't I always been ready to assist you with help, both spiritual and material, as far as lay within my power? Answer! Haven't I?
ENGSTRAND. Things would often have looked black for me if it hadn't been for your Reverence.
MANDERS. And this is how you reward me! You cause me to enter false statements in the parish register, and withhold from me over a period of years the information which you owed both to me and to the cause of truth! Your conduct has been completely indefensible, Engstrand. From now on, I wash my hands of you.
ENGSTRAND [*with a sigh*]. Yes, of course, sir. I appreciate that.
MANDERS. I mean, how could you possibly justify yourself?
ENGSTRAND. But wouldn't it have made things even worse for poor Johanna if the truth had been allowed to come out? Now just imagine if your Reverence had been in the same situation as her—
MANDERS. I!
ENGSTRAND. Oh, for heaven's sake, I don't mean exactly the same. But I mean, suppose your Reverence had something to be ashamed of in the eyes of the world, as the saying goes. We men mustn't judge a poor woman too harshly, your Reverence.
MANDERS. But I'm not. It's you I'm reproaching.
ENGSTRAND. May I ask your Reverence a tiny question?
MANDERS. Yes, yes, what is it?
ENGSTRAND. Isn't it right and proper for a man to raise up the fallen?
MANDERS. Of course it is.
ENGSTRAND. And isn't it a man's duty to stand by his word?
MANDERS. Certainly it is: but—
ENGSTRAND. That time when Johanna fell into misfortune through that Englishman—or maybe he was an American, or a Russian, as they call them—well, she came up to town. Poor creature, she'd turned up her nose at me once or twice; for she only looked at what was handsome and fine, poor thing; and of course I had this thing wrong with my leg. Well, your Reverence will remember how I'd ventured into a dancing hall where foreign sailors were indulging in drunkenness and excess, as the saying goes. And when I tried to exhort them to start leading a better life—
MRS. ALVING [*by the window*]. Hm—

MANDERS. I know, Engstrand. The ruffians threw you down the stairs. You've told me about it before. Your injury is something to be proud of.

ENGSTRAND. Oh, I take no pride in it, your Reverence. But what I was going to say was, so she came along and poured out all her troubles to me amid weeping and gnashing of teeth. I'll be frank, your Reverence; it nearly broke my heart to listen to her.

MANDERS. Did it really, Engstrand? Well, go on.

ENGSTRAND. Yes, well, so I said to her: "This American is a vagrant on the sea of life," I said. "And you, Johanna, you've committed a sin and are a fallen creature. But Jacob Engstrand," I said, "he's got both feet firmly on the ground"—speaking figuratively, you understand—

MANDERS. I understand you perfectly. Go on.

ENGSTRAND. Well, that's how I raised her up and made an honest woman of her so that people shouldn't get to know the wanton way she'd behaved with foreigners.

MANDERS. You acted very handsomely. The only thing I can't understand is how you could bring yourself to accept money—

ENGSTRAND. Money? I? Not a penny!

MANDERS [*glances questioningly at* MRS. ALVING]. But—!

ENGSTRAND. Oh yes, wait a moment—now I remember. Johanna did have a few shillings with her. But I wouldn't have any of it. "Fie!" I said, "that's Mammon, that's the wages of sin. We'll throw that wretched gold—or notes, or whatever it was—back in the American's face," I said. But he'd taken his hook and disappeared across the wild sea, your Reverence.

MANDERS. Had he, my dear Engstrand?

ENGSTRAND. Oh yes. And so Johanna and I agreed that the money was to be used to bring up the child, and that's what happened; and I can account for every shilling of it.

MANDERS. But this puts quite a different face on things.

ENGSTRAND. That's the way it was, your Reverence. And I think I can say I've been a real father to Regina—as far as stood within my power—for unfortunately I'm an ailing man.

MANDERS. Now, now, my dear Engstrand—

ENGSTRAND. But this I can say, that I've brought up the child tenderly and been a loving husband to poor Johanna and ordered my household the way the good book says. But it would never have entered my head to go along to your Reverence in sinful pride and boast that for once I too had done a good deed. No, when anything of that kind happens to Jacob Engstrand, he keeps quiet about it. I don't suppose that's always the way, more's the pity. And when I do go to see Pastor Manders I've always more than enough of wickedness and weakness to talk to him about. For I said it just now and I say it again—a man's conscience can be a real beggar now and then.

MANDERS. Give me your hand, Jacob Engstrand.

ENGSTRAND. Why, good heavens, Pastor—!

MANDERS. No argument, now. [*Presses his hand*] There!

ENGSTRAND. And if I was to go down on my bended knees and humbly to beg your Reverence's forgiveness—?

MANDERS. You? No, on the contrary. It is I who must ask your pardon—

ENGSTRAND. Oh no, really—

MANDERS. Indeed, yes. And I do so with all my heart. Forgive me that I could ever have misjudged you so. And if there is any way in which I can show the sincerity of my regrets and of my good will towards you—

ENGSTRAND. Would your Reverence really do that?

MANDERS. Most gladly.

ENGSTRAND. Well, in that case there's a real opportunity just now. With the money I've managed to put aside through the blessed work here, I'm thinking of starting a kind of home for sailors in the city.

MANDERS. *You* are?

ENGSTRAND. Yes, a kind of refuge like the one here, in a manner of speaking. The temptations for a sailor wandering on shore are so manifold. But in this house, with me there, it'd be like them having a father to take care of them, I thought.

MANDERS. What have you to say to that, Mrs. Alving!

ENGSTRAND. My means are rather limited, God knows. But if only someone would stretch out a helping hand—

MANDERS. Yes, well, let us consider the matter more closely. Your project interests me very deeply. But go along now and get everything in order and light candles so as to make the place cheerful, and we'll have a little edification together, my dear Engstrand. For now I think you're in the right frame of mind.

ENGSTRAND. Yes, I think I am. Well, good-bye, Mrs. Alving, and thank you for everything. And take good care of Regina for me. [*Wipes a tear from his eye*] Poor Johanna's child! Hm—it's strange, but—it's just as though she'd grown to be a part of me. It is really, yes. [*Touches his forehead and goes out through the door*]

MANDERS. Well, what have you to say about that man now, Mrs. Alving? That was quite a different explanation we were given there.

MRS. ALVING. It was indeed.

MANDERS. You see how terribly careful one must be about condemning

one's fellows. But then, again, it is a deep joy to discover that one has been mistaken. Or what do you say?
MRS. ALVING. I say: you are a great baby, Manders. And you always will be.
MANDERS. I?
MRS. ALVING [*places both her hands on his shoulders*]. And I say: I'd like to throw both my arms round your neck.
MANDERS [*frees himself quickly*]. No, no, bless you! Such impulses—!
MRS. ALVING [*with a smile*]. Oh, you needn't be frightened of me.
MANDERS [*by the table*]. You have such an extravagant way of expressing yourself sometimes. Now let me just gather these documents together and put them in my case. [*Does so*] There! And now, all revoir. Keep your eyes open when Oswald comes back. I'll be with you again presently. [*Takes his hat and goes out through the hall*]
MRS. ALVING [*sighs, looks out of the window for a moment, tidies the room a little and is about to go into the dining room, but stops in the doorway and calls softly*]. Oswald, are you still at table?
OSWALD [*offstage*]. I'm just finishing my cigar.
MRS. ALVING. I thought you'd gone for a little walk.
OSWALD. In this weather?

[*There is the clink of a glass.* MRS. ALVING *leaves the door open and sits down with her sewing on the sofa by the window.*]

OSWALD [*still offstage*]. Wasn't that Pastor Manders who left just now?
MRS. ALVING. Yes, he's gone down to the Orphanage.
OSWALD. Hm. [*Clink of decanter and glass again*]
MRS. ALVING [*with a worried glance*]. Oswald dear, you ought to be careful with that liqueur. It's strong.
OSWALD. It keeps out the damp.
MRS. ALVING. Won't you come in and talk to me?
OSWALD. I can't smoke in there.
MRS. ALVING. You know I don't mind cigars.
OSWALD. All right, I'll come, then. Just one tiny drop more. There. [*He enters with his cigar and closes the door behind him. Short silence*]
OSWALD. Where's the Pastor gone?
MRS. ALVING. I told you, he went down to the Orphanage.
OSWALD. Oh yes, so you did.
MRS. ALVING. You oughtn't to sit at table so long, Oswald.
OSWALD [*holding his cigar behind his back*]. But I think it's so nice, mother. [*Strokes and pats her*] To come home, and sit at my mother's own table, in my mother's dining room, and eat my mother's beautiful food.

MRS. ALVING. My dear, dear boy.

OSWALD [*walks and smokes a trifle impatiently*]. And what else is there for me to do here? I can't work—

MRS. ALVING. Can't you?

OSWALD. In this weather? Not a glimmer of sunlight all day. [*Walks across the room*] That's the worst thing about it—not to be able to work—

MRS. ALVING. Perhaps you shouldn't have come home.

OSWALD. Yes, mother, I had to.

MRS. ALVING. I'd ten times rather sacrifice the happiness of having you with me than that you should—

OSWALD [*stops by the table*]. Tell me, mother. Does it really make you so happy to have me home?

MRS. ALVING. Does it make me happy?

OSWALD [*crumples a newspaper*]. I think it must be almost the same for you whether I'm alive or not.

MRS. ALVING. How can you have the heart to say that to your mother, Oswald?

OSWALD. But you managed so well to live without me before.

MRS. ALVING. Yes. I have lived without you. That is true.

[*Silence. Dusk begins to gather slowly.* OSWALD *paces up and down the room. He has put down his cigar.*]

OSWALD [*stops beside* MRS. ALVING]. Mother, may I sit down on the sofa with you?

MRS. ALVING [*makes room for him*]. Yes, of course, my dear boy.

OSWALD [*sits*]. There's something I have to tell you, mother.

MRS. ALVING [*tensely*]. Yes?

OSWALD [*stares vacantly ahead of him*]. I can't keep it to myself any longer.

MRS. ALVING. What? What do you mean?

OSWALD [*as before*]. I couldn't bring myself to write to you about it; and since I came home I—

MRS. ALVING [*grips his arm*]. Oswald, what is this?

OSWALD. Yesterday and today I've been trying to forget. To escape. But it's no good.

MRS. ALVING [*rises*]. Tell me the truth, Oswald.

OSWALD [*pulls her down on to the sofa again*]. Sit still and I'll try to tell you about it. I've complained so much about how tired I felt after the journey—

MRS. ALVING. Yes. Well?

OSWALD. But it isn't that that's wrong with me. It isn't any ordinary tiredness—

MRS. ALVING [*tries to rise*]. You're not ill, Oswald!

OSWALD [*pulls her down again*]. Sit still, mother. Just keep calm. No, I'm not really ill; not what people usually call ill. [*Clasps his hands to his head*] Mother, I'm spiritually broken—I'm ruined—I shall never be able to work any more!

[*He throws himself into her lap, with his hands over his face, and sobs.*]

MRS. ALVING [*pale and trembling*]. Oswald! Look at me! No, no, it isn't true!

OSWALD [*looks up at her despairingly*]. Never to be able to work again! Never. Never. To be dead while I'm still alive. Mother, can you imagine anything so dreadful?

MRS. ALVING. My poor boy. How did this frightful thing happen to you?

OSWALD [*sits upright again*]. Yes, that's just what I can't understand. I've never lived intemperately. Not in any way. You mustn't believe that of me, mother. I've never done that.

MRS. ALVING. Of course I don't believe it, Oswald.

OSWALD. And yet it's happened to me. This dreadful thing.

MRS. ALVING. Oh, but my dear, dear boy, it'll be all right. You've just overworked. You take my word for it.

OSWALD [*heavily*]. That's what I thought at first. But it isn't that.

MRS. ALVING. Tell me the whole story.

OSWALD. I shall, yes.

MRS. ALVING. When did you first notice it?

OSWALD. It was soon after the last time I'd been home, and had gone back again to Paris. I began to feel the most violent pains in my head —mostly at the back of my head, it seemed. It was as though a tight iron ring had been screwed round my neck and just above it.

MRS. ALVING. Yes?

OSWALD. At first I thought it was just the usual headaches I used to have so often while I was a child.

MRS. ALVING. Yes, yes—

OSWALD. But it wasn't. I soon realized that. I couldn't work any more. I wanted to begin on a new painting, but it was as though my powers had failed me. It was as though I was paralyzed—I couldn't see anything clearly—everything went misty and began to swim in front of my eyes. Oh, it was dreadful! In the end I sent for the doctor. And he told me the truth.

MRS. ALVING. How do you mean?

OSWALD. He was one of the leading doctors down there. I had to tell him how I felt. And then he began to ask me a lot of questions, which seemed to me to have absolutely nothing to do with it. I didn't understand what the man was driving at—

MRS. ALVING. Yes!

OSWALD. In the end he said: "You've been worm-eaten from birth." That was the word he used: *vermoulu*.

MRS. ALVING [*tensely*]. What did he mean by that?

OSWALD. I didn't understand either, and asked him to explain more clearly. And then the old cynic said—[*clenches his fist*] Oh—!

MRS. ALVING. What did he say?

OSWALD. He said: "The sins of the fathers shall be visited on the children."

MRS. ALVING [*rises slowly*]. The sins of the fathers—!

OSWALD. I nearly hit him in the face—

MRS. ALVING [*walks across the room*]. The sins of the fathers—

OSWALD [*smiles sadly*]. Yes, what do you think of that? Of course I assured him it was quite out of the question. But do you think he gave in? No, he stuck to his opinion; and it was only when I brought out your letters and translated to him all the passages that dealt with father—

MRS. ALVING. But then he—?

OSWALD. Yes, then of course he had to admit he was on the wrong track. And then I learned the truth. The incredible truth! This wonderfully happy life with my comrades, I should have abstained from. It had been too much for my strength. In other words, I have only myself to blame.

MRS. ALVING. Oswald! Oh, no, you mustn't think that!

OSWALD. There was no other explanation possible, he said. That's the dreadful thing. Beyond cure—ruined for life—because of my own folly. Everything I wanted to accomplish in the world—not even to dare to think of it—not to be *able* to think of it. Oh, if only I could start my life over again, and undo it all!

[*Throws himself face down on the sofa.* MRS. ALVING *wrings her hands and walks to and fro, fighting silently with herself.*]

OSWALD [*after a while, looks up and remains half-leaning on his elbow*]. If it had been something I'd inherited. Something I wasn't myself to blame for. But this! To have thrown away in this shameful, thoughtless, light-hearted way one's whole happiness and health, everything in the world—one's future, one's life—

MRS. ALVING. No, no, my dear, blessed boy—this is impossible! [*Leans over him*] Things are not as desperate as you think.

OSWALD. Oh, you don't know—! [*Jumps up*] And then, mother, that

I should cause you all this grief! I've often almost wished and hoped that you didn't care very much about me.

MRS. ALVING. I, Oswald! My only son! The only possession I have in the world—the only thing I care about!

OSWALD [*seizes both her hands and kisses them*]. Yes, yes, I know. When I am at home, of course I know it. And that's one of the hardest things to bear. But now you know. And now we won't talk about it any more today. I can't bear to think about it for long. [*Walks across the room*] Get me something to drink, mother.

MRS. ALVING. Drink? What do you want to drink now?

OSWALD. Oh, anything. You have some cold punch in the house, haven't you?

MRS. ALVING. Yes, but, my dear Oswald—

OSWALD. Oh, mother, don't be difficult. Be nice now! I *must* have something to help me forget these worries. [*Goes into the conservatory*] Oh, how—how dark it is in here! [MRS. ALVING *pulls a bellrope, right.*] And this incessant rain. It goes on week after week; sometimes for months. Never to see the sun! In all the years I've been at home I don't remember ever having seen the sun shine.

MRS. ALVING. Oswald! You are thinking of leaving me!

OSWALD. Hm—[*Sighs deeply*] I'm not thinking about anything. I *can't* think about anything. [*Softly*] I take good care not to.

REGINA [*enters from the dining room*]. Did you ring, madam?

MRS. ALVING. Yes, bring in the lamp.

REGINA. Yes, madam, at once. I've already lit it. [*Goes*]

MRS. ALVING [*goes over to* OSWALD]. Oswald, don't hide anything from me.

OSWALD. I'm not, mother. [*Goes over to the table*] Haven't I told you enough?

[REGINA *enters with the lamp and puts it on the table.*]

MRS. ALVING. Oh, Regina, you might bring us half a bottle of champagne.

REGINA. Very good, madam. [*Goes.*]

OSWALD [*takes* MRS. ALVING'*s head in his hands*]. That's the way. I knew my mother wouldn't let her boy go thirsty.

MRS. ALVING. My poor, dear Oswald! How could I deny you anything now?

OSWALD [*eagerly*]. Is that true, mother? Do you mean it?

MRS. ALVING. Mean what?

OSWALD. That you wouldn't deny me anything?

MRS. ALVING. But, my dear Oswald—

OSWALD. Ssh!
REGINA [*brings a tray with a half-bottle of champagne and two glasses, and puts it down on the table*]. Shall I open—?
OSWALD. No, thank you, I'll do it myself.

[REGINA *goes.*]

MRS. ALVING [*sits down at the table*]. What did you mean just now, when you said I mustn't deny you anything?
OSWALD [*busy trying to open the bottle*]. Let's taste this first.

[*The cork jumps out. He fills one glass and is about to do likewise with the other.*]

MRS. ALVING [*puts her hand over it*]. Thank you, not for me.
OSWALD. Well, for me, then. [*Empties the glass, refills it and empties it again. Then he sits down at the table.*]
MRS. ALVING [*tensely*]. Well?
OSWALD [*not looking at her*]. Tell me, mother—I thought you and Pastor Manders looked so strange—hm—quiet—at dinner.
MRS. ALVING. Did you notice?
OSWALD. Yes—hm. [*Short silence*] Tell me—what do you think of Regina?
MRS. ALVING. What do I think?
OSWALD. Yes, isn't she splendid?
MRS. ALVING. Oswald dear, you don't know her as well as I do—
OSWALD. Oh?
MRS. ALVING. Regina spent too much time at home, I'm afraid. I ought to have brought her here to live with me sooner.
OSWALD. Yes, but isn't she splendid to look at, mother? [*Fills his glass*]
MRS. ALVING. Regina has many great faults—
OSWALD. Oh, what does that matter? [*Drinks again*]
MRS. ALVING. But I'm fond of her all the same. And I am responsible for her. I'd rather anything in the world happened than that she should come to any harm.
OSWALD [*jumps up*]. Mother, Regina's my only hope!
MRS. ALVING [*rises*]. What do you mean by that?
OSWALD. I can't bear all this misery alone.
MRS. ALVING. But you have your mother to bear it with you.
OSWALD. Yes, that's what I thought. And that's why I came home to you. But it won't work. I can see it; it won't work. I can't bear this life here.
MRS. ALVING. Oswald!
OSWALD. Oh, I must live differently, mother. That's why I have to leave you. I don't want you to see.

MRS. ALVING. My poor, sick boy! Oh, but Oswald, as long as you're not well—
OSWALD. If it was just the illness, I'd stay with you, mother. You're the best friend I have in the world.
MRS. ALVING. Yes, I am, Oswald, aren't I?
OSWALD [*walks around restless*]. But it's all the remorse, the gnawing, the self-reproach. And then the fear! Oh—this dreadful fear!
MRS. ALVING [*follows him*]. Fear? What fear? What do you mean?
OSWALD. Oh, don't ask me any more about it. I don't know. I can't describe it.

[MRS. ALVING *crosses right and pulls the bell-rope.*]

OSWALD. What do you want?
MRS. ALVING. I want my boy to be happy. He shan't sit here and brood. [*To* REGINA *who appears in the doorway*] More champagne. A whole bottle.

[REGINA *goes.*]

OSWALD. *Mother!*
MRS. ALVING. Do you think we don't know how to live here, too?
OSWALD. Isn't she splendid to look at? The way she's made! And so healthy and strong!
MRS. ALVING [*sits at the table*]. Sit down, Oswald, and let's talk calmly together.
OSWALD [*sits*]. You don't know this, mother, but I have done Regina a wrong. And I've got to put it right.
MRS. ALVING. A wrong?
OSWALD. Well, a little thoughtlessness—whatever you care to call it. Quite innocently, really. When I was home last—
MRS. ALVING. Yes?
OSWALD. She asked me so often about Paris, and I told her this and that about the life down there. And I remember, one day I happened to say: "Wouldn't you like to come there yourself?"
MRS. ALVING. Oh?
OSWALD. Well, she blushed violently, and then she said: "Yes, I'd like to very much." "Well, well," I replied, "that might be arranged"—or something of the sort.
MRS. ALVING. Yes?
OSWALD. Well, of course I forgot the whole thing. But the day before yesterday, when I asked her if she was glad that I was going to stay at home so long—
MRS. ALVING. Yes?

oswald. She gave me such a strange look and then she asked: "But then, what's going to become of my trip to Paris?"
mrs. alving. Her trip!
oswald. And then I got it out of her that she'd taken the whole thing seriously, that she'd been going around here thinking about me the whole time, and that she'd begun to learn French—
mrs. alving. I see—
oswald. Mother—when I saw that splendid, handsome, healthy girl standing there in front of me—well, I'd never really noticed her before—but now, when she stood there, so to speak, with open arms ready to receive me—
mrs. alving. Oswald!
oswald. Then I realized that in her I could find salvation; for I saw that she was full of the joy of life.
mrs. alving [*starts*]. The joy of life! But how could that help?
regina [*enters from the dining room with a bottle of champagne*]. I'm sorry I was so long. I had to go down to the cellar—[*Puts the bottle on the table*]
oswald. And fetch another glass.
regina [*looks at him, surprised*]. There is Mrs. Alving's glass.
oswald. But fetch one for yourself, Regina.

[regina *starts and throws a quick glance at* mrs. alving.]

oswald. Well?
regina [*quietly, hesitantly*]. Do you wish me to, madam?
mrs. alving. Fetch the glass, Regina.

[regina *goes into the dining room.*]

oswald [*watches her go*]. Do you see how she walks? With such purpose and gaiety!
mrs. alving. This must not happen, Oswald.
oswald. It's already decided. Surely you can see. It's no use trying to stop it.

[regina *enters with an empty glass, which she keeps in her hand.*]

oswald. Sit down, Regina. [*She glances questioningly at* mrs. alving.]
mrs. alving. Sit down.

[regina *sits on a chair by the dining-room door, with the empty glass still in her hand.*]

mrs. alving. Oswald, what was it you were saying about the joy of life?

OSWALD. Oh, yes—the joy of life, mother—you don't know much about that here. I never feel it here.
MRS. ALVING. Not when you are with me?
OSWALD. Not when I'm at home. But you don't understand that.
MRS. ALVING. Oh, yes—I think I do now—almost.
OSWALD. The joy of life and the love of one's work. They're practically the same thing. But that you don't know anything about, either.
MRS. ALVING. No, I don't suppose we do. Oswald, tell me more about this.
OSWALD. Well, all I mean is that here people are taught to believe that work is a curse and a punishment, and that life is a misery which we do best to get out of as quickly as possible.
MRS. ALVING. A vale of tears, yes. And we do our best to make it one.
OSWALD. But out there, people don't fell like that. No one there believes in that kind of teaching any longer. They feel it's wonderful and glorious just to be alive. Mother, have you noticed how everything I've painted is concerned with the joy of life? Always, always, the joy of life. Light and sunshine and holiday—and shining, contented faces. That's what makes me afraid to be here at home with you.
MRS. ALVING. Afraid? What are you afraid of here with me?
OSWALD. I'm afraid that everything in me will degenerate into ugliness here.
MRS. ALVING [looks hard at him]. You think that would happen?
OSWALD. I know it. Live the same life here as down there, and it wouldn't be the same life.
MRS. ALVING [who has listened intently, rises, her eyes large and thoughtful]. Now I see.
OSWALD. What do you see?
MRS. ALVING. Now I understand for the first time. And now I can speak.
OSWALD [rises]. Mother, I don't follow you.
REGINA [who has also risen]. Shall I go?
MRS. ALVING. No, stay. Now I can speak. Now, my boy, you shall know everything. And then you can choose. Oswald! Regina!
OSWALD. Ssh! The Pastor—!
MANDERS [enters from the hall]. Well, we've had a most splendid and profitable hour down there.
OSWALD. So have we.
MANDERS. We must assist Engstrand with this sailors' home. Regina must go and help him—
REGINA. No thank you, Pastor.
MANDERS [notices her for the first time]. What! You here! And with a glass in your hand!

REGINA [*puts the glass down quickly*]. Oh, pardon—
OSWALD. Regina is leaving with me, sir.
MANDERS. Leaving! With you!
OSWALD. Yes. As my wife. If she so wishes.
MANDERS. But, good heavens—!
REGINA. It isn't my doing, sir.
OSWALD. Or she will stay here, if I stay.
REGINA [*involuntarily*]. Here?
MANDERS. I am petrified at you, Mrs. Alving.
MRS. ALVING. She will neither leave with you nor stay with you. Now I can speak the truth.
MANDERS. But you mustn't! No, no, no!
MRS. ALVING. I can and I will. And I shan't destroy any ideals, either.
OSWALD. Mother, what have you been hiding from me?
REGINA [*listens*]. Madam! Listen! People are shouting outside!

[*She goes into the conservatory and looks out.*]

OSWALD [*at the window, left*]. What's going on? Where's that light coming from?
REGINA [*cries*]. The Orphanage is on fire!
MRS. ALVING [*at the window*]. On fire!
MANDERS. On fire? Impossible! I've only just left it.
OSWALD. Where's my hat? Oh, never mind! Father's Orphanage—! [*Runs out through the garden door*]
MRS. ALVING. My shawl, Regina! The whole building's alight!
MANDERS. Terrible! Mrs Alving, there blazes the judgment of God upon this sinful house!
MRS. ALVING. Yes, I agree. Come, Regina. [*She and* REGINA *hurry out through the hall.*]
MANDERS [*clasps his hands*]. And not insured either! [*He follows them.*]

ACT THREE

The same. All the doors are standing open. The lamp is still burning on the table. Outside it is dark, with only a faint glow from the fire in the background, left. MRS. ALVING, *with a big shawl over her head, standing in the conservatory, looking out.* REGINA, *also with a shawl round her, stands a little behind her.*

MRS. ALVING. All burnt to the ground.
REGINA. It's still burning in the basement.
MRS. ALVING. Why doesn't Oswald come back? There's nothing to save.
REGINA. Would you like me to go down and take him his hat?
MRS. ALVING. Hasn't he even got his hat?
REGINA [*points to the hall*]. No, it's hanging there.
MRS. ALVING. Let it hang. He must come up now. I'll go and look for him myself. [*Goes out through the garden door.*]
MANDERS [*enters from hall*]. Isn't Mrs. Alving here?
REGINA. She's just this minute gone into the garden.
MANDERS. This is the most terrible night I have ever experienced.
REGINA. Yes, sir, isn't it a dreadful tragedy?
MANDERS. Oh, don't talk about it? I hardly dare even to think about it.
REGINA. But how can it have happened—?
MANDERS. Don't ask me, Miss Engstrand. How can I know? Are you, too, going to—? Isn't it enough that your father—?
REGINA. What's he done?
MANDERS. Oh, he's completely confused me.
ENGSTRAND [*enters from the hall*]. Your Reverence—
MANDERS [*turns, alarmed*]. Are you still pursuing me?
ENGSTRAND. Yes, well, God rot me if—oh, good heavens! But this is a terrible business, your Reverence.
MANDERS [*walks up and down*]. It is indeed, it is indeed.
REGINA. What is?
ENGSTRAND. Well, you see, it all began with this prayer service. [*Aside*] Now we've got him, my girl! [*Aloud*] Fancy me being to blame for Pastor Manders being to blame for something like this.
MANDERS. But I assure you, Engstrand—
ENGSTRAND. But there was no one except your Reverence mucking around with the candles down there.
MANDERS [*stops*]. Yes, so you keep on saying. But I'm sure I don't remember ever having had a candle in my hand.
ENGSTRAND. And I saw as plain as plain could be your Reverence take the candle and snuff it with your fingers and throw the wick right down among the shavings.
MANDERS. And you saw this?
ENGSTRAND. Yes, with these eyes.
MANDERS. That I cannot understand. It's not usually my habit to snuff out candles with my fingers.
ENGSTRAND. Yes, it looked a bit careless, I thought. But it can't really be as bad as you say, can it, your Reverence?
MANDERS [*paces uneasily up and down*]. Oh, don't ask me.

ENGSTRAND [*walks with him*]. And of course you haven't insured it, either?

MANDERS [*still walking*]. No, no, no. I've told you.

ENGSTRAND [*still with him*]. Not insured. And then to go straight over and set fire to it all. Oh, good heavens, what a tragedy.

MANDERS [*wipes the sweat from his forehead*]. Yes, Engstrand, you may well say that.

ENGSTRAND. And that such a thing should happen to a charitable institution which was to have served the city as well as the countryside. The newspapers won't be too gentle with your Reverence, I'm afraid.

MANDERS. No, that's just what I'm thinking. That's almost the worst part of it. All these hateful attacks and accusations—Oh, it's frightful to think about.

MRS. ALVING [*enters from the garden*]. I can't persuade him to come away from the fire.

MANDERS. Ah, it's you, Mrs. Alving.

MRS. ALVING. Well, now you won't have to make that speech after all, Pastor Manders.

MANDERS. Oh, I'd have been only too happy to—

MRS. ALVING [*in a subdued voice*]. It was all for the best. Nothing good would have come of this Orphanage.

MANDERS. You think not?

MRS. ALVING. What do you think?

MANDERS. Nevertheless, it was a terrible tragedy.

MRS. ALVING. We'll discuss it simply as a business matter. Are you waiting for the Pastor, Engstrand?

ENGSTRAND [*in the doorway to the hall*]. That's right, madam.

MRS. ALVING. Well, sit down, then.

ENGSTRAND. Thank you, I'm happy standing.

MRS. ALVING [*to* MANDERS]. I suppose you'll be leaving with the steamer?

MANDERS. Yes. In an hour.

MRS. ALVING. Would you be kind enough to take all the papers along with you? I don't want to hear another word about this. Now I have other things to think about—

MANDERS. Mrs. Alving—

MRS. ALVING. I'll send you a power of attorney so that you can take any measures you think fit.

MANDERS. I shall be only too happy to shoulder that responsibility. I fear the original purpose of the endowment will now have to be completely changed.

MRS. ALVING. I appreciate that.

MANDERS. Yes, I'm provisionally thinking of arranging for the Solvik property to be handed over to the parish. The freehold cannot by any means be said to be without value. It can always be put to some purpose or other. And the interest from the capital in the savings bank I could perhaps most suitably employ in supporting some enterprise or other which could be said to be of benefit to the town.

MRS. ALVING. As you please. It's a matter of complete indifference to me.

ENGSTRAND. Remember my home for sailors, your Reverence.

MANDERS. Yes, indeed, you have a point there. We shall have to consider that possibility carefully.

ENGSTRAND. Consider? To hell with—oh, good heavens!

MANDERS [*with a sigh*]. And I'm afraid I don't know how long these matters will remain in my hands. Public opinion may force me to withdraw. It all depends on the outcome of the enquiry into the cause of the fire.

MRS. ALVING. What are you saying?

MANDERS. And one cannot possibly predict the outcome.

ENGSTRAND [*comes closer*]. Oh, yes one can. Don't I stand here, and isn't my name Jacob Engstrand?

MANDERS. Yes, yes, but—

ENGSTRAND [*more quietly*]. And Jacob Engstrand isn't the man to fail his blessed benefactor in his time of need, as the saying goes.

MANDERS. But, my dear man, how—?

ENGSTRAND. Jacob Engstrand can be likened to an angel of deliverance, as you might say, your Reverence.

MANDERS. No, no, I really cannot accept this.

ENGSTRAND. Oh, that's the way it's going to be. I know someone who's taken the blame for another man's wickedness once before.

MANDERS. Jacob! [*Presses his hand*] You are indeed a rare person. Well, you too shall receive a helping hand. For your seamen's home. That you can rely upon.

[ENGSTRAND *wants to thank him, but is too moved to speak.*]

MANDERS [*hangs his traveling bag on his shoulder*]. Well, let's be off. We two shall go together.

ENGSTRAND [*at the dining-room door, says quietly to* REGINA]. You come with me, my girl. You'll live as tight as the yolk in an egg.

REGINA [*tosses her head*]. Merci! [*Goes into the hall and fetches* MANDERS'*s overcoat*]

MANDERS. Farewell, Mrs. Alving. And may the spirit of law and order soon enter into this house.

MRS. ALVING. Good-bye, Manders.

[*She goes toward the conservatory, as she sees* OSWALD *come in through the garden door.*]

ENGSTRAND [*while he and* REGINA *help* MANDERS *on with his overcoat*]. Good-bye, my child. And if ever you find yourself in any trouble, you know where Jacob Engstrand is to be found. [*Quietly*] Little Harbour Street—hm—! [*To* MRS. ALVING *and* OSWALD] And the house for wandering sailors is going to be called Captain Alving's Home. And if I am allowed to run it according to my ideas, I think I can promise you it'll be a worthy memorial to him, God rest his soul.

MANDERS [*in the doorway*]. Hm—hm! Come along, my dear Engstrand. Good-bye, good-bye. [*He and* ENGSTRAND *go out through the hall.*]

OSWALD [*goes over toward the table*]. What was that he was talking about?

MRS. ALVING. Some kind of home that he and Pastor Manders are going to found.

OSWALD. It'll burn down just like this one.

MRS. ALVING. Why do you say that?

OSWALD. Everything will burn. There will be nothing left to remind people of father. I, too, am burning.

[REGINA *starts and stares at him.*]

MRS. ALVING. Oswald! You ought not to have stayed down there so long, my poor boy.

OSWALD [*sits down at the table*]. I think you're right.

MRS. ALVING. Let me wipe your face, Oswald. It's soaking wet. [*She dries him with her handkerchief.*]

OSWALD [*stares indifferently ahead of him*]. Thank you, mother.

MRS. ALVING. Aren't you tired, Oswald? Wouldn't you like to go upstairs and sleep?

OSWALD [*frightened*]. No, no, I won't sleep. I never sleep. I only pretend to. [*Heavily*] It'll come soon enough.

MRS. ALVING [*looks worried at him*]. My dear boy, you really are ill.

REGINA [*tensely*]. Is Mr. Alving ill?

OSWALD [*impatiently*]. And shut all the doors! Oh, this fear that haunts me—!

MRS. ALVING. Close them, Regina.

[REGINA *closes the doors and remains standing by the hall door.* MRS. ALVING *takes off her shawl.* REGINA *does likewise.*]

MRS. ALVING [*brings a chair over to* OSWALD'S *and sits down beside him*]. There, now. I'll sit beside you—

OSWALD. Yes, do. And Regina must stay here too. Regina must always be near me. You'll save me, Regina. Won't you?
REGINA. I don't understand—
MRS. ALVING. Save you—?
OSWALD. Yes. When the time comes.
MRS. ALVING. But Oswald, you have your mother.
OSWALD. You? [*Smiles*] No, mother, you wouldn't do this for me. [*Laughs heavily*] You? Ha, ha! [*Looks earnestly at her*] Though really you're the one who ought to. [*Violently*] Why don't you speak to me as though I was your friend, Regina? Why don't you call me Oswald?
REGINA [*quietly*]. I don't think Mrs. Alving would like it.
MRS. ALVING. You may do so presently. Come over and sit down here with us. [REGINA *sits quietly and diffidently on the other side of the table.*] And now, my poor, tormented boy, now I shall remove the burden from your mind—
OSWALD. You, mother?
MRS. ALVING [*continues*]. All this remorse and self-reproach you speak of—
OSWALD. You think you can do that?
MRS. ALVING. Yes, Oswald, now I can. You spoke of the joy of life; and that seemed to throw a new light over everything that has happened to me in my life.
OSWALD [*shakes his head*]. I don't understand.
MRS. ALVING. You should have known your father when he was a young lieutenant. He was full of the joy of life, Oswald.
OSWALD. Yes, I know.
MRS. ALVING. It was like a sunny morning just to see him. And the untamed power and the vitality he had!
OSWALD. Yes?
MRS. ALVING. And this happy, carefree child—for he was like a child, then—had to live here in a little town that had no joy to offer him, only diversions. He had to live here with no purpose in life; simply a position to keep up. He could find no work into which he could throw himself heart and soul—just keeping the wheels of business turning. He hadn't a single friend capable of knowing what the joy of life means; only idlers and drinking-companions—
OSWALD. Mother—!
MRS. ALVING. And in the end the inevitable happened.
OSWALD. The inevitable?
MRS. ALVING. You said yourself this evening what would happen to you if you stayed at home.
OSWALD. You mean that father—?

MRS. ALVING. Your poor father never found any outlet for the excess of vitality in him. And I didn't bring any sunshine into his home.
OSWALD. You didn't?
MRS. ALVING. They had taught me about duty and things like that, and I sat here for too long believing in them. In the end everything became a matter of duty—*my* duty, and *his* duty, and—I'm afraid I made his home intolerable for your poor father, Oswald.
OSWALD. Why did you never write and tell me about this?
MRS. ALVING. Until now I never saw it as something that I could tell you, because you were his son.
OSWALD. And how did you see it?
MRS. ALVING [*slowly*]. I only saw that your father was a depraved man before you were born.
OSWALD [*quietly*]. Ah—! [*Gets up and goes over to the window*]
MRS. ALVING. And day in and day out I thought of only one thing, that Regina really belonged here in this house—just as much as my own son.
OSWALD [*turns swiftly*]. Regina—!
REGINA [*jumps up and asks softly*]. I?
MRS. ALVING. Yes, now you both know.
OSWALD. Regina!
REGINA [*to herself*]. So mother was one of them.
MRS. ALVING. Your mother was in many ways a good woman, Regina.
REGINA. Yes, but still, she was one of them. Yes, I've sometimes wondered; but—! Well, madam, if you'll allow me I think I'd better leave. At once.
MRS. ALVING. Do you really want to, Regina?
REGINA. Yes, I certainly do.
MRS. ALVING. Of course you must do as you please, but—
OSWALD [*goes over to* REGINA]. Go now? But you belong here.
REGINA. *Merci*, Mr. Alving—yes, I suppose I'm allowed to say Oswald now. But it certainly isn't the way I'd hoped.
MRS. ALVING. Regina, I haven't been open with you—
REGINA. I should say not. If I'd known that Oswald was ill like this, I—Now that there can never be anything serious between us—No, I'm not going to stay out here in the country and wear myself out looking after invalids.
OSWALD. Not even for someone who is so close to you?
REGINA. I should say not. A poor girl has got to make the best of her life while she's young. Otherwise she'll be left high and dry before she knows where she is. And I've got the joy of life in me too, Mrs. Alving.

MRS. ALVING. Yes, I'm afraid you have. But don't throw yourself away, Regina.
REGINA. Oh, what will be will be. If Oswald takes after his father, I shouldn't be surprised but what I'll take after my mother. May I ask, madam, does Pastor Manders know this about me?
MRS. ALVING. Pastor Manders knows everything.
REGINA [begins to put on her shawl]. Well then, I'd better get down to the steamer as quick as I can. The Pastor's such a nice man to get along with. And I'm sure I've as much a right to a little of that money as he has—that awful carpenter.
MRS. ALVING. I'm sure you're very welcome to it, Regina.
REGINA [looks spitefully at her]. You might have brought me up like the daughter of a gentleman. It'd have been more appropriate considering. [Tosses her head] Oh, what the hell does it matter? [With a bitter glance at the bottle, still unopened] I can still drink champagne with gentlemen.
MRS. ALVING. And if ever you need a home, Regina, come to me.
REGINA. No thank you, madam. Pastor Manders will take care of me. And if things go really wrong, I know a house where I belong.
MRS. ALVING. Where is that?
REGINA. In Captain Alving's home for sailors.
MRS. ALVING. Regina—I can see it. You will destroy yourself.
REGINA. Oh, rubbish. *Adieu!* [Curtseys and goes out through the hall.]
OSWALD [stands by the window, looking out]. Has she gone?
MRS. ALVING. Yes.
OSWALD [mumbles to himself]. I think it was wrong, all this.
MRS. ALVING [goes over behind him and places her hands on his shoulders]. Oswald, my dear boy, has this news upset you very much?
OSWALD [turns his face toward her]. All this about father, you mean?
MRS. ALVING. Yes, about your poor father. I'm so afraid it may have been too much for you.
OSWALD. What on earth makes you think that? Of course it came as a great surprise to me. But I can't really feel it makes any difference.
MRS. ALVING [takes her hands away]. No difference! That your father was so miserably unhappy!
OSWALD. I feel sorry for him of course, as I would for anyone, but—
MRS. ALVING. Nothing else? For your own father!
OSWALD [impatiently]. Oh, father, father! I never knew anything about father. I don't remember anything about him, except that once he made me sick.
MRS. ALVING. This is terrible! Surely a child ought to love its father whatever may happen?

OSWALD. Even when a child has nothing to thank its father for? Has never known him? Do you really cling to that old superstition—you, who are otherwise so enlightened?

MRS. ALVING. Do you really think it's only a superstition—?

OSWALD. Yes, mother, surely you realize that. It's one of those truisms people hand down to their children—

MRS. ALVING [*shudders*]. Ghosts!

OSWALD [*walks across the room*]. Yes, that's not a bad word for them. Ghosts.

MRS. ALVING [*emotionally*]. Oswald! Then you don't love me either!

OSWALD. At least I know you—

MRS. ALVING. Know me, yes. But is that all?

OSWALD. And of course I know how fond you are of me; and for that I must be grateful to you. And you can do so much for me now that I'm ill.

MRS. ALVING. Yes, Oswald, I can, can't I? Oh, I could almost bless your sickness for bringing you home to me. I realize it now. You aren't mine. I must win you.

OSWALD [*impatiently*]. Yes, yes, yes. These are just empty phrases. You must remember I'm sick, mother. I can't be expected to bother about others. I've enough worry thinking about myself.

MRS. ALVING [*quietly*]. I shall be patient and undemanding.

OSWALD. And cheerful, mother!

MRS. ALVING. Yes, my dear boy—I know. [*Goes over to him*] Have I freed you from all your anxiety and self-reproach now?

OSWALD. Yes, you have. But who will take away the fear?

MRS. ALVING. The fear?

OSWALD [*walks across the room*]. Regina would have done it for the asking.

MRS. ALVING. I don't understand you. What's all this about fear—and Regina?

OSWALD. Is it very late, mother?

MRS. ALVING. It's early morning. [*Looks out into the conservatory*] The dawn's beginning to show upon the mountains. It's going to be a fine day, Oswald. In a little while you'll be able to see the sun.

OSWALD. I'll look forward to that. Oh, there's still so much for me to look forward to and live for—

MRS. ALVING. Of course there is!

OSWALD. Even if I can't work, there's—

MRS. ALVING. Oh, you'll soon be able to work again, my dear boy. You haven't all these gnawing and oppressing thoughts to brood over any longer now.

OSWALD. No, it was a good thing you managed to rid me of all those ideas. Once I've got over this one thing—! [*Sits on the sofa*] Let's sit down and talk, mother.

MRS. ALVING. Yes, let's. [*Moves an armchair over to the sofa, and sits close to him*]

OSWALD. And while we talk the sun will rise. And then you'll know. And then I won't have this fear any longer.

MRS. ALVING. What will I know?

OSWALD [*not listening to her*]. Mother, didn't you say earlier tonight that there wasn't anything in the world you wouldn't do for me if I asked you?

MRS. ALVING. Certainly I did.

OSWALD. And you'll keep your promise, mother?

MRS. ALVING. Of course I will, my dearest, my only boy. I've nothing else to live for. Only you.

OSWALD. Yes, well, listen then. Mother, you're brave and strong, I know that. Now you must sit quite still while I tell you.

MRS. ALVING. But what is this dreadful thing you—?

OSWALD. You mustn't scream. You hear? Promise me that. We'll sit and talk about it quite calmly. Do you promise me that, mother?

MRS. ALVING. Yes, yes, I promise. Only tell me.

OSWALD. Well then, all that business about being tired—and not being able to think about work—that isn't the real illness—

MRS. ALVING. What is the real illness?

OSWALD. The illness which is my inheritance—[*Points to his forehead and says quite quietly*] That's in here.

MRS. ALVING [*almost speechless*]. Oswald! No! No!

OSWALD. Don't scream. I can't bear it. Yes, mother, it sits in here, watching and waiting. And it may break out any time; any hour.

MRS. ALVING. Oh, how horrible—!

OSWALD. Now keep calm. That's the way it is—

MRS. ALVING [*jumps up*]. It isn't true, Oswald! It's impossible! It can't be true!

OSWALD. I had one attack down there. It soon passed. But when I found out what I had been like, this raging fear began to haunt me; and that's why I came back home to you as quickly as I could.

MRS. ALVING. So that's the fear—

OSWALD. Yes—it's so unspeakably repulsive, you see. Oh, if only it had been an ordinary illness that would have killed me—! Because I'm not so frightened of dying; though I'd like to live as long as I can.

MRS. ALVING. Yes, yes, Oswald, you must!

OSWALD. But this is so revolting. To be turned back into a slobbering baby; to have to be fed, to have to be—! Oh—! I can't think about it—!

MRS. ALVING. The child has its mother to nurse it.
OSWALD [*jumps up*]. No, never! That's just what I won't allow! I can't bear to think that I might stay like that for years, growing old and gray. And perhaps you might die and leave me. [*Sits in* MRS. ALVING's *chair*] It might not mean that I'd die at once, the doctor said. He called it a softening of the brain or something. [*Smiles sadly*] I think that sounds so beautiful. I shall always think of cherry-colored velvet curtains—something delicious to stroke.
MRS. ALVING [*screams*]. Oswald!
OSWALD [*jumps up again and walks across the room*]. And now you've taken Regina from me. If only I had her! She would have saved me. I know.
MRS. ALVING [*goes over to him*]. What do you mean by that, my beloved boy? Is there anything I wouldn't do to save you?
OSWALD. When I had recovered from the attack down there, the doctor told me that when it comes again—and it will come again—then there's no more hope.
MRS. ALVING. How could he be so heartless as to—?
OSWALD. I made him tell me. I told him I had arrangements to make. [*Smiles cunningly*] And so I had. [*Takes a small box from his inside breast pocket*] Mother, do you see this?
MRS. ALVING. What's that?
OSWALD. Morphine powders.
MRS. ALVING [*looks at him in horror*]. Oswald—my boy—!
OSWALD. I've managed to collect twelve capsules—
MRS. ALVING [*tries to take it*]. Give that box to me, Oswald.
OSWALD. Not yet, mother. [*Puts it back in his pocket*]
MRS. ALVING. I can't bear this!
OSWALD. You must bear it. If Regina had been here now, I'd have told her how things were with me—and asked her to do me this last service. I'm sure she would have helped me.
MRS. ALVING. Never!
OSWALD. When the horror was on me and she saw me lying there like a newborn baby, helpless, lost—beyond all hope—
MRS. ALVING. Regina would never have done it.
OSWALD. She would have. Regina was so splendidly carefree. And she would soon have got bored with looking after an invalid like me.
MRS. ALVING. Then thank God that Regina is not here!
OSWALD. Yes, well, so now you will have to do this last service for me, mother.
MRS. ALVING [*screams aloud*]. I?
OSWALD. Who else?
MRS. ALVING. I! Your mother!

OSWALD. Exactly.
MRS. ALVING. I, who gave you life!
OSWALD. I didn't ask you for life. And what kind of a life have you given me? I don't want it. Take it back.
MRS. ALVING. Help! Help! [*Runs out into the hall*]
OSWALD [*goes after her*]. Don't leave me! Where are you going?
MRS. ALVING [*in the hall*]. To fetch the doctor, Oswald. Let me go!
OSWALD [*also offstage*]. You're not going anywhere. And no one's coming here. [*A key is turned.*]
MRS. ALVING [*comes back*]. Oswald! Oswald—my child!
OSWALD [*follows her*]. If you have a mother's love for me, how can you see me suffer like this?
MRS. ALVING [*after a moment's silence, says in a controlled voice*]. Very well. [*Takes his hand*] I give you my word.
OSWALD. You promise?
MRS. ALVING. If it becomes necessary. But it won't be. No, no, it's impossible.
OSWALD. Yes, let us hope so. And let us live together as long as we can. Thank you, mother.

[*He sits in the armchair, which* MRS. ALVING *has moved over to the sofa. The day breaks. The lamp continues to burn on the table.*]

MRS. ALVING [*approaches him cautiously*]. Do you feel calm now?
OSWALD. Yes.
MRS. ALVING [*leans over him*]. You've just imagined these dreadful things, Oswald. You've imagined it all. All this suffering has been too much for you. But now you shall rest. At home with your own mother, my own dear, blessed boy. Point at anything you want and you shall have it, just like when you were a little child. There, there. Now the attack is over. You see how easily it passed! Oh, I knew it! And, Oswald, do you see what a beautiful day we're going to have? Bright sunshine. Now you can really see your home.

[*She goes over to the table and puts out the lamp. The sun rises. The glacier and the snow-capped peaks in the background glitter in the morning light.*]

OSWALD [*sits in the armchair facing downstage, motionless. Suddenly he says*]. Mother, give me the sun.
MRS. ALVING [*by the table, starts and looks at him*]. What did you say?
OSWALD [*repeats dully and tonelessly*]. The sun. The sun.
MRS. ALVING [*goes over to him*]. Oswald, how are you feeling?

[OSWALD *seems to shrink small in his chair. All his muscles go slack. His face is expressionless. His eyes stare emptily.*]

MRS. ALVING [*trembles with fear*]. What's this? [*Screams loudly*] Oswald! What is it? [*Throws herself on her knees beside him and shakes him*] Oswald! Oswald! Look at me! Don't you know me?
OSWALD [*tonelessly as before*]. The sun. The sun.
MRS. ALVING [*jumps to her feet in despair, tears her hair with both hands and screams*]. I can't bear this! [*Whispers as though numbed*] I can't bear it! No! [*Suddenly*] Where did he put them? [*Fumbles quickly across his breast*] Here! [*Shrinks a few steps backwards and screams*] No; no; no! Yes! No; no! [*She stands a few steps away from him with her hands twisted in her hair, speechless, and stares at him in horror.*]
OSWALD [*still motionless*]. The sun. The sun.

THE MISER

by MOLIÈRE

TRANSLATED FROM THE FRENCH BY *H. Baker and J. Miller*

Translation by H. Baker and J. Miller, adapted for use in the production presented by The Repertory Theater of Lincoln Center, New York, under the direction of Jules Irving, in their 1968–1969 season at the Vivian Beaumont Theater, New York. Copyright © 1971 by Harcourt Brace Jovanovich, Inc. Professional and amateur dramatic rights are strictly reserved. Inquiries on these rights should be addressed to The Repertory Theater of Lincoln Center, New York, N.Y. 10023.

Photos by Martha Swope of production presented by The Repertory Theater of Lincoln Center, under the direction of Jules Irving, in their 1968–1969 season at the Vivian Beaumont Theater, New York.

Recording of this text available through Caedmon Records, Inc., 505 Eighth Avenue, New York, N.Y. 10018.

France's greatest comic playwright, Molière, the professional name of Jean Baptiste Poquelin, was a seventeenth-century actor-manager who for the latter part of his life enjoyed the patronage of Louis XIV, the "Sun King." Molière satirized hypocrisy and social pretension, and in such plays as *The Misanthrope, Tartuffe, The School for Women,* and *The Doctor in Spite of Himself* his satire cut so deeply that even with the king's protection outraged victims of his comic attacks managed to have some of his plays altered or temporarily suppressed.

The theater of Molière derives from a long tradition of Latin, Italian, and early French writers of comedy. But his basic situation is always a rational world in which one or more persons suffer from an obsessive monomania, a deviation from good sense. *The Miser* dramatizes the folly of this irrational behavior. The aged Harpagon is obsessed with money for money's sake. He never once considers what money can provide, but gloats over the mere possession of his box of golden coins, suffering constantly from the fear that it will be stolen. When it is missing, he accuses the whole world of theft, saying that if such crimes are permitted to go unpunished, the most sacred things are no longer safe. And his depraved use of parental authority produces genuine frustration in his son and daughter, Cleante and Elise, and in their lovers, Mariane and Valere.

In order to enjoy the full flavor of Molière's play, the modern reader must dispense with ideas of realism. In *The Miser* Master Jacque, coachman and cook for Harpagon, can run between Valere and Harpagon who are standing only a few feet apart on the stage and deliberately misrepresent what is being said by each. Or La Fleche can speak clearly enough for the audience to understand and still distort his meaning to Harpagon who is standing only a short distance away. These are stage conventions and their absurdity lends a hilarious air to the action and a subtle insight into Harpagon's character. As avaricious and suspicious as he is, he is still easily deceived by flattery and cajoled by youth.

The Miser was first presented in 1668 at the Palais Royale, in the luxurious theater Louis XIV had provided for Molière and his acting company. Apparently the knife cut a little too closely, however, for immediate enthusiasm from his audience. We seldom find our own vices amusing. The leering, coughing, howling, hand-wringing Harpagon must have reminded too many money-lenders of their business tactics and too many fathers of sons who were awaiting inheritances for the play to have been an instant success. But before Molière died, five years later, *The Miser* had been acclaimed as a masterpiece.

Characters

HARPAGON, *father of Cleante and Elise, in love with Mariane*
CLEANTE, *Harpagon's son, in love with Mariane*
ELISE, *Harpagon's daughter, in love with Valere*
VALERE, *Anselme's son, in love with Elise*
MARIANE, *Anselme's daughter, in love with Cleante*
ANSELME, *father of Valere and Mariane*
FROSINE, *a woman of intrigue*
MR. SIMON, *a broker*
MASTER JACQUE, *Harpagon's cook and coachman*
LA FLECHE, *Cleante's valet*
DAME CLAUDE, *Harpagon's maid*
BRINDAVOINE, *Harpagon's lackey*
LA MERLUCHE, *Harpagon's lackey*
A COMMISSARY *and* HIS CLERK

The scene throughout is in Harpagon's house in Paris.

ACT ONE

SCENE I. VALERE, ELISE.

VALERE. What, my charming Elise, grown melancholy, after the obliging assurance you gave me of your love? I see you sighing, in the midst of my joy! And do you repent that engagement which my passion forced from you?
ELISE. No, Valere.
VALERE. Good!
ELISE. I cannot regret anything I do for you. I find myself drawn by a force too enchanting, and I am not able, even to form a wish that what is done should be undone. But to say the truth, the consequence gives me some worry; and I am afraid of loving you a little more than I ought to do.
VALERE. Elise. What can you fear in the love you bear me?
ELISE. A hundred things. The resentments of a father; the reproaches of my family; the censures of the world; but above all, Valere, a change in your affection; that criminal coldness with which those of your sex most frequently repay the too warm proofs of an innocent love.
VALERE. Ah! do me not that wrong, to judge me by others. Suspect me of anything, Elise, except failure in my duty to you. I love you too much for that; and my love for you shall be as lasting as my life.
ELISE. Ah! Valere, all men are alike in their words; and only their actions that prove them different.
VALERE. Since our actions alone prove what we are, wait at least and judge my heart by them; allow me time to convince you, by a thousand and a thousand proofs, of the sincerity of my love.
ELISE. How easily are we persuaded by those we love! Yes, Valere, I believe you love me with a real passion, and that you will ever be constant to me. All that concerns me, is the censure which people may pass on me.
VALERE. But why this uneasiness?
ELISE. I should have nothing to fear, would all the world look upon you with my eyes; I see enough in your person to vindicate everything I do for you. I call to mind every moment your surprising generosity which made you risk your own life, to snatch mine from the fury of the waves; your most tender concern after you had dragged me out of the water; your ardent love, which neither time

233

nor difficulties could discourage, and neglecting both family and country, detains you in this place, and made you take upon you the employment of a domestic of my father's. All this is sufficient, in my eyes, to justify that marriage contract, which I signed with you: but 'tis not enough, perhaps, to justify it to others; I am not sure they will share my sentiments.

VALERE. Your father himself takes care enough to justify you to all the world; his excess of avarice, and the austere manner with which he lives with his children, would allow for things even more daring than what you did for me. If I can find my family again, we shall have no great trouble to gain him on our side. I expect some news of them with great impatience; and if they should stay much longer, I myself will go in search of them to Naples.

ELISE. Ah! Valere, do not leave me, I entreat you; I think only how to work yourself into my father's favor.

VALERE. You saw what artful compliance I made use of, to enter into his service; and you see what part I perpetually act with him in order to win his heart. I succeed to admiration; I find that to be in the good graces of men, there's no better way than to praise their foibles, and applaud everything they do. The slyest people are always grand dupes on the side of flattery; there's nothing so impertinent or so ridiculous which we cannot make them swallow, when we season it with praise. Sincerity suffers a little by the trade I follow. But when we have need of men, we must suit ourselves to their taste; so it is not the fault of those who flatter, but of those who want to be flattered.

ELISE. But why don't you also gain my brother for a support, in case the maid should take it into her head to betray our secret?

VALERE. There is no managing them both at once; the temper of the father, and that of the son, are things so opposite, that it is difficult to win the confidence of both at the same time. But you, can transact the business with your brother, and take the advantage of his friendship to bring him over to our interests.

ELISE. I don't know whether I have the courage to lay myself thus open to him.

VALERE. Let him no further into our affair than you think advisable.

SCENE 2. CLEANTE, ELISE.

CLEANTE. Sister.

ELISE. Brother.

CLEANTE. A world of things, sister, comprehended in one word—I am burning with impatience to speak with you.

ELISE. What is it you have to tell me?
CLEANTE. A world of things, sister, comprehended in one word—I am in love.
ELISE. You, in love?
CLEANTE. Yes, in love: but, before I go any further, I know that I depend on a father, and that the name of son subjects me to his will; that we ought not to engage ourselves, without his consent; that we ought rather to trust to the eyes of his prudence, than to the blindness of our passion; and that the heat of youth very often draws us upon dangerous precipices. I say all this to you, sister, that you should not take the trouble of saying it to me; for in short, my love will listen to nothing.
ELISE. Have you engaged yourself, brother, with her you love?
CLEANTE. No, but I have determined to do it; and I beg you once more to bring me no reasons to dissuade me from it.
ELISE. Am I so strange a person, brother?
CLEANTE. No, sister, but you are not in love; you are ignorant of that sweet violence which the tender passion commits upon our hearts, and I am afraid of your prudence.
ELISE. Brother, not a word about my prudence. And if I lay open my heart to you, I should perhaps appear much less prudent in your eyes.
CLEANTE. Ah! Would Heaven your heart, like mine—
ELISE. Let us finish your affair first; tell me who is the person you are in love with.
CLEANTE. A young girl who lodges of late in this neighborhood. Her name is Mariane, and she lives with her mother, who is almost always sick; this dear girl waits upon her, bemoans her, comforts her with a tenderness that would touch you to the very soul. She goes about everything she does with an air the most charming in the world; a sweetness most winning, a good nature all engaging, a modesty adorable, a—Ah! sister, I wish you had but seen her.
ELISE. I see a great deal of her, dear brother, in what you've told me; and it's sufficient for me that you love her.
CLEANTE. I have heard that she and her mother are in very serious financial straits. Imagine, sister, what joy it must be to raise the fortune of a person one loves; and to contribute in a handsome manner, some small relief to the modest necessities of a virtuous family, but by the avarice of a father, I am unable to taste this joy, and to offer to this girl any testimony of my love.
ELISE. Yes, brother, I understand your anger.
CLEANTE. Ah! sister, it is greater than one can believe. Can anything be more cruel, than that rigorous close-fisted economy with which

we are kept under; and what good will it do us to have means, at a time when we are past the prime of enjoying them? I am forced for my necessary support, to run myself in debt with everybody around me. You and I are reduced to hunt about daily for relief from tradesmen, to clothe ourselves decently. In short, I want you to help me sound out father; and if he opposes me, I am determined to go elsewhere, with this lovely creature, and make the best of that fortune which heaven shall throw in our way. I'm ransacking high and low to borrow money for this purpose; and if your affair, sister, resembles mine, and father opposes our inclinations, we'll both leave him, and free ourselves from that tyranny.

ELISE. It is very true, brother, he gives us every day more and more reason to regret the loss of our mother, and that—

CLEANTE. I hear his cough. In my room, we'll discuss our affairs thoroughly and afterwards we'll join our attack on the stubbornness of his temper.

SCENE 3. HARPAGON, LA FLECHE.

HARPAGON. Get out this moment, march out of my house, you sworn rascal, you true gallows-swinger.

LA FLECHE. Never did I see anything so villainous as this cursed old fool; I think he's possessed of the devil.

HARPAGON. Do you mutter between your teeth?

LA FLECHE. Why do you drive me out?

HARPAGON. It well becomes you, scoundrel, to ask me reasons, indeed; get out.

LA FLECHE. My master, your son, has given me orders to wait for him.

HARPAGON. Wait for him in the street, and not in my house, planted bolt upright like a stake. I won't have a spy in my house, a traitor, whose cursed eyes ferret about in every corner to see where there's anything they can steal.

LA FLECHE. How the devil can anyone steal from you? You who keep everything under lock and key, and stand guard day and night; it can't be done.

HARPAGON. I will lock up what I think proper, and stand guard as I please. [*Aside*] I tremble for fear he has suspected something about my money. Don't you spread stories that I have money hidden in my house.

LA FLECHE. Have you money hidden?

HARPAGON. No, rascal, I don't say so. I only ask that you will not maliciously spread a rumor that I have.

LA FLECHE. What matters it to us that you have, or that you have not; we don't see any of it either way.
HARPAGON. Ho! You turn philosopher, do you? I'll philosophize on your ears. [*Lifting up his hand to give* LA FLECHE *a box on the ear*] Get out!
LA FLECHE. Well, I'm going.
HARPAGON. Stay, have you carried nothing away from me?
LA FLECHE. What should I carry away from you?
HARPAGON. Come here that I may see; show me your hands.
LA FLECHE. There.
HARPAGON. The other.
LA FLECHE. The other?
HARPAGON. Yes.
LA FLECHE. There.
HARPAGON. Have you crammed nothing in here? [*Pointing to* LA FLECHE's *breeches*]
LA FLECHE. See for yourself.
HARPAGON [*feeling the knees of his breeches*]. These wide-kneed breeches are proper receivers of stolen goods—
LA FLECHE [*aside*]. Ah! Such a fellow deserves to get what he expects and what a pleasure it would be to rob him!
HARPAGON. Heh?
LA FLECHE. What?
HARPAGON. What is it you talk of robbing?
LA FLECHE. I say that you feel pretty well round about, to see if I have robbed you.
HARPAGON. That's what I will do. [*Feels in* LA FLECHE's *pockets*]
LA FLECHE [*aside*]. The plague take all stinginess, and stingy curs.
HARPAGON. How? What do you say?
LA FLECHE. What do I say?
HARPAGON. Yes. What do you say of stinginess, and stingy curs?
LA FLECHE. I say the plague take all stinginess, and stingy curs.
HARPAGON. Whom do you speak of?
LA FLECHE. Of the stingy.
HARPAGON. And who are those stingy?
LA FLECHE. Villains, and skinflints.
HARPAGON. But who do you mean by that?
LA FLECHE. What are you uneasy about?
HARPAGON. I am uneasy about what I ought to be.
LA FLECHE. You believe I mean you?
HARPAGON. I believe what I believe; but you should tell me whom you speak to, when you say that.
LA FLECHE. I speak—I speak—to my hat.

HARPAGON. And I'll speak to your head. HOLD YOUR TONGUE!
LA FLECHE. I mentioned no names.
HARPAGON. A word more I'll break your bones.
LA FLECHE. If the hat fits—
HARPAGON. Not done yet?
LA FLECHE. Yes, much against my will. [*Showing him one of his waistcoat pockets*] Wait; here's another pocket; are you satisfied?
HARPAGON. Come, give it to me, without the trouble of rummaging for it.
LA FLECHE. What?
HARPAGON. What you have taken from me.
LA FLECHE. I've taken nothing at all from you.
HARPAGON. Really?
LA FLECHE. Really.
HARPAGON. Adieu then, and go to the devil.
LA FLECHE [*aside*]. So; I am blessedly dismissed.
HARPAGON. I nevertheless put it on your conscience.

SCENE 4.

HARPAGON [*alone*]. There's a rascal of a valet, who is a constant vexation to me. I don't like to see him around here. 'Tis no small trouble to keep a great sum of money at home; but I'm not sure that I've done the right thing to bury the cashbox in my garden, a cashbox with 30,000 francs, which were paid to me yesterday. Happy is he who has all his money well invested, and keeps no more cash at home than he needs for common expenses. It's hard to find in an entire house a secure hiding place for it, and safes are, to me, very suspicious; I would never trust them. I look upon them to be mere bait for thieves, and they are always the first things they head for.

SCENE 5. HARPAGON, ELISE, *and* CLEANTE *talking together at the farther part of the stage.*

HARPAGON [*thinking himself alone*]. Thirty thousand francs in cash is a sum sufficiently— [*Seeing the brother and sister whispering together*] O Heavens! I have betrayed myself; as I was thinking just now, did I speak out loud? [*To* CLEANTE *and* ELISE] What's the matter?
CLEANTE. Nothing, father.
HARPAGON. Have you been there long?

ELISE. We have just come in, father.
HARPAGON. Did you overhear?
CLEANTE. What, father?
HARPAGON. What I—
ELISE. What?
HARPAGON. What I was just now saying.
CLEANTE. No.
HARPAGON. You did, you did.
ELISE. With submission we did not.
HARPAGON. I was discoursing to myself about the difficulty, nowadays, of coming by money, and I was saying, that happy is he who has thirty thousand francs in his house.
CLEANTE. We were afraid of coming up to you, for fear we should interrupt you.
HARPAGON. I am very glad to tell you with what I said, that you might not take things the wrong way, and fancy I said 'twas I who had thirty thousand francs.
CLEANTE. We don't pry into your affairs.
HARPAGON. Would I had them, those thirty thousand francs.
CLEANTE. I don't believe—
HARPAGON. They would be of great service to me.
ELISE. You are—
HARPAGON. And I should make no complaints, as I do now, that the times are hard.
CLEANTE. My God! father, you have no reason to complain; the world knows you do well enough.
HARPAGON. What! Well enough? They that say it are liars. There's nothing more false, and they are rascals who spread all these rumors.
ELISE. There's no need to throw yourself into a passion.
HARPAGON. 'Tis strange that my own children should betray me, and turn my enemies!
CLEANTE. Is it being your enemy, to tell you that you do well enough?
HARPAGON. Yes: such talk and your expenses will be the reason, one of these days, of people coming to cut my throat, thinking that I am stuffed with gold.
CLEANTE. What expenses?
HARPAGON. What expenses? Is there anything more scandalous than those sumptuous clothes which you flaunt about town? I was scolding your sister yesterday, but this is ten times worse. Were one to take you from head to foot, one might find enough to purchase an annuity for life. I've told you twenty times, son, that all your ways very much displease me. You give yourself the airs of a nobleman, and you must certainly rob me, to go dressed as you do.

CLEANTE. How could I rob you?
HARPAGON. How should I know? Where can you get the money to live as you do?
CLEANTE. Me, father? By gambling: and since I am very lucky, I lay out all the money I win upon my back.
HARPAGON. 'Tis very ill done. If you're lucky at gambling, you should invest the money you win at honest interest. I should be glad to know to what purpose serve all these ribbons, and such a wig. I'll wager that in wigs and in ribbons, there are at least 480 francs: and 480 francs bring in at least 55 francs, 6 sous, and 8 denier per annum, at only eight percent interest.
CLEANTE. Yes, that's very true.
HARPAGON. No more of this, let's talk of other business. [*Aside, seeing* CLEANTE *and* ELISE *making signs to one another*] Can it be! They are making signs to one another to pick my pocket? [*Aloud*] What mean these gestures?
ELISE. We are bargaining, my brother and I, who shall speak first; and we have each of us, something to say to you.
HARPAGON. And I have something to say to each of you.
CLEANTE. It is about marriage, father, that we wish to talk with you.
HARPAGON. 'Tis about marriage that I have to talk to you.
ELISE. Ah! father.
HARPAGON. Why that Ah? Is it the word, daughter, that frightens you, or the thing itself?
CLEANTE. Matrimony may be frightful in both respects, in the manner you may intend it; and we are afraid our feelings mayn't agree with your choice.
HARPAGON. A little patience. Don't frighten yourselves. I know what is proper for you both; and you shall have no reason, to complain of anything I intend to do. [*To* CLEANTE] And to begin at the beginning. Have you seen a young person whose name is Mariane, who lodges not far from here?
CLEANTE. Yes, father.
HARPAGON. And you?
ELISE. I've heard of her, father.
HARPAGON. How do you like her, son?
CLEANTE. She is a very fine creature.
HARPAGON. Her looks?
CLEANTE. Honest and sprightly.
HARPAGON. Her air and manner?
CLEANTE. Admirable, undoubtedly.
HARPAGON. Don't you think that such a girl deserves to be considered?
CLEANTE. Yes, father.

HARPAGON. That this would be a desirable match?
CLEANTE. Most desirable.
HARPAGON. That she has all the appearance of making an excellent housewife?
CLEANTE. Yes.
HARPAGON. And that a husband might live comfortably with her?
CLEANTE. Most comfortably.
HARPAGON. There is a trifling difficulty. I am afraid she has not so much money, as one might reasonably expect.
CLEANTE. Oh! father, money is not important when the question is of marrying a person of virtue.
HARPAGON. Now, now, there is much to be said for a good dowry, but her honest deportment, and sweetness of temper have gained my heart; and provided she has something of a dowry, I am resolved to marry her.
CLEANTE. Euh!
HARPAGON. What?
CLEANTE. You are resolved, what did you say?
HARPAGON. To marry Mariane.
CLEANTE. Who, you? you?
HARPAGON. Yes, me, me, me. What can all this mean?
CLEANTE. I am a bit dizzy, and I'll withdraw a little.
HARPAGON. Go into the kitchen, and drink a large glass of plain water.

SCENE 6. HARPAGON, ELISE.

HARPAGON. These are your flimsy fops, they have no more stamina than a chicken. This, daughter, is what I resolved for myself. As to your brother, I have decided upon a certain widow for him, and for you, daughter, I'll give you to Signor Anselme.
ELISE. To Signor Anselme?
HARPAGON. Yes. A staid, prudent, and wise man, who is not above fifty, and is reported to be very rich.
ELISE [*curtsying*]. I have no inclination to marry, father, if you please.
HARPAGON [*curtsying again*]. And I've an inclination, my little girl, that you should marry, if you please.
ELISE [*curtsying again*]. I beg your pardon, father.
HARPAGON. I beg your pardon, daughter.
ELSIE. I am Signor Anselme's most humble servant. [*Curtsying again*] But, with your leave, I will not marry him.
HARPAGON. I am your most humble slave. [*Curtsying again*] But, with your leave, you shall marry him this very night.

ELISE. This very night?
HARPAGON. This very night.
ELISE [*curtsying again*]. This won't be, father.
HARPAGON [*curtsying again*]. This will be, daughter.
ELISE. No.
HARPAGON. Yes.
ELISE. No, I tell you.
HARPAGON. Yes, I tell you.
ELISE. You shall never force me to do this.
HARPAGON. I will force you to do this.
ELISE. I'll sooner kill myself, than marry such a man.
HARPAGON. You shall not kill yourself, and you shall marry him. Did ever anybody see a daughter speak this way to a father?
ELISE. Did ever anybody see a father marry his daughter in this way?
HARPAGON. 'Tis a match to which there can be no objection; and I'll wager all the world will approve my choice.
ELISE. And I'll wager that it can't be approved by any reasonable person.
HARPAGON. Daughter, shall we make Valere a judge between us in this affair.
ELISE. With all my heart.
HARPAGON. Will you submit to his judgment?
ELISE. Yes. I'll agree to whatever he says.
HARPAGON. Done.

SCENE 7. VALERE, HARPAGON, ELISE.

HARPAGON. Come here, Valere, we have chosen you to tell us who is right, my daughter, or me.
VALERE. 'Tis you, sir, beyond all dispute.
HARPAGON. Do you know what we are talking about?
VALERE. No. But you can't be wrong, you are reason itself.
HARPAGON. This evening I want to give her a husband who is equally rich and wise; and the baggage tells me to my face, she won't have him. What do you say to that?
VALERE. What do I say?
HARPAGON. Yes.
VALERE. Eh, eh?—
HARPAGON. What?
VALERE. I say that basically, I am of your opinion, and you can't possibly fail of being right. But at the same time, she is not absolutely in the wrong; and—
HARPAGON. How so? Signor Anselm is a gentleman of nobility, sweet-

tempered, staid, wise, and very well off, and he has no child by his former marriage. Could she be better fitted?

VALERE. That's true. But she might tell you, that this is hurrying things a bit; and that some time should have been given to see whether her inclination might reconcile itself with—

HARPAGON. 'Tis an opportunity which we must catch quickly by the forelock. I find an advantage here, which I should not find elsewhere; he'll take her with no dowry.

VALERE. No dowry?

HARPAGON. Yes.

VALERE. Oh! I say not a word more. You see here is a reason absolutely convincing.

HARPAGON. This is a considerable saving to me.

VALERE. Most certainly, there is no contradiction. 'Tis true, your daughter may tell you, that marriage is a more important affair, than people are apt to conceive; and that an engagement which is to last till death, should never be made without great precaution.

HARPAGON. No dowry.

VALERE. You are right. That's what decides all, that's taken for granted. There are people who might tell you, that on such occasions, the inclination of a daughter is, doubtless, this thing which ought to be regarded; and that this great disparity of age, of humor, and of feelings, makes a marriage subject to most unpleasant accidents.

HARPAGON. No dowry.

VALERE. It's true. That stops every mouth; no dowry. Show me a way to withstand such an argument.

HARPAGON [*aside, looking toward the garden*]. Oh, the dog is barking; there must be someone after my money! [*To* VALERE] Don't move, I'll be back immediately.

SCENE 8. ELISE, VALERE.

ELISE. Are you mocking me, Valere, to talk to him as you do?

VALERE. If I don't exasperate him, I may achieve my end the better. Directly to fall foul of his sentiments is the way to spoil everything. Some people must be taken only the roundabout way. Seem to consent to what he has in mind and you'll gain your point the better; and—

ELISE. But this marriage, Valere?

VALERE. We'll find some way to break it off.

ELISE. But what can we find, if it must be concluded this evening?

VALERE. You must gain a delay; feign some disorder.

ELISE. But they'll discover the counterfeit, if they call in the doctors.
VALERE. Do doctors know anything? Come! You may have what illness you please for all them; they'll find you reasons for the cause of it.

SCENE 9. HARPAGON, ELISE, VALERE.

HARPAGON [*aside, at the farther part of the stage*]. 'Tis nothing, thank Heaven.
VALERE [*not seeing* HARPAGON]. Our last resort is, flight; and if your love, Elise, is capable of—[*spying* HARPAGON] a daughter should be obedient to her father; she ought by no means to mind the looks of a husband; and when the substantial argument of no dowry is offered, she ought to take anything given to her.
HARPAGON. Good. That was admirably said.
VALERE. Sir, I beg your pardon, if I took the liberty to talk to her in this way.
HARPAGON. I am delighted and I want you to take her absolutely under your charge. [*To* ELISE] It won't help to run away. I give him the same authority over you that Heaven has given me, and you must comply with everything he directs—

SCENE 10. HARPAGON, VALERE.

VALERE. I'll give her more of the same lectures.
HARPAGON. Do so. You'll oblige me.
VALERE. 'Tis good to keep a strict hand over her.
HARPAGON. Do, do. I'm going to take a short walk to the city, and shall be back again shortly.
VALERE [*going toward that side of the stage where* ELSIE *went off, and speaking as to her*]. It's true! Money is the most valuable thing in this world; and you ought to thank Heaven for the father it has bestowed on you. He knows what life is all about. When a gentleman offers to take a daughter with no dowry, one ought to look no further. Everything is included in that. No dowry takes the place of beauty, youth, pedigree, honor, wisdom, and integrity.
HARPAGON [*alone*]. Ah! brave boy! Speaks like an oracle. Happy is he who has such a servant.

ACT TWO

SCENE I. CLEANTE, LA FLECHE.

CLEANTE. Hey! Rascal! Where have you been thrusting in your impertinent nose? Did I not tell you?—

LA FLECHE. Yes, sir, and I came here to attend you; but your father, a most ungracious mortal, drove me out and I ran the risk of being beaten up.

CLEANTE. How goes our affair? Things are more urgent than ever; and since I left you, I have discovered that my father is my rival.

LA FLECHE. Your father in love?

CLEANTE. Yes; with Mariane and I had all the difficulty in the world to conceal from him the disorder into which I was thrown by this news.

LA FLECHE. He dabble in love-affairs! What the Devil does he think of! Was love made for people like him?

CLEANTE. It must be, for my sins, that this passion should have got into his head. But what answer have they made you?

LA FLECHE. Sir, borrowing money is a miserable business; and anyone who is reduced to borrowing as you are must bear with strange things when passing through the hands of a money-lender.

CLEANTE. Won't the job be done at all then?

LA FLECHE. Pardon me. Our Mr. Simon the broker, who is recommended to us as an active, stirring fellow, tells me he has left no stone unturned to serve you, and protests that your looks alone have gained his heart.

CLEANTE. I shall have the 15,000 francs then?

LA FLECHE. Yes; but upon some trifling conditions, which it's necessary you should accept.

CLEANTE. He brought you to the man who was to lend the money?

LA FLECHE. No truly, this business is not transacted in that fashion. He takes even more pains to keep hidden than you do. Mr. Simon would by no means tell me his name: But he is to be brought to an interview with you today at an appointed place, to be informed from your own mouth of your substance and your family; and I have no doubt, but the name only of your father, will make things very easy for you.

CLEANTE. And chiefly of my mother's estate which nobody can keep from me.

LA FLECHE. Here are some articles which the lender himself dictated to our Master Simon to be shown to you, before anything can be done.

> On supposition that the lender sees all his securities good, and the borrower be of age, of a family whose estate is great, solid, free from all encumbrances, a punctual contract shall be executed before an honest notary.

CLEANTE. There's nothing to be said against this.

LA FLECHE. The lender, not to load his conscience with the least scruple, will lend out his money at not more than six percent.

CLEANTE. At six percent! That's very reasonable.

LA FLECHE. Very reasonable.

> But as the lender aforesaid has not by him the sum under debate, he himself is necessitated to borrow of another, at the rate of eighteen and one-half percent, 'twill be but reasonable that the said first borrower pay that interest, as it is only to oblige him that the said lender engages himself to make this loan at all.

CLEANTE. What the devil! That's more than twenty percent.

LA FLECHE. Twenty-four and one-half percent precisely; you had better think on it.

CLEANTE. What would you have me consider? I need money, and I must agree to it all.

LA FLECHE. That very answer I made him.

CLEANTE. Is there anything more?

LA FLECHE. One small article only.

> Of the fifteen thousand francs required, the lender will not be able to pay in cash more than twelve thousand; and as to the three thousand francs remaining, the borrower must take them out in household stuff, furniture, and trinkets; listed in the following inventory.

CLEANTE. What?

LA FLECHE. Hear the inventory:

> Imprimis: One four-legged bed with curtains of green velour, edged in Hungarian lace; six chairs with matching embroidery, all in fair condition, and a bedspread with a taffeta lining woven in the national colors.

[*Moves up*]

> Item: one small trundle bed complete with tassels and fringes of silk.

CLEANTE. What would he have me do with this?

LA FLECHE [*to* CLEANTE]. Hold.
  Item: one set of tapestry hangings, depicting the amours of Abelard and Heloise.
CLEANTE. Abelard and Heloise—
LA FLECHE.
  Item: one expandable table made from petrified wood, supported by twelve corkscrew legs or pillars, with its half-dozen stools under it.
CLEANTE. Petrified wood!
LA FLECHE. Have patience.
  Item: one brick furnace, with two cauldrons and three hand-irons, very useful for those interested in alchemy.
CLEANTE [*crosses left*]. I shall go mad.
LA FLECHE. Gently.
  Item: One chess board, one fox and goose table, with the play of the goose, restored from the Greeks, very proper to pass away the time, when one has nothing to do.

  [*Crosses up*]

  Item: One lizard skin with three feet and a half, legs stuffed with hay; very suitable to hang from the ceiling of a bedchamber. The total above mentioned being honestly worth four thousand five hundred francs, is reduced, through the generosity of the lender, to the value of three thousand francs.
CLEANTE. The plague choke him with his generosity. He is not satisfied with the cruel interest he demands, but he forces me to take the old lumber he has heaped together, at the rate of three thousand francs? I shan't get six hundred francs for the lot.
LA FLECHE. Three hundred at the most.
CLEANTE. Three hundred?!! And yet, I must agree to his terms; for he is in a position to make me accept anything; the jackal has me by the throat.
LA FLECHE. Sir, without offense, you are exactly on the road to disaster.
CLEANTE. What would you have me do? See what young fellows are reduced to by the monstrous avarice of fathers! Is there any wonder that their children wish them dead?
LA FLECHE. I must confess that yours would incense the calmest men in the world against his villainy. I have not, Heaven be praised, inclinations strongly bent toward hanging; and amongst my comrades, whom I see dabbling pretty much in the small-craft way, I've dexterity enough to withdraw myself from all gallantries which taste ever so little of the gallows; but, to tell the truth, he would even tempt

me to rob him; and I should think, in robbing him, I did a meritorious deed.

CLEANTE. Give me that inventory, that I may look it over again.

SCENE 2. HARPAGON, MR. SIMON, CLEANTE, LA FLECHE, *at the farther part of the stage.*

MR. SIMON. No fear of that, sir; no fear of that! Yes, sir, tis a young man in need of money. His affairs force him to take it up, and he'll accept whatever terms you prescribe for him.

HARPAGON. But you do believe, Master Simon, there's no hazard run in this case? And do you know the name, the estate, and the family of him you speak for?

MR. SIMON. No, I can't well let you thoroughly into that; and it was only by chance I came to know him; but you will be made acquainted with everything by himself; and this man assured me that when you come to know him you would be satisfied. All I can tell you, is, that his family is very rich, that he has no mother, and that he will certify, if you insist upon it, that his father shall die within eight months.

HARPAGON. That's something, indeed. Christian charity, Mr. Simon, obliges us to gratify people when it is in our power.

LA FLECHE [*aside to* CLEANTE]. What's the meaning of this? Our Master Simon talking to your father!

MR. SIMON. That, of course, goes without saying.

LA FLECHE [*low to* CLEANTE, *seeing* MR. SIMON]. What's the meaning of this?

CLEANTE [*low to* LA FLECHE]. Can they have informed him who I am? Did you betray me?

MR. SIMON [*to* LA FLECHE]. Hah! You are hard pressed! Who told you this was the house? [*To* HARPAGON] It is not me, sir; however, they learned your name and your lodging; but in my opinion there's no great harm done; they are discreet people, and here you may discuss business.

HARPAGON. How!

MR. SIMON [*pointing to* CLEANTE]. This is the gentleman who'd borrow the fifteen thousand francs of you, that I was speaking of.

HARPAGON. Is it you that abandon yourself to these filthy dealings?

CLEANTE. Is it you father that descend to these base actions?

[MR. SIMON *makes off, and* LA FLECHE *goes to hide himself.*]

SCENE 3.   HARPAGON, CLEANTE.

HARPAGON. Is it you who would ruin yourself, by such rascally borrowings?
CLEANTE. Is it you who seek to enrich yourself by such villainous usury?
HARPAGON. Dare you, after this, appear before me?
CLEANTE. Dare you, after this, show yourself to the world?
HARPAGON. Are you not ashamed to descend to these debaucheries? To run headlong into horrible expenses, and scandalously squander that substance, which your parents have amassed for you with the sweat of their brows?
CLEANTE. Don't you blush to disgrace your rank by the trade you drive? To sacrifice honor and reputation to the insatiable lust of heaping coin upon coin, and to outdo, in point of interest, the most notorious usurers?
HARPAGON. Begone out of my sight, rascal, out of my sight. Out, out, get out and stay out.
CLEANTE. Who do you think is the greater criminal, he who borrows the money he really needs, or he, who steals the money he has no use for?
HARPAGON. Out, I say, and don't torment my ears—

[*Exit* CLEANTE]

I'm not at all sorry for this adventure, 'twill be a warning to me, to keep a stricter eye than ever upon all his actions.

SCENE 4.   FROSINE, HARPAGON.

FROSINE. Sir.
HARPAGON. Stay a moment, I'll come back and talk with you presently. [*Aside*] It's time I should make a short trip to my money.

SCENE 5.   LA FLECHE, FROSINE.

LA FLECHE [*not seeing* FROSINE]. He must have something out there.
FROSINE [*seeing him*]. Ha! Is it you, my poor La Fleche! What are you doing here?
LA FLECHE. Hah! Hah! Is it you, Frosine! What are you doing here?
FROSINE. What I do everywhere else; to play the go-between in affairs, make myself serviceable to people, and take the best advantage I possibly can of the small talents I have. In this world we must live by

our wits and to such as I am Heaven has given no other income but intrigue, and hard work.

LA FLECHE. Have you any business with the master of this house?

FROSINE. Yes, I'm transacting a small affair for him for which I expect some reward.

LA FLECHE. From him? You'll be very clever if you extract anything from him; and I must tell you that money is amazingly scarce in this house.

FROSINE. There are certain services which are marvelously appealing.

LA FLECHE. Granted, but you don't know Signor Harpagon. Signor Harpagon is of all human creatures the least humane; of all mortals the hardest, and most tight-fisted. No service can push his gratitude to the extremity of unclenching his hands. And "give" is a word for which he has conceived so strong an aversion, that he never says, I *give you* a good-day, but I *lend you* a good-day.

FROSINE. I've the art of milking men. I've the secret of tickling their hearts, to find on which side they are the softest.

LA FLECHE. No use here! I defy you to melt the man we're speaking of. You may burst him before ye can move him; in a word, he loves money more than reputation, honor, and virtue, and the mere sight of a person who has any demands upon him, throws him into convulsions; it wounds him in the mortal part, pierces him to the heart, tears out his very entrails; and if—but he returns; I must be gone.

[*Exit* LA FLECHE]

SCENE 6. HARPAGON, FROSINE.

HARPAGON [*aside*]. Everything is as it should be. [*Aloud*] Well, Frosine? How is it?

FROSINE. Bless me! You look so well! You are the very picture of health.

HARPAGON. Who, me?

FROSINE. Never did I see you look so fresh and jolly.

HARPAGON. Indeed?

FROSINE. Indeed? You were never so young in your life as you are now. I see fellows of twenty-five who are older than you.

HARPAGON. For all that, Frosine, I am well in my sixties.

FROSINE. Sixties! What's that? It is the very prime of man!

HARPAGON. Twenty years less would do me no harm, I think.

FROSINE. You joke, you're built to last a hundred years.

HARPAGON. Do you think so?

FROSINE. Most certainly; look at me. Ha! There it is—just between your two eyes—the token of long life!

HARPAGON. Are you skilled that way?
FROSINE. Certainly. Show me your hand. Mercy oh me, what a life line.
HARPAGON. What?
FROSINE. Don't you see what a vast way that line goes?
HARPAGON. Well, what does that signify?
FROSINE. I said a hundred years, but you'll go beyond a hundred and twenty.
HARPAGON. Is it possible?
FROSINE. I tell you they will have to beat you to death! You'll live to bury your children, and your children's children.
HARPAGON. So much the better. Well Frosine, how goes our affair?
FROSINE. Need you ask? Does anybody see me meddle with a thing I don't bring to bear? I've above all, a wondrous talent at matchmaking. There aren't two people in the world that I can't couple in a trice; I could even marry the grand Turk with the republic Venice —but there was no such great difficulty in this affair. As I'm very intimate with the ladies, I've had deep discourse with them both about you. I told the mother of your intentions on Mariane, since you saw her pass along the street, and take the air at her window.
HARPAGON. And did she reply?
FROSINE. She received the proposal with joy; and allowed Mariane to be present this evening at the signing of your daughter's marriage contract. She has trusted her to my care.
HARPAGON. Well, Frosine, I'm obliged to give Signor Anselm a supper tonight and I should be glad to have Mariane partake of the treat.
FROSINE. That is very reasonable. In the afternoon she'll pay your daughter a visit, from here she intends to go to the fair, and we'll return for supper.
HARPAGON. But, Frosine, have you talked to the mother about the dowry she can give her daughter? Have you told her she must drive a little, and bleed for such an occasion as this? For I tell you again, nobody marries a girl unless she bring something with her.
FROSINE. Something? She will bring you in twelve thousand francs per annum.
HARPAGON. Twelve thousand francs per annum?
FROSINE. Yes. First of all, she has been reared in great scantiness of feeding. She's a girl used to live upon salad, bread, and apples; and consequently there will be no need of a table well served up, nor your exquisite jellies, nor any other delicacies that another woman must have; and this is not such a trifling matter, but it will amount to three thousand francs per annum, at least. Item: She has no curiosity for anything beyond great simplicity, and loves none of your magnificent dresses, nor rich jewels, nor sumptuous furniture, which other

girls are addicted to with great eagerness; and this is worth more than four thousand francs a year. Item: She has a horrible aversion to gambling, which is not common with the ladies nowadays; and I know one of them in our neighborhood who has lost thirty thousand francs this year. But let's only take one-fourth of that; five thousand francs, and four thousand francs in dresses and jewels, that makes nine thousand francs; and three thousand francs for food, is not there your twelve thousand francs a year, hard cash?

HARPAGON. Yes, that's not bad; but this computation has nothing real in it.

FROSINE. Excuse me. Is it nothing real if a wife brings into marriage a dowry of no appetite, the investment of simplicity in dress, and an estate of great hatred for gambling?

HARPAGON. 'Tis mere jest to make me up her dowry out of all the expenses she won't put me to; I must have something I can put my hands on.

FROSINE. You shall put your hands on plenty. I have heard them talk of a certain country where they have property of which you will be the owner.

HARPAGON. I must look into that. But, Frosine, there is one thing more which gives me uneasiness. The girl is young; young people generally covet only their own company. I'm afraid a man of my age will not strike her taste; and this may produce certain little disorders that would not be agreeable to me.

FROSINE. How little do you know her! She has a terrible aversion to all young folks, and loves none but old men.

HARPAGON. She!

FROSINE. Yes, she. She can't bear the sight of a young fellow. She is never more ravished, she says, than when she sees a fine old man with a venerable beard; with her the oldest have the greatest charms, and I warn you not to make yourself younger than you are; not four months ago on the point of marriage, she broke the match off when she discovered that the fiancé was only fifty-six and didn't need spectacles to sign the contract.

HARPAGON. Only on that account?

FROSINE. Yes. She says fifty-six will not satisfy her; and, moreover, she adores noses that wear spectacles.

HARPAGON. I have never heard of such a thing.

FROSINE. This goes even further than I can tell you. There are several pictures and prints in her bedchamber. But what would you imagine they are? Adonis? Paris? Apollo? No. Your handsome portraits of King Priam, of old Nestor, and good father Anchises upon his son's shoulders.

HARPAGON. I should never have dreamt it; and I'm very pleased to find she's of this humor. In truth, had I been a woman, I should never have loved young fellows.
FROSINE. I believe it.
HARPAGON. For my part, I can't comprehend that there are women who are so fond of them.
FROSINE. They must be out of their minds to think youth attractive. Are they men, these young fops? And can people be attracted to such animals as these?
HARPAGON. That's what I always say, with their effeminate voices, and their three little bits of a beard turned up like a cat's whiskers, their curled wigs, their beribboned breeches, and their shirts hanging open.
FROSINE. Compared with a person like yourself! There's something like a man! There's what will gratify the eye! This is the make and dress to inspire love.
HARPAGON. Do you think me attractive?
FROSINE. Do I? You are ravishing, and your picture ought to be painted. Turn a little if you please; let me see you walk. Here's a body, trim, graceful, and degagé as it ought to be, and not the least imperfection.
HARPAGON. I have very few, thank heaven. Only my catarrh . . . from time to time.
FROSINE. That's nothing at all. Your catarrh fits you; and you cough with grace.
HARPAGON. Tell me. Has not Mariane seen me yet? Has she not noticed me as I passed by?
FROSINE. No, no. But we'd a great deal of discourse about your person. And I was setting forth your merits and the advantage it would be to her to have such a husband.
HARPAGON. You did well, and I thank you.
FROSINE. Sir, I have a small request to make to you. I have a lawsuit, that I'm in great danger of losing for want of a little money.

[HARPAGON *looks grave.*]

And you could easily gain me this suit. You can't think the pleasure she'll have to see you.

[*He resumes a gay air.*]

How you will please her! What an admirable effect will that antique ruff of yours have upon her fancy. But of all things she'll be charmed with your breeches tagged to your doublet with hooks and eyes. A hook-and-eye lover will be most appetizing for her.
HARPAGON. You put me in raptures by this talk.
FROSINE. Really, sir, this lawsuit is absolutely of the greatest importance.

[HARPAGON *looks grave again.*]

I'm undone if I lose it; and some small assistance—I wish you had seen the rapture she was in to hear me speak of you.

[HARPAGON *looks gay again.*]

Joy sparkled in her eyes at the recital of your good qualities; and I made her extremely impatient to see this marriage fully consummated.

HARPAGON. You have done me an exceeding kind office, Frosine; and I have all the obligations in the world to you.

FROSINE. I beseech you, sir, grant me the small assistance I request of you.

[HARPAGON *looks serious.*]

'Twill set me on my feet again, and I should be eternally obliged for it.

HARPAGON. Adieu. I must finish my dispatches.

FROSINE. I do assure you, sir, you can never help me in a greater necessity.

HARPAGON. I'll give the orders for my coach to be ready to carry you to the fair.

FROSINE. I would not bother you were I not forced to do it. Don't refuse me this favor. You can't imagine, sir, the pleasure that—

HARPAGON. I must go. They're calling me. Farewell.

FROSINE [*alone*]. The plague on you and go to the devil. You dog! The skinflint was deft against all my attacks: but I need not give up this business because I still have the other side, and I'm sure of getting a good reward.

ACT THREE

SCENE I. HARPAGON, CLEANTE, ELISE, VALERE, DAME CLAUDE *with a broom in her hand.* MASTER JACQUE, BRINDAVOINE, LA MERLUCHE.

HARPAGON. Come, come here all of you, that I may give you my orders of the day, and regulate your employments. A little closer, Dame Claude. I'll begin with you. Good, you are well armed I see. The task of cleaning everything I assign to you: and take care not to rub the furniture too hard, for fear of wearing it out. Furthermore, I give you the jurisdiction of the bottles, during supper; and if anyone is missing, or anything is broken, I shall take it out of your wages.

MASTER JACQUE [*aside*]. That's a clever punishment.

HARPAGON [*to* DAME CLAUDE]. Go.

SCENE 2. HARPAGON, CLEANTE, ELISE, VALERE, MASTER JACQUE, BRINDAVOINE, LA MERLUCHE.

HARPAGON. You Brindavoine, and you La Merluche, I put you in charge of rinsing the glasses and serving the wine; but only when someone is thirsty, and not like certain impertinent servants who stimulate people to drink. Wait till they call for it again and again, and remember always to mix a great deal of water with it.

MASTER JACQUE [*aside*]. Yes, pure wine goes to the head.

LA MERLUCHE. Shall we take off our canvas frocks, sir?

HARPAGON. Yes, when you see the guests coming; and take special care not to spoil your clothes.

BRINDAVOINE. You very well know, sir, that one of the foreflaps of my doublet is covered with a great blotch of lamp oil.

LA MERLUCHE. And I, sir, have my pants so torn behind, that saving your presence, they may see my—

HARPAGON. Peace, turn it toward the wall, and always show your forepart to the world. [HARPAGON *holds his hat before his doublet to show* BRINDAVOINE *how he should hide the blotch of oil.*] And you, Brindavoine, always hold your cap in this fashion, when you serve at table.

SCENE 3. HARPAGON, CLEANTE, ELISE, VALERE, MASTER JACQUE.

HARPAGON. As for you, daughter, keep an eye on what is left at table and take care there be no waste. That's very becoming to young women. But in the meantime prepare yourself to receive my fiancée, who is to pay you a visit, and attend her to the fair. Do you hear what I say?

ELISE. Yes, father.

SCENE 4. HARPAGON, CLEANTE, VALERE, MASTER JACQUE.

HARPAGON. And you my fop of a son, don't you go take it into your head to make sour faces.

CLEANTE. I sour faces, father; and for what reason?

HARPAGON. Come, come, I know the ways of children whose fathers marry again; and with what eye they look upon a stepmother. But if you wish me to forget your last prank, I recommend to you to entertain this lady with a cheerful countenance.

CLEANTE. To tell you the truth, father, I can by no means promise you to be pleased should she become my stepmother. I would lie, if I told you so: but as for receiving her handsomely, and looking upon her cheerfully, I do promise to obey you most punctually.

HARPAGON. Take care of that, at least.

SCENE 5. HARPAGON, VALERE, MASTER JACQUE.

HARPAGON. Valere, help me with this business—ho! Master Jacque, come here, I kept you for the last.

MASTER JACQUE. Is it your coachman, sir, or your cook, you would speak to? For I am both.

HARPAGON. To both of them.

MASTER JACQUE. But to which one of them first?

HARPAGON. To the cook.

MASTER JACQUE. Wait then, if you please. [*Takes off his coachman's long great coat, and appears dressed as a cook.*]

HARPAGON. What nonsense of a ceremony's this?

MASTER JACQUE. You've nothing to do but give your orders.

HARPAGON. I've committed myself, Master Jacque, to give a supper to-night.

MASTER JACQUE [*aside*]. A miracle!

HARPAGON. Can you give us a good meal?

MASTER JACQUE. Yes, if you'll give me a good deal of money.

HARPAGON. What the devil! always money! They have nothing else to say; money, money, money. Not a word but money, Valere. Their favorite song is money.

VALERE. I never heard a more impertinent answer. To make a good meal with a good deal of money is the easiest thing in the world; any poor bungler could do as much; but a man of skill prepares a good meal with a little money.

MASTER JACQUE. A good meal with little money?

VALERE. Yes.

MASTER JACQUE [*to* VALERE]. Mr. Steward, you'll oblige us by letting us into this secret, and taking my place of cook! You are so meddlesome to make yourself factotum here.

HARPAGON. Hold your tongue. What must we have?

MASTER JACQUE. There's your factotum, sir, he will make you a good meal for a little money.
HARPAGON. You will answer me; answer me!
MASTER JACQUE. How many will there be of you at table?
HARPAGON. We shall be eight or ten: but you need only reckon on eight. When there's enough for eight, there's plenty for ten.
VALERE. Very right.
MASTER JACQUE. Well then, we must have four large soups, and five entrées. Soups—a bisque, partridge broth, fresh vegetable soup, duck and carrot soup; entrées—chicken fricassé, pigeon pie, sweet breads. . . .
HARPAGON. The devil! That's enough to feed the whole town.
MASTER JACQUE. A pyramid of roast meats—a whole loin of veal, 6 fat fowl, 6 large pheasants, 24 plump pigeons, 25 tender chickens, 11 succulent rabbits.
HARPAGON [*clapping his hand on his mouth*]. Ha! he's cooking me out of house and home.
MASTER JACQUE. —and the fishes—
HARPAGON. What, more? [*Clapping his hand again upon his mouth*]
VALERE [*to* MASTER JACQUE]. Has the master invited people to murder them by mere force of cramming? Ask the physicians whether there is anything more dangerous to men than eating to excess.
HARPAGON. He's right.
VALERE. Learn, Master Jacque, that a table overcharged with food is a cut-throat; if we are true friends of those we invite, frugality should reign through the whole repast; and that according to the saying of one of the ancients, "We must eat to live, and not live to eat."
HARPAGON. Excellently said! Come, and let me kiss you for that. It is the finest sentence I ever heard in my life. We must live to eat, and not eat to li— No, that is not it. How was it you said?
VALERE. That we must eat to live, and not live to eat.
HARPAGON [*to* MASTER JACQUE]. Right! [*to* VALERE] Who is the great man who said that?
VALERE. I don't recall his name at present.
HARPAGON. Write out those words for me; I'll have them engraved in letters of gold over the mantlepiece of my dining room.
VALERE. I won't fail. And as to your supper, you need only leave it to me. I'll order all as it should be.
HARPAGON. Do so.
MASTER JACQUE. So much the better; it shall be the less trouble for me.
HARPAGON [*to* VALERE]. There must be such things as people can't eat much of, and that cloy them immediately; a carrot stew, a pot pie well garnished with green chestnuts, a—

VALERE. Leave it to me.

HARPAGON. Now, Master Jacque, you must go clean my coach.

MASTER JACQUE. This is directed to the coachmen? [*He puts on his coachman's greatcoat.*]

HARPAGON. Yes, you must clean my coach, and get my horses ready to drive to the fair—

MASTER JACQUE. Your horses, sir? They're not in a condition for stirring anywhere. I won't tell you that they are down on their litter, for the poor beasts have none; you make them keep such austere fasts, that they are nothing but phantoms, or shadows of horses.

HARPAGON. Ill indeed; and yet they do nothing.

MASTER JACQUE. And because they do nothing, sir, must they eat nothing? 'Twould be much better for them, poor souls, to work a great deal, and eat accordingly. It breaks my very heart to see them grown so thin; for I have a tender affection for my horses. Not a day passes but I take the bread out of my own mouth to feed them.

HARPAGON. 'Twill be no great labor, just to go to the fair.

MASTER JACQUE. No, sir, I ha'n't the heart to drive them, 'twould go against my conscience to give them the whip, in the condition they are.

VALERE. Sir, I'll oblige our neighbor le Picard to drive them.

MASTER JACQUE. Good! I'd much rather they should die under the hand of another, than under mine.

VALERE. Master Jacque affects being considerate.

MASTER JACQUE. Mr. Steward affects being necessary.

HARPAGON. Have done.

MASTER JACQUE. Sir, I can't endure flatterers; and I see that all he does, his perpetual counting the bread and wine, the wood, the salt and candles, is for nothing but to curry favor with you. It makes me mad; and I am grieved to hear daily what people say of you; for I find I have a great fondness for you, in spite of myself; and, next to my horses, you are the person I love most.

HARPAGON. Master Jacque, what is it people say of me?

MASTER JACQUE. I'd tell you, sir, if I were sure it would not make you angry.

HARPAGON. No, not in the least.

MASTER JACQUE. Excuse me; I know very well I'll throw you in a passion.

HARPAGON. Not at all; on the contrary, I'm glad to hear what the world says of me.

MASTER JACQUE. Sir, since you will have it, I tell you frankly, that people everywhere make fun of you; they are never more delighted than when they tell stories without end of your stingy tricks. One says you have calendars printed on purpose, wherein you double the holy weeks and vigils, to take advantage of the fasts you oblige your folks to. Another, that you have a quarrel always ready to pick with your servants at Christmas, or when they leave you, to find an excuse to give them nothing. One tells a story that you ordered a cat of one of your neighbors to be cited in court, for having eaten the remains of a leg of mutton. Another, that you were caught one night stealing your horses' oats, and that your coachman, who was my predecessor, gave you, in the dark, a thorough thrashing. In short, do you want me to . . . ? You are the laughing stock of all the world, and you're never spoken of, but by the names of miser, skinflint, penny-pincher, and extortioner.

HARPAGON [*beating him*]. You're an idiot, a rascal, a scoundrel, and an impertinent puppy.

MASTER JACQUE. I told you that I should put you in a passion by telling you the truth.

HARPAGON. That will teach you to hold your tongue.

SCENE 6. MASTER JACQUE, VALERE.

VALERE [*laughing*]. As far as I can see, Master Jacque, your frankness was scurvily rewarded.

MASTER JACQUE. Mr. Upstart, 'tis none of your business; laugh at your own beating when you get it, and don't come here to laugh at mine.

VALERE. Dear Master Jacque, don't put yourself in a passion, I beseech you.

MASTER JACQUE [*aside*]. He is a sneak; I'll pretend to be brave, and if he's fool enough to be afraid of me, I'll drub him a little. [*Aloud*] Very well, Mr. Joker, I don't think it's funny; and if you provoke me further, it will be my turn to laugh.

[MASTER JACQUE *pushes* VALERE *to the farther end of the stage, threatening him.*]

VALERE. Gently!
MASTER JACQUE. How, gently? Suppose I've no mind to 't?
VALERE. Please!
MASTER JACQUE. You're impertinent.
VALERE. Monsieur Master Jacque.
MASTER JACQUE. There's no such person as Monsieur Master Jacque. If I take a stick, I shall tan your hide, with your importance.
VALERE. A stick! [VALERE *driving him back.*]
MASTER JACQUE. Yes, a stick.

VALERE. One stick! Do you know that I can tan your hide?
MASTER JACQUE. I don't doubt it.
VALERE. And that you are but a scrub of a cook?
MASTER JACQUE. I know it very well.
VALERE. And you will tan my hide, you said?
MASTER JACQUE. I was joking.
VALERE. And I've no relish for your joking. [*Cudgels him*] Learn that you are but a scurvy joker.
MASTER JACQUE [*alone*]. A plague on sincerity, 'tis a wretched trade. From today on I'll renounce it, and will speak truth no more. My master has the right to beat me. But as for this Mr. Steward, I'll be revenged on him, if I can.

SCENE 7. FROSINE, MARIANE, MASTER JACQUE.

FROSINE. Do you know, Master Jacque, whether your master is at home?
MASTER JACQUE. Yes, he is; I know it but too well.
FROSINE. Tell him, pray, that we are here.

SCENE 8. MARIANE, FROSINE.

MARIANE. Ah! Frosine, what a strange state I am in! If I may speak what I feel, I am dreading this interview!
FROSINE. But why! What is there to worry about?
MARIANE. Can't you imagine the feelings of a person just entering in view of the rack on which she is to be fixed?
FROSINE. I agree that Harpagon is not the sort of rack you would embrace to die happily; and I know by your expression that the young fop you were speaking of is still on your mind.
MARIANE. Yes, Frosine, I don't pretend to deny it; the respectful visits he paid us have made some impression on my mind.
FROSINE. But have you learnt who he is?
MARIANE. No, I don't know who he is; but I know he is formed to inspire love; if it could be my choice, I should take him before another; and he contributes not a little to the horrible dread of the husband I have to take.
FROSINE. Good lord! these young fops are all pleasant enough, and play their part very well; but most of them are poor as rats, and it would suit you much better to take an old man, who'll make you a good settlement. I admit that the senses won't find very much satisfaction.

Certain disgusting trifles must be endured with such a husband; but this won't last long. And, believe me, his death will soon put you in a position to take an attractive man who will compensate you for everything.

MARIANE. Bless me, Frosine, 'tis a strange affair, when, to be happy, we must wait for somebody's death; and death does not always comply with our wishes.

FROSINE. You joke sure! You marry him on the condition of making you a widow very soon; this ought to be in the marriage contract. 'Twould be downright impertinent of him not to die in three months. But here he comes in person.

MARIANE. Ah! Frosine! What a face!

SCENE 9. HARPAGON, MARIANE, FROSINE.

HARPAGON [*to* MARIANE]. Be not offended my fair one, if I approach you with my spectacles on. I know that your charms are visible enough by themselves, and that there is no need of spectacles to discover them; but 'tis with glasses we observe the stars; and I do maintain and guarantee that you are a star, but a star, the fairest star in the whole country of stars. Frosine, she answers not a word, nor does she betray the least joy at the sight of me.

FROSINE. She is yet all surprise. Maids are always ashamed of declaring, at first sight, what they have in their soul.

HARPAGON. You're right. [*To* MARIANE.] Here is my daughter, pretty dearie, to wait upon you.

SCENE 10. HARPAGON, ELISE, MARIANE, FROSINE.

MARIANE. I'm very late, madam, in paying this visit.

ELISE. You've done, madam, what I ought to have done, and 'twas my place to visit with you.

HARPAGON. You see what a great girl she is. Ill weeds always grow fast.

MARIANE [*aside to* FROSINE]. Abominable man!

HARPAGON [*to* FROSINE]. What says my pretty one?

FROSINE. That she finds you admirable.

HARPAGON. 'Tis too much honor you do me, adorable darling.

MARIANE [*aside*]. Beast!

HARPAGON. I'm very obliged to you for these sentiments.

MARIANE. I can't stand it any longer.

SCENE II. HARPAGON, MARIANE, ELISE, CLEANTE, VALERE, FROSINE, BRINDAVOINE.

HARPAGON. Here's my son, too, who comes to pay his respects.
MARIANE [*aside to* FROSINE]. Ah! Frosine, what an accident! 'Tis the very man I spoke to you about.
FROSINE [*to* MARIANE]. The adventure is wonderful.
HARPAGON. I see you're astonished to see me have children so big. But I shall soon be rid of them both.
CLEANTE [*to* MARIANE]. Madam, to tell you the truth, this is an adventure, which I by no means expected; and my father did not a little surprise me, when he told me just now of his intentions.
MARIANE. I can say the same. 'Tis an unforeseen accident, which has surprised me as much as you.
CLEANTE. It's true, madam, my father could not make a better choice; and that the honor of seeing you is a sensible joy to me; but for all this, I will not assure you that I'm glad of your becoming my stepmother. The compliment is too difficult for me, and this is a title, begging your pardon, which I don't wish you. This might appear rude in the eyes of certain people; but I am assured you will look on it as you should do. It is a marriage, madam, which I have an aversion to. I should tell you, with my father's permission, that if things depend on me, this match should not be made.
HARPAGON. A very impertinent compliment! What a confession to make to the lady!
MARIANE. If you should have an aversion to see me your stepmother, I should have no less to see you my stepson. If I were not forced by an absolute power, I give you my word, I would not consent to a match which causes you distress.
HARPAGON. She's right. A silly compliment deserves a silly reply. I ask your pardon for the impertinence of my son; he's a young puppy who doesn't yet know the consequence of what he says.
MARIANE. He has by no means been offensive to me; on the contrary he has done me a pleasure by explaining his real sentiments; and had he spoken in another manner, I should have esteemed him much less.
HARPAGON. Time will make him wiser, and you will see that he'll change his sentiments.
CLEANTE. No, sir, I'm not capable of changing them; and I most earnestly desire the lady to believe me so.
HARPAGON. Will you at least change the subject.
CLEANTE. Well, since you will have me talk in another way, I will put myself in the place of my father. I never saw anything in the world so charming I can conceive of; nothing equal to the happiness of

pleasing you; and the title of your husband is a glory, a felicity, which I would prefer to the destiny of the greatest princes on earth. Yes, madam, the happiness of possessing you is, in my view, the fairest of all fortunes. There is nothing I should not be capable of doing for so valuable a conquest, and the greatest of obstacles—

HARPAGON. Softly, son, if you please.

CLEANTE. 'Tis a compliment I make the lady for you.

HARPAGON. I've a tongue of my own, and don't need an interpreter. You are a star. . . . Valere, bring chairs.

FROSINE. No, 'twill be better to go directly to the fair, that we may return the sooner and have the whole time afterwards to entertain ourselves.

HARPAGON [to VALERE]. Have the horses hitched to the coach. Quickly, quickly.

SCENE 12. HARPAGON, MARIANE, ELISE, CLEANTE, VALERE, FROSINE.

HARPAGON [to MARIANE]. I beg your pardon, sweetheart, if I forgot to give you a small refreshment before you set out.

CLEANTE. I have provided one, father, and have ordered some plates of china oranges, sweet lemons, and preserves, which I have charged to your account.

HARPAGON [aside to VALERE]. Valere.

VALERE [to HARPAGON]. He's out of his wits.

CLEANTE. Don't you think this enough, father? The lady will be so good to excuse it.

MARIANE. 'Twas not necessary.

HARPAGON. Son . . .

CLEANTE. Did you ever see, madam, a diamond more lively than that my father has upon his finger?

MARIANE. Indeed it sparkles very much.

CLEANTE [taking the diamond off his father's finger and giving it to MARIANE]. You should look on it a little nearer.

MARIANE. It is very fine, indeed; it casts a great luster.

CLEANTE [steps before MARIANE, who would restore it]. Madam, 'tis in hands too beautiful. My father makes it a gift to you.

HARPAGON. Me?

CLEANTE. Is it not true, sir, that you wish the lady should keep it for your sake?

HARPAGON [aside to his son]. What?

CLEANTE [to MARIANE]. He tells me that I should force you to accept it.

MARIANE. I would not—

CLEANTE [*hindering* MARIANE *from returning it*]. No, I tell you, it will offend him.
MARIANE. —Please.
CLEANTE. By no means.
HARPAGON [*aside*]. Valere. . . .
CLEANTE. He is perfectly shocked at your refusal.
HARPAGON [*low to his son*]. Ah, traitor!
CLEANTE [*to* MARIANE]. You see he's losing his patience.
HARPAGON [*aside to his son, threatening him*]. Villain!
CLEANTE. It is not my fault, father; I do all I can to oblige her to keep it.
HARPAGON [*aside to his son in a rage*]. Scoundrel!
CLEANTE. You are the cause, madam, of my father's quarreling with me.
HARPAGON [*aside to his son with the same sour looks*]. Rascal!
CLEANTE [*to* MARIANE]. For goodness sake, madam, resist no longer, you'll throw him into fits.
FROSINE [*to* MARIANE]. Good lord! Keep the ring, since the gentleman will have it so.
MARIANE [*to* HARPAGON]. I shall keep it for the present, and shall take another opportunity to restore it.

SCENE 13. HARPAGON, MARIANE, ELISE, CLEANTE, VALERE, FROSINE, BRINDAVOINE.

BRINDAVOINE. Sir, here's a man wants to speak with you.
HARPAGON. Tell him I'm busy.
BRINDAVOINE. He says he brings you some money.
HARPAGON [*to* MARIANE]. I beg your pardon. I shall be back presently.

SCENE 14. HARPAGON, MARIANE, ELISE, CLEANTE, VALERE, FROSINE, LA MERLUCHE.

LA MERLUCHE [*comes running, and throws* HARPAGON *down*]. Sir—
HARPAGON. Oh! I'm killed!
CLEANTE. What's the matter, father? Have you hurt yourself?
HARPAGON. The rascal has certainly been paid by my debtors to break my neck.
VALERE [*to* HARPAGON]. There's no harm done—
LA MERLUCHE [*to* HARPAGON]. Sir, I beg your pardon, I thought I did right to hurry.
HARPAGON. What do you come here for, hang-dog?
LA MERLUCHE. To tell you that both your horses are without shoes.

HARPAGON. Take them to the smith then quickly.
CLEANTE. While we wait for their shoeing, I'll do the honors of the house, sir; in your place, let the refreshments be served.

SCENE 15. HARPAGON, VALERE.

HARPAGON. Valere, keep an eye a little upon all this, and take care to save me as much as you can, that we may send it back to the merchants.
VALERE. Rest assured!
HARPAGON. O impertinent son! have you a mind to ruin me?

ACT FOUR

SCENE 1. CLEANTE, MARIANE, ELISE, FROSINE.

ELISE. Madam, my brother has disclosed to me the passion he has for you. I assure you, your adventure has all my sympathy.
CLEANTE. There's not one suspicious person around now, and we can speak with freedom.
FROSINE. You both are unlucky people, not to have told me of your affair before all this. I certainly would not have carried matters as far as they are.
CLEANTE. What would you have me do? My evil destiny would have it so. But, fair Mariane, what is your decision?
MARIANE. Am I in a position of making decisions? Dependent as I am, can I do anything but hope?
CLEANTE. Have I no support in your heart but bare hope? No pity? No kindness? No active affection?
MARIANE. What can I say to you? Put yourself in my place, and see what I can do. But don't ask anything of me, but what honor and decency will permit.
CLEANTE. Honor and decency! Of what use are these peevish sentiments of rigorous honor and scrupulous decency.
MARIANE. But what would you have me do? Though I could get over several scruples to which our sex is obliged, I've a regard for my mother. She brought me up with an extreme tenderness; I can't bring myself to cause her any grief. Treat, transact the business with her. Employ all your efforts to gain her approval; you may do and

say everything you please, I give you liberty; and if it only depends on my declaring in your favor, I readily consent to disclose to her my true feelings.

CLEANTE. Frosine, dear Frosine, would you help us?

FROSINE. Need you ask it? I'd do it with all my soul. You know I am humane enough, and when I see people who love one another truly and honorably. But what could we do in this case?

CLEANTE. Think a little. I beg you.

MARIANE. Show us some escape.

ELISE. Trump up some invention to unravel what you have done.

FROSINE [*to* MARIANE]. 'Tis difficult enough. As to your mother, she's not altogether unreasonable, and perhaps one might make her transfer to the son the gift she intended for the father. [*To* CLEANTE] But the trouble is, that your father is your father.

CLEANTE. That's very true. [*To* MARIANE] My fair Mariane, let us win over your mother. Make use of all those charms which Heaven has placed in your eyes and lips.

MARIANE. I'll do all I can.

SCENE 2. HARPAGON, CLEANTE, MARIANE, ELISE, FROSINE.

HARPAGON [*aside and unseen*]. My son kisses the hand of his intended stepmother, and she does not much object. Can there be something in this?

ELISE. Here comes father.

HARPAGON. The coach is quite ready; you may leave when you please.

CLEANTE. Since you're not going, I'll attend them myself.

HARPAGON. No, stay. They may go very well alone; I need you.

SCENE 3. HARPAGON, CLEANTE.

HARPAGON. Well, setting aside the consideration of a stepmother, what do you think of her?

CLEANTE. What do I think of her?

HARPAGON. Yes, of her manner, her build, her beauty, her wit?

CLEANTE. So so.

HARPAGON. No, speak out.

CLEANTE. To be frank, father, I did not find her what I once thought her. Her manner is quite flirtatious, her build awkward enough, her beauty very mediocre, and her wit most common. Don't think, father, that I say this to make you dislike her, for as a stepmother, I like her as well as another.

HARPAGON. And yet just now you told her—

CLEANTE. I did pay some compliments to her in your name, but 'twas just to please you.

HARPAGON. So, you do not have the least inclination for her?

CLEANTE. I? not at all.

HARPAGON. Well. . . . I'm sorry for it. I was reflecting, when I saw her here, upon my age; and was thinking that people would find fault with my marrying a young girl. This consideration almost made me change my mind; and had you not such an aversion to her, I would have given her to you.

CLEANTE. To me?

HARPAGON. To you.

CLEANTE. In marriage?

HARPAGON. In marriage.

CLEANTE. Listen, it's true she's not much to my taste. But to oblige you, father, I'll marry her, if you please.

HARPAGON. I? I'm more reasonable than you think; I won't force you.

CLEANTE. Excuse me, I'll force myself out of respect to you.

HARPAGON. No, no, marriage can never be happy where there is no inclination for love.

CLEANTE. But, father, they say that love is often the fruit of marriage.

HARPAGON. No, that ought not to be risked by the man; and there are embarrassing consequences, to which I wouldn't expose you; had you the least inclination for her, I would have forced you to marry her, in my stead. But as this is not the case, I shall have to marry her myself.

CLEANTE. Well, father, since matters have come to this, I must reveal my heart to you; I must let you into this secret of ours. The truth is, I've been in love with Mariane from the day I saw her in the park; I would have asked her of you for a wife, but the declaration of your sentiments, and the fear of displeasing you, kept me from it.

HARPAGON. Did you visit her?

CLEANTE. Yes, father.

HARPAGON. Very often?

CLEANTE. Often enough, considering the short time I've known her.

HARPAGON. Did she receive you well?

CLEANTE. Very well, but without knowing who I was; that was the occasion of Mariane's surprise just now.

HARPAGON. Did you declare your inclination to her, and your plan to marry her?

CLEANTE. Most certainly; and I even made some faint overtures to her mother.
HARPAGON. Did she listen to your proposals concerning her daughter?
CLEANTE. Yes, very civilly.
HARPAGON. And did the daughter sympathize with your love?
CLEANTE. If I may believe appearances, father, she has some kindness for me.
HARPAGON. I'm very glad to have learnt the secret; that is exactly what I was after. Very well, son, do you know what you must do? You must abandon your love; for the person I have chosen for myself; and marry the person I have assigned you.
CLEANTE. So, father, that is how you toy with me? Well, since matters have come to that, I declare that I will not abandon the love I have for Mariane; and that there is no extremity to which I will not go to defeat you in this; and if you have the consent of a mother on your side, I shall have other advantages, perhaps, on mine.
HARPAGON. Am I not your father? And don't you owe me respect?
CLEANTE. These are not things in which children must pay deference to their fathers; and love respects no one.
HARPAGON. I'll make you respect me with my stick.
CLEANTE. All your threats won't help.
HARPAGON. Will you renounce Mariane?
CLEANTE. Not at all.
HARPAGON. Give me that stick.

SCENE 4. HARPAGON, CLEANTE, MASTER JACQUE.

MASTER JACQUE. Hold! hold! hold gentlemen! What's this? What d'you mean?
CLEANTE. I don't care anymore.
MASTER JACQUE [*to* CLEANTE]. What, to your father?
HARPAGON. Let me at him!
MASTER JACQUE [*to* HARPAGON]. What, to your son? It's not me you're dealing with.
HARPAGON. I'll make you judge, Master Jacque, in this affair to prove how right I am.
MASTER JACQUE. Agreed. [*To* CLEANTE] Step back a little.
HARPAGON. You know I love a girl whom I have a mind to marry; and this rascal has the impudence to love the same person, and to propose to her in spite of me.
MASTER JACQUE. Ah! He's certainly wrong.
HARPAGON. Is't not a horrid thing, for a son to compete with his father?

MASTER JACQUE. You're right. Let me speak to him, but stay you there.
CLEANTE [*to* MASTER JACQUE, *who is coming up to him*]. Well, since he wants you to be the judge, I don't refuse it; 'tis nothing to me who it is.
MASTER JACQUE. 'Tis a great honor you do me.
CLEANTE. I am in love with a young lady, who tenderly accepted the offer of my heart; but my father takes it into his head to demand her for a wife.
MASTER JACQUE. He's absolutely wrong.
CLEANTE. Is he not ashamed, at his age, to think of marriage? Should he not leave this business to young people?
MASTER JACQUE. You're right, he must be joking. Let me speak two words with him. [*He returns to* HARPAGON.] Well, your son is not so difficult as you say; he'll listen to reason. He knows the respect he owes you; and he was only carried away by the first heat of passion; he'll by no means refuse to submit to anything you please, provided you would treat him better than you do and give him some person in marriage with whom he'll be satisfied.
HARPAGON. Oh! tell him, Master Jacque, that he may have anything from me, and that, Mariane excepted, I give him the liberty of choosing whom he pleases.
MASTER JACQUE. I'll take care of it. [*To* CLEANTE] Well, your father is not so unreasonable as you make him; and only your fierceness threw him into a passion; he will be very glad to grant you your wishes, provided you pay him the respect and submission that a son owes to his father.
CLEANTE. Ah! Master Jacque, tell him that if he grants me Mariane, he shall always find me the most submissive of sons and that I shall never do anything but according to his pleasure.
MASTER JACQUE [*to* HARPAGON]. 'Tis done; he consents to what you say.
HARPAGON. This is the happiest thing in the world.
MASTER JACQUE [*to* CLEANTE]. It's settled; he's satisfied with your promises.
CLEANTE. Heaven be praised.
MASTER JACQUE. Gentlemen, your agreement is completed; and you were just at daggers-drawn, for want of understanding one another.
CLEANTE. Master Jacque, I shall be obliged to you all my life.
MASTER JACQUE. There's no reason, sir.
HARPAGON. You have done me a favor, Master Jacque, and it deserves a reward.

[HARPAGON *fumbling in his pocket.* MASTER JACQUE *holds out his hand, but* HARPAGON *only pulls out his handkerchief.*]

Go, I shall remember it, I assure you.
MASTER JACQUE. I kiss your hand, sir.

SCENE 5. HARPAGON, CLEANTE.

CLEANTE. I ask your pardon, father, for the fit of temper I threw.
HARPAGON. 'Tis nothing.
CLEANTE. I assure you it gives me all the concern in the world.
HARPAGON. And it gives me all the joy in the world, to see you so reasonable.
CLEANTE. What kindness to forget my fault so soon!
HARPAGON. A father soon forgets the faults of children, when they return to their duty.
CLEANTE. I promise you, father, that I shall remember your kindness, even to my grave.
HARPAGON. And I promise you, there's nothing you mayn't obtain of me.
CLEANTE. Ah! father, I ask nothing more of you. You gave me everything when you gave me Mariane.
HARPAGON. Who talks of giving you Mariane?
CLEANTE. You, father.
HARPAGON. I?
CLEANTE. Most certainly.
HARPAGON. Did you not renounce her?
CLEANTE. I renounce her?
HARPAGON. Yes.
CLEANTE. Not at all.
HARPAGON. Haven't you given up all claims to her?
CLEANTE. On the contrary, I'm more determined than ever.
HARPAGON. What, rascal, again?
CLEANTE. Nothing can change me.
HARPAGON. I forbid you ever seeing me again.
CLEANTE. Do what you please.
HARPAGON. Out of my sight!
CLEANTE. The sooner the better.
HARPAGON. I abandon you.
CLEANTE. Abandon me.
HARPAGON. I renounce you for my son.
CLEANTE. Be it so.
HARPAGON. I disinherit you.
CLEANTE. What you will.

HARPAGON. I give you my curse.
CLEANTE. Spare me your gifts.

SCENE 6. CLEANTE, LA FLECHE.

LA FLECHE [*coming out of the garden with a casket*]. Ah! sir, I find you in the nick of time.
CLEANTE. What's this?
LA FLECHE. Follow me, I tell you, we're all right.
CLEANTE. What?
LA FLECHE. Here's your business.
CLEANTE. What?
LA FLECHE. I've had an eye on't all day.
CLEANTE. What is it?
LA FLECHE. Your father's cashbox, I've pinched it.
CLEANTE. How have you done it?
LA FLECHE. You shall know all; let's get away.

SCENE 7.

HARPAGON [*from the garden, crying thieves*]. Thieves, thieves, murder, assassination!! Justice, just Heaven! I'm undone, I'm murdered, they've cut my throat, they've stolen my money. My poor money, my poor money, my dear friend, they've bereaved me of you. Without you, 'tis impossible to live. I die, I'm dead, I'm buried. Is there nobody will bring me to life again, and give me back my dear money, or tell me who has taken it? Who can it be? Where does he hide himself? What shall I do to find him? Is he there? Is he there? Who's this? [*To himself, laying hold of his own arm*] 'Tis myself. My mind's disturbed; and I don't know where I am, who I am, or what I do. Whoever did it must have picked the opportunity with a great deal of care; when I was talking to my son. I'll go demand justice, and order my whole family to be put to the torture; my maids, my servants, my son, my daughter, and myself, too. What a crowd! I can't look on anybody without suspicion, they all look like thieves. Heh! what are they talking about? Of him that robbed me? What noise is up there? Is't my thief that's there? For Heaven's sake, if you know my thief, you tell me. Is he not hiding there among you? They all stare at me, and laugh in my face. You are all a part of this crime no doubt. Here, quick, commissaries, police, provosts, judges, racks, gallows, and hangmen. I'll hang all the world; and if I don't find my money again, I'll hang myself afterwards.

ACT FIVE

SCENE 1. HARPAGON, A COMMISSARY.

COMMISSARY. Let me alone, thank Heaven I know my business. 'Tis not the first time that I've investigated a theft; and I wish that I had as many thousand franc bags as I have hanged people.
HARPAGON. There isn't a magistrate who shouldn't be eager to take this case in hand; and if they don't find me my money, I'll demand justice on justice itself.
COMMISSARY. We must follow all the procedures as prescribed by the law. You say that there was in this cashbox—
HARPAGON. Thirty thousand francs.
COMMISSARY. Thirty thousand francs.
HARPAGON [*weeping*]. Thirty thousand francs.
COMMISSARY. A considerable robbery.
HARPAGON. There's no punishment great enough for the enormity of this crime; if it remains unpunished, nothing sacred will ever more be safe.
COMMISSARY. In what coin was the sum?
HARPAGON. In gold pieces, and certified silver.
COMMISSARY. Whom do you suspect?
HARPAGON. Everyone. I want you to arrest the whole city and suburbs.
COMMISSARY. You must not scare people too much; but fish for evidence softly, to proceed afterwards with more vigor.

SCENE 2. HARPAGON, COMMISSARY, MASTER JACQUE.

MASTER JACQUE [*at the end of the stage, turning back to the door he came out of*]. I shall be back. Cut his throat immediately; singe his feet, put him into boiling water, and hang him from the ceiling.
HARPAGON. Who? He that robbed me? Who? Who? Tell me who?
MASTER JACQUE. I speak of a sucking pig, which your steward has just sent me, and I'll prepare him for you after my own recipe.

HARPAGON. That's not the question. You must speak to this gentleman about something else.

COMMISSARY. Don't be frightened. I'm not a man who will scandalize you.

MASTER JACQUE. Is the gentleman to dine with you?

COMMISSARY. My dear friend, you must hide nothing from your master.

MASTER JACQUE. If I don't make you as good a supper as I would, 'tis the fault of your Mr. Steward, who has clipped my wings with the scissors of his economy.

HARPAGON. Traitor, we're concerned about other matters than supper; and I want the money they've taken from me.

MASTER JACQUE. Have they taken your money?

HARPAGON. Yes, scoundrel; and I'll have you hanged if you do not give it back.

COMMISSARY. My God, don't intimidate him. [*To* HARPAGON] I see, by the look of him, he's an honest fellow; and that, without being sent to gaol, he'll tell all you want to know. Yes, friend, if you confess, no harm shall come to you, and you shall be properly rewarded by your master. They've stolen his money from him today, and you must know something about it?

MASTER JACQUE [*aside*]. Exactly what I need to be revenged on that steward.

HARPAGON. What are you mumbling about?

COMMISSARY. Let him alone. He's going to satisfy you; I told you he was an honest fellow.

MASTER JACQUE. Sir, do you want me to speak out? I believe 'tis your Mr. Steward who has done this business.

HARPAGON. What, Valere?

MASTER JACQUE. Yes.

HARPAGON. He who appears so trustworthy?

MASTER JACQUE. The very same. I believe 'tis he that has robbed you.

HARPAGON. On what grounds do you believe so?

MASTER JACQUE. On what grounds?

HARPAGON. Yes.

MASTER JACQUE. I believe it—because I do believe it.

COMMISSARY. You must produce the evidence you know.

HARPAGON. Did you see him hovering about the place where I had put my money?

MASTER JACQUE. Yes, indeed. Where was your money?

HARPAGON. In the garden.

MASTER JACQUE. Exactly; I saw him sneaking about the garden. And what was this money in?

HARPAGON. In a cashbox.
MASTER JACQUE. The very thing. I saw him with a cashbox.
HARPAGON. And how was this cashbox made? I shall easily see whether it is mine.
MASTER JACQUE. How was it made?
HARPAGON. Yes.
MASTER JACQUE. It was made—it was made like a cashbox.
COMMISSARY. You must illuminate it a little.
MASTER JACQUE. It was a large cashbox.
HARPAGON. The one they stole from me was small.
MASTER JACQUE. Why, yes, it is small if you take it in that way; but I call it large for what it contains.
COMMISSARY. What color is it?
MASTER JACQUE. What color?
COMMISSARY. Yes.
MASTER JACQUE. A color—'Tis of a certain color, there—Could you not help me out?
HARPAGON. Heh?
MASTER JACQUE. Isn't it red?
HARPAGON. No, gray.
MASTER JACQUE. Why, yes, gray-red; that's what I meant to say.
HARPAGON. There's no doubt. That's certainly it. Write, sir, write down his testimony. Heavens! Whom to trust here! After this I believe that I could rob myself.
MASTER JACQUE [*to* HARPAGON]. Here he comes sir. Don't tell him that I told you this.

SCENE 3. HARPAGON, VALERE, COMMISSARY, MASTER JACQUE.

HARPAGON. Here, come and confess the blackest, the most horrible crime ever committed.
VALERE. What do y' mean, sir?
HARPAGON. What, traitor, not blush at your crime?
VALERE. What crime are you speaking of?
HARPAGON. Of what crime am I speaking, scoundrel, as if you did not know. You pretend to deny it. The business is out, and they have just now told me everything. How could you abuse my kindness this way and introduce yourself into my house to betray me.
VALERE. Sir, since everything has been discovered, I won't try to deny it.
MASTER JACQUE. Oh! hoh! Could I have invented the truth without knowing it!
VALERE. It was my intention to speak to you about it. And I was wait-

ing for a favorable opportunity. But, I implore you not to ruffle yourself and to hear my reasons.

HARPAGON. And what reasons can you give me, infamous thief?

VALERE. Sir, I deserve no such name. 'Tis true, I have committed an offense against you. But, when you have heard me, you'll see the harm is not so great as you make it.

HARPAGON. The harm not so great as I make it? What! my blood, my bowels, villain?

VALERE. Your blood, sir, is not fallen into bad hands. I'm of a rank not to do it injury; there's nothing in all this, but what I can well make amends for.

HARPAGON. So you shall; and you restore to me what you have stolen from me. But, tell me, what moved you to this action?

VALERE. Do you ask me?

HARPAGON. Yes, I do ask you.

VALERE. A god who carries the excuse for everything he makes us do. Love.

HARPAGON. Love!

VALERE. Yes.

HARPAGON. Fine love, fine love, ah yes! Love of my gold.

VALERE. No, sir, your riches have dazzled me; and I vow never to demand any of your wealth, provided you would leave me in possession of what I already have.

HARPAGON. I will not do it, what insolence, to desire to keep what he has robbed me of.

VALERE. Do you call this robbery?

HARPAGON. Do I call it robbery? A treasure such as this?

VALERE. 'Tis a treasure, 'tis true, and the most precious one you have. On my knees I beg for this most charming treasure; and nothing but death can separate us.

HARPAGON. He is absolutely bewitched with my money, but I'll file proper charges and justice will make you pay for it.

VALERE. I am ready to suffer all the violence you please; but I beg of you, at least to believe, that 'tis only me you are to accuse; and that your daughter is not, in the least, to blame in all this.

HARPAGON. 'Twould be very strange had my daughter been accomplice in such a crime. But confess whither you've carried my treasure.

VALERE. I? I have not carried it anywhere, 'tis still at home.

HARPAGON [*aloud*]. It hasn't gone from the house?

VALERE. No, sir.

HARPAGON. Heh, tell me, have you not been dabbling?

VALERE. I dabbling? Ah! You wrong us both; I burn, but purely and respectfully.

HARPAGON [*aside*]. Burn for my cashbox!
VALERE. All my desires were limited to the pleasure of sight; and nothing criminal has profaned the love those fair eyes have inspired me with.
HARPAGON [*aside*]. The fair eyes of my cashbox!
VALERE. Dame Claude knows the whole truth and she can bear witness.
HARPAGON. What! my maid an accomplice in the affair?
VALERE. Yes, sir, she was witness to our engagement; she assisted me in persuading your daughter to give me her pledge, and receive mine.
HARPAGON. Why do you bring my daughter into this?
VALERE. I say, sir, that I had all the difficulty in the world to bring her modesty to consent to my love.
HARPAGON. The modesty of whom?
VALERE. Of your daughter; yesterday she signed a marriage contract.
HARPAGON. My daughter signed a marriage contract?
VALERE. Yes, sir, as I signed one to her.
HARPAGON. O Heavens! Another disaster!
MASTER JACQUE [*to the* COMMISSARY]. Write, sir, write.
HARPAGON. Misfortune upon misfortune! [*To the* COMMISSARY] Come, sir, do your duty, and indict him as a felon, and a seducer.
MASTER JACQUE. As a felon and a seducer.
VALERE. These names don't belong to me; and when you know who I am—

SCENE 4. HARPAGON, ELISE, MARIANE, VALERE, FROSINE, MASTER JACQUE, COMMISSARY.

HARPAGON. Ah? Shameless child! Daughter unworthy of such a father! Is it thus you put in practice the lessons I've given you? Do you engage yourself to an infamous thief, without my consent? But you shall be well rewarded, both of you. [*To* ELISE] Four strong walls shall guarantee me for your conduct; [*to* VALERE] and a good gallows shall do justice to your impudence.
VALERE. Your passion will not judge me; and they'll hear me, at least before they condemn me.
HARPAGON. I was wrong to say a gallows, you shall be broken alive on the wheel.
ELISE [*kneeling to her father*]. Ah! father—
MASTER JACQUE [*aside*]. He'll pay me every blow of that stick.
ELISE. Don't be carried away by the first impulse of your passion; but give yourself time to consider what you do. Take the pains of looking more closely into the person you're so enraged at. He's quite

another man than he appears to you; and you will find it less strange I should have given myself to him, when you know that without him you would have lost me for ever. Yes, father, 'tis he saved me from the water; and to him you owe the life of that very daughter, who—

HARPAGON. It had been much better for me, had he let you drown, than to do what he has done.

ELISE. I implore you, father, by your paternal love—

HARPAGON. No, no, I won't hear anything; and justice must take its course.

FROSINE [*aside*]. What an embarrassing incident!

SCENE 5. ANSELME, HARPAGON, ELISE, MARIANE, FROSINE, VALERE, COMMISSARY, MASTER JACQUE.

ANSELME. What's the matter here, Signor Harpagon? You are very much ruffled, I see.

HARPAGON. Ah! Signor Anselme, I am the most unfortunate of men; I'm assassinated in my fortune, I'm assassinated in my honor; and there's a traitor, a villain, who has sneaked himself into my family under the title of servant, to rob me of my money and to seduce my daughter.

VALERE. Who cares about your money, that you make such a fuss about?

HARPAGON. Yes, they've made each other a promise of marriage. This affront concerns you, Signor Anselme; and you ought to prosecute him at your own expense.

ANSELME. It is not my way to force myself upon anybody, or make any pretenses to a heart which has already bestowed itself. But as to your interests, I'm ready to support them as if they were my own.

HARPAGON. This gentleman is a very honest Commissary, he'll omit nothing which concerns the duty of his office. [*To the* COMMISSARY, *pointing to* VALERE] Charge him, sir, and make things very criminal.

VALERE. I don't see what crime you can make of the love I have for your daughter; and when you know who I am—

HARPAGON. I don't care who you are; the world nowadays is full of imposters, who take advantage of the first important name that pops into their heads.

VALERE. I have a heart too noble to claim anything which does not belong to me; all Naples can bear witness of my birth.

ANSELME. Soft and fair, sir, soft and fair, take care what you are going to say. You speak before a person to whom all Naples is known, and who can easily see through your story.

VALERE. If you know Naples, you know who Don Thomas d'Alburcy was.

ANSELME. I know him, and few people knew him better than I.

HARPAGON. I care not a bit for your Don Thomas; or your Don Martins. [*Seeing two candles burning, he blows out one.*]

ANSELME. Let him speak; we shall see what he'll say of him.

VALERE. I would say, that he was my father.

ANSELME. He?

VALERE. Yes.

ANSELME. Come, come; find some other story that may succeed better for you; and don't try to save yourself by this piece of imposture.

VALERE. It is no imposture; and I claim nothing here, that I cannot justify.

ANSELME. How dare you call yourself son of Don Thomas d'Alburcy?

VALERE. Yes, I dare; and I am ready to maintain this truth against any person whatsoever.

ANSELME. His audacity is marvelous. Know, then, to your confusion, that it is sixteen years ago at least that the person you speak of was lost at sea with his wife and children. He tried to save their lives from the cruel persecutions which accompanied the troubles at Naples and caused the exile of many noble families.

VALERE. Yes. But know to your confusion that his son, with a servant, was saved from that shipwreck by a Spanish vessel; and that this son is the person who speaks to you. The captain of this vessel brought me up as his own son; and the army has been my employment ever since I was capable. I have learnt recently that my father was not dead; passing through Paris in search of him, an adventure sent by Heaven brought me to the sight of the charming Elise; and this sight made me slave to her beauty. The violence of my love, and the severities of her father, made me stay to introduce myself into his house and send the servant in search of my parents.

ANSELME. But what evidence may assure us that this is not a fable built upon a truth?

VALERE. The Spanish captain; a ruby seal which belonged to my father; an agate bracelet which my mother put on my arm; and old Pedro, the servant who was saved with me.

MARIANE. I myself can answer here for what you've said, that you do not impose upon us; and everything you say proves clearly that you are my brother.

VALERE. You are my sister?

MARIANE. Yes, my heart was touched from the moment you opened your mouth; and our mother who will be overjoyed at sight of you, has a thousand times told me of the misfortunes of our family. Heaven so willed that we not perish in that shipwreck; but it saved our lives at the expense of our liberty; it was corsairs took up my mother and myself from the wreck of our vessel. After ten years of slavery, a lucky accident gave us our liberty, and we returned to Naples, where we found all our property sold and no news of our father. We took passage for Genoa, whither my mother went to pick up the remains of a family estate that had been torn to pieces; then flying from the barbarous injustice of her relations, she came to Paris, where she has lived in perpetual ailing ever since.

ANSELME. Oh Heaven! How great are the miracles of thy power! Embrace me, my children, and mix your joys with those of your father!

VALERE. You are our father?

MARIANE. Is it you our mother wept for.

ANSELME. Yes, my daughter, yes, my son, I am Don Thomas d'Alburcy, whom Heaven saved from the waves, with all the money he had with him; having thought you all dead for more than sixteen years, I settled myself here, under the name of Anselme, and I endeavored to forget that other name, which caused me so many crosses.

HARPAGON [*to* ANSELME]. Is that your son?

ANSELME. Yes.

HARPAGON. I shall make you pay me the thirty thousand francs he has robbed me of.

ANSELME. He robbed you!

HARPAGON. The very same.

VALERE. Who told you so?

HARPAGON. Master Jacque.

VALERE. Did you tell him so?

MASTER JACQUE. You see that I say nothing.

HARPAGON. Yes. There's a commissary who has taken down his testimony.

VALERE. Can you think me capable of so base an action?

HARPAGON. Capable, or not capable, I want my money.

SCENE 6. HARPAGON, ANSELME, ELISE, MARIANE, CLEANTE, VALERE, FROSINE, COMMISSARY, MASTER JACQUE, LA FLECHE.

CLEANTE. Father! Don't torment yourself, accuse nobody. I've had news of your cashbox; and I come to tell you that your money shall be restored you, if you will let me marry Mariane.

HARPAGON. Where is it?

CLEANTE. Never mind. 'Tis in a place I can answer for; but everything depends on me alone. Now you have your choice, either to give me Mariane or lose your cashbox.

HARPAGON. Have they taken nothing out of it?

CLEANTE. Nothing at all. What's your decision? Do you consent to our marriage?

MARIANE [*to* CLEANTE]. But this consent alone is not sufficient; because Heaven, with a brother, as you see [*pointing to* VALERE], has restored me a father [*pointing to* ANSELME], from whom you are to obtain me.

ANSELME. Heaven, my children, has not restored me to you to oppose your desires. Signor Harpagon, you know very well that the choice of a young person will fall upon the son, sooner than upon the father. Come, don't force us to tell you what is embarrassing to hear. Consent, as I do, to this double marriage.

HARPAGON. Before I decide anything, I must see my cashbox.

CLEANTE. You shall see it safe and sound.

HARPAGON. I have no money to give my children any dowry.

ANSELME. Well, I have enough for them, let not that worry you.

HARPAGON. You'll oblige yourself to pay the whole expense of these two marriages?

ANSELME. Yes, I do oblige myself. Are you satisfied?

HARPAGON. Yes, provided you will order me new clothes for the wedding.

ANSELME. Agreed. Come, let's enjoy this happy day with your mother.

COMMISSARY. Hold, gentlemen, hold. Who pays me for my writings.

HARPAGON. We have nothing to do with your writings.

COMMISSARY. Indeed! But I won't do them for nothing.

HARPAGON [*pointing to* MASTER JACQUE]. There's a fellow I'll give you to hang for payment.

MASTER JACQUE. Ah! What must one do then? They beat me for speaking truth; and they would hang me for lying.

ANSELME. Signor Harpagon, we must forgive him this piece of imposture.

HARPAGON. You'll pay the Commissary then.

ANSELME. Done. Off to your mother's, this joy will mend her.

HARPAGON. Ah, my cashbox, my joy!

END

ROMEO

AND

JULIET

by WILLIAM SHAKESPEARE

ROMEO AND JULIET From *Shakespeare: The Complete Works* edited by G. B. Harrison, copyright, 1948, 1952, by Harcourt Brace Jovanovich, Inc. and reprinted with their permission.

Photos © 1968 Paramount Pictures Corporation. A Franco Zeffirelli Production.

Recording of this text (with Albert Finney and Claire Bloom) available through Caedmon Records, Inc., 505 Eighth Avenue, New York, N.Y. 10018.

A large proportion of the world's literature consists of love stories, and of these Shakespeare's *Romeo and Juliet*, written around 1594, is probably the most famous. The play's popularity is not difficult to understand for the two young people not only fall passionately in love with one another but, because their fathers are sworn enemies, they must overcome a formidable obstacle in order to achieve their desired union. It is a very old story, and in spite of its understandable popularity it is hard to tell in a fresh and convincing manner. But Shakespeare was not content simply to recount this basic rhythm of life. A poem, *The Tragical History of Romeus and Juliet* by Arthur Brooke, published in 1562, which was Shakespeare's source, had done just that, but the poem is the skeleton that Shakespeare covered with flesh.

The most obvious improvements are the characters: Shakespeare's are vital, passionate human beings. Their vitality is matched by the tempo of the play, which moves with the impetuosity of the lovers' passion. Brooke's poem covers nine months; Shakespeare compressed his story into five days, producing a sense of urgency appropriate to the impatience of youth. And always there is the magic of the Shakespearean language charged with unprecedented energy and beauty.

Shakespeare was not acquainted with the word "psychology," which did not enter the English language until a hundred years after he had written *Romeo and Juliet*. But if by psychology we mean the careful scrutiny and analysis of the psyche, or soul, Shakespeare was the greatest psychological writer who ever lived. In this play which does not search into the complexities of the human psyche as deeply as do his later tragedies, each character is a distinct individual with the irrational impulses, the follies, and the strengths that we see in contemporary man. Shakespeare, inexhaustible in his creativity, introduces a wide world of characters. There are the fathers, Capulet and Montague, determined to continue an absurd feud regardless of the consequences. There is the alluring young Juliet whose extreme youth—she is not yet 14—may strain modern credibility, although the young matured early in Shakespeare's day. And although Romeo, when he first appears, is obviously suffering from an appalling attack of first-love, his character deepens into determination and maturity as the play develops. Even insignificant characters like the servants who open the play but spend less than ten minutes on the stage have a sort of blundering charm, although their acts are cowardly and their punning salacious. Other minor characters like the volatile Mercutio and the bawdy old Nurse, whose language and stories seem so indelicate for the chaste ears of Juliet, come to spectacular life in a good performance or a careful reading.

This is a play about youth and age, written by a man who himself was just 30. As age persists in its folly, youth tries to escape through love. The violence that results from the conflict of these forces quickly mounts to tragic proportions.

But even with such abundance of characters and so skillfully organized a plot, *Romeo and Juliet* would not be the masterpiece it is if it were not for the richness of the language. The basic situation of the play is contrast, and contrasts, particularly of lightness and darkness, abound, supported by a rhetorical device that expresses the fundamental predicament in the lives of the two lovers. This device—linked opposites (*oxymoron*)—appears with significant frequency in such phrases as "loving hate," "heavy lightness," "cold fire," and "sick health." This fusing of opposites conveys a meaning that Shakespeare clearly intended to dominate the play. It is implicit in the struggle between youth and age, in opposing versions of human love offered, in the fact that love between Romeo and Juliet flourishes in spite of the enmity of their fathers, even in the accident that to find love Romeo goes to the house of his enemy. The final love scene is the culminating oxymoron of the play, for it takes place in the house of death, the tomb.

In the prologue Shakespeare speaks of "a pair of star-crossed lovers," suggesting the opinion widely held in the Renaissance that man's destiny was determined by the stars. *Romeo and Juliet* is an interesting illustration of Shakespeare's attitude toward this belief, since the play is marked by numerous accidents and coincidences that seem to be directed by a perverse fate, and yet it is also made obvious that human decisions affect the outcome of the action—that the combined forces of character and destiny lead to tragedy.

Characters

ESCALUS, *Prince of Verona*
PARIS, *a young nobleman, kinsman to the Prince*
MONTAGUE \} *heads of two houses at variance with each other*
CAPULET
AN OLD MAN, *of the Capulet family*
ROMEO, *son to Montague*
MERCUTIO, *kinsman to the Prince, and friend to Romeo*
BENVOLIO, *nephew to Montague, and friend to Romeo*
TYBALT, *nephew to Lady Capulet*
FRIAR LAURENCE, *a Franciscan*
FRIAR JOHN, *of the same order*
BALTHASAR, *servant to Romeo*
SAMPSON \} *servants to Capulet*
GREGORY
PETER, *servant to Juliet's nurse*
ABRAHAM, *servant to Montague*
AN APOTHECARY
THREE MUSICIANS
PAGE *to Paris; another* PAGE; *an* OFFICER

LADY MONTAGUE, *wife to Montague*
LADY CAPULET, *wife to Capulet*
JULIET, *daughter to Capulet*
NURSE *to Juliet*

CITIZENS *of Verona:* KINSFOLK *of both houses;* MASKERS, GUARDS, WATCHMEN, *and* ATTENDANTS

CHORUS

SCENE—*Verona; Mantua.*

PROLOGUE

[*Enter* CHORUS.°]

CHORUS. Two households, both alike in dignity,
In fair Verona, where we lay our scene,
From ancient grudge break to new mutiny,°
Where civil blood makes civil hands unclean.
From forth the fatal loins of these two foes   5
A pair of star-crossed ° lovers take their life,
Whose misadventured piteous overthrows
Do with their death bury their parents' strife.
The fearful passage of their death-marked love,
And the continuance of their parents' rage,   10
Which, but their children's end, naught could remove,
Is now the two hours' ° traffic° of our stage;
The which if you with patient ears attend,
What here shall miss, our toil shall strive to mend.°

ACT ONE

SCENE I. *Verona. A public place.*

[*Enter* SAMPSON *and* GREGORY, *of the House of Capulet, with swords and bucklers.*]

SAMPSON. Gregory, on my word, we'll not carry coals.°
GREGORY. No, for then we should be colliers.°
SAMPSON. I mean, an we be in choler,° we'll draw.
GREGORY. Aye, while you live, draw your neck out o' the collar.
SAMPSON. I strike quickly, being moved.   5

PROLOGUE: *Chorus:* A Chorus or Prologue was seldom used by Shakespeare to introduce and explain the action of a play, but it was usual with other dramatists. 3. *mutiny:* quarrel. 6. *star-crossed:* thwarted by evil stars. 12. *two hours:* the normal playing time taken for a performance in the Elizabethan playhouse, where there was no scenery to change and the actors spoke rapidly. *traffic:* business. 14. *What . . . mend:* i.e., if you find shortcomings in our play, we will try to set them right.

ACT ONE, SC. I: 1. *carry coals:* do dirty work, be put upon. 2. *colliers:* coal dealers, notorious for their dirty tricks. 3–4. *choler . . . collar:* Puns on "collier," "choler" (wrath) and "collar" (halter) are common.

GREGORY. But thou art not quickly moved to strike.
SAMPSON. A dog of the house of Montague moves me.
GREGORY. To move is to stir, and to be valiant is to stand. Therefore if thou art moved, thou runn'st away.
SAMPSON. A dog of that house shall move me to stand. I will take the wall° of any man or maid of Montague's. 11
GREGORY. That shows thee a weak slave, for the weakest goes to the wall.°
SAMPSON. 'Tis true, and therefore women, being the weaker vessels, are ever thrust to the wall. Therefore I will push Montague's men from the wall and thrust his maids to the wall. 16
GREGORY. The quarrel is between our masters and us their men.
SAMPSON. 'Tis all one, I will show myself a tyrant. When I have fought with the men, I will be cruel with the maids. I will cut off their heads. 20
GREGORY. The heads of the maids?
SAMPSON. Aye, the heads of the maids, or their maiden heads—take it in what sense thou wilt.
GREGORY. They must take it in sense that feel it.
SAMPSON. Me they shall feel while I am able to stand. And 'tis known I am a pretty piece of flesh. 26
GREGORY. 'Tis well thou art not fish. If thou hadst, thou hadst been poor John.° Draw thy tool. Here comes two of the house of Montagues.

[*Enter* ABRAHAM *and* BALTHASAR.]

SAMPSON. My naked weapon is out. Quarrel—I will back thee. 30
GREGORY. How! Turn thy back and run?
SAMPSON. Fear me not.
GREGORY. No, marry,° I fear thee!
SAMPSON. Let us take the law of our sides. Let them begin.
GREGORY. I will frown as I pass by, and let them take it as they list. 35
SAMPSON. Nay, as they dare. I will bite my thumb° at them, which is a disgrace to them, if they bear it.
ABRAHAM. Do you bite your thumb at us, sir?
SAMPSON. I do bite my thumb, sir.
ABRAHAM. Do you bite your thumb at us, sir? 40
SAMPSON [*aside to* GREGORY]. Is the law of our side, if I say aye?

10–11. *take the wall:* go on the inside of the sidewalk, where the ground was higher and less muddy, and so show superiority.   12–13. *weakest . . . wall:* Gregory retorts with another proverb.   28. *poor John:* dried salted hake, a cheap food.   33. *marry:* Mary; by the Virgin Mary.   36. *bite my thumb:* an insulting gesture, made by snicking the thumbnail on the upper teeth.

GREGORY. No.
SAMPSON. No, sir, I do not bite my thumb at you, sir; but I bite my thumb, sir.
GREGORY. Do you quarrel, sir? 45
ABRAHAM. Quarrel, sir! No, sir.
SAMPSON. But if you do, sir, I am for you. I serve as good a man as you.
ABRAHAM. No better.
SAMPSON. Well, sir.

[*Enter* BENVOLIO.]

GREGORY [*aside to* SAMPSON]. Say "Better." Here comes one of my master's kinsmen. 51
SAMPSON. Yes, better, sir.
ABRAHAM. You lie.
SAMPSON. Draw, if you be men. Gregory, remember thy swashing° blow. 55

[*They fight.*]

BENVOLIO. Part, fools! [*Beating down their weapons.*] Put up your swords. You know not what you do.

[*Enter* TYBALT.]

TYBALT. What, art thou drawn among these heartless hinds°?
Turn thee, Benvolio, look upon thy death.
BENVOLIO. I do but keep the peace. Put up thy sword, 60
Or manage it to part these men with me.
TYBALT. What, drawn, and talk of peace! I hate the word
As I hate Hell, all Montagues, and thee.
Have at thee, coward! [*They fight.*]

[*Enter several of both houses, who join the fray; then enter* CITIZENS *and* PEACE OFFICERS, *with clubs.*]

FIRST OFFICER. Clubs, bills, and partisans! Strike! Beat them down! 65
Down with the Capulets! Down with the Montagues!

[*Enter old* CAPULET *in his gown, and* LADY CAPULET.]

CAPULET. What noise is this? Give me my long sword, ho!
LADY CAPULET. A crutch, a crutch! Why call you for a sword?
CAPULET. My sword, I say! Old Montague is come,
And flourishes his blade in spite of me. 70

54. *swashing:* smashing.   58. *heartless hinds:* a fourfold pun; hind means "servant" and "female deer" and heartless "without feelings" and "without harts" (male deer). This play is packed with phrases that carry two or more meanings, often bawdy.

[*Enter old* MONTAGUE *and* LADY MONTAGUE.]
MONTAGUE. Thou villain Capulet!—Hold me not, let me go.
LADY MONTAGUE. Thou shalt not stir one foot to seek a foe.
[*Enter* PRINCE ESCALUS, *with his train.*]
PRINCE. Rebellious subjects, enemies to peace,
Profaners of this neighbor-stainèd steel °—
Will they not hear? What ho! You men, you beasts, 75
That quench the fire of your pernicious rage
With purple fountains issuing from your veins,
On pain of torture, from those bloody hands
Throw your mistempered ° weapons to the ground,
And hear the sentence of your movèd prince. 80
Three civil brawls, bred of an airy° word,
By thee, old Capulet and Montague,
Have thrice disturbed the quiet of our streets,
And made Verona's ancient citizens
Cast by their grave beseeming ornaments 85
To wield old partisans, in hands as old,
Cankered with peace, to part your cankered ° hate.
If ever you disturb our streets again,
Your lives shall pay the forfeit of the peace.
For this time, all the rest depart away. 90
You, Capulet, shall go along with me,
And, Montague, come you this afternoon,
To know our further pleasure in this case,
To old Freetown, our common judgment place.
Once more, on pain of death, all men depart. 95

[*Exeunt all but* MONTAGUE, LADY MONTAGUE, *and* BENVOLIO.]
MONTAGUE. Who set this ancient quarrel new abroach°?
Speak, Nephew, were you by when it began?
BENVOLIO. Here were the servants of your adversary
And yours close fighting ere I did approach.
I drew to part them. In the instant came 100
The fiery Tybalt, with his sword prepared,
Which as he breathed defiance to my ears,
He swung about his head and cut the winds,

74. *Profaners . . . steel:* who profane (disgrace) your swords by staining them with the blood of your neighbors. 79. *mistempered:* "wrathful" and "made for a bad purpose." 81. *airy:* light as air. 87. *Cankered . . . cankered:* corroded . . . malignant. 96. *abroach:* on foot.

Who, nothing hurt withal, hissed him in scorn.
While we were interchanging thrusts and blows, 105
Came more and more, and fought on part and part
Till the Prince came, who parted either part.
LADY MONTAGUE. Oh, where is Romeo? Saw you him today?
Right glad I am he was not at this fray.
BENVOLIO. Madam, an hour before the worshiped sun 110
Peered forth the golden window of the east,
A troubled mind drave me to walk abroad,
Where, underneath the grove of sycamore
That westward rooteth from the city's side,
So early walking did I see your son. 115
Towards him I made; but he was ware of me,
And stole into the covert of the wood.
I, measuring his affections by my own,
That most are busied when they're most alone,
Being one too many by my weary self, 120
Pursued my humor,° not pursuing his,
And gladly shunned who gladly fled from me.
MONTAGUE. Many a morning hath he there been seen,
With tears augmenting the fresh morning's dew,
Adding to clouds more clouds with his deep sighs. 125
But all so soon as the all-cheering sun
Should in the farthest east begin to draw
The shady curtains from Aurora's° bed,
Away from light steals home my heavy son,
And private in his chamber pens himself, 130
Shuts up his windows, locks fair daylight out,
And makes himself an artificial night.
Black and portentous must this humor prove
Unless good counsel may the cause remove.
BENVOLIO. My noble uncle, do you know the cause? 135
MONTAGUE. I neither know it nor can learn of him.
BENVOLIO. Have you impórtuned ° him by any means?
MONTAGUE. Both by myself and many other friends.
But he, his own affections' counselor,
Is to himself—I will not say how true— 140
But to himself so secret and so close,
So far from sounding and discovery,
As is the bud bit with an envious worm
Ere he can spread his sweet leaves to the air,

121. *humor:* mood.   128. *Aurora's:* of the dawn.   137. *impórtuned:* asked repeatedly.

Or dedicate his beauty to the sun. 145
Could we but learn from whence his sorrows grow,
We would as willingly give cure as know.

[*Enter* ROMEO.]

BENVOLIO. See where he comes. So please you, step aside.
I'll know his grievance, or be much denied.
MONTAGUE. I would thou wert so happy° by thy stay 150
To hear true shrift.° Come, madam, let's away.

[*Exeunt* MONTAGUE *and* LADY.]

BENVOLIO. Good morrow, Cousin.
ROMEO.   Is the day so young?
BENVOLIO. But new struck nine.
ROMEO.   Aye me, sad hours seem long!
Was that my father that went hence so fast?
BENVOLIO. It was. What sadness lengthens Romeo's hours? 155
ROMEO. Not having that which, having, makes them short.
BENVOLIO. In love?
ROMEO. Out—
BENVOLIO. Of love?
ROMEO. Out of her favor where I am in love. 160
BENVOLIO. Alas that love, so gentle in his view,°
Should be so tyrannous and rough in proof! °
ROMEO. Alas that love, whose view is muffled still,°
Should without eyes see pathways to his will!
Where shall we dine? Oh me! What fray was here? 165
Yet tell me not, for I have heard it all.
Here's much to do with hate, but more with love.
Why then, O brawling love! O loving hate!
O anything, of nothing first create!
O heavy lightness! Serious vanity! 170
Misshapen chaos of well-seeming forms!
Feather of lead, bright smoke, cold fire, sick health!
Still-waking sleep, that is not what it is!
This love feel I, that feel no love in this.
Dost thou not laugh?
BENVOLIO.   No, Coz,° I rather weep. 175
ROMEO. Good heart, at what?
BENVOLIO.   At thy good heart's oppression.
ROMEO. Why, such is love's transgression.

---

150. *happy:* fortunate. 151. *shrift:* confession. 161. *view:* appearance. 162. *in proof:* i.e., when experienced. 163. *view . . . still:* sight is blindfolded always. 175. *Coz:* cousin.

Griefs of mine own lie heavy in my breast,
Which thou wilt propagate,° to have it pressed
With more of thine. This love that thou hast shown   180
Doth add more grief to too much of mine own.
Love is a smoke raised with the fume of sighs;
Being purged, a fire sparkling in lovers' eyes;
Being vexed, a sea nourished with lovers' tears.
What is it else? A madness most discreet,   185
A choking gall and a preserving sweet.
Farewell, my coz.
BENVOLIO.   Soft! I will go along.
And if you leave me so, you do me wrong.
ROMEO. Tut, I have lost myself, I am not here.
This is not Romeo, he's some other where.   190
BENVOLIO. Tell me in sadness,° who is that you love?
ROMEO. What, shall I groan and tell thee?
BENVOLIO.   Groan! Why, no,
But sadly tell me who.
ROMEO. Bid a sick man in sadness make his will.
Ah, word ill urged to one that is so ill!   195
In sadness, Cousin, I do love a woman.
BENVOLIO. I aimed so near when I supposed you loved.
ROMEO. A right good mark-man! And she's fair I love.
BENVOLIO. A right fair mark, fair Coz, is soonest hit.
ROMEO. Well, in that hit you miss. She'll not be hit   200
With Cupid's arrow. She hath Dian's° wit,
And in strong proof of chastity well armed,
From love's weak childish bow she lives unharmed.
She will not stay the siege of loving terms,
Nor bide the encounter of assailing eyes,   205
Nor ope her lap to saint-seducing gold.
Oh, she is rich in beauty, only poor
That when she dies, with beauty dies her store.°
BENVOLIO. Then she hath sworn that she will still live chaste?
ROMEO. She hath, and in that sparing makes huge waste;   210
For beauty, starved with her severity,
Cuts beauty off from all posterity.
She is too fair, too wise, wisely too fair,
To merit bliss by making me despair.
She hath forsworn° to love, and in that vow   215

179. *propagate:* increase.   191. *in sadness:* seriously.   201. *Dian:* Diana, the Virgin huntress goddess, was not interested in men.   208. *with . . . store:* i.e., she will leave no offspring to carry on her beauty.   215. *forsworn:* sworn that she will not.

Do I live dead, that live to tell it now.
BENVOLIO. Be ruled by me, forget to think of her.
ROMEO. Oh, teach me how I should forget to think.
BENVOLIO. By giving liberty unto thine eyes.
   Examine other beauties.
ROMEO.   'Tis the way   220
   To call hers exquisite, in question more.°
   These happy masks° that kiss fair ladies' brows,
   Being black, put us in mind they hide the fair.
   He that is stricken blind cannot forget
   The precious treasure of his eyesight lost.   225
   Show me a mistress that is passing° fair,
   What doth her beauty serve but as a note
   Where I may read who passed that passing fair?
   Farewell. Thou canst not teach me to forget.   229
BENVOLIO. I'll pay that doctrine,° or else die in debt.   [*Exeunt.*]

SCENE 2. *A street.*

[*Enter* CAPULET, PARIS, *and* SERVANT.]

CAPULET. But Montague is bound as well as I,
   In penalty alike, and 'tis not hard, I think,
   For men so old as we to keep the peace.
PARIS. Of honorable reckoning° are you both,
   And pity 'tis you lived at odds so long.   5
   But now, my lord, what say you to my suit?
CAPULET. But saying o'er what I have said before.
   My child is yet a stranger in the world—
   She hath not seen the change of fourteen years.
   Let two more summers wither in their pride   10
   Ere we may think her ripe to be a bride.
PARIS. Younger than she are happy mothers made.
CAPULET. And too soon marred are those so early made.
   The earth hath swallowed all my hopes but she,
   She is the hopeful lady of my earth.°   15
   But woo her, gentle Paris, get her heart.

220–21. *'Tis . . . more:* to examine their beauty is the way to realize her greater beauty.   222. *masks:* Elizabethan ladies, admiring an ivory complexion, wore masks in the open air to preserve their faces from the sun. These masks were usually black, but sometimes colored.   226. *passing:* exceedingly.   230. *I'll . . . doctrine:* I will pay for that teaching; i.e., I will have you convinced that you are wrong.
   sc. 2: 4. *Of . . . reckoning:* reckoned honorable.   15. *earth:* body.

My will to her consent is but a part;
An she agree, within her scope of choice
Lies my consent and fair according voice.
This night I hold an old accustomed feast, 20
Whereto I have invited many a guest
Such as I love, and you among the store,
One more, most welcome, makes my number more.
At my poor house look to behold this night
Earth-treading stars that make dark heaven light. 25
Such comfort as do lusty young men feel
When well-appareled April on the heel
Of limping winter treads, even such delight
Among fresh female buds shall you this night
Inherit at my house. Hear all, all see, 30
And like her most whose merit most shall be.
Which on more view, of many mine, being one,
May stand in number, though in reckoning none.°
Come, go with me. [*To* SERVANT, *giving a paper*]
    Go, sirrah, trudge about
Through fair Verona. Find those persons out 35
Whose names are written there, and to them say
My house and welcome on their pleasure stay.

                   [*Exeunt* CAPULET *and* PARIS.]

SERVANT. Find them out whose names are written here! It is written that the shoemaker should meddle with his yard and the tailor with his last, the fisher with his pencil and the painter with his nets; but I am sent to find those persons whose names are here writ, and can never find what names the writing person hath here writ. I must to the learned. In good time.° 43

    [*Enter* BENVOLIO *and* ROMEO.]

BENVOLIO. Tut, man, one fire burns out another's burning,
    One pain is lessened by another's anguish.
Turn giddy, and be holp° by backward turning,
    One desperate grief cures with another's languish.
Take thou some new infection to thy eye,
And the rank poison of the old will die.
ROMEO. Your plantain° leaf is excellent for that. 50

32–33. *Which . . . none:* i.e., my daughter will be one amongst the beauties whom you will see, but none will be worth more.   43. *In good time:* what a lucky chance; i.e., the arrival of the two gentlemen.   46. *holp:* helped.   50. *plantain:* a weed with broad, flat leaves, a popular remedy for bruises and nettle stings.

BENVOLIO. For what, I pray thee?
ROMEO. For your broken shin.
BENVOLIO. Why, Romeo, art thou mad?
ROMEO. Not mad, but bound more than a madman is,
Shut up in prison, kept without my food,
Whipped and tormented and—Godden,° good fellow. 55
SERVANT. God gi' godden. I pray, sir, can you read?
ROMEO. Aye, mine own future in my misery.
SERVANT. Perhaps you have learned it without book, but I pray, can you read anything you see?
ROMEO. Aye, if I know the letters and the language. 60
SERVANT. Ye say honestly. Rest you merry!°
ROMEO. Stay, fellow, I can read. [*Reads.*]

"Signior Martino and his wife and daughters; County° Anselme and and his lovely nieces; Mercutio and his brother Valentine; mine uncle Capulet, his wife, and daughters; my fair niece Rosaline; Livia; Signior Valentio and his cousin Tybalt; Lucio and the lively Helena." 67

A fair assembly. Whither should they come?
SERVANT. Up.
ROMEO. Whither? 70
SERVANT. To supper, to our house.
ROMEO. Whose house?
SERVANT. My master's.
ROMEO. Indeed I should have asked you that before. 74
SERVANT. Now I'll tell you without asking. My master is the great rich Capulet, and if you be not of the House of Montagues, I pray come and crush a cup of wine. Rest you merry! [*Exit.*]
BENVOLIO. At this same ancient feast of Capulet's
Sups the fair Rosaline whom thou so lovest,
With all the admirèd beauties of Verona. 80
Go thither, and with unattained eye
Compare her face with some that I shall show,
And I will make thee think thy swan a crow.
ROMEO. When the devout religion of mine eye
Maintains such falsehood, then turn tears to fires, 85
And these, who, often drowned, could never die,
Transparent heretics, be burned for liars!
One fairer than my love! The all-seeing sun
Ne'er saw her match since first the world begun.

55. *Godden:* good evening; a form of greeting used in the afternoon. 61. *Rest you merry:* God keep you merry. 63. *County:* Count.

BENVOLIO. Tut, you saw her fair, none else being by, 90
  Herself poised ° with herself in either eye.
  But in that crystal scales let there be weighed
  Your lady's love against some other maid
  That I will show you shining at this feast,
  And she shall scant show well that now seems best. 95
ROMEO. I'll go along, no such sight to be shown,
  But to rejoice in splendor of mine own.   [*Exeunt.*]

SCENE 3. *A room in* CAPULET's *house.*

[*Enter* LADY CAPULET *and* NURSE.]

LADY CAPULET. Nurse, where's my daughter? Call her forth to me.
NURSE. Now, by my maidenhead at twelve year old,
  I bade her come. What, lamb! What, ladybird! °—God forbid!—
  Where's this girl? What, Juliet!

[*Enter* JULIET.]

JULIET. How now! Who calls? 5
NURSE. Your mother.
JULIET. Madam, I am here. What is your will?
LADY CAPULET. This is the matter. Nurse, give leave awhile,
  We must talk in secret.—Nurse, come back again,
  I have remembered me, thou'st hear our counsel. 10
  Thou know'st my daughter's of a pretty age.
NURSE. Faith, I can tell her age unto an hour.
LADY CAPULET. She's not fourteen.
NURSE.   I'll lay fourteen of my teeth—
  And yet, to my teen° be it spoken, I have but four—
  She is not fourteen. How long is it now 15
  To Lammastide? °
LADY CAPULET.   A fortnight and odd days.
NURSE. Even or odd, of all days in the year,
  Come Lammas Eve at night shall she be fourteen.
  Susan and she—God rest all Christian souls!—
  Were of an age. Well, Susan is with God. 20

---

91. *poised:* balanced.
  sc. 3: 3. *ladybird:* lit., a small round insect with bright red spots; a pretty little thing. It also has a bad meaning, "tart." The Nurse, realizing that she has used the wrong word, continues abruptly: "God forbid!" 14. *teen:* sorrow. 16. *Lammastide:* August 1. Shakespeare deliberately sets the story in the hot season, when "the mad blood is stirring." In *Romeus and Juliet* the incident occurred on Easter Sunday.

She was too good for me.—But, as I said,
On Lammas Eve at night shall she be fourteen.
That shall she, marry, I remember it well.
'Tis since the earthquake now eleven years,
And she was weaned—I never shall forget it— 25
Of all the days of the year, upon that day.
For I had then laid wormwood to my dug,
Sitting in the sun under the dovehouse wall;
My lord and you were then at Mantua.—
Nay, I do bear a brain.°—But, as I said, 30
When it did taste the wormwood on the nipple
Of my dug, and felt it bitter, pretty fool,
To see it tetchy,° and fall out with the dug!
Shake, quoth the dovehouse.° 'Twas no need, I trow,°
To bid me trudge. 35
And since that time it is eleven years;
For then she could stand high-lone°—nay, by the rood,°
She could have run and waddled all about,
For even the day before, she broke her brow,
And then my husband—God be with his soul! 40
A'° was a merry man—took up the child.
"Yea," quoth he, "dost thou fall upon thy face?
Thou wilt fall backward when thou hast more wit,
Wilt thou not, Jule?" And, by my holidame,°
The pretty wretch left crying, and said "Aye." 45
To see now how a jest shall come about!
I warrant an I should live a thousand years,
I never should forget it. "Wilt thou not, Jule?" quoth he,
And, pretty fool, it stinted,° and said "Aye."
LADY CAPULET. Enough of this. I pray thee hold thy peace. 50
NURSE. Yes, madam, yet I cannot choose but laugh
To think it should leave crying, and say "Aye."
And yet, I warrant, it had upon its brow
A bump as big as a young cockerel's stone,
A perilous° knock, and it cried bitterly. 55
"Yea," quoth my husband, "fall'st upon thy face?
Thou wilt fall backward when thou comest to age,
Wilt thou not, Jule?" It stinted, and said "Aye."

30. *I . . . brain:* I have a head.   33. *tetchy:* peevish.   34. *Shake . . . dovehouse:* a dovecote, where the lord of the manor bred pigeons for his own table.   *trow:* guess.   37. *high-lone:* quite alone.   *rood:* crucifix.   41. *A':* he.   44. *holidame:* halidom, holy relic, upon which an oath was sworn.   49. *stinted:* stopped.   55. *perilous:* grievous.

JULIET. And stint thou too, I pray thee, Nurse, say I.
NURSE. Peace, I have done. God mark° thee to His grace! 60
 Thou wast the prettiest babe that e'er I nursed.
 An I might live to see thee married once,
 I have my wish.
LADY CAPULET. Marry, that "marry" is the very theme
 I came to talk of. Tell me, daughter Juliet, 65
 How stands your disposition to be married?
JULIET. It is an honor that I dream not of.
NURSE. An honor! Were not I thine only nurse,
 I would say thou hadst sucked wisdom from thy teat.
LADY CAPULET. Well, think of marriage now. Younger than you 70
 Here in Verona, ladies of esteem,
 Are made already mothers. By my count,
 I was your mother much upon these years
 That you are now a maid. Thus then in brief—
 The valiant Paris seeks you for his love. 75
NURSE. A man, young lady! Lady, such a man
 As all the world—Why, he's a man of wax.°
LADY CAPULET. Verona's summer hath not such a flower.
NURSE. Nay, he's a flower, in faith, a very flower.
LADY CAPULET. What say you? Can you love the gentleman? 80
 This night you shall behold him at our feast.
 Read o'er the volume° of young Paris' face,
 And find delight writ there with beauty's pen.
 Examine every married lineament,°
 And see how one another lends content, 85
 And what obscured in this fair volume lies
 Find written in the margent° of his eyes.
 This precious book of love, this unbound lover,
 To beautify him, only lacks a cover.
 The fish lives in the sea, and 'tis much pride 90
 For fair without the fair within to hide.
 That book in many's eyes doth share the glory
 That in gold clasps locks in the golden story.
 So shall you share all that he doth possess,
 By having him making yourself no less. 95
NURSE. No less! Nay, bigger. Women grow by men.

60. *mark:* select. 77. *man of wax:* like a model in wax; i.e., perfect. 82–93. *volume . . . story:* The elaborate metaphor of Paris as a book is continued throughout these lines. 84. *married lineament:* perfectly united part. 87. *margent:* margin.

LADY CAPULET. Speak briefly. Can you like of Paris' love?
JULIET. I'll look to like, if looking liking move.
  But no more deep will I endart mine eye
  Than your consent gives strength to make it fly.   100
  [*Enter a* SERVINGMAN.]
SERVINGMAN. Madam, the guests are come, supper served up, you called, my young lady asked for, the nurse cursed in the pantry, and everything in extremity. I must hence to wait. I beseech you, follow straight.°
LADY CAPULET. We follow thee.   [*Exit* SERVINGMAN.]
  Juliet, the County stays.°   105
NURSE. Go, girl, seek happy nights to happy days.   [*Exeunt.*]

SCENE 4. *A street.*

  [*Enter* ROMEO, MERCUTIO, BENVOLIO, *with five or six other* MASKERS, *and* TORCHBEARERS.]

ROMEO. What, shall this speech be spoke for our excuse?
  Or shall we on without apology?
BENVOLIO. The date is out of such prolixity.°
  We'll have no Cupid hoodwinked° with a scarf,
  Bearing a Tartar's painted bow of lath,   5
  Scaring the ladies like a crow-keeper;
  Nor no without-book prologue, faintly spoke
  After the prompter, for our entrance.
  But let them measure us by what they will,
  We'll measure them a measure, and be gone.   10
ROMEO. Give me a torch. I am not for this ambling.°
  Being but heavy,° I will bear the light.
MERCUTIO. Nay, gentle Romeo, we must have you dance.
ROMEO. Not I, believe me. You have dancing shoes
  With nimble soles. I have a soul of lead   15

---

104. *straight:* at once, straightaway.   105. *stays:* waits for you.
  sc. 4: 1–3. *What . . . prolixity:* Elizabethan entertainments were elaborate. When uninvited maskers wished to attend, it was customary for them to announce their coming by sending in a messenger, symbolically costumed, to make an appropriate speech. Benvolio says that such an elaborate device ("prolixity") is out of date. His party will not provide someone dressed up as Cupid.   4. *hoodwinked:* blindfolded.   11. *ambling:* mincing.   12. *heavy:* sad.

So stakes me to the ground I cannot move.
MERCUTIO. You are a lover. Borrow Cupid's wings,
  And soar with them above a common bound.°
ROMEO. I am too sore empiercèd with his shaft
  To soar with his light feathers, and so bound, 20
  I cannot bound a pitch° above dull woe.
  Under love's heavy burden do I sink.
MERCUTIO. And to sink in it, should you burden love,
  Too great oppression for a tender thing.
ROMEO. Is love a tender thing? It is too rough, 25
  Too rude, too boisterous, and it pricks like thorn.
MERCUTIO. If love be rough with you, be rough with love.
  Prick love for pricking, and you beat love down.
  Give me a case to put my visage° in.
  A visor for a visor!° What care I 30
  What curious eye doth quote° deformities?
  Here are the beetle brows shall blush for me.
BENVOLIO. Come, knock and enter, and no sooner in
  But every man betake him to his legs.
ROMEO. A torch for me. Let wantons light of heart 35
  Tickle the senseless rushes° with their heels,
  For I am proverbed with a grandsire phrase.°
  I'll be a candleholder,° and look on.
  The game was ne'er so fair, and I am done.°
MERCUTIO. Tut, dun's the mouse, the constable's own word. 40
  If thou art dun, we'll draw thee from the mire
  Of this sir-reverence love wherein thou stick'st
  Up to the ears. Come, we burn daylight,° ho.
ROMEO. Nay, that's not so.
MERCUTIO.   I mean, sir, in delay
  We waste our lights in vain, like lamps by day. 45
  Take our good meaning, for our judgment sits
  Five times in that ere once in our five wits.°
ROMEO. And we mean well in going to this mask,
  But 'tis no wit to go.
MERCUTIO.   Why, may one ask?

18. *bound:* leap. 21. *pitch:* flight. 29. *visage:* face. Here the party put on grotesque masks. 30. *visor . . . visor:* mask for an ugly face. 31. *quote:* note. 36. *rushes:* the floors were commonly covered with rushes. 37. *am . . . phrase:* am provided with an old proverb. 38. *candleholder:* onlooker. 39. *The . . . done:* be the game never so fair, I am too tired for it. 43. *burn daylight:* waste time. 46–47. *Take . . . wits:* Accept the best meaning of my words, for we are judged five times for our reputation before we are judged once for our intellect.

ROMEO. I dreamed a dream tonight.
MERCUTIO.   And so did I.
ROMEO. Well, what was yours?
MERCUTIO.   That dreamers often lie.
ROMEO. In bed asleep, while they do dream things true.
MERCUTIO. Oh then, I see Queen Mab° hath been with you.
    She is the fairies' midwife, and she comes
    In shape no bigger than an agate stone
    On the forefinger of an alderman,
    Drawn with a team of little atomies°
    Athwart men's noses as they lie asleep—
    Her wagon spokes made of long spinners'° legs;
    The cover, of the wings of grasshoppers;
    Her traces, of the smallest spider's web;
    Her collars, of the moonshine's watery beams;
    Her whip, of cricket's bone; the lash, of film;°
    Her wagoner, a small gray-coated gnat
    Not half so big as a round little worm
    Pricked from the lazy finger of a maid.°
    Her chariot is an empty hazelnut,
    Made by the joiner squirrel or old grub,
    Time out o' mind the fairies' coachmakers.
    And in this state she gallops night by night
    Through lovers' brains, and then they dream of love;
    O'er courtiers' knees, that dream on curtseys straight;
    O'er lawyers' fingers, who straight dream on fees;
    O'er ladies' lips, who straight on kisses dream,
    Which oft the angry Mab with blisters plagues
    Because their breaths with sweetmeats tainted are.
    Sometime she gallops o'er a courtier's nose,
    And then dreams he of smelling out a suit.°
    And sometime comes she with a tithe pig's° tail
    Tickling a parson's nose as a' lies asleep,
    Then dreams he of another benefice.
    Sometime she driveth o'er a soldier's neck,
    And then dreams he of cutting foreign throats,
    Of breaches, ambuscadoes, Spanish blades,

---

53. *Queen Mab:* the fairy *queen.* 57. *atomies:* tiny creatures; lit., motes in a sunbeam. 59. *spinners':* spiders'. 63. *film:* spider's thread. 65–66. *worm . . . maid:* Lazy maids were said to grow maggots in their fingers. 78. *suit:* with the double meaning of "fine clothes" and "petition for favor." 79. *tithe pig's:* The parson was entitled to a tithe, or tenth of the produce of his parishioners, which he often took in kind.

Of healths five fathom deep; and then anon 85
Drums in his ear, at which he starts and wakes,
And being thus frighted swears a prayer or two,
And sleeps again. This is that very Mab
That plaits the manes of horses in the night,
And bakes the elflocks° in foul sluttish hairs, 90
Which once untangled much misfortune bodes.
This is the hag, when maids lie on their backs,
That presses them and learns them first to bear,
Making them women of good carriage.
This is she—
ROMEO.   Peace, peace, Mercutio, peace! 95
Thou talk'st of nothing.
MERCUTIO.   True, I talk of dreams,
Which are the children of an idle brain,
Begot of nothing but vain fantasy,
Which is as thin of substance as the air
And more inconstant than the wind, who woos 100
Even now the frozen bosom of the North,
And, being angered, puffs away from thence,
Turning his face to the dew-dropping South.
BENVOLIO. This wind you talk of blows us from ourselves.
Supper is done, and we shall come too late. 105
ROMEO. I fear, too early. For my mind misgives
Some consequence, yet hanging in the stars,
Shall bitterly begin his fearful date
With this night's revels, and expire the term
Of a despisèd life closed in my breast 110
By some vile forfeit of untimely death.
But He that hath the steerage of my course
Direct my sail! On, lusty gentlemen.
BENVOLIO. Strike, drum.   [*Exeunt.*]

SCENE 5. *A hall in* CAPULET'*s house.*

[MUSICIANS *waiting. Enter* SERVINGMEN, *with napkins.*]

FIRST SERVINGMAN. Where's Potpan, that he helps not to take away? He shift a trencher! ° He scrape a trencher!

---

90. *elflocks:* The knots in the manes of horses and uncombed human hair were sometimes attributed to mischievous fairies.
   sc. 5: 2. *trencher:* wooden platter.

SECOND SERVINGMAN. When good manners shall lie all in one or two men's hands, and they unwashed too, 'tis a foul thing.
FIRST SERVINGMAN. Away with the joint stools,° remove the court cupboard, look to the plate. Good thou, save me a piece of marchpane.° And, as thou lovest me, let the porter let in Susan Grindstone and Nell, Antony, and Potpan! 8
SECOND SERVINGMAN. Aye, boy, ready.
FIRST SERVINGMAN. You are looked for and called for, asked for and sought for, in the great chamber. 11
THIRD SERVINGMAN. We cannot be here and there too. Cheerly, boys. Be brisk a while, and the longer liver take all. [*They retire behind.*]

[*Enter* CAPULET, *with* JULIET *and others of his house, meeting the* GUESTS *and* MASKERS.]

CAPULET. Welcome, gentlemen! Ladies that have their toes
Unplagued with corns will have a bout with you. 15
Ah ha, my mistresses! Which of you all
Will now deny to dance? She that makes dainty,°
She, I'll swear, hath corns—am I come near ye now?
Welcome, gentlemen! I have seen the day
That I have worn a visor, and could tell 20
A whispering tale in a fair lady's ear
Such as would please. 'Tis gone, 'tis gone, 'tis gone.
You are welcome, gentlemen! Come, musicians, play.
A hall, a hall! ° Give room! And foot it, girls.

[*Music plays, and they dance.*]

More light, you knaves, and turn the tables up, 25
And quench the fire, the room is grown too hot.
Ah, sirrah, this unlooked-for sport comes well.
Nay, sit, nay, sit, good Cousin Capulet,
For you and I are past our dancing days.
How long is 't now since last yourself and I 30
Were in a mask?
SECOND CAPULET. By 'r Lady, thirty years.
CAPULET. What, man! 'Tis not so much, 'tis not so much.
'Tis since the nuptial of Lucentio,
Come Pentecost as quickly as it will,

---

5. *joint stools:* stools made of joiners' work. 6. *marchpane:* marzipan, a mixture of almond paste, often in an elaborate shape. 17. *makes dainty:* pretends to be shy. 24. *A hall, a hall!:* Clear the hall for dancing!

                    Some five and twenty years, and then we masked.   35
SECOND CAPULET. 'Tis more, 'tis more. His son is elder, sir,
   His son is thirty.
CAPULET.   Will you tell me that?
   His son was but a ward two years ago.
ROMEO [*to a* SERVINGMAN]. What lady's that which doth enrich the hand
   Of yonder knight?   40
SERVINGMAN. I know not, sir.
ROMEO. Oh, she doth teach the torches to burn bright!
   It seems she hangs upon the cheek of night
   Like a rich jewel in an Ethiop's ear—
   Beauty too rich for use, for earth too dear!   45
   So shows a snowy dove trooping with crows
   As yonder lady o'er her fellows shows.
   The measure done, I'll watch her place of stand,
   And, touching hers, make blessèd my rude hand.
   Did my heart love till now? Forswear it, sight!   50
   For I ne'er saw true beauty till this night.
TYBALT. This, by his voice, should be a Montague.
   Fetch me my rapier, boy. What dares the slave
   Come hither, covered with an antic face,°
   To fleer° and scorn at our solemnity?   55
   Now, by the stock and honor of my kin,
   To strike him dead I hold it not a sin.
CAPULET. Why, how now, kinsman! Wherefore storm you so?
TYBALT. Uncle, this is a Montague, our foe,
   A villain, that is hither come in spite   60
   To scorn at our solemnity this night.
CAPULET. Young Romeo, is it?
TYBALT.   'Tis he, that villain Romeo.
CAPULET. Content thee, gentle Coz, let him alone,
   He bears him like a portly gentleman.
   And, to say truth, Verona brags of him   65
   To be a virtuous and well-governed youth.
   I would not for the wealth of all this town
   Here in my house do him disparagement.
   Therefore be patient, take no note of him.
   It is my will, the which if thou respect,   70
   Show a fair presence and put off these frowns,
   An ill-beseeming semblance° for a feast.

54. *antic face:* grotesque mask.   72. *semblance:* appearance.

TYBALT. It fits when such a villain is a guest.
I'll not endure him.
CAPULET.   He shall be endured.
What, goodman boy° I say he shall. Go to,   75
Am I the master here, or you? Go to.
You'll not endure him! God shall mend my soul,
You'll make a mutiny among my guests!
You will set cock-a-hoop! ° You'll be the man!
TYBALT. Why, Uncle, 'tis a shame.
CAPULET.   Go to, go to,   80
You are a saucy boy. Is't so, indeed?
This trick° may chance to scathe° you, I know what.
You must contrary me! Marry, 'tis time.
Well said, my hearts! You are a princox,° go.
Be quiet, or—More light, more light! For shame!   85
I'll make you quiet. What, cheerly, my hearts!
TYBALT. Patience perforce with willful choler meeting
Makes my flesh tremble in their different greeting.
I will withdraw. But this intrusion shall,   89
Now seeming sweet, convert to bitterest gall.   [*Exit.*]
ROMEO [*to* JULIET]. If I profane with my unworthiest hand
This holy shrine, the gentle fine is this,
My lips, two blushing pilgrims, ready stand
To smooth that rough touch with a tender kiss.
JULIET. Good pilgrim, you do wrong your hand too much,   95
Which mannerly devotion shows in this;
For saints have hands that pilgrims' hands do touch,
And palm to palm is holy palmers'° kiss.
ROMEO. Have not saints lips, and holy palmers too?
JULIET. Aye, pilgrim, lips that they must use in prayer.   100
ROMEO. Oh then, dear saint, let lips do what hands do.
They pray. Grant thou, lest faith turn to despair.
JULIET. Saints do not move, though grant for prayers' sake.
ROMEO. Then move not while my prayer's effect I take.   104
Thus from my lips by thine my sin is purged.   [*Kissing her.*]

---

75. *goodman boy:* a contemptuous phrase. Goodman indicated a man under the rank of gentleman, but above that of a laborer; boy, a youngster, an insulting term. 79. *cock-a-hoop:* an ancient phrase of doubtful origin. In the sixteenth century it meant "to take the spigot out of the barrel, and so let the liquor flow without interruption," hence, "be utterly reckless." 82. *trick:* habit, i.e., of quarreling. *scathe:* injure. 84. *princox:* conceited boy. 98. *palmer:* a pilgrim who carried a palm leaf as a sign that he had made the journey to the Holy Land.

JULIET. Then have my lips the sin that they have took.
ROMEO. Sin from my lips? Oh, trespass sweetly urged!
  Give me my sin again.
JULIET.   You kiss by the book.°
NURSE. Madam, your mother craves a word with you.
ROMEO. What is her mother?
NURSE.   Marry, bachelor,   110
  Her mother is the lady of the house,
  And a good lady, and a wise and virtuous.
  I nursed her daughter, that you talked withal.
  I tell you, he that can lay hold of her.
  Shall have the chinks.°
ROMEO.   Is she a Capulet?   115
  Oh, dear° account! My life is my foe's debt.°
BENVOLIO. Away, be gone. The sport is at the best.
ROMEO. Aye, so I fear. The more is my unrest.
CAPULET. Nay, gentlemen, prepare not to be gone,
  We have a trifling foolish banquet° toward.   120
  Is it e'en so? Why then, I thank you all,
  I thank you, honest gentlemen. Good night.
  More torches here! Come on, then, let's to bed.
  Ah, sirrah, by my fay,° it waxes late.   124
  I'll to my rest.   [Exeunt all but JULIET and NURSE.]
JULIET. Come hither, Nurse. What is yond gentleman?
NURSE. The son and heir of old Tiberio.
JULIET. What's he that now is going out of door?
NURSE. Marry, that, I think, be young Petruchio.
JULIET. What's he that follows there, that would not dance?   130
NURSE. I know not.
JULIET. Go ask his name. If he be marrièd,
  My grave is like to be my wedding bed.
NURSE. His name is Romeo, and a Montague,
  The only son of your great enemy.   135
JULIET. My only love sprung from my only hate!
  Too early seen unknown, and known too late!
  Prodigious° birth of love it is to me,
  That I must love a loathèd enemy.
NURSE. What's this? What's this?
JULIET.   A rhyme I learned even now   140

---

108. *by the book:* according to the book of instructions; i.e., you are merely being gallant.   115. *chinks:* cash.   116. *dear:* in the double meaning of "costly" and "beloved."   *foe's debt:* owed to my foe.   120. *banquet:* light refreshments.   124. *fay:* faith.   138. *Prodigious:* monstrous, unnatural.

Of one I danced withal.   [*One calls within,* "Juliet."]
NURSE.   Anon, anon!
Come, let's away, the strangers all are gone.   [*Exeunt.*]

ACT TWO

PROLOGUE

[*Enter* CHORUS.]

CHORUS. Now old desire doth in his deathbed lie,
    And young affection gapes to be his heir.
That fair for which love groaned for and would die,
    With tender Juliet matched, is now not fair.
Now Romeo is beloved and loves again,   5
    Alike° bewitchèd by the charm of looks,
But to his foe supposed he must complain,
    And she steal love's sweet bait from fearful hooks.
Being held a foe, he may not have access
    To breathe such vows as lovers use to swear,   10
And she as much in love, her means much less
    To meet her new belovèd anywhere.
But passion lends them power, time means, to meet,
    Tempering extremities with extreme sweet.   [*Exit.*]

SCENE I. *A lane by the wall of* CAPULET'S *orchard.*

[*Enter* ROMEO, *alone.*]

ROMEO. Can I go forward when my heart is here?
Turn back, dull earth,° and find thy center° out.   [*Exit.*]

    [*Enter* BENVOLIO *with* MERCUTIO.]

BENVOLIO. Romeo! My cousin Romeo!
MERCUTIO.   He is wise,
And, on my life, hath stol'n him home to bed.

ACT TWO, PRO.: 6. *Alike:* equally.
sc. 1: 2. *dull earth:* my body.   *center:* the absolute center of the universe; i.e., Juliet.

BENVOLIO. He ran this way, and leaped this orchard wall. 5
　Call, good Mercutio.
MERCUTIO. 　　　　　　Nay, I'll conjure° too.
　Romeo! Humors! Madman! Passion! Lover!
　Appear thou in the likeness of a sigh.
　Speak but one rhyme, and I am satisfied,
　Cry but "aye me!" pronounce but "love" and "dove," 10
　Speak to my gossip° Venus one fair word,
　One nickname for her purblind° son and heir,
　Young Adam Cupid, he that shot so trim
　When King Cophetua° loved the beggar maid!
　He heareth not, he stirreth not, he moveth not. 15
　The ape is dead, and I must conjure him.
　I conjure thee by Rosalind's bright eyes,
　By her high forehead and her scarlet lip,
　By her fine foot, straight leg, and quivering thigh,
　And the demesnes° that there adjacent lie, 20
　That in thy likeness thou appear to us!
BENVOLIO. An if he hear thee, thou wilt anger him.
MERCUTIO. This cannot anger him. 'Twould anger him
　To raise a spirit in his mistress' circle
　Of some strange nature, letting it there stand 25
　Till she had laid it and conjured it down.
　That were some spite. My invocation
　Is fair and honest, and in his mistress' name
　I conjure only but to raise up him.
BENVOLIO. Come, he hath hid himself among these trees, 30
　To be consorted with the humorous° night.
　Blind is his love, and best befits the dark.
MERCUTIO. If love be blind, love cannot hit the mark.
　Now will he sit under a medlar° tree,
　And wish his mistress were that kind of fruit 35
　As maids call medlars when they laugh alone.
　Oh, Romeo, that she were, Oh, that she were
　An open et cetera, thou a poperin° pear!

6. *conjure:* call up a spirit.　11. *gossip:* friend with whom one can exchange confidences and scandal.　12. *purblind:* dim-sighted.　14. *King Cophetua:* the hero of a popular ballad; he fell in love with a beggar maid, whom he married.　20. *demesnes:* domains.　31. *humorous:* moody.　34. *medlar:* a tree that produces a fruit like a small brown apple, only eaten when it has grown soft; used here with a quibble on meddler.　38. *poperin:* lit., a pear from Poperinghe in Flanders, but used obscenely for the male parts.

Romeo, good night. I'll to my truckle bed,°
This field bed is too cold for me to sleep. 40
Come, shall we go?
BENVOLIO. Go then, for 'tis in vain
To seek him here that means not to be found. [*Exeunt.*]

SCENE 2. CAPULET's *orchard.*

[*Enter* ROMEO.]

ROMEO. He jests at scars that never felt a wound.

[JULIET *appears above at a window.*]

But, soft! What light through yonder window breaks?
It is the east, and Juliet is the sun!
Arise, fair sun, and kill the envious moon,
Who is already sick and pale with grief 5
That thou her maid art far more fair than she.
Be not her maid, since she is envious.
Her vestal° livery is but sick and green,
And none but fools do wear it. Cast it off.
It is my lady, oh, it is my love! 10
Oh, that she knew she were!
She speaks, yet she says nothing. What of that?
Her eye discourses, I will answer it.
I am too bold, 'tis not to me she speaks.
Two of the fairest stars in all the heaven, 15
Having some business, do entreat her eyes
To twinkle in their spheres till they return.
What if her eyes were there, they in her head?
The brightness of her cheek would shame those stars
As daylight doth a lamp; her eyes in heaven 20
Would through the airy region stream so bright
That birds would sing and think it were not night.
See how she leans her cheek upon her hand!
Oh, that I were a glove upon that hand,
That I might touch that cheek!
JULIET. Aye me!
ROMEO. She speaks. 25

39. *truckle bed:* trundle bed, a bed on casters, pushed under the great bed in the daytime.
    sc. 2: 8. *vestal:* virgin.

Oh, speak again, bright angel! For thou art
As glorious to this night, being o'er my head,
As is a wingèd messenger of Heaven
Unto the white-upturnèd wondering eyes
Of mortals that fall back to gaze on him 30
When he bestrides the lazy-pacing clouds
And sails upon the bosom of the air.

JULIET. O Romeo, Romeo, wherefore art thou Romeo?
Deny thy father and refuse thy name,
Or, if thou wilt not, be but sworn my love 35
And I'll no longer be a Capulet.

ROMEO [*aside*]. Shall I hear more, or shall I speak at this?

JULIET. 'Tis but thy name that is my enemy.
Thou art thyself, though not a Montague.
What's Montague? It is nor hand, nor foot, 40
Nor arm, nor face, nor any other part
Belonging to a man. Oh, be some other name!
What's in a name? That which we call a rose
By any other name would smell as sweet.
So Romeo would, were he not Romeo called, 45
Retain that dear perfection which he owes°
Without that title. Romeo, doff thy name,
And for thy name, which is no part of thee,
Take all myself.

ROMEO.   I take thee at thy word.
Call me but love, and I'll be new baptized. 50
Henceforth I never will be Romeo.

JULIET. What man art thou that, thus bescreened in night,
So stumblest on my counsel?

ROMEO.   By a name
I know not how to tell thee who I am.
My name, dear saint, is hateful to myself 55
Because it is an enemy to thee.
Had I it written, I would tear the word.

JULIET. My ears have yet not drunk a hundred words
Of thy tongue's uttering, yet I know the sound.
Art thou not Romeo, and a Montague? 60

ROMEO. Neither, fair saint, if either thee dislike.

JULIET. How camest thou hither, tell me, and wherefore?
The orchard walls are high and hard to climb,
And the place death, considering who thou art,

---

46. *owes:* owns.

If any of my kinsmen find thee here.
ROMEO. With love's light wings did I o'erperch° these walls,
For stony limits cannot hold love out.
And what love can do, that dares love attempt,
Therefore thy kinsmen are no let° to me.
JULIET. If they do see thee, they will murder thee.
ROMEO. Alack, there lies more peril in thine eye
Than twenty of their swords. Look thou but sweet,
And I am proof ° against their enmity.
JULIET. I would not for the world they saw thee here.
ROMEO. I have night's cloak to hide me from their eyes,
And but° thou love me, let them find me here.
My life were better ended by their hate
Than death prorogued,° wanting of thy love.
JULIET. By whose direction found'st thou out this place?
ROMEO. By love, that first did prompt me to inquire.
He lent me counsel, and I lent him eyes.
I am no pilot, yet wert thou as far
As that vast shore washed with the farthest sea,
I would adventure for such merchandise.
JULIET. Thou know'st the mask of night is on my face,
Else would a maiden blush bepaint my cheek
For that which thou hast heard me speak tonight.
Fain would I dwell on form, fain, fain deny
What I have spoke. But farewell compliment! °
Dost thou love me? I know thou wilt say "Aye,"
And I will take thy word. Yet if thou swear'st,
Thou mayst prove false. At lovers' perjuries
They say Jove laughs. O gentle Romeo,
If thou dost love, pronounce it faithfully.
Or if thou think'st I am too quickly won,
I'll frown and be perverse and say thee nay,
So thou wilt woo; but else, not for the world.
In truth, fair Montague, I am too fond,
And therefore thou mayst think my 'havior light.
But trust me, gentleman, I'll prove more true
Than those that have more cunning to be strange.°
I should have been more strange, I must confess,
But that thou overheard'st, ere I was ware,

---

66. *o'erperch:* fly over.   69. *let:* hindrance.   73. *proof:* armored.   76. *And but:* if only.   78. *prorogued:* postponed.   89. *compliment:* polite behavior.   101. *strange:* outwardly cold.

My true love's passion. Therefore pardon me,
And not impute this yielding to light love,
Which the dark night hath so discovered.
ROMEO. Lady, by yonder blessed moon I swear,
  That tips with silver all these fruit-tree tops—
JULIET. Oh, swear not by the moon, th' inconstant moon,
  That monthly changes in her circled orb,
  Lest that thy love prove likewise variable.
ROMEO. What shall I swear by?
JULIET.   Do not swear at all.
  Or, if thou wilt, swear by thy gracious self,
  Which is the god of my idolatry,
  And I'll believe thee.
ROMEO.   If my heart's dear love—
JULIET. Well, do not swear. Although I joy in thee,
  I have no joy of this contráct° tonight.
  It is too rash, too unadvised, too sudden,
  Too like the lightning, which doth cease to be
  Ere one can say "It lightens." Sweet, good night!
  This bud of love, by summer's ripening breath,
  May prove a beauteous flower when next we meet.
  Good night, good night! As sweet repose and rest
  Come to thy heart as that within my breast!
ROMEO. Oh, wilt thou leave me so unsatisfied?
JULIET. What satisfaction canst thou have tonight?
ROMEO. The exchange of thy love's faithful vow for mine.
JULIET. I gave thee mine before thou didst request it,
  And yet I would it were to give again.
ROMEO. Wouldst thou withdraw it? For what purpose, love?
JULIET. But to be frank, and give it thee again.
  And yet I wish but for the thing I have.
  My bounty is as boundless as the sea,
  My love as deep; the more I give to thee,
  The more I have, for both are infinite.
  I hear some noise within. Dear love, adieu!

  [NURSE *calls within.*]

  Anon, good Nurse! Sweet Montague, be true.
  Stay but a little, I will come again.   [*Exit.*]
ROMEO. Oh, blessed, blessed night! I am afeard,
  Being in light, all this is but a dream,
  Too flattering-sweet to be substantial.

117. *contráct:* betrothal.

[*Re-enter* JULIET, *above.*]

JULIET. Three words, dear Romeo, and good night indeed.
  If that thy bent° of love be honorable,
  Thy purpose marriage, send me word tomorrow
  By one that I'll procure to come to thee, 145
  Where and what time thou wilt perform the rite,
  And all my fortunes at thy foot I'll lay,
  And follow thee my lord throughout the world.
NURSE [*within*]. Madam! 149
JULIET. I come, anon.—But if thou mean'st not well, I do beseech thee—
NURSE [*within*]. Madam!
JULIET.   By and by, I come—
  To cease thy suit, and leave me to my grief.
  Tomorrow will I send.
ROMEO.   So thrive my soul—
JULIET. A thousand times good night! [*Exit.*]
ROMEO. A thousand times the worse, to want thy light. 155
  Love goes toward love as schoolboys from their books,
  But love from love toward school with heavy looks.
          [*Retiring slowly.*]

[*Re-enter* JULIET, *above.*]

JULIET. Hist! Romeo, hist!—Oh, for a falconer's voice,
  To lure this tassel-gentle° back again!
  Bondage is hoarse,° and may not speak aloud, 160
  Else would I tear the cave where Echo lies
  And make her airy tongue more hoarse than mine
  With repetition of my Romeo's name.
ROMEO. It is my soul that calls upon my name.
  How silver-sweet sound lovers' tongues by night, 165
  Like softest music to attending ears!
JULIET. Romeo!
ROMEO.   My dear?
JULIET.   At what o'clock tomorrow
  Shall I send to thee?
ROMEO.   At the hour of nine.
JULIET. I will not fail. 'Tis twenty years till then.
  I have forgot why I did call thee back. 170
ROMEO. Let me stand here till thou remember it.

143. *bent:* intention. 159. *tassel-gentle:* male peregrine falcon. 160. *Bondage is hoarse:* i.e., being under the control of my parents, I can only whisper.

314 WILLIAM SHAKESPEARE

JULIET. I shall forget, to have thee still stand there,
  Remembering how I love thy company.
ROMEO. And I'll still stay, to have thee still forget,
  Forgetting any other home but this.   175
JULIET. 'Tis almost morning. I would have thee gone,
  And yet no farther than a wanton's° bird,
  Who lets it hop a little from her hand,
  Like a poor prisoner in his twisted gyves,°
  And with a silk thread plucks it back again,   180
  So loving-jealous of his liberty.
ROMEO. I would I were thy bird.
JULIET.   Sweet, so would I.
  Yet I should kill thee with much cherishing.
  Good night, good night! Parting is such sweet sorrow   184
  That I shall say good night till it be morrow.   [Exit.]
  Sleep dwell upon thine eyes, peace in thy breast!
  Would I were sleep and peace, so sweet to rest!
  Hence will I to my ghostly° father's cell,
  His help to crave and my dear hap° to tell.   [Exit.]

SCENE 3.   FRIAR LAURENCE's cell.

[Enter FRIAR LAURENCE, with a basket.]

FRIAR LAURENCE. The gray-eyed morn smiles on the frowning night,
  Checkering the eastern clouds with streaks of light,
  And fleckèd° darkness like a drunkard reels
  From forth day's path and Titan's° fiery wheels.
  Now, ere the sun advance his burning eye,   5
  The day to cheer and night's dank dew to dry,
  I must upfill° this osier cage° of ours
  With baleful weeds and precious-juicèd flowers.
  The earth that's Nature's mother is her tomb,
  What is her burying grave, that is her womb.   10
  And from her womb children of divers kind
  We sucking on her natural bosom find,
  Many for many virtues excellent,
  None but for some, and yet all different.
  Oh, mickle° is the powerful grace that lies   15

177. *wanton:* spoiled child.   179. *gyves:* fetters.   188. *ghostly:* spiritual.   189. *hap:* luck.
sc. 3: 3. *fleckèd:* dappled.   4. *Titan:* the sun.   7. *upfill:* fill up.   *osier cage:* wicker basket.   15. *mickle:* mighty.

In herbs, plants, stones, and their true qualities.
For naught so vile that on the earth doth live,
But to the earth some special good doth give;
Nor aught so good but, strained from that fair use,
Revolts from true birth, stumbling on abuse. 20
Virtue itself turns vice, being misapplied,
And vice sometime's by action dignified.
Within the infant rind of this small flower
Poison hath residence, and medicine power.
For this, being smelt, with that part cheers each part, 25
Being tasted, slays all senses with the heart.
Two such opposèd kings encamp them still
In man as well as herbs, grace° and rude will;°
And where the worser is predominant,
Full soon the canker° death eats up that plant. 30

[Enter ROMEO.]

ROMEO. Good morrow, Father.
FRIAR LAURENCE.   Benedicite!
What early tongue so sweet saluteth me?
Young son, it argues a distempered head
So soon to bid good morrow to thy bed.
Care keeps his watch in every old man's eye, 35
And where care lodges, sleep will never lie;
But where unbruisèd youth with unstuffed brain
Doth couch his limbs, there golden sleep doth reign.
Therefore thy earliness doth me assure
Thou art uproused by some distemperature. 40
Or if not so, then here I hit it right,
Our Romeo hath not been in bed tonight.
ROMEO. That last is true. The sweeter rest was mine.
FRIAR LAURENCE. God pardon sin! Wast thou with Rosaline?
ROMEO. With Rosaline, my ghostly father? No. 45
I have forgot that name and that name's woe.
FRIAR LAURENCE. That's my good son. But where hast thou been, then?
ROMEO. I'll tell thee ere thou ask it me again.
I have been feasting with mine enemy,
Where on a sudden one hath wounded me 50
That's by me wounded. Both our remedies
Within thy help and holy physic° lies.
I bear no hatred, blessed man, for, lo,

28. *grace:* the power of goodness.   *rude will:* man's natural desire for evil.   30. *canker:* cankerworm.   52. *physic:* remedy.

    My intercession likewise steads° my foe.
FRIAR LAURENCE. Be plain, good son, and homely in thy drift.   55
    Riddling confession finds but riddling shrift.°
ROMEO. Then plainly know my heart's dear love is set
    On the fair daughter of rich Capulet.
    As mine on hers, so hers is set on mine,
    And all combined save what thou must combine   60
    By holy marriage. When, and where, and how,
    We met, we wooed and made exchange of vow,
    I'll tell thee as we pass; but this I pray,
    That thou consent to marry us today.
FRIAR LAURENCE. Holy Saint Francis, what a change is here!   65
    Is Rosaline, that thou didst love so dear,
    So soon forsaken? Young men's love then lies
    Not truly in their hearts, but in their eyes.
    Jesu Maria, what a deal of brine
    Hath washed thy sallow cheeks for Rosaline!   70
    How much salt water thrown away in waste,
    To season love, that of it doth not taste!
    The sun not yet thy sighs from heaven clears,
    Thy old groans ring yet in mine ancient ears.
    Lo, here upon thy cheek the stain doth sit   75
    Of an old tear that is not washed off yet.
    If e'er thou wast thyself and these woes thine,
    Thou and these woes were all for Rosaline.
    And art thou changed? Pronounce this sentence then—
    Women may fall when there's no strength in men.   80
ROMEO. Thou chid'st me oft for loving Rosaline.
FRIAR LAURENCE. For doting, not for loving, pupil mine.
ROMEO. And bad'st me bury love.
FRIAR LAURENCE.   Not in a grave
    To lay one in, another out to have.
ROMEO. I pray thee, chide not. She whom I love now   85
    Doth grace for grace and love for love allow.
    The other did not so.
FRIAR LAURENCE.   Oh, she knew well
    Thy love did read by rote and could not spell.°
    But come, young waverer, come, go with me,
    In one respect I'll thy assistant be;   90
    For this alliance may so happy prove,

---

54. *steads:* benefits.   56. *shrift:* absolution.   88. *love . . . spell:* your love was merely repeating phrases by heart (by rote), like a child that pretends to read because it knows the words.

To turn your household's rancor to pure love.
ROMEO. Oh, let us hence. I stand on sudden haste.
FRIAR LAURENCE. Wisely and slow. They stumble that run fast.
[Exeunt.]

SCENE 4. *A street.*

[Enter BENVOLIO *and* MERCUTIO.*]*

MERCUTIO. Where the devil should this Romeo be?
Came he not home tonight?
BENVOLIO. Not to his father's, I spoke with his man.
MERCUTIO. Ah, that same pale hardhearted wench, that Rosaline,
Torments him so that he will sure run mad. 5
BENVOLIO. Tybalt, the kinsman of old Capulet,
Hath sent a letter to his father's house.
MERCUTIO. A challenge, on my life.
BENVOLIO. Romeo will answer it.
MERCUTIO. Any man that can write may answer a letter. 10
BENVOLIO. Nay, he will answer the letter's master, how he dares being dared.
MERCUTIO. Alas, poor Romeo, he is already dead! Stabbed with a white wench's black eye, shot thorough the ear with a love song, the very pin° of his heart cleft with the blind bowboy's butt shaft.° And is he a man to encounter Tybalt? 16
BENVOLIO. Why, what is Tybalt?
MERCUTIO. More than Prince of Cats,° I can tell you. Oh, he's the courageous captain of compliments.° He fights as you sing prick song,° keeps time, distance, and proportion; rests me his minim° rest, one, two, and the third in your bosom. The very butcher of a silk button, a duelist, a duelist, a gentleman of the very first house,° of the first and second cause.° Ah, the immortal passado! The punto reverso! The hai!° 24
BENVOLIO. The what?

sc. 4: 15. *pin:* center of the target. *butt shaft:* unpointed arrow, used for target practice. 18. *Prince of Cats:* In the tale of Reynard the Fox, Tibert (or Tybalt) is the Prince of Cats. 19. *captain of compliments:* expert in the niceties of fashionable behavior. 20. *prick song:* melody accompanying a song. *minim:* the shortest note in music. 21–24. *butcher . . . hai:* A professional fencer would undertake to touch his opponent on any button of his doublet. Mercutio mocks Tybalt because he is an expert with the new-fashioned rapier. 22. *first house:* finest school. 23. *first . . . cause:* the reasons which (according to the exact rules of honor) caused a gentleman to issue a challenge.

MERCUTIO. The pox of such antic, affecting fantasticoes,° these new tuners of accents; "By Jesu, a very good blade! A very tall° man! A very good whore!" Why, is not this a lamentable thing, Grandsire, that we should be thus afflicted with these strange flies, these fashionmongers, these perdona-mi's,° who stand so much on the new form that they cannot sit at ease on the old bench? Oh, their bones,° their bones! 32

[*Enter* ROMEO.]

BENVOLIO. Here comes Romeo, here comes Romeo.
MERCUTIO. Without his roe, like a dried herring. Oh, flesh, flesh, how art thou fishified! Now is he for the numbers° that Petrarch flowed in. Laura to his lady was but a kitchen wench—marry, she had a better love to berhyme her—Dido, a dowdy;° Cleopatra, a gypsy; Helen and Hero, hildings and harlots; Thisbe, a gray eye or so, but not to the purpose. Signior Romeo, *bon jour!*—there's a French salutation to your French slop.° You gave us the counterfeit° fairly last night. 41
ROMEO. Good morrow to you both. What counterfeit did I give you?
MERCUTIO. The slip, sir, the slip. Can you not conceive?
ROMEO. Pardon, good Mercutio, my business was great, and in such a case as mine a man may strain courtesy. 45
MERCUTIO. That's as much as to say, Such a case as yours constrains a man to bow in the hams.
ROMEO. Meaning, to curtsy.
MERCUTIO. Thou hast most kindly hit it.
ROMEO. A most courteous exposition. 50
MERCUTIO. Nay, I am the very pink of courtesy.
ROMEO. Pink for flower.
MERCUTIO. Right.
ROMEO. Why, then is my pump well flowered.° 54
MERCUTIO. Well said. Follow me this jest now till thou hast worn out thy pump, that, when the single sole of it is worn, the jest may remain, after the wearing, solely singular.
ROMEO. Oh, single-soled jest, solely singular for the singleness!
MERCUTIO. Come between us, good Benvolio. My wits faint.

26. *fantasticoes:* fantastical fellows. 27. *tall:* brave. 30. *perdona-mi's:* Italian for "pardon me." The man of fashion affected foreign languages. 31. *bones:* with a pun on the French *bon.* 35. *numbers:* verses. 37. *dowdy:* slut. 40. *slop:* baggy breeches. 40–43. *counterfeit . . . slip:* a counterfeit coin was called a slip. 54. *pump well flowered:* my shoe is pinked (punched) with a pattern of flowers.

ROMEO. Switch and spurs,° switch and spurs, or I'll cry a match.°   60
MERCUTIO. Nay, if thy wits run the wild-goose chase, I have done; for thou hast more of the wild goose in one of thy wits than, I am sure, I have in my whole five. Was I with you there for the goose?°
ROMEO. Thou wast never with me for anything when thus wast not there for the goose.   65
MERCUTIO. I will bite thee by the ear for that jest.
ROMEO. Nay, good goose, bite not.
MERCUTIO. Thy wit is a very bitter sweeting, it is a most sharp sauce.
ROMEO. And is it not well served in to a sweet goose?   69
MERCUTIO. Oh, here's a wit of cheveril,° that stretches from an inch narrow to an ell broad!
ROMEO. I stretch it out for that word "broad," which, added to the goose, proves thee far and wide a broad goose.   73
MERCUTIO. Why, is not this better now than groaning for love? Now art thou sociable, now art thou Romeo; now art thou what thou art, by art as well as by nature. For this driveling love is like a great natural° that runs lolling up and down to hide his bauble° in a hole.
BENVOLIO. Stop there, stop there.
MERCUTIO. Thou desirest me to stop in my tale against the hair.°   80
BENVOLIO. Thou wouldst else have made thy tale large.°
MERCUTIO. Oh, thou art deceived—I would have made it short. For I was come to the whole depth of my tale, and meant indeed to occupy the argument no longer.
ROMEO. Here's goodly gear!°   85

[*Enter* NURSE *and* PETER.]

MERCUTIO. A sail, a sail!
BENVOLIO. Two, two—a shirt and a smock.°
NURSE. Peter!
PETER. Anon?
NURSE. My fan, Peter.   90
MERCUTIO. Good Peter, to hide her face, for her fan's the fairer face.
NURSE. God ye good morrow, gentlemen.

---

60. *Switch and spurs:* at full gallop urge your wits on.   *match:* wager. Romeo means: If you can't keep up this wit contest, I claim the wager.   63. *Was . . . goose?:* Have I proved you to be a goose?   70. *cheveril:* kidskin.   77. *natural:* fool.   *bauble:* the fool's stick, ornamented with a doll's head.   80. *against the hair:* contrary to the natural life of the hair, as when one strokes a cat from the tail forward.   81. *large:* licentious.   85. *gear:* stuff.   87. *shirt . . . smock:* man and a woman.

MERCUTIO. God ye good-den, fair gentlewoman.
NURSE. Is it good-den?° 94
MERCUTIO. 'Tis no less, I tell you, for the bawdy hand of the dial is now upon the prick° of noon.
NURSE. Out upon you! What a man are you!
ROMEO. One, gentlewoman, that God hath made himself to mar.
NURSE. By my troth, it is well said. "For himself to mar," quoth a'? Gentlemen, can any of you tell me where I may find the young Romeo? 101
ROMEO. I can tell you, but young Romeo will be older when you have found him than he was when you sought him. I am the youngest of that name, for fault of a worse.
NURSE. You say well. 105
MERCUTIO. Yea, is the worst well? Very well took, i' faith—wisely, wisely.
NURSE. If you be he, sir, I desire some confidence° with you.
BENVOLIO. She will indite° him to some supper.
MERCUTIO. A bawd, a bawd, a bawd! So ho!° 110
ROMEO. What hast thou found?
MERCUTIO. No hare,° sir, unless a hare, sir, in a lenten pie, that is something stale and hoar° ere it be spent. [*Sings.*]
"An old hare hoar,
And an old hare hoar, 115
Is very good meat in Lent.
But a hare that is hoar,
Is too much for a score
When it hoars ere it be spent." 119
Romeo, will you come to your father's? We'll to dinner thither.
ROMEO. I will follow you.
MERCUTIO. Farewell, ancient lady, farewell [*singing*], "lady, lady, lady."
[*Exeunt* MERCUTIO *and* BENVOLIO.]
NURSE. Marry, farewell! I pray you, sir, what saucy merchant was this, that was so full of his ropery?° 124
ROMEO. A gentleman, Nurse, that loves to hear himself talk, and will speak more in a minute than he will stand to in a month.
NURSE. An a' speak anything against me, I'll take him down, an a' were lustier than he is, and twenty such Jacks;° and if I cannot, I'll find those that shall. Scurvy knave! I am none of his flirt-gills,° I am

---

94. *Is it good-den?:* Is it afternoon? 96. *prick:* point. 108. *confidence:* for "conference." The old Nurse loves long words, but is not always sure of their meaning. 109. *indite:* for "invite." 110. *So ho!:* the hunter's cry signifying he has spied game. 112. *hare:* prostitute. 113. *hoar:* moldy. 124. *ropery:* for "roguery." 128. *Jacks:* knaves. 129. *flirt-gills:* loose women.

none of his skainsmates.° [*Turning to* PETER] And thou must stand
by too, and suffer every knave to use me at his pleasure?   131
PETER. I saw no man use you at his pleasure. If I had, my weapon
should quickly have been out, I warrant you. I dare draw as soon as
another man, if I see occasion in a good quarrel and the law on my
side.   135
NURSE. Now, afore God, I am so vexed that every part about me
quivers. Scurvy knave! Pray you, sir, a word. And as I told you, my
young lady bade me inquire you out—what she bade me say, I will
keep to myself. But first let me tell ye, if ye should lead her into a
fool's paradise, as they say, it were a very gross kind of behavior, as
they say. For the gentlewoman is young, and therefore if you should
deal double with her, truly it were an ill thing to be offered to any
gentlewoman, and very weak dealing.   143
ROMEO. Nurse, commend me to thy lady and mistress. I protest° unto
thee—   145
NURSE. Good heart, and, i' faith, I will tell her as much. Lord, Lord,
she will be a joyful woman.
ROMEO. What wilt thou tell her, Nurse? Thou dost not mark° me.
NURSE. I will tell her, sir, that you do protest, which, as I take it, is a
gentlemanlike offer.   150
ROMEO. Bid her devise
Some means to come to shrift this afternoon,
And there she shall at Friar Laurence' cell
Be shrived and married. Here is for thy pains.
NURSE. No, truly, sir, not a penny.   155
ROMEO. Go to, I say you shall.
NURSE. This afternoon, sir? Well, she shall be there.
ROMEO. And stay, good Nurse, behind the abbey wall.
Within this hour my man shall be with thee,
And bring thee cords made like a tackled stair,°   160
Which to the high topgallant° of my joy
Must be my convoy in the secret night.
Farewell. Be trusty, and I'll quit thy pains.°
Farewell, commend me to thy mistress.
NURSE. Now God in Heaven bless thee! Hark you, sir.   165
ROMEO. What say'st thou, my dear nurse?
NURSE. Is your man secret? Did you ne'er hear say
Two may keep counsel, putting one away?
ROMEO. I warrant thee, my man's as true as steel.   169

130. *skainsmates:* gangsters.   144. *protest:* declare.   148. *mark:* pay attention to.
160. *tackled stair:* rope ladder, as on a sailing ship.   161. *topgallant:* small mast
fixed to the top of the mainmast.   163. *quit thy pains:* reward your trouble.

NURSE. Well, sir, my mistress is the sweetest lady—Lord, Lord, when 'twas a little prating thing—Oh, there is a nobleman in town, one Paris, that would fain lay knife aboard;° but she, good soul, had as lieve° see a toad, a very toad, as see him. I anger her sometimes, and tell her that Paris is the properer man. But I'll warrant you, when I say so, she looks as pale as any clout° in the versal world.° Doth not rosemary and Romeo begin both with a letter? 176
ROMEO. Aye, Nurse, what of that? Both with an R.
NURSE. Ah, mocker! That's the dog's name.° R is for the—No, I know it begins with some other letter—and she hath the prettiest sententious° of it, of you and rosemary, that it would do you good to hear it. 181
ROMEO. Commend me to thy lady.
NURSE. Aye, a thousand times.   [*Exit* ROMEO.]
  Peter!
PETER. Anon?   185
NURSE. Peter, take my fan, and go before, and apace.°   [*Exeunt*.]

SCENE 5. CAPULET's *orchard*.

[*Enter* JULIET.]

JULIET. The clock struck nine when I did send the nurse.
  In half an hour she promised to return.
  Perchance she cannot meet him. That's not so.
  Oh, she is lame! Love's heralds should be thoughts,
  Which ten times faster glide than the sun's beams,   5
  Driving back shadows over lowering° hills.
  Therefore do nimble-pinioned° doves draw love,
  And therefore hath the wind-swift Cupid wings.
  Now is the sun upon the highmost hill
  Of this day's journey, and from nine till twelve   10
  Is three long hours; yet she is not come.
  Had she affections and warm youthful blood,
  She would be as swift in motion as a ball,
  My words would bandy° her to my sweet love,
  And his to me.   15

172. *lay knife aboard:* get her for himself.   173. *lieve:* soon.   175. *clout:* cloth. *versal world:* universe.   178. *dog's name:* The letter "R" was called the dog's letter because it makes a growling sound.   180. *sententious:* for "sentence"; proverb.   186. *apace:* quickly.
  sc. 5: 6. *lowering:* frowning.   7. *nimble-pinioned:* swift winged.   14. *bandy:* hit back, as a tennis ball.

But old folks, many feign as they were dead,
Unwieldy, slow, heavy and pale as lead.

[*Enter* NURSE, *with* PETER.]

Oh, God, she comes! O honey Nurse, what news?
Hast thou met with him? Send thy man away.   19
NURSE. Peter, stay at the gate.   [*Exit* PETER.]
JULIET. Now, good sweet Nurse—Oh, Lord, why look'st thou sad?
Though news be sad, yet tell them merrily;
If good, thou shamest the music of sweet news
By playing it to me with so sour a face.
NURSE. I am aweary, give me leave° a while.   25
Fie, how my bones ache! What a jaunce° have I had!
JULIET. I would thou hadst my bones and I thy news.
Nay, come, I pray thee, speak, good, good Nurse, speak.
NURSE. Jesu, what haste? Can you not stay a while?
Do you not see that I am out of breath?   30
JULIET. How art thou out of breath when thou hast breath
To say to me that thou art out of breath?
The excuse that thou dost make in this delay
Is longer than the tale thou dost excuse.
Is thy news good, or bad? Answer to that.   35
Say either, and I'll stay the circumstance.°
Let me be satisfied, is 't good or bad?
NURSE. Well, you have made a simple choice. You know not how to choose a man. Romeo! No, not he, though his face be better than any man's, yet his leg excels all men's; and for a hand, and a foot, and a body, though they be not to be talked on, yet they are past compare. He is not the flower of courtesy, but, I'll warrant him, as gentle as a lamb. Go thy ways, wench, serve God. What, have you dined at home?
JULIET. No, no. But all this did I know before.   45
What says he of our marriage? What of that?
NURSE. Lord, how my head aches! What a head have I!
It beats as it would fall in twenty pieces.
My back o' t' other side—ah, my back, my back!
Beshrew° your heart for sending me about   50
To catch my death with jauncing up and down!
JULIET. I' faith, I am sorry that thou art not well.
Sweet, sweet, sweet Nurse, tell me, what says my love?

25. *give me leave:* let me alone.   26. *jaunce:* running to and fro.   36. *stay the circumstance:* wait for details.   50. *Beshrew:* plague on.

NURSE. Your love says, like an honest gentleman, and a courteous, and
a kind, and a handsome, and, I warrant, a virtuous—Where is your
mother?   56
JULIET. Where is my mother! Why, she is within,
Where should she be? How oddly thou repliest!
"Your love says, like an honest gentleman,
Where is your mother?"
NURSE.   Oh, God's Lady dear! °   60
Are you so hot°? Marry, come up,° I trow.
Is this the poultice for my aching bones?
Henceforward do your messages yourself.
JULIET. Here's such a coil! ° Come, what says Romeo?
NURSE. Have you got leave to go to shrift today?   65
JULIET. I have.
NURSE. Then hie° you hence to Friar Laurence' cell,
There stays a husband to make you a wife.
Now comes the wanton blood up in your cheeks,
They'll be in scarlet straight at any news.   70
Hie you to church, I must another way,
To fetch a ladder by the which your love
Must climb a bird's nest soon when it is dark.
I am the drudge, and toil in your delight,
But you shall bear the burden soon at night.   75
Go, I'll to dinner, hie you to the cell.
JULIET. Hie to high fortune! Honest Nurse, farewell.   [*Exeunt.*]

SCENE 6. FRIAR LAURENCE's *cell.*

[*Enter* FRIAR LAURENCE *and* ROMEO.]

FRIAR LAURENCE. So smile the Heavens upon this holy act
That afterhours with sorrow chide us not!
ROMEO. Amen, amen! But come what sorrow can,
It cannot countervail ° the exchange of joy
That one short minute gives me in her sight.   5
Do thou but close our hands with holy words,
Then love-devouring death do what he dare,
It is enough I may but call her mine.
FRIAR LAURENCE. These violent delights have violent ends,

---

60. *God's . . . dear:* by God's dear Mother; i.e., the Virgin Mary.   61. *hot:* eager.
Marry . . . up: an expression of angry impatience.   64. *coil:* fuss.   67. *hie:* hasten.
   sc. 6: 4. *countervail:* counterbalance.

And in their triumph die, like fire and powder° 10
Which as they kiss consume. The sweetest honey
Is loathsome in his own deliciousness,
And in the taste confounds the appetite.
Therefore, love moderately, long love doth so,
Too swift arrives as tardy as too slow. 15
  [*Enter* JULIET.]
Here comes the lady. Oh, so light a foot
Will ne'er wear out the everlasting flint.
A lover may bestride the gossamer
That idles in the wanton summer air,
And yet not fall, so light is vanity. 20
JULIET. Good even to my ghostly confessor.
FRIAR LAURENCE. Romeo shall thank thee, daughter, for us both.
JULIET. As much to him, else is his thanks too much.
ROMEO. Ah, Juliet, if the measure of thy joy
  Be heaped like mine, and that thy skill be more 25
  To blazon° it, then sweeten with thy breath
  This neighbor air, and let rich music's tongue
  Unfold the imagined happiness that both
  Receive in either by this dear encounter.
JULIET. Conceit,° more rich in matter than in words, 30
  Brags of his substance, not of ornament.
  They are but beggars that can count their worth,
  But my true love is grown to such excess,
  I cannot sum up sum of half my wealth. 34
FRIAR LAURENCE. Come, come with me, and we will make short work,
  For, by your leaves, you shall not stay alone
  Till Holy Church incorporate two in one. [*Exeunt.*]

ACT THREE

SCENE I. *A public place.*

  [*Enter* MERCUTIO, BENVOLIO, PAGE, *and* SERVANTS.]

BENVOLIO. I pray thee, good Mercutio, let's retire.
  The day is hot, the Capulets abroad,

---

10. *fire and powder:* Elizabethan cannon were discharged by applying a lighted match to loose gunpowder.   30. *Conceit:* understanding.

And if we meet, we shall not 'scape a brawl;
For now these hot days is the mad blood stirring. 4
MERCUTIO. Thou art like one of those fellows that when he enters the confines of a tavern claps me his sword upon the table and says, "God send me no need of thee!" and by the operation of the second cup draws it on the drawer,° when indeed there is no need.
BENVOLIO. Am I like such a fellow? 9
MERCUTIO. Come, come, thou art as hot a Jack in thy mood as any in Italy, and as soon moved to be moody, and as soon moody to be moved.
BENVOLIO. And what to? 13
MERCUTIO. Nay, an there were two such, we should have none shortly, for one would kill the other. Thou! Why, thou wilt quarrel with a man that hath a hair more, or a hair less, in his beard than thou hast. Thou wilt quarrel with a man for cracking nuts, having no other reason but because thou hast hazel eyes. What eye but such an eye would spy out such a quarrel? Thy head is as full of quarrels as an egg is full of meat, and yet thy head hath been beaten as addle as an egg for quarreling. Thou hast quarreled with a man for coughing in the street, because he hath wakened thy dog that hath lain asleep in the sun. Didst thou not fall out with a tailor for wearing his new doublet before Easter? With another for tying his new shoes with old ribbon? And yet thou wilt tutor me from quarreling! ° 25
BENVOLIO. An I were so apt to quarrel as thou art, any man should buy the fee simple° of my life for an hour and a quarter.
MERCUTIO. The fee simple! Oh, simple!

[*Enter* TYBALT *and others.*]

BENVOLIO. By my head, here come the Capulets.
MERCUTIO. By my heel, I care not. 30
TYBALT. Follow me close, for I will speak to them. Gentlemen, good-den—a word with one of you.
MERCUTIO. And but one word with one of us? Couple it with something—make it a word and a blow.
TYBALT. You shall find me apt enough to that, sir, an you will give me occasion. 36
MERCUTIO. Could you not take some occasion without giving?
TYBALT. Mercutio, thou consort'st° with Romeo—

ACT THREE, SC. 1: 8. *drawer:* potboy who fetches the drinks in a tavern. 25. *tutor . . . quarreling:* instruct me how to avoid quarreling. 27. *fee simple:* absolute possession, a legal phrase meaning "holding in perpetuity." 38. *consort'st:* you are a companion of. Mercutio takes up the other meaning of consort: a party of musicians playing different instruments.

MERCUTIO. Consort! What, dost thou make us minstrels? An thou
make minstrels of us, look to hear nothing but discords. Here's my
fiddlestick,° here's that shall make you dance. Zounds,° consort! 41
BENVOLIO. We talk here in the public haunt of men.
Either withdraw unto some private place,
And reason coldly of your grievances,
Or else depart. Here all eyes gaze on us. 45
MERCUTIO. Men's eyes were made to look, and let them gaze.
I will not budge for no man's pleasure, I.

[*Enter* ROMEO.]

TYBALT. Well, peace be with you, sir. Here comes my man.
MERCUTIO. But I'll be hanged, sir, if he wear your livery.
Marry, go before to field, he'll be your follower. 50
Your worship in that sense may call him man.
TYBALT. Romeo, the hate I bear thee can afford
No better term than this—thou art a villain.
ROMEO. Tybalt, the reason that I have to love thee
Doth much excuse the appertaining rage 55
To such a greeting. Villain am I none,
Therefore farewell. I see thou know'st me not.
TYBALT. Boy, this shall not excuse the injuries
That thou hast done me, therefore turn and draw.
ROMEO. I do protest I never injured thee, 60
But love thee better than thou canst devise°
Till thou shalt know the reason of my love.
And so, good Capulet—which name I tender°
As dearly as mine own—be satisfied.
MERCUTIO. Oh, calm, dishonorable, vile submission! 65
Alla stocatta° carries it away. [*Draws.*]
Tybalt, you ratcatcher, will you walk?
TYBALT. What wouldst thou have with me?
MERCUTIO. Good King of Cats, nothing but one of your nine lives, that
I mean to make bold withal, and, as you shall use me hereafter, dry-
beat the rest of the eight. Will you pluck your sword out of his
pilcher° by the ears? Make haste, lest mine be about your ears ere it
be out.
TYBALT. I am for you. [*Drawing.*]

41. *fiddlestick:* i.e., rapier.   *Zounds:* by God's wounds, a common oath.   61.
devise: think.   63. *tender:* regard.   66. *Alla stocata:* a thrust. Mercutio thinks
that Tybalt with his newfangled skill with the rapier has terrified Romeo into
behaving like a coward.   72. *pilcher:* scabbard; lit., a leather coat.

ROMEO. Gentle Mercutio, put thy rapier up. 75
MERCUTIO. Come, sir, your passado. [*They fight.*]
ROMEO. Draw, Benvolio, beat down their weapons.
  Gentlemen, for shame, forbear this outrage!
  Tybalt, Mercutio, the Prince expressly hath
  Forbid this bandying° in Verona streets. 80
  Hold, Tybalt, good Mercutio!

[TYBALT *under* ROMEO's *arm stabs* MERCUTIO *and flies with his followers.*]

MERCUTIO.   I am hurt.
  A plague o' both your houses! I am sped.°
  Is he gone, and hath nothing?
BENVOLIO.   What, art thou hurt?
MERCUTIO. Aye, aye, a scratch, a scratch—marry, 'tis enough.
  Where is my page? Go, villain, fetch a surgeon. [*Exit* PAGE.]
ROMEO. Courage, man, the hurt cannot be much. 86
MERCUTIO. No, 'tis not so deep as a well nor so wide as a church door, but 'tis enough, 'twill serve. Ask for me tomorrow and you shall find me a grave man.° I am peppered, I warrant, for this world. A plague o' both your houses! 'Zounds, a dog, a rat, a mouse, a cat, to scratch a man to death! A braggart, a rogue, a villain, that fights by the book of arithmetic!° Why the devil came you between us! I was hurt under your arm.
ROMEO. I thought all for the best.
MERCUTIO. Help me into some house, Benvolio, 95
  Or I shall faint. A plague o' both your houses!
  They have made worms' meat of me. I have it,
  And soundly too—your houses! [*Exeunt* MERCUTIO *and* BENVOLIO.]
ROMEO. This gentleman, the Prince's near ally,
  My very friend, hath got his mortal hurt 100
  In my behalf, my reputation stained
  With Tybalt's slander—Tybalt, that an hour
  Hath been my kinsman. O sweet Juliet,
  Thy beauty hath made me effeminate,
  And in my temper softened valor's steel! 105

[*Re-enter* BENVOLIO.]

BENVOLIO. O Romeo, Romeo, brave Mercutio's dead!

80. *bandying:* quarreling. 82. *sped:* done for. 89. *grave man:* Mercutios' last pun. 92. *book of arithmetic:* exact rules of fencing.

That gallant spirit hath aspired° the clouds,
Which too untimely here did scorn the earth.
ROMEO. This day's black fate on more days doth depend,°
This but begins the woe others must end. 110

[*Re-enter* TYBALT.]

BENVOLIO. Here comes the furious Tybalt back again.
ROMEO. Alive, in triumph! And Mercutio slain!
Away to Heaven, respective lenity,°
And fire-eyed fury be my conduct° now!
Now, Tybalt, take the "villain" back again 115
That late thou gavest me; for Mercutio's soul
Is but a little way above our heads,
Staying for thine to keep him company.
Either thou, or I, or both, must go with him.
TYBALT. Thou, wretched boy, that didst consort him here, 120
Shalt with him hence.
ROMEO. This shall determine that.

[*They fight;* TYBALT *falls.*]

BENVOLIO. Romeo, away, be gone!
The citizens are up, and Tybalt slain.
Stand not amazed. The Prince will doom thee death
If thou art taken. Hence, be gone, away! 125
ROMEO. Oh, I am fortune's fool!°
BENVOLIO. Why dost thou stay? [*Exit* ROMEO.]

[*Enter* CITIZENS, *etc.*]

FIRST CITIZEN. Which way ran he that killed Mercutio?
Tybalt, that murderer, which way ran he?
BENVOLIO. There lies that Tybalt.
FIRST CITIZEN. Up, sir, go with me. 130
I charge thee in the Prince's name, obey.

[*Enter* PRINCE, *attended;* MONTAGUE, CAPULET, *their* WIVES, *and others.*]

PRINCE. Where are the vile beginners of this fray?
BENVOLIO. O noble Prince, I can discover° all

107. *aspired:* soared to. 109. *This . . . depend:* i.e., This day is but the beginning of many more fateful days. 113. *respective lenity:* considerate mercy; i.e., I will no longer make allowances for Tybalt as Juliet's kinsman. 114. *conduct:* guide. 126. *fortune's fool:* fooled by fortune. 133. *discover:* reveal.

The unlucky manage° of this fatal brawl.
There lies the man, slain by young Romeo, 135
That slew thy kinsman, brave Mercutio.
LADY CAPULET. Tybalt, my cousin! Oh, my brother's child!
O Prince! O Cousin! Husband! Oh, the blood is spilt
Of my dear kinsman! Prince, as thou art true,
For blood of ours shed blood of Montague. 140
O Cousin, Cousin!
PRINCE. Benvolio, who began this bloody fray?
BENVOLIO. Tybalt, here slain, whom Romeo's hand did slay—
Romeo that spoke him fair, bade him bethink
How nice° the quarrel was, and urged withal 145
Your high displeasure. All this uttered
With gentle breath, calm look, knees humbly bowed,
Could not take truce with the unruly spleen°
Of Tybalt deaf to pace, but that he tilts
With piercing steel at bold Mercutio's breast, 150
Who, all as hot, turns deadly point to point,
And, with a martial scorn, with one hand beats
Cold death aside and with the other sends
It back to Tybalt, whose dexterity
Retorts it. Romeo, he cries aloud, 155
"Hold, friends! Friends, part!" and, swifter than his tongue,
His agile arm beats down their fatal points,
And 'twixt them rushes. Underneath whose arm
An envious° thrust from Tybalt hit the life
Of stout Mercutio, and then Tybalt fled, 160
But by and by comes back to Romeo,
Who had but newly entertained revenge,
And to 't they go like lightning. For ere I
Could draw to part them was stout Tybalt slain,
And as he fell, did Romeo turn and fly. 165
This is the truth, or let Benvolio die.
LADY CAPULET. He is a kinsman to the Montague,
Affection makes him false, he speaks not true.
Some twenty of them fought in this black strife,
And all those twenty could but kill one life. 170
I beg for justice, which thou, Prince, must give.
Romeo slew Tybalt, Romeo must not live.

---

134. *manage:* management, circumstances. 145. *nice:* trifling. 148. *spleen:* fiery temper. 159. *envious:* hateful.

PRINCE. Romeo slew him, he slew Mercutio.
  Who now the price of his dear blood doth owe?
MONTAGUE. Not Romeo, Prince, he was Mercutio's friend. 175
  His fault concludes but what the law should end,
  The life of Tybalt.
PRINCE. And for that offense
  Immediately we do exile him hence.
  I have an interest in your hate's proceeding,
  My blood for your rude brawls doth lie a-bleeding. 180
  But I'll amerce° you with so strong a fine
  That you shall all repent the loss of mine.
  I will be deaf to pleading and excuses,
  Nor tears nor prayers shall purchase out° abuses.
  Therefore use none. Let Romeo hence in haste, 185
  Else, when he's found, that hour is his last.
  Bear hence this body, and attend our will.°
  Mercy but murders, pardoning those that kill. [*Exeunt.*]

SCENE 2. CAPULET's *orchard.*

[*Enter* JULIET.]

JULIET. Gallop apace, you fiery-footed steeds,
  Toward Phoebus'° lodging. Such a wagoner
  As Phaëton° would whip you to the west,
  And bring in cloudy night immediately.
  Spread thy close curtain, love-performing night, 5
  That runaways' eyes may wink, and Romeo
  Leap to these arms, untalked of and unseen.
  Lovers can see to do their amorous rites
  By their own beauties; or, if love be blind,
  It best agrees with night. Come, civil night, 10
  Thou sober-suited matron, all in black,
  And learn me how to lose a winning match
  Played for a pair of stainless maidenhoods.
  Hood my unmanned blood bating in my cheeks
  With thy black mantle, till strange love grown bold 15

181. *amerce:* punish. 184. *purchase out:* pay for. 187. *attend our will:* come to receive my judgment.
  sc. 2: 2. *Phoebus:* Phoebus, the sun, was daily drawn across the sky in his chariot. 3. *Phaëton:* the sun god's son, who tried to drive his father's chariot, but the horses bolted.

Think true love acted simple modesty.
Come, night, come, Romeo, come, thou day in night,
For thou wilt lie upon the wings of night
Whiter than new snow on a raven's back.
Come, gentle night, come, loving, black-browed night, 20
Give me my Romeo; and when he shall die,
Take him and cut him out in little stars,
And he will make the face of heaven so fine
That all the world will be in love with night,
And pay no worship to the garish sun. 25
Oh, I have bought the mansion of a love,
But not possessed it, and though I am sold,
Not yet enjoyed. So tedious is this day
As is the night before some festival
To an impatient child that hath new robes 30
And may not wear them. Oh, here comes my nurse,
And she brings news, and every tongue that speaks
But Romeo's name speaks heavenly eloquence.

[*Enter* NURSE, *with cords.*]

Now, Nurse, what news? What hast thou there? The cords
That Romeo bid thee fetch? 35
NURSE. Aye, aye, the cords. [*Throws them down.*]
JULIET. Aye me! What news? Why dost thou wring thy hands?
NURSE. Ah, welladay! He's dead, he's dead, he's dead.
We are undone, lady, we are undone.
Alack the day! He's gone, he's killed, he's dead. 40
JULIET. Can Heaven be so envious?
NURSE.   Romeo can,
Though Heaven cannot. O Romeo, Romeo!
Who ever would have thought it? Romeo!
JULIET. What devil art thou that dost torment me thus?
This torture should be roared in dismal Hell. 45
Hath Romeo slain himself? Say thou but "I,"°
And that bare vowel "I" shall poison more
Than the death-darting eye of cockatrice.°
I am not I, if there be such an I,
Or those eyes shut, that make thee answer "I." 50
If he be slain, say "I," or if not, no.
Brief sounds determine of my weal or woe.

46. *Say . . . "I"*: Puns on "aye" and "I" are common. 48. *cockatrice:* a fabulous serpent so deadly that it could slay by its mere glance.

NURSE. I saw the wound, I saw it with mine eyes—
　　God save the mark!—here on his manly breast.
　　A piteous corse, a bloody piteous corse,　　　　　　　　55
　　Pale, pale as ashes, all bedaubed in blood,
　　All in gore blood. I swounded at the sight.
JULIET. Oh, break, my heart! Poor bankrupt, break at once!
　　To prison, eyes, ne'er look on liberty!
　　Vile earth to earth resign, end motion here,　　　　　　60
　　And thou and Romeo press one heavy bier!
NURSE. O Tybalt, Tybalt, the best friend I had!
　　O courteous Tybalt! Honest gentleman!
　　That ever I should live to see thee dead!
JULIET. What storm is this that blows so contrary?　　　　65
　　Is Romeo slaughtered, and is Tybalt dead?
　　My dear-loved cousin, and my dearer lord?
　　Then, dreadful trumpet, sound the general doom! °
　　For who is living if those two are gone?
NURSE. Tybalt is gone, and Romeo banishèd—　　　　　　70
　　Romeo that killed him, he is banishèd.
JULIET. Oh, God! Did Romeo's hand shed Tybalt's blood?
NURSE. It did, it did. Alas the day, it did!
JULIET. Oh, serpent heart, hid with a flowering face!
　　Did ever dragon keep so fair a cave?　　　　　　　　　　75
　　Beautiful tyrant! Fiend angelical!
　　Dove-feathered raven! Wolvish-ravening lamb!
　　Despisèd substance of divinest show!
　　Just opposite to what thou justly seem'st,
　　A damnèd saint, an honorable villain!　　　　　　　　　80
　　O Nature, what hadst thou to do in Hell
　　When thou didst bower° the spirit of a fiend
　　In mortal paradise of such sweet flesh?
　　Was ever book containing such vile matter
　　So fairly bound? Oh, that deceit should dwell　　　　　85
　　In such a gorgeous palace!
NURSE.　　　　　　　　　There's no trust,
　　No faith, no honesty in men—all perjured,
　　All forsworn, all naught, all dissemblers.°
　　Ah, where's my man? Give me some aqua vitae.°
　　These griefs, these woes, these sorrows, make me old.　90
　　Shame come to Romeo!
JULIET.　　　　　　　　Blistered be thy tongue

---

82. *bower:* embower.　88. *dissemblers:* hypocrites.　89. *aqua vitae:* spirits.

    For such a wish! He was not born to shame.
    Upon his brow shame is ashamed to sit,
    For 'tis a throne where honor may be crowned
    Sole monarch of the universal earth. 95
    Oh, what a beast was I to chide at him!
NURSE. Will you speak well of him that killed your cousin?
JULIET. Shall I speak ill of him that is my husband?
    Ah, poor my lord, what tongue shall smooth thy name
    When I, thy three-hours wife, have mangled it? 100
    But wherefore, villain, didst thou kill my cousin?
    That villain cousin would have killed my husband.
    Back, foolish tears, back to your native spring,
    Your tributary drops belong to woe
    Which you mistaking offer up to joy. 105
    My husband lives, that Tybalt would have slain,
    And Tybalt's dead, that would have slain my husband.
    All this is comfort, wherefore weep I, then?
    Some word there was, worser than Tybalt's death,
    That murdered me. I would forget it fain, 110
    But, oh, it presses to my memory
    Like damnèd guilty deeds to sinners' minds.
    "Tybalt is dead, and Romeo banishèd."
    That "banishèd," that one word "banishèd,"
    Hath slain ten thousand Tybalts. Tybalt's death 115
    Was woe enough if it had ended there.
    Or, if sour woe delights in fellowship,
    And needly° will be ranked with other griefs,
    Why followed not, when she said "Tybalt's dead,"
    Thy father, or thy mother, nay, or both, 120
    Which modern° lamentation might have moved?
    But with a rearward following Tybalt's death,
    "Romeo is banishèd." To speak that word
    Is father, mother, Tybalt, Romeo, Juliet,
    All slain, all dead. "Romeo is banishèd." 125
    There is no end, no limit, measure, bound,
    In that word's death; no words can that woe sound.
    Where is my father, and my mother, Nurse?
NURSE. Weeping and wailing over Tybalt's corse.
    Will you go to them? I will bring you thither. 130
JULIET. Wash they his wounds with tears. Mine shall be spent,
    When theirs are dry, for Romeo's banishment.

---

118. *needly:* necessarily.   121. *modern:* ordinary.

Take up those cords. Poor ropes, you are beguiled,
Both you and I, for Romeo is exiled.
He made you for a highway to my bed, 135
But I, a maid, die maiden-widowèd.
Come, cords, come Nurse, I'll to my wedding bed,
And death, not Romeo, take my maidenhead!
NURSE. Hie to your chamber. I'll find Romeo
To comfort you. I wot° well where he is. 140
Hark ye, your Romeo will be here at night.
I'll to him—he is hid at Laurence' cell.
JULIET. Oh, find him! Give this ring to my true knight,
And bid him come to take his last farewell. [*Exeunt.*]

SCENE 3. FRIAR LAURENCE'*s cell*.

[*Enter* FRIAR LAURENCE.]

FRIAR LAURENCE. Romeo, come forth, come forth, thou fearful man.
Affliction is enamored of thy parts,°
And thou art wedded to calamity.

[*Enter* ROMEO.]

ROMEO. Father, what news? What is the Prince's doom?°
What sorrow craves acquaintance at my hand 5
That I yet know not?
FRIAR LAURENCE. Too familiar
Is my dear son with such sour company.
I bring thee tidings of the Prince's doom.
ROMEO. What less than Doomsday is the Prince's doom?
FRIAR LAURENCE. A gentler judgment vanished from his lips, 10
Not body's death, but body's banishment.
ROMEO. Ha, banishment! Be merciful, say "death,"
For exile hath more terror in his look,
Much more, than death. Do not say "banishment."
FRIAR LAURENCE. Hence from Verona art thou banishèd. 15
Be patient, for the world is broad and wide.
ROMEO. There is no world without Verona walls,
But Purgatory, torture, Hell itself.

---

140. *wot:* know.
sc. 3: 2. *Affliction . . . parts:* Sorrow has fallen in love with your good qualities. 4. *doom:* degree, punishment.

Hence banishèd from the world,
And world's exile is death. Then "banishèd"
Is death mistermed. Calling death "banishèd,"
Thou cut'st my head off with a golden ax,
And smilest upon the stroke that murders me.
FRIAR LAURENCE. Oh, deadly sin! Oh, rude unthankfulness!
Thy fault our law calls death, but the kind Prince,
Taking thy part, hath rushed° aside the law,
And turned that black word "death" to "banishment."
This is dear mercy, and thou seest it not.
ROMEO. 'Tis torture, and not mercy. Heaven is here,
Where Juliet lives, and every cat and dog
And little mouse, every unworthy thing,
Live here in Heaven and may look on her,
But Romeo may not. More validity,
More honorable state, more courtship, lives
In carrion flies than Romeo. They may seize
On the white wonder of dear Juliet's hand,
And steal immortal blessing from her lips,
Who, even in pure and vestal modesty,
Still blush, as thinking their own kisses sin.
But Romeo may not, he is banishèd.
This may flies do, but I from this must fly.
They are free men, but I am banishèd.
And say'st thou yet that exile is not death?
Hadst thou no poison mixed, no sharp-ground knife,
No sudden mean of death, though ne'er so mean,
But "banishèd" to kill me?—"Banishèd"?
O Friar, the damnèd use that word in Hell,
Howling attends it. How hast thou the heart,
Being a divine, a ghostly confessor,
A sin-absolver, and my friend professed,
To mangle me with that word "banishèd"?
FRIAR LAURENCE. Thou fond° madman, hear me but speak a word.
ROMEO. Oh, thou wilt speak again of banishment.
FRIAR LAURENCE. I'll give thee armor to keep off that word,
Adversity's sweet milk, philosophy,
To comfort thee, though thou art banishèd.
ROMEO. Yet "banishèd"? Hang up philosophy!
Unless philosophy can make a Juliet,
Displant° a town, reverse a Prince's doom,

26. *rushed:* brushed.   52. *fond:* foolish.

It helps not, it prevails not. Talk no more. 60
FRIAR LAURENCE. Oh, then I see that madmen have no ears.
ROMEO. How should they when that wise men have no eyes?
FRIAR LAURENCE. Let me dispute with thee of thy estate.°
ROMEO. Thou canst not speak of that thou dost not feel.
    Wert thou as young as I, Juliet thy love, 65
    An hour but married, Tybalt murderèd,
    Doting like me, and like me banishèd,
    Then mightst thou speak, then mightst thou tear thy hair
    And fall upon the ground, as I do now,
    Taking the measure of an unmade grave. 70
                    [*Knocking within.*]
FRIAR LAURENCE. Arise, one knocks. Good Romeo, hide thyself.
ROMEO. Not I, unless the breath of heartsick groans
    Mistlike enfold me from the search of eyes.   [*Knocking.*]
FRIAR LAURENCE. Hark how they knock! Who's there? Romeo, arise,
    Thou wilt be taken.—Stay awhile!—Stand up, [*Knocking.*] 75
    Run to my study.—By and by!—God's will,
    What simpleness is this!—I come, I come!   [*Knocking.*]
    Who knocks so hard? Whence come you? What's your will?
NURSE [*within*]. Let me come in, and you shall know my errand.
    I come from Lady Juliet.
FRIAR LAURENCE.   Welcome, then. 80

[*Enter* NURSE.]

NURSE. O holy Friar, oh, tell me, holy Friar,
    Where is my lady's lord, where's Romeo?
FRIAR LAURENCE. There on the ground, with his own tears made drunk.
NURSE. Oh, he is even in my mistress' case,
    Just in her case!
FRIAR LAURENCE. Oh, woeful sympathy! 85
    Piteous predicament!
NURSE.   Even so lies she,
    Blubbering and weeping, weeping and blubbering.
    Stand up, stand up, stand, an you be a man.
    For Juliet's sake, for her sake, rise and stand.
    Why should you fall into so deep an O?° 90
ROMEO. Nurse!
NURSE. Ah sir, ah sir! Well, death's the end of all.
ROMEO. Spakest thou of Juliet? How is it with her?

59. *Displant:* remove.   63. *estate:* circumstances.   90. *an O:* a great sigh.

  Doth she not think me an old° murderer,
  Now I have stained the childhood of our joy   95
  With blood removed but little from her own?
  Where is she? And how doth she? And what says
  My concealed lady to our canceled love?
NURSE. Oh, she says nothing, sir, but weeps and weeps,
  And now falls on her bed, and then starts up   100
  And Tybalt calls, and then on Romeo cries,
  And then down falls again.
ROMEO.   As if that name,
  Shot from the deadly level of a gun,
  Did murder her, as that name's cursèd hand
  Murdered her kinsman. Oh, tell me, Friar, tell me,   105
  In what vile part of this anatomy
  Doth my name lodge? Tell me, that I may sack
  The hateful mansion.   [*Drawing his dagger.*]
FRIAR LAURENCE.   Hold thy desperate hand.
  Art thou a man? Thy form cries out thou art.
  Thy tears are womanish, thy wild acts denote   110
  The unreasonable fury of a beast.
  Unseemly woman in a seeming man!
  Or ill-beseeming beast in seeming both!
  Thou hast amazed me. By my holy order,
  I thought thy disposition better tempered.   115
  Hast thou slain Tybalt? Wilt thou slay thyself?
  And slay thy lady too that lives in thee,
  By doing damnèd hate upon thyself?
  Why rail'st thou on thy birth, the Heaven and earth?
  Since birth and Heaven and earth all three do meet   120
  In thee at once, which thou at once wouldst lose.
  Fie, fie, thou shamest thy shape, thy love, thy wit,
  Which, like a usurer,° abound'st in all,
  And usest none in that true use indeed
  Which should bedeck thy shape, thy love, thy wit.   125
  Thy noble shape is but a form of wax,
  Digressing from the valor of a man;
  Thy dear love sworn, but hollow perjury,
  Killing that love which thou hast vowed to cherish;
  Thy wit, that ornament to shape and love,   130
  Misshapen in the conduct of them both,
  Like powder in a skill-less soldier's flask,

---

94. *Old:* veritable; lit., experienced.   123. *usurer:* miser.

Is set afire by thine own ignorance,
And thou dismembered with thine own defense.°
What, rouse thee, man! Thy Juliet is alive, 135
For whose dear sake thou wast but lately dead.
There art thou happy. Tybalt would kill thee,
But thou slew'st Tybalt. There art thou happy too.
The law, that threatened death, becomes thy friend
And turns it to exile. There art thou happy. 140
A pack of blessings lights upon thy back,
Happiness courts thee in her best array;
But, like a misbehaved and sullen wench,
Thou pout'st upon thy fortune and thy love.
Take heed, take heed, for such die miserable. 145
Go, get thee to thy love, as was decreed,
Ascend her chamber—hence and comfort her.
But look thou stay not till the watch be set,°
For then thou canst not pass to Mantua,
Where thou shalt live till we can find a time 150
To blaze° your marriage, reconcile your friends,
Beg pardon of the Prince, and call thee back
With twenty hundred thousand times more joy
Than thou went'st forth in lamentation.
Go before, Nurse. Commend me to thy lady, 155
And bid her hasten all the house to bed,
Which heavy sorrow makes them apt unto.
Romeo is coming.
NURSE. Oh Lord, I could have stayed here all the night
To hear good counsel. Oh, what learning is! 160
My lord, I'll tell my lady you will come.
ROMEO. Do so, and bid my sweet prepare to chide.
NURSE. Here, sir, a ring she bid me give you, sir.
Hie you, make haste, for it grows very late. [*Exit.*]
ROMEO. How well my comfort is revived by this! 165
FRIAR LAURENCE. Go hence, good night, and here stands all your state.
Either be gone before the watch be set,
Or by the break of day disguised from hence.
Sojourn in Mantua. I'll find out your man,
And he shall signify from time to time 170
Every good hap to you that chances here.
Give me thy hand, 'tis late. Farewell, good night.

134. *dismembered . . . defense:* blown to pieces by your own weapon. 148. *watch be set:* The watch go on duty at the gates for the night. 151. *blaze:* make public.

ROMEO. But that a joy past joy calls out on me,
  It were a grief so brief to part with thee.
  Farewell.   [*Exeunt.*] 175

  SCENE 4. *A room in* CAPULET's *house.*

  [*Enter* CAPULET, LADY CAPULET, *and* PARIS.]

CAPULET. Things have fall'n out, sir, so unluckily,
  That we have had no time to move° our daughter.
  Look you, she loved her kinsman Tybalt dearly,
  And so did I. Well, we were born to die.
  'Tis very late, she'll not come down tonight.   5
  I promise you, but for your company
  I would have been abed an hour ago.
PARIS. These times of woe afford no time to woo.
  Madam, good night. Commend me to your daughter.
LADY CAPULET. I will, and know her mind early tomorrow; 10
  Tonight she's mewed° up to her heaviness.
CAPULET. Sir Paris, I will make a desperate tender°
  Of my child's love. I think she will be ruled
  In all respects by me—nay, more, I doubt it not.
  Wife, go you to her ere you go to bed,   15
  Acquaint her here of my son Paris' love,
  And bid her, mark you me, on Wednesday next—
  But, soft! what day is this?
PARIS.   Monday, my lord.
CAPULET. Monday! Ha, ha! Well, Wednesday is too soon.
  O' Thursday let it be. O' Thursday, tell her,   20
  She shall be married to this noble Earl.
  Will you be ready? Do you like this haste?
  We'll keep no great ado, a friend or two;
  For, hark you, Tybalt being slain so late,
  It may be thought we held him carelessly,   25
  Being our kinsman, if we revel much.
  Therefore we'll have some half a dozen friends,
  And there an end. But what say you to Thursday?
PARIS. My lord, I would that Thursday were tomorrow.
CAPULET. Well, get you gone. O' Thursday be it, then.   30
  Go you to Juliet ere you go to bed,

---

sc. 4: 2. *move:* make the proposal to.   11. *mewed:* lit., caged like a hawk.
12. *desperate tender:* bold offer.

Prepare her, wife, against° this wedding day.
Farewell, my lord. Light to my chamber, ho!
Afore me,° it is so very very late
That we may call it early by and by.   35
Good night.   [*Exeunt.*]

SCENE 5. CAPULET's *orchard.*

[*Enter* ROMEO *and* JULIET, *above, at the window.*]

JULIET. Wilt thou be gone? It is not yet near day.
It was the nightingale, and not the lark,
That pierced the fearful hollow of thine ear.
Nightly she sings on yond pomegranate tree.
Believe me, love, it was the nightingale.   5
ROMEO. It was the lark, the herald of the morn,
No nightingale. Look, love, what envious streaks
Do lace the severing clouds in yonder east.
Night's candles are burnt out, and jocund day
Stands tiptoe on the misty mountaintops.   10
I must be gone and live, or stay and die.
JULIET. Yond light is not daylight, I know it, I.
It is some meteor that the sun exhales,
To be to thee this night a torchbearer
And light thee on thy way to Mantua.   15
Therefore stay yet—thou need'st not to be gone.
ROMEO. Let me be ta'en, let me be put to death,
I am content, so thou wilt have it so.
I'll say yon gray is not the morning's eye,
'Tis but the pale reflex of Cynthia's° brow;   20
Nor that is not the lark whose notes do beat
The vaulty heaven so high above our heads.
I have more care to stay than will to go.
Come, death, and welcome! Juliet wills it so.
How is 't, my soul? Let's talk. It is not day.   25
JULIET. It is, it is. Hie hence, be gone, away!
It is the lark that sings so out of tune,
Straining harsh discords and unpleasing sharps.
Some say the lark makes sweet division.°

32. *against:* in readiness for. 34. *Afore me:* an oath meaning "before God."
sc. 5: 20. *Cynthia's:* the moon's. 29. *division:* melody.

This doth not so, for she divideth us. 30
Some say the lark and loathèd toad change eyes.
Oh, now I would they had changed voices too!
Since arm from arm that voice doth us affray,°
Hunting thee hence with hunt's-up° to the day.
Oh, now be gone, more light and light it grows. 35
ROMEO. More light and light. More dark and dark our woes!

[*Enter* NURSE, *to the chamber.*]

NURSE. Madam!
JULIET. Nurse?
NURSE. Your lady mother is coming to your chamber.
  The day is broke, be wary, look about.   [*Exit.*] 40
JULIET. Then, window, let day in, and let life out.
ROMEO. Farewell, farewell! One kiss, and I'll descend. [*Descends.*]
JULIET. Art thou gone so? Love, lord, ay, husband, friend!
  I must hear from thee every day in the hour,
  For in a minute there are many days. 45
  Oh, by this count I shall be much in years
  Ere I again behold my Romeo!
ROMEO. Farewell!
  I will omit no opportunity
  That may convey my greetings, love, to thee. 50
JULIET. Oh, think'st thou we shall ever meet again?
ROMEO. I doubt it not, and all these woes shall serve.
  For sweet discourses in our time to come.
JULIET. Oh God! I have an ill-divining soul.
  Methinks I see thee, now thou art below, 55
  As one dead in the bottom of a tomb.
  Either my eyesight fails or thou look'st pale.
ROMEO. And trust me, love, in my eye so do you.
  Dry sorrow drinks our blood.° Adieu, adieu!   [*Exit.*]
JULIET. O Fortune, Fortune, all men call thee fickle. 60
  If thou art fickle, what dost thou with him
  That is renowned for faith? Be fickle, Fortune,
  For then, I hope, thou wilt not keep him long,
  But send him back.
LADY CAPULET [*within*]. Ho, daughter! Are you up? 65
JULIET. Who is't that calls? It is my lady mother!

---

33. *affray:* frighten.   34. *hunt's-up:* a song played or sung in the early morning to arouse the hunters.   59. *Dry . . . blood:* Sighing was supposed to consume the heart's blood, hence Juliet's pallor.

Is she not down so late, or up so early?
What unaccustomed cause procures her hither?

[*Enter* LADY CAPULET.]

LADY CAPULET. Why, how now, Juliet!
JULIET. Madam, I am not well.
LADY CAPULET. Evermore weeping for your cousin's death? 70
What, wilt thou wash him from his grave with tears?
And if thou couldst, thou couldst not make him live,
Therefore have done. Some grief shows much of love,
But much of grief shows still some want of wit.
JULIET. Yet let me weep for such a feeling° loss. 75
LADY CAPULET. So shall you feel the loss, but not the friend
Which you weep for.
JULIET. Feeling so the loss,
I cannot choose but ever weep the friend.
LADY CAPULET. Well, girl, thou weep'st not so much for his death
As that the villain lives which slaughtered him. 80
JULIET. What villain, madam?
LADY CAPULET. That same villain, Romeo.
JULIET [*aside*]. Villain and he be many miles asunder.
God pardon him! I do, with all my heart,
And yet no man like he doth grieve my heart.
LADY CAPULET. That is because the traitor murderer lives. 85
JULIET. Aye, madam, from the reach of these my hands.
Would none but I might venge my cousin's death!
LADY CAPULET. We will have vengeance for it, fear thou not.
Then weep no more. I'll send to one in Mantua,
Where that same banished runagate° doth live, 90
Shall give him such an unaccustomed dram°
That he shall soon keep Tybalt company.
And then I hope thou wilt be satisfied.
JULIET. Indeed I never shall be satisfied
With Romeo till I behold him—dead— 95
Is my poor heart so for a kinsman vexed.
Madam, if you could find out but a man
To bear a poison, I would temper° it,
That Romeo should, upon receipt thereof,
Soon sleep in quiet. Oh, how my heart ahbors 100
To hear him named and cannot come to him,
To wreak° the love I bore my cousin

75. *feeling:* deeply felt. 90. *runagate:* runaway. 91. *unaccustomed dram:* unexpected dose. 98. *temper:* mix.

Upon his body that hath slaughtered him!
LADY CAPULET. Find thou the means, and I'll find such a man.
But now I'll tell thee joyful tidings, girl.
JULIET. And joy comes well in such a needy time.
What are they, I beseech your ladyship?
LADY CAPULET. Well, well, thou hast a careful father, child,
One who, to put thee from thy heaviness,
Hath sorted out a sudden day of joy,
That thou expect'st not, nor I looked not for.
JULIET. Madam, in happy time, what day is that?
LADY CAPULET. Marry, my child, early next Thursday morn,
The gallant, young, and noble gentleman,
The County Paris, at Saint Peter's Church,
Shall happily make thee there a joyful bride.
JULIET. Now, by Saint Peter's Church, and Peter too,
He shall not make me there a joyful bride.
I wonder at this haste, that I must wed
Ere he that should be husband comes to woo.
I pray you tell my lord and father, madam,
I will not marry yet. And when I do, I swear
It shall be Romeo, whom you know I hate,
Rather than Paris. These are news indeed!
LADY CAPULET. Here comes your father, tell him so yourself
And see how he will take it at your hands.

[*Enter* CAPULET *and* NURSE.]

CAPULET. When the sun sets, the air doth drizzle dew,
But for the sunset of my brother's son
It rains downright.
How now! A conduit,° girl? What, still in tears?
Evermore showering? In one little body
Thou counterfeit'st° a bark,° a sea, a wind.
For still thy eyes, which I may call the sea,
Do ebb and flow with tears; the bark thy body is,
Sailing in this salt flood; the winds, thy sighs,
Who raging with thy tears, and they with them,
Without a sudden calm will overset
Thy tempest-tossed body. How now, wife!
Have you delivered to her our decree?
LADY CAPULET. Aye, sir, but she will none, she gives you thanks.

102. *wreak:* revenge. 130. *conduit:* fountain. 132. *counterfeit'st:* imitatest.
bark: boat.

    I would the fool were married to her grave!
CAPULET. Soft! Take me with you, take me with you,° wife.
    How! Will she none? Doth she not give us thanks?
    Is she not proud? Doth she not count her blest,
    Unworthy as she is, that we have wrought 145
    So worthy a gentleman to be her bridegroom?
JULIET. Not proud you have, but thankful that you have.
    Proud can I never be of what I hate,
    But thankful even for hate that is meant love.
CAPULET. How, how! How, how! Chop-logic!° What is this? 150
    "Proud," and "I thank you," and "I thank you not."
    And yet "not proud." Mistress minion,° you,
    Thank me no thankings, nor proud me no prouds,
    But fettle your fine joints 'gainst Thursday next,
    To go with Paris to Saint Peter's Church, 155
    Or I will drag thee on a hurdle° thither.
    Out, you green-sickness carrion! Out, you baggage!
    You tallow-face!
LADY CAPULET.   Fie, fie! What, are you mad?
JULIET. Good Father, I beseech you on my knees,
    Hear me with patience but to speak a word. 160
CAPULET. Hang thee, young baggage! Disobedient wretch!
    I tell thee what. Get thee to church o' Thursday
    Or never after look me in the face.
    Speak not, reply not, do not answer me.
    My fingers itch. Wife, we scarce thought us blest 165
    That God had lent us but this only child,
    But now I see this one is one too much,
    And that we have a curse in having her.
    Out on her, hilding!
NURSE.   God in Heaven bless her!
    You are to blame, my lord, to rate° her so. 170
CAPULET. And why, my lady wisdom? Hold your tongue,
    Good prudence. Smatter° with your gossips, go.
NURSE. I speak no treason.
CAPULET.   Oh, God ye godden.
NURSE. May not one speak?
CAPULET.   Peace, you mumbling fool!

142. *Take . . . you:* Let me understand you.   150. *Chop-logic:* One who splits hairs in an argument.   152. *Mistress minion:* saucy miss.   156. *hurdle:* a wooden frame (like the hurdle used in foot races) on which criminals were drawn to execution.   170. *rate:* abuse.   172. *Smatter:* prattle.

  Utter your gravity o'er a gossip's bowl,   175
 For here we need it not.
LADY CAPULET.   You are too hot.
CAPULET. God's bread! It makes me mad.
 Day, night, hour, tide, time, work, play,
 Alone, in company, still° my care hath been
 To have her matched. And having now provided   180
 A gentleman of noble parentage,
 Of fair demesnes, youthful, and nobly trained,
 Stuffed, as they say, with honorable parts,
 Proportioned as one's thought would wish a man—
 And then to have a wretched puling° fool,   185
 A whining mammet,° in her fortune's tender,°
 To answer "I'll not wed, I cannot love,
 I am too young, I pray you, pardon me."
 But an you will not wed, I'll pardon you.
 Graze where you will, you shall not house with me.   190
 Look to 't, think on 't, I do not use to jest.
 Thursday is near. Lay hand on heart, advise.°
 An you be mine, I'll give you to my friend.
 An you be not, hang, beg, starve, die in the streets,
 For, by my soul, I'll ne'er acknowledge thee,   195
 Nor what is mine shall never do thee good—
 Trust to 't, bethink you, I'll not be forsworn.°   [*Exit.*]
JULIET. Is there no pity sitting in the clouds
 That sees into the bottom of my grief?
 O sweet my mother, cast me not away!   200
 Delay this marriage for a month, a week;
 Or, if you do not, make the bridal bed
 In that dim monument where Tybalt lies.
LADY CAPULET. Talk not to me, for I'll not speak a word.
 Do as thou wilt, for I have done with thee.   [*Exit.*] 205
JULIET. Oh, God!—O Nurse, how shall this be prevented?
 My husband is on earth, my faith in Heaven.
 How shall that faith return again to earth
 Unless that husband send it me from Heaven
 By leaving earth? Comfort me, counsel me.   210
 Alack, alack, that Heaven should practice stratagems°
 Upon so soft a subject as myself!

---

179. *still:* always.   185. *puling:* whining.   186. *mammet:* doll.   *her . . . tender:* when good fortune is offered her.   192. *advise:* be advised.   197. *forsworn:* break my oath.   211. *stratagems:* violent deeds.

What say'st thou? Hast thou not a word of joy?
Some comfort, Nurse.
NURSE.   Faith, here it is.
Romeo is banished, and all the world to nothing° 215
That he dares ne'er come back to challenge° you;
Or if he do, it needs must be by stealth.
Then, since the case so stands as now it doth,
I think it best you married with the County.
Oh, he's a lovely gentleman! 220
Romeo's a dishclout to him. An eagle, madam,
Hath not so green, so quick, so fair an eye
As Paris hath. Beshrew my very heart,
I think you are happy in this second match,
For it excels your first. Or if it did not, 225
Your first is dead, or 'twere as good he were
As living here and you no use of him.
JULIET. Speakest thou from thy heart?
NURSE. And from my soul too, else beshrew them both.
JULIET. Amen!
NURSE.   What? 229
JULIET.   Well, thou hast comforted me marvelous much.
Go in, and tell my lady I am gone,
Having displeased my father, to Laurence' cell,
To make confession and to be absolved.
NURSE. Marry, I will, and this is wisely done.   [*Exit.*]
JULIET. Ancient damnation! ° Oh, most wicked fiend! 235
Is it more sin to wish me thus forsworn,
Or to dispraise my lord with that same tongue
Which she hath praised him with above compare
So many thousand times? Go, counselor.
Thou and my bosom henceforth shall be twain. 240
I'll to the Friar, to know his remedy.
If all else fail, myself have power to die.   [*Exit.*]

215. *all . . . nothing:* there is no chance.   216. *challenge:* claim.   235. *Ancient damnation:* damnable old woman.

ACT FOUR

SCENE I. FRIAR LAURENCE'S *cell.*

[*Enter* FRIAR LAURENCE *and* PARIS.]

FRIAR LAURENCE. On Thursday, sir? The time is very short.
PARIS. My father Capulet will have it so,
   And I am nothing slow to slack his haste.
FRIAR LAURENCE. You say you do not know the lady's mind.
   Uneven is the course, I like it not.
PARIS. Immoderately she weeps for Tybalt's death,
   And therefore have I little talked of love,
   For Venus smiles not in a house of tears.
   Now, sir, her father counts it dangerous
   That she doth give her sorrow so much sway,
   And in his wisdom hastes our marriage,
   To stop the inundation of her tears,
   Which, too much minded by herself alone,
   May be put from her by society.
   Now do you know the reason of this haste.
FRIAR LAURENCE [*aside*]. I would I knew not why it should be slowed.
   Look, sir, here comes the lady toward my cell.

[*Enter* JULIET.]

PARIS. Happily met, my lady and my wife!
JULIET. That may be, sir, when I may be a wife.
PARIS. That may be must be, love, on Thursday next.
JULIET. What must be shall be.
FRIAR LAURENCE.   That's a certain text.
PARIS. Come you to make confession to this Father?
JULIET. To answer that, I should confess to you.
PARIS. Do not deny to him that you love me.
JULIET. I will confess to you that I love him.
PARIS. So will ye, I am sure, that you love me.
JULIET. If I do so, it will be of more price
   Being spoke behind your back than to your face.
PARIS. Poor soul, thy face is much abused with tears.
JULIET. The tears have got small victory by that,
   For it was bad enough before their spite.
PARIS. Thou wrong'st it more than tears with that report.

JULIET. That is no slander, sir, which is a truth,
  And what I spake, I spake it to my face.
PARIS. Thy face is mine, and thou hast slandered it.   35
JULIET. It may be so, for it is not mine own.
  Are you at leisure, holy Father, now,
  Or shall I come to you at evening mass?
FRIAR LAURENCE. My leisure serves me, pensive daughter, now.
  My lord, we must entreat the time alone.   40
PARIS. God shield° I should disturb devotion!
  Juliet, on Thursday early will I rouse ye.
  Till then, adieu, and keep this holy kiss.   [*Exit.*]
JULIET. Oh, shut the door, and when thou hast done so,
  Come weep with me—past hope, past cure, past help!   45
FRIAR LAURENCE. Ah, Juliet, I already know thy grief,
  It strains me past the compass of my wits.
  I hear thou must, and nothing may prorogue it,
  On Thursday next be married to this County.
JULIET. Tell me not, Friar, that thou hear'st of this,   50
  Unless thou tell me how I may prevent it.
  If in thy wisdom thou canst give no help,
  Do thou but call my resolution wise,
  And with this knife I'll help it presently.
  God joined my heart and Romeo's, thou our hands,   55
  And ere this hand, by thee to Romeo's sealed,
  Shall be the label to another deed,°
  Or my true heart with treacherous revolt
  Turn to another, this shall slay them both.
  Therefore, out of thy long-experienced time,   60
  Give me some present counsel; or, behold,
  'Twixt my extremes and me this bloody knife
  Shall play the umpire, arbitrating that
  Which the commission° of thy years and art
  Could to no issue of true honor bring.   65
  Be not so long to speak, I long to die
  If what thou speak'st speak not of remedy.
FRIAR LAURENCE. Hold, daughter. I do spy a kind of hope,
  Which craves as desperate an execution
  As that is desperate which we would prevent.   70
  If, rather than to marry County Paris,
  Thou hast the strength of will to slay thyself,

ACT FOUR, SC. I: 41. *shield:* forbid.   56–57. *ere . . . deed:* before my hand consents to another contract.   64. *commission:* authority.

Then is it likely thou wilt undertake
A thing like death to chide away this shame,
That copest with death himself to 'scape from it. 75
And, if thou darest, I'll give thee remedy.
JULIET. Oh, bid me leap, rather than marry Paris,
From off the battlements of yonder tower;
Or walk in thievish ways; or bid me lurk
Where serpents are; chain me with roaring bears; 80
Or shut me nightly in a charnel house,°
O'ercover'd quite with dead men's rattling bones,
With reeky° shanks and yellow chapless° skulls;
Or bid me go into a new-made grave,
And hide me with a dead man in his shroud— 85
Things that to hear them told have made me tremble—
And I will do it without fear or doubt,
To live an unstained wife to my sweet love.
FRIAR LAURENCE. Hold, then, go home, be merry, give consent
To marry Paris. Wednesday is tomorrow. 90
Tomorrow night look that thou lie alone,
Let not thy nurse lie with thee in thy chamber.
Take thou this vial, being then in bed,
And this distillèd liquor drink thou off,
When presently through all thy veins shall run 95
A cold and drowsy humor;° for no pulse
Shall keep his native progress, but surcease.°
No warmth, no breath, shall testify thou livest.
The roses in thy lips and cheeks shall fade
To paly ashes, thy eyes' windows fall, 100
Like death when he shuts up the day of life.
Each part, deprived of supple government,
Shall, stiff and stark and cold, appear like death.
And in this borrowed likeness of shrunk death
Thou shalt continue two and forty hours, 105
And then awake as from a pleasant sleep.
Now, when the bridegroom in the morning comes
To rouse thee from thy bed, there art thou dead.
Then, as the manner of our country is,
In thy best robes uncovered on the bier 110

---

81. *charnel house:* bone shed. In Shakespeare's time the churchyard was used again and again; bones disinterred in making a new grave were thrown into the charnel house. 83. *reekly:* stinking. *chapless:* without jaws. 96. *humor:* without moisture. 97. *surcease:* cease.

Thou shalt be borne to that same ancient vault
Where all the kindred of the Capulets lie.
In the meantime, against thou shalt awake,
Shall Romeo by my letters know our drift,°
And hither shall he come, and he and I 115
Will watch thy waking, and that very night
Shall Romeo bear thee hence to Mantua.
And this shall free thee from this present shame,
If no inconstant toy° nor womanish fear
Abate thy valor in the acting it. 120
JULIET. Give me, give me! Oh, tell not me of fear!
FRIAR LAURENCE. Hold, get you gone, be strong and prosperous
In this resolve. I'll send a friar with speed
To Mantua, with my letters to thy lord.
JULIET. Love give me strength! And strength shall help afford. 125
Farewell, dear Father! [*Exeunt.*]

SCENE 2. *Hall in* CAPULET'*s house.*

[*Enter* CAPULET, LADY CAPULET, NURSE, *and two* SERVINGMEN.]

CAPULET. So many guests invite as here are writ.
[*Exit* FIRST SERVANT.]
Sirrah, go hire me twenty cunning cooks.
SECOND SERVINGMAN. You shall have none ill, sir, for I'll try if they can lick their fingers.
CAPULET. How canst thou try them so? 5
SECOND SERVINGMAN. Marry, sir, 'tis an ill cook that cannot lick his own fingers. Therefore he that cannot lick his fingers goes not with me.
CAPULET. Go, be gone. [*Exit* SECOND SERVANT.]
We shall be much unfurnished° for this time.
What, is my daughter gone to Friar Laurence? 10
NURSE. Aye, forsooth.
CAPULET. Well, he may chance to do some good on her. A peevish self-willed harlotry° it is.

[*Enter* JULIET.]

NURSE. See where she comes from shrift with merry look. 14
CAPULET. How now, my headstrong! Where have you been gadding?

---

114. *drift:* intention.   119. *inconstant toy:* fickle fancy.
sc. 2: 9. *unfurnished:* unprovided.   13. *harlotry:* hussy.

JULIET. Where I have learned me to repent the sin
  Of disobedient opposition
  To you and your behests, and am enjoined
  By holy Laurence to fall prostrate here,
  To beg your pardon. Pardon, I beseech you!   20
  Henceforward I am ever ruled by you.
CAPULET. Send for the County, go tell him of this.
  I'll have this knot knit up tomorrow morning.
JULIET. I met the youthful lord at Laurence' cell,
  And gave him what becomèd° love I might,   25
  Not stepping o'er the bounds of modesty.
CAPULET. Why, I am glad on 't, this is well. Stand up.
  This is as 't should be. Let me see the County.
  Aye, marry, go, I say, and fetch him hither.
  Now, afore God, this reverend holy Friar,   30
  All our whole city is much bound to him.
JULIET. Nurse, will you go with me into my closet,°
  To help me sort such needful ornaments
  As you think fit to furnish me tomorrow?
LADY CAPULET. No, not till Thursday, there is time enough.   35
CAPULET. Go, Nurse, go with her. We'll to church tomorrow.
                    [*Exeunt* JULIET *and* NURSE.]
LADY CAPULET. We shall be short in our provision.
  'Tis now near night.
CAPULET.   Tush, I will stir about,
  And all things shall be well, I warrant thee, wife.
  Go thou to Juliet, help to deck up her.   40
  I'll not to bed tonight, let me alone,
  I'll play the housewife for this once. What ho!
  They are all forth. Well, I will walk myself
  To County Paris, to prepare him up
  Against tomorrow. My heart is wondrous light   45
  Since this same wayward girl is so reclaimed.   [*Exeunt.*]

SCENE 3. JULIET'*s chamber.*

[*Enter* JULIET *and* NURSE.]

JULIET. Aye, those attires are best. But, gentle Nurse,
  I pray thee leave me to myself tonight;
  For I have need of many orisons°

---
25. *becomèd:* suitable.
  sc. 3: 3. *orisons:* prayers.

To move the Heavens to smile upon my state,
Which, well thou know'st, is cross° and full of sin. 5

[*Enter* LADY CAPULET.]

LADY CAPULET. What, are you busy, ho? Need you my help?
JULIET. No, madam, we have culled ° such necessaries
As are behooveful° for our state° tomorrow.
So please you, let me now be left alone,
And let the nurse this night sit up with you, 10
For I am sure you have your hands full all
In this so sudden business.
LADY CAPULET.   Goodnight.
Get thee to bed and rest, for thou hast need.

[*Exeunt* LADY CAPULET *and* NURSE.]

JULIET. Farewell! God knows when we shall meet again.
I have a faint cold fear thrills through my veins 15
That almost freezes up the heat of life.
I'll call them back again to comfort me.
Nurse!—What should she do here?
My dismal scene I needs must act alone.
Come, vial. 20
What if this mixture do not work at all?
Shall I be married then tomorrow morning?
No, no, this shall forbid it. Lie thou there. [*Laying down a dagger.*]
What if it be a poison which the Friar
Subtly hath ministered to have me dead, 25
Lest in this marriage he should be dishonored
Because he married me before to Romeo?
I fear it is. And yet methinks it should not,
For he hath still been tried° a holy man.
How if, when I am laid into the tomb, 30
I wake before the time that Romeo
Come to redeem me? There's a fearful point.
Shall I not then be stifled in the vault,
To whose foul mouth no healthsome air breathes in,
And there die strangled ere my Romeo comes? 35
Or if I live, is it not very like,
The horrible conceit° of death and night,
Together with the terror of the place,
As in a vault, an ancient receptacle,

---

5. *cross:* thwarted.   7. *culled:* selected.   8. *behooveful:* fit.   *state:* poison.   29. *still been tried:* always been proved.   37. *conceit:* idea.

Where for this many hundred years the bones 40
Of all my buried ancestors are packed;
Where bloody Tybalt, yet but green in earth,
Lies festering in his shroud; where, as they say,
At some hours in the night spirits resort—
Alack, alack, is it not like that I 45
So early waking, what with loathsome smells
And shrieks like mandrakes'° torn out of the earth,
That living mortals hearing them run mad?
Oh, if I wake, shall I not be distraught,
Environèd with all these hideous fears, 50
And madly play with my forefathers' joints,
And pluck the mangled Tybalt from his shroud,
And in this rage, with some great kinsman's bone,
As with a club, dash out my desperate brains?
Oh, look! Methinks I see my cousin's ghost 55
Seeking out Romeo, that did spit his body
Upon a rapier's point. Stay, Tybalt, stay!
Romeo, I come! This do I drink to thee.
[*She falls upon her bed, within the curtains.*]

SCENE 4. *Hall in* CAPULET'S *house.*

[*Enter* LADY CAPULET *and* NURSE.]

LADY CAPULET. Hold, take these keys, and fetch more spices, Nurse.
NURSE. They call for dates and quinces in the pastry.°

[*Enter* CAPULET.]

CAPULET. Come, stir, stir, stir! The second cock hath crowed,
  The curfew bell hath rung, 'tis three o'clock.
  Look to the baked meats, good Angelica. 5
  Spare not for cost.
NURSE.   Go, you cotquean,° go,
  Get you to bed. Faith, you'll be sick tomorrow
  For this night's watching.
CAPULET. No, not a whit. What! I have watched ere now
  All night for lesser cause, and ne'er been sick. 10

---

47. *mandrakes:* mandragora, a narcotic root.
  SC. 4: 2. *pastry:* bakehouse. 6. *cotquean:* a man who meddles with women's affairs.

LADY CAPULET. Aye, you have been a mousehunt° in your time,
But I will watch you from such watching now.
                              [*Exeunt* LADY CAPULET *and* NURSE.]
CAPULET. A jealoushood,° a jealoushood!

[*Enter three or four* SERVINGMEN, *with spits, and logs, and baskets.*]

                              Now, fellow, what's there?
FIRST SERVINGMAN. Things for the cook, sir, but I know not what.
CAPULET. Make haste, make haste. [*Exit* FIRST SERVINGMAN.] Sirrah,
    fetch drier logs.   15
Call Peter, he will show thee where they are.
SECOND SERVINGMAN. I have a head, sir, that will find out logs
And never trouble Peter for the matter.
CAPULET. Mass,° and well said, a merry whoreson,° ha!
Thou shalt be loggerhead. [*Exit* SECOND SERVINGMAN.] Good faith, 'tis
    day.   20
The County will be here with music straight,
For so he said he would. [*Music within.*] I hear him near.
Nurse! Wife! What ho! What, Nurse, I say!

[*Re-enter* NURSE.]

Go waken Juliet, go and trim her up.
I'll go and chat with Paris. Hie, make haste,   25
Make haste. The bridegroom he is come already.
Make haste, I say.   [*Exeunt.*]

SCENE 5. JULIET'*s chamber.*

[*Enter* NURSE.]

NURSE. Mistress! What, mistress! Juliet! Fast, I warrant her, she.
Why, lamb! Why, lady! Fie, you slugabed!
Why, love, I say! Madam! Sweetheart! Why, bride!
What, not a word? You take your pennyworths now,
Sleep for a week; for the next night, I warrant,   5
The County Paris hath set up his rest°

11. *mousehunt:* one who follows the girls; in today's slang, "a wolf."   13. *jealoushood:* "Mrs. Jealousy."   19. *Mass:* by the mass.   *whoreson:* lit., bastard, but not used seriously.
    SC. 5: 6. *set . . . rest:* to hold one's hand, a metaphor from primero, a card game; hence, "to be determined."

That you shall rest but little. God forgive me,
Marry and amen, how sound is she asleep!
I needs must wake her. Madam, madam, madam!
Aye, let the County take you in your bed, 10
He'll fright you up, i'faith. Will it not be? [*Undraws the curtains.*]
What, dressed! And in your clothes! And down again!
I must needs wake you. Lady, lady, lady!
Alas, alas! Help, help! My lady's dead!
Oh, welladay that ever I was born! 15
Some aqua vitae, ho! My lord! My lady!

   [*Enter* LADY CAPULET.]

LADY CAPULET. What noise is here?
NURSE.   Oh, lamentable day!
LADY CAPULET. What is the matter?
NURSE.   Look, look! Oh, heavy day!
LADY CAPULET. Oh me, oh me! My child, my only life,
  Revive, look up, or I will die with thee. 20
  Help! help! Call help.

   [*Enter* CAPULET.]

CAPULET. For shame, bring Juliet forth, her lord is come.
NURSE. She's dead, deceased, she's dead, alack the day!
LADY CAPULET. Alack the day, she's dead, she's dead, she's dead!
CAPULET. Ha! Let me see her. Out, alas! She's cold. 25
  Her blood is settled and her joints are stiff.
  Life and these lips have long been separated.
  Death lies on her like an untimely frost
  Upon the sweetest flower of all the field.
NURSE. Oh, lamentable day!
LADY CAPULET.   Oh, woeful time! 30
CAPULET. Death, that hath ta'en her hence to make me wail,
  Ties up my tongue and will not let me speak.

   [*Enter* FRIAR LAURENCE *and* PARIS, *with* MUSICIANS.]

FRIAR LAURENCE. Come, is the bride ready to go to church?
CAPULET. Ready to go, but never to return.
  O son, the night before thy wedding day 35
  Hath death lain with thy wife. See, there she lies,
  Flower as she was, deflowerèd by him.
  Death is my son-in-law, Death is my heir,
  My daughter he hath wedded. I will die,
  And leave him all—life, living, all is Death's. 40

PARIS. Have I thought long to see this morning's face
   And doth it give me such a sight as this?
LADY CAPULET. Accurst, unhappy, wretched, hateful day!
   Most miserable hour that e'er time saw
   In lasting labor of his pilgrimage!
   But one, poor one, one poor and loving child,
   But one thing to rejoice and solace in,
   And cruel death hath catched it from my sight!
NURSE. Oh, woe! Oh, woeful, woeful, woeful day!
   Most lamentable day, most woeful day,
   That ever, ever, I did yet behold!
   Oh, day, oh, day, oh, day! Oh, hateful day!
   Never was seen so black a day as this.
   Oh, woeful day, oh, woeful day!
PARIS. Beguiled, divorced, wronged, spited, slain!
   Most detestable death, by thee beguiled,
   By cruel cruel thee quite overthrown!
   Oh, love! Oh, life! Not life, but love in death!
CAPULET. Despised, distressed, hated, martyred, killed!
   Uncomfortable time, why camest thou now
   To murder, murder our solemnity?
   O child! O child! My soul, and not my child!
   Dead art thou! Alack, my child is dead,
   And with my child my joys are burièd!
FRIAR LAURENCE. Peace ho, for shame! Confusion's cure lives not
   In these confusions. Heaven and yourself
   Had part in this fair maid, now Heaven hath all,
   And all the better is it for the maid.
   Your part in her you could not keep from death,
   But Heaven keeps his part in eternal life.
   The most you sought was her promotion,
   For 'twas your heaven she could be advanced.
   And weep ye now, seeing she is advanced
   Above the clouds, as high as Heaven itself?
   Oh, in this love, you love your child so ill
   That you run mad, seeing that she is well.
   She's not well married that lives married long,
   But she's best married that dies married young.
   Dry up your tears, and stick your rosemary°
   On this fair corse, and, as the custom is,
   In all her best array bear her to church.

79. *rosemary:* Rosemary was carried both for weddings and funerals.

For though fond nature bids us all lament,
Yet nature's tears are reason's merriment.°
CAPULET. All things that we ordainèd festival
Turn from their office to black funeral.   85
Our instruments to melancholy bells,
Our wedding cheer to a sad burial feast,
Our solemn hymns to sullen dirges change,
Our bridal flowers serve for a buried corse,
And all things change them to the contrary.   90
FRIAR LAURENCE. Sir, go you in, and, madam, go with him.
And go, Sir Paris, everyone prepare
To follow this fair corse unto her grave.
The Heavens do lour upon you for some ill;
Move them no more by crossing their high will.   95

[*Exeunt* CAPULET, LADY CAPULET, PARIS, *and* FRIAR.]

FIRST MUSICIAN. Faith, we may put on our pipes, and be gone.
NURSE. Honest good fellows, ah, put up, put up.
For well you know this is a pitiful case.   [*Exit.*]
SECOND MUSICIAN. Aye, by my troth, the case° may be amended.

[*Enter* PETER.]

PETER. Musicians, oh, musicians, "Heart's ease,° heart's ease." Oh, an
you will have me live, play "Heart's ease."   101
FIRST MUSICIAN. Why "Heart's ease"?
PETER. Oh, musicians, because my heart itself plays "My heart is full of
woe." Oh, play me some merry dump,° to comfort me.
FIRST MUSICIAN. Not a dump we, 'tis no time to play now.   105
PETER. You will not, then?
FIRST MUSICIAN. No.
PETER. I will then give it you soundly.
FIRST MUSICIAN. What will you give us?   109
PETER. No money, on my faith, but the gleek.° I will give you the minstrel.°
FIRST MUSICIAN. Then will I give you the serving creature.
PETER. Then will I lay the serving creature's dagger on your pate. I will
carry no crotchets.° I'll re you, I'll fa you, do you note me?

---

83. *nature's . . . merriment:* Though it is natural to weep, it is reasonable to rejoice because she has gone to a better place.   98-99. *case . . . case:* a pun on case-"affair" and case-"instrument box."   100. *"Heart's ease":* a popular song of the time.   104. *dump:* doleful ditty.   110. *gleek:* mock.   110-111. *I . . . minstrel:* i.e., I'll beat you.   114. *carry no crotchets:* not put up with your whims.

FIRST MUSICIAN. An you re us and fa us, you note us.   115
SECOND MUSICIAN. Pray you put up your dagger, and put out your wit.
PETER. Then have at you with my wit! I will dry-beat you with an iron wit, and put up my iron dagger. Answer me like men:
"When griping grief the heart doth wound
And doleful dumps the mind oppress,   120
Then music with her silver sound—"
Why "silver sound"? Why "music with her silver sound"?—What say you, Simon Catling?°
FIRST MUSICIAN. Marry, sir, because silver hath a sweet sound.
PETER. Pretty! What say you, Hugh Rebeck?°   125
SECOND MUSICIAN. I say "silver sound" because musicians sound for silver.
PETER. Pretty too! What say you, James Soundpost?°
THIRD MUSICIAN. Faith, I know not what to say.   129
PETER. Oh, I cry you mercy, you are the singer. I will say for you. It is "music with her silver sound" because musicians have no gold for sounding.
"Then music with her silver sound
With speedy help doth lend redress."   [*Exit.*]
FIRST MUSICIAN. What a pestilent knave is this same!   135
SECOND MUSICIAN. Hang him, Jack! Come, we'll in here. Tarry for the mourners, and stay° dinner.   [*Exeunt.*]

ACT FIVE

SCENE I. *Mantua. A street.*

[*Enter* ROMEO.]

ROMEO. If I may trust the flattering truth of sleep,
My dreams presage some joyful news at hand.
My bosom's lord° sits lightly in his throne,
And all this day an unaccustomed spirit
Lifts me above the ground with cheerful thoughts.   5
I dreamed my lady came and found me dead—
Strange dream, that gives a dead man leave to think!—

---

123. *Catling:* catgut fiddle string.   125. *Rebeck:* a three-stringed fiddle.   128. *Soundpost:* part of a violin.   137. *stay:* wait for.
ACT FIVE, SC. I: 3. *bosom's lord:* heart.

And breathed such life with kisses in my lips
That I revived and was an emperor.
Ah me, how sweet is love itself possessed   10
When but love's shadows are so rich in joy!

[*Enter* BALTHASAR, *booted.°*]

News from Verona! How now, Balthasar!
Dost thou not bring me letters from the Friar?
How doth my lady? Is my father well?
How fares my Juliet? That I ask again;   15
For nothing can be ill if she be well.
BALTHASAR. Then she is well, and nothing can be ill.
Her body sleeps in Capels' monument,
And her immortal part with angels lives.
I saw her laid low in her kindred's vault,   20
And presently took post° to tell it you.
Oh, pardon me for bringing these ill news,
Since you did leave it for my office, sir.
ROMEO. Is it e'en so? Then I defy you, stars!°
Thou know'st my lodging. Get me ink and paper,   25
And hire post horses. I will hence tonight.
BALTHASAR. I do beseech you, sir, have patience.
Your looks are pale and wild, and do import
Some misadventure.
ROMEO.   Tush, thou art deceived.
Leave me, and do the thing I bid thee do.   30
Hast thou no letters to me from the Friar?
BALTHASAR. No, my good lord.
ROMEO.   No matter. Get thee gone,
And hire those horses. I'll be with thee straight.   [*Exit* BALTHASAR.]
Well, Juliet, I will lie with thee tonight.
Let's see for means.—O mischief, thou art swift   35
To enter in the thoughts of desperate men!
I do remember an apothecary,
And hereabouts he dwells, which late I noted
In tattered weeds,° with overwhelming° brows,
Culling of simples.° Meager were his looks,   40
Sharp misery had worn him to the bones.

---

12. s.d., *booted:* wearing riding boots, an indication that he has ridden far.   21. *took post:* rode fast.   24. *defy . . . stars:* Romeo throughout has been star-crossed by malignant fate. Now he finally defies fate to do him any worse injury.   39. *weeds:* garments.   *overwhelming:* overhanging.   40. *simples:* herbs.

And in his needy shop a tortoise hung,
An alligator stuffed and other skins
Of ill-shaped fishes; and about his shelves
A beggarly account° of empty boxes, 45
Green earthen pots, bladders, and musty seeds,
Remnants of packthread and old cakes of roses,°
Were thinly scattered, to make up a show.
Noting this penury, to myself I said,
"An if a man did need a poison now, 50
Whose sale is present death in Mantua,
Here lives a caitiff° wretch would sell it him."
Oh, this same thought did but forerun my need,
And this same needy man must sell it me.
As I remember, this should be the house. 55
Being holiday, the beggar's shop is shut.
What ho! Apothecary!
  [*Enter* APOTHECARY.]
APOTHECARY.   Who calls so loud?
ROMEO. Come hither, man. I see that thou art poor.
  Hold, there is forty ducats. Let me have
  A dram of poison, such soon-speeding gear° 60
  As will disperse itself through all the veins,
  That the life-weary taker may fall dead,
  And that the trunk° may be discharged of breath
  As violently as hasty powder fired
  Doth hurry from the fatal cannon's womb. 65
APOTHECARY. Such mortal drugs I have, but Mantua's law
  Is death to any he that utters° them.
ROMEO. Art thou so bare and full of wretchedness,
  And fear'st to die? Famine is in thy cheeks,
  Need and oppression starveth in thy eyes, 70
  Contempt and beggary hangs upon thy back,
  The world is not thy friend, nor the world's law.
  The world affords no law to make thee rich,
  Then be not poor, but break it, and take this.
APOTHECARY. My poverty, but not my will, consents. 75
ROMEO. I pay thy poverty and not thy will.
APOTHECARY. Put this in any liquid thing you will,
  And drink it off, and if you had the strength
  Of twenty men, it would dispatch you straight.

45. *account:* number.   47. *cakes of roses:* dried rose leaves compressed into a cake, used as a perfume.   52. *caitiff:* miserable creature.   60. *gear:* stuff.   63. *trunk:* body.   67. *utters:* sells.

ROMEO. There is thy gold, worse poison to men's souls, 80
   Doing more murder in this loathsome world
   Than these poor compounds that thou mayst not sell.
   I sell thee poison, thou hast sold me none.
   Farewell. Buy food, and get thyself in flesh.
   Come, cordial and not poison, go with me 85
   To Juliet's grave, for there must I use thee. [*Exeunt.*]

SCENE 2. FRIAR LAURENCE's *cell*.

[*Enter* FRIAR JOHN.]

FRIAR JOHN. Holy Franciscan friar! Brother, ho!

[*Enter* FRIAR LAURENCE.]

FRIAR LAURENCE. This same should be the voice of Friar John.
   Welcome from Mantua. What says Romeo?
   Or if his mind be writ, give me his letter.
FRIAR JOHN. Going to find a barefoot brother out, 5
   One of our order, to associate° me
   Here in this city visiting the sick,
   And finding him, the searchers of the town,
   Suspecting that we both were in a house
   Where the infectious pestilence° did reign, 10
   Sealed up the doors and would not let us forth,
   So that my speed to Mantua there was stayed.
FRIAR LAURENCE. Who bare my letter, then, to Romeo?
FRIAR JOHN. I could not send it—here it is again—
   Nor get a messenger to bring it thee, 15
   So fearful were they of infection.
FRIAR LAURENCE. Unhappy fortune! By my brotherhood,
   The letter was not nice,° but full of charge°
   Of dear import,° and the neglecting it
   May do much danger. Friar John, go hence. 20
   Get me an iron crow° and bring it straight
   Unto my cell.
FRIAR JOHN. Brother, I'll go and bring it thee. [*Exit.*]
FRIAR LAURENCE. Now must I to the monument alone.
   Within this three hours will fair Juliet wake. 25

sc. 2: 6. *associate:* accompany. 10. *pestilence:* the plague. 18. *nice:* trifling.
full of charge: weighty. 19. *dear import:* great importance. 21. *crow:* crowbar.
26. *beshrew:* blame.

She will beshrew° me much that Romeo
Hath had no notice of these accidents.
But I will write again to Mantua,
And keep her at my cell till Romeo come.
Poor living corse, closed in a dead man's tomb! [*Exit.*] 30

SCENE 3. *A churchyard; in it a monument belonging to the* CAPULETS.

[*Enter* PARIS *and his* PAGE, *bearing flowers and a torch.*]

PARIS. Give me thy torch, boy. Hence, and stand aloof.
Yet put it out, for I would not be seen.
Under yond yew trees lay thee all along,°
Holding thine ear close to the hollow ground.
So shall no foot upon the churchyard tread, 5
Being loose, unfirm, with digging up of graves,
But thou shalt hear it. Whistle then to me,
As signal that thou hear'st something approach.
Give me those flowers. Do as I bid thee, go.
PAGE [*aside*]. I am almost afraid to stand alone 10
Here in the churchyard, yet I will adventure. [*Retires.*]
PARIS. Sweet flower, with flowers thy bridal bed I strew—
Oh, woe! Thy canopy is dust and stones—
Which with sweet water nightly I will dew,
Or, wanting that, with tears distilled by moans. 15
The obsequies° that I for thee will keep
Nightly shall be to strew thy grave and weep.

[*The* PAGE *whistles.*]

The boy gives warning something doth approach.
What cursèd foot wanders this way tonight,
To cross° my obsequies and true love's rite? 20
What, with a torch! Muffle° me, night, awhile. [*Retires.*]

[*Enter* ROMEO *and* BALTHASAR, *with a torch, mattock,° etc.*]

ROMEO. Give me that mattock and the wrenching iron.
Hold, take this letter. Early in the morning
See thou deliver it to my lord and father.
Give me the light. Upon thy life, I charge thee, 25
Whate'er thou hear'st or seest, stand all aloof,

SC. 3: 3. *all along:* at full length.   16. *obsequies:* funeral rites.   20. *cross:* thwart.   21. *Muffle:* conceal.   22. s.d., *mattock:* a tool like a pick, but with a broad end.

And do not interrupt me in my course.
Why I descend into this bed of death
Is partly to behold my lady's face,
But chiefly to take thence from her dead finger 30
A precious ring, a ring that I must use
In dear employment. Therefore hence, be gone.
But if thou, jealous,° dost return to pry
In what I farther shall intend to do,
By Heaven, I will tear thee joint by joint 35
And strew this hungry churchyard with thy limbs.
The time and my intents are savage-wild,
More fierce and more inexorable far
Than empty° tigers or the roaring sea.
BALTHASAR. I will be gone, sir, and not trouble you. 40
ROMEO. So shalt thou show me friendship. Take thou that.
Live, and be prosperous, and farewell, good fellow.
BALTHASAR [*aside*]. For all this same, I'll hide me hereabout.
His looks I fear, and his intents I doubt. [*Retires.*]
ROMEO. Thou detestable maw,° thou womb of death, 45
Gorged with the dearest morsel of the earth,
Thus I enforce thy rotten jaws to open,
And in despite° I'll cram thee with more food. [*Opens the tomb.*]
PARIS. This is that banished haughty Montague
That murdered my love's cousin, with which grief 50
It is supposèd the fair creature died,
And here is come to do some villainous shame
To the dead bodies. I will apprehend him. [*Comes forward.*]
Stop thy unhallowed toil, vile Montague!
Can vengeance be pursued further than death? 55
Condemnèd villain, I do apprehend thee.
Obey, and go with me, for thou must die.
ROMEO. I must indeed, and therefore came I hither.
Good gentle youth, tempt not a desperate man.
Fly hence and leave me. Think upon these gone, 60
Let them affright thee. I beseech thee, youth,
Put not another sin upon my head,
By urging me to fury. Oh, be gone!
By Heaven, I love thee better than myself,
For I come hither armed against myself. 65
Stay not, be gone. Live, and hereafter say
A madman's mercy bid thee run away.

33. *jealous:* curious. 39. *empty:* hungry. 45. *maw:* stomach. 48. *despite:* scorn.

PARIS. I do defy thy conjurations
    And apprehend thee for a felon here.   69
ROMEO. Wilt thou provoke me? Then have at thee, boy! [*They fight.*]
PAGE. Oh, Lord, they fight! I will go call the watch.   [*Exit.*]
PARIS. Oh, I am slain! [*Falls.*] If thou be merciful,
    Open the tomb, lay me with Juliet.   [*Dies.*]
ROMEO. In faith, I will. Let me peruse this face.
    Mercutio's kinsman, noble County Paris!   75
    What said my man, when my betossèd soul
    Did not attend° him as we rode? I think
    He told me Paris should have married Juliet.
    Said he not so? Or did I dream it so?
    Or am I mad, hearing him talk of Juliet,   80
    To think it was so? Oh, give me thy hand,
    One writ with me in sour misfortune's book!
    I'll bury thee in a triumphant grave—
    A grave? Oh, no, a lantern,° slaughtered youth;
    For here lies Juliet, and her beauty makes   85
    This vault a feasting presence° full of light.
    Death, lie thou there, by a dead man interred. [*Laying* PARIS *in the monument.*]
    How oft when men are at the point of death
    Have they been merry! Which their keepers call
    A lightning before death. Oh, how may I   90
    Call this a lightning? O my love! My wife!
    Death, that hath sucked the honey of thy breath,
    Hath had no power yet upon thy beauty.
    Thou art not conquered; beauty's ensign yet
    Is crimson in thy lips and in thy cheeks,   95
    And death's pale flag is not advancèd there.
    Tybalt, liest thou there in thy bloody sheet?
    Oh, what more favor can I do to thee
    Than with that hand that cut thy youth in twain
    To sunder his that was thine enemy?   100
    Forgive me, Cousin! Ah, dear Juliet,
    Why art thou yet so fair? Shall I believe
    That unsubstantial death is amorous,
    And that the lean abhorrèd monster keeps
    Thee here in dark to be his paramour?   105
    For fear of that, I still will stay with thee,

---

77. *attend:* listen to.   84. *lantern:* dome or small turret with windows, set in the roof of a hall to give additional light.   86. *presence:* Presence Chamber, where the Queen held public court.

And never from this palace of dim night
Depart again. Here, here will I remain
With worms that are thy chambermaids. Oh, here
Will I set up my everlasting rest, 110
And shake the yoke of inauspicious stars
From this world-wearied flesh. Eyes, look your last!
Arms, take your last embrace! And lips, O you
The doors of breath, seal with a righteous kiss
A dateless bargain to engrossing death! 115
Come, bitter conduct,° come, unsavory guide!
Thou desperate pilot, now at once run on
The dashing rocks thy seasick weary bark.
Here's to my love! [*Drinks.*] O true apothecary!
Thy drugs are quick. Thus with a kiss I die. [*Dies.*] 120

[*Enter, at the other end of the churchyard,* FRIAR LAURENCE, *with a lantern, crow, and spade.*]

FRIAR LAURENCE. Saint Francis be my speed! How oft tonight
  Have my old feet stumbled at graves! Who's there?
BALTHASAR. Here's one a friend, and one that knows you well.
FRIAR LAURENCE. Bliss be upon you! Tell me, good my friend,
  What torch is yond that vainly lends his light 125
  To grubs and eyeless skulls? As I discern,
  It burneth in the Capel's monument.
BALTHASAR. It doth so, holy sir, and there's my master,
  One that you love.
FRIAR LAURENCE.   Who is it?
BALTHASAR.   Romeo.
FRIAR LAURENCE. How long hath he been there?
BALTHASAR.   Full half an hour. 130
FRIAR LAURENCE. Go with me to the vault.
BALTHASAR.   I dare not, sir.
  My master knows not but I am gone hence,
  And fearfully did menace me with death
  If I did stay to look on his intents.
FRIAR LAURENCE. Stay, then, I'll go alone. Fear comes upon me— 135
  Oh, much I fear some ill unlucky thing.
BALTHASAR. As I did sleep under this yew tree here,
  I dreamed my master and another fought,
  And that my master slew him.
FRIAR LAURENCE.   Romeo! [*Advances.*]

116. *conduct:* guide.

Alack, alack, what blood is this which stains 140
The stony entrance of this sepulcher?
What mean these masterless and gory swords
To lie discolored by this place of peace?
[*Enters the tomb.*] Romeo! Oh, pale! Who else? What, Paris too?
And steeped in blood? Ah, what an unkind hour 145
Is guilty of this lamentable chance!
The lady stirs.

[JULIET *wakes.*]

JULIET. O comfortable Friar! Where is my lord?
I do remember well where I should be,
And there I am. Where is my Romeo? 150

[*Noise within.*]

FRIAR LAURENCE. I hear some noise. Lady, come from that nest
Of death, contagion, and unnatural sleep.
A greater power than we can contradict
Hath thwarted our intents. Come, come away.
Thy husband in thy bosom there lies dead, 155
And Paris too. Come, I'll dispose of thee
Among a sisterhood of holy nuns.
Stay not to question, for the watch is coming.
Come, go, good Juliet, I dare no longer stay.
JULIET. Go, get thee hence, for I will not away. 160
[*Exit* FRIAR LAURENCE.]
What's here? A cup, closed in my true love's hand?
Poison, I see, hath been his timeless° end.
O churl! Drunk all, and left no friendly drop
To help me after? I will kiss thy lips—
Haply° some poison yet doth hang on them 165
To make me die with a restorative. [*Kisses him.*]
Thy lips are warm.
FIRST WATCH [*within*]. Lead, boy. Which way?
JULIET. Yea, noise? Then I'll be brief. O happy dagger!
[*Snatching* ROMEO'*s dagger.*]
This is thy sheath. [*Stabs herself.*] There rust, and let me die. 170
[*Falls on* ROMEO'*s body, and dies.*]

[*Enter* WATCH, *with the* PAGE *of* PARIS.]

162. *timeless:* untimely.   165. *Haply:* perhaps.

PAGE. This is the place—there, where the torch doth burn.
FIRST WATCH. The ground is bloody. Search about the churchyard.
Go, some of you, whoe'er you find attach.°
Pitiful sight! Here lies the County slain,
And Juliet bleeding, warm, and newly dead, 175
Who here hath lain this two days burièd.
Go tell the Prince. Run to the Capulets,
Raise up the Montagues. Some others search.
We see the ground whereon these woes do lie,
But the true ground of all these piteous woes 180
We cannot without circumstance° descry.

[*Re-enter some of the* WATCH, *with* BALTHASAR.]

SECOND WATCH. Here's Romeo's man. We found him in the churchyard.
FIRST WATCH. Hold him in safety till the Prince come hither.

[*Re-enter* FRIAR LAURENCE, *and another* WATCHMAN.]

THIRD WATCH. Here is a friar that trembles, sighs, and weeps.
We took this mattock and this spade from him 185
As he was coming from this churchyard's side.
FIRST WATCH. A great suspicion. Stay the friar too.

[*Enter the* PRINCE *and* ATTENDANTS.]

PRINCE. What misadventure is so early up
That calls our person from our morning rest?

[*Enter* CAPULET, LADY CAPULET, *and others.*]

CAPULET. What should it be that they so shriek abroad? 190
LADY CAPULET. The people in the street cry Romeo,
Some Juliet, and some Paris, and all run
With open outcry toward our monument.
PRINCE. What fear is this which startles in our ears?
FIRST WATCH. Sovereign, here lies the County Paris slain, 195
And Romeo dead, and Juliet, dead before,
Warm and new-killed.
PRINCE. Search, seek, and know how this foul murder comes.
FIRST WATCH. Here is a friar, and slaughtered Romeo's man,
With instruments upon them fit to open 200
These dead men's tombs.
CAPULET. Oh, heavens! O wife, look how our daughter bleeds!
This dagger hath mista'en, for, lo, his house°

173. *attach:* arrest.   181. *circumstance:* knowledge of the facts.   203. *house:* i.e., scabbard.

Is empty on the back of Montague,
And it missheathèd in my daughter's bosom! 205
LADY CAPULET. Oh me! This sight of death is as a bell
That warns my old age to a sepulcher.

[*Enter* MONTAGUE *and others.*]

PRINCE. Come, Montague, for thou art early up,
To see thy son and heir more early down.
MONTAGUE. Alas, my liege, my wife is dead tonight, 210
Grief of my son's exile hath stopped her breath.
What further woe conspires against mine age?
PRINCE. Look, and thou shalt see.
MONTAGUE. O thou untaught! What manners is in this,
To press before thy father to a grave? 215
PRINCE. Seal up the mouth of outrage° for a while
Till we can clear these ambiguities
And know their spring, their head, their true descent.
And then will I be general of your woes,
And lead you even to death. Meantime forbear, 220
And let mischance be slave to patience.
Bring forth the parties of suspicion.
FRIAR LAURENCE. I am the greatest, able to do least,
Yet most suspected, as the time and place
Doth make against me, of this direful murder. 225
And here I stand, both to impeach and purge°
Myself condemnèd and myself excused.
PRINCE. Then say at once what thou dost know in this.
FRIAR LAURENCE. I will be brief, for my short date of breath°
Is not so long as is a tedious tale. 230
Romeo, there dead, was husband to that Juliet,
And she, there dead, that Romeo's faithful wife.
I married them, and their stol'n marriage day
Was Tybalt's doomsday, whose untimely death
Banished the new-made bridegroom from this city, 235
For whom, and not for Tybalt, Juliet pined.
You, to remove that siege of grief from her,
Betrothed and would have married her perforce
To County Paris. Then comes she to me,
And with wild looks bid me devise some mean 240
To rid her from this second marriage,

---

216. *Seal . . . outrage:* At these words, the curtains at the back of the stage are closed to conceal the three bodies.   226. *purge:* clear.   229. *short . . . breath:* the little life still left to me.

Or in my cell there would she kill herself.
Then gave I her, so tutored by my art,
A sleeping potion, which so took effect
As I intended, for it wrought on her   245
The form of death. Meantime I writ to Romeo
That he should hither come as this dire night,
To help to take her from her borrowed grave,
Being the time the potion's force should cease.
But he which bore my letter, Friar John,   250
Was stayed by accident, and yesternight
Returned my letter back. Then all alone
At the prefixèd hour of her waking
Came I to take her from her kindred's vault,
Meaning to keep her closely at my cell   255
Till I conveniently could send to Romeo.
But when I came, some minute ere the time
Of her awaking, here untimely lay
The noble Paris and true Romeo dead.
She wakes, and I entreated her come forth,   260
And bear this work of Heaven with patience.
But then a noise did scare me from the tomb,
And she too desperate would not go with me,
But, as it seems, did violence on herself.
All this I know, and to the marriage   265
Her nurse is privy.° And if aught in this
Miscarried by my fault, let my old life
Be sacrificed some hour before his time
Unto the rigor of severest law.
PRINCE. We still° have known thee for a holy man. 270
  Where's Romeo's man? What can he say in this?
BALTHASAR. I brought my master news of Juliet's death,
  And then in post he came from Mantua
  To this same place, to this same monument.
  This letter he early bid me give his father,   275
  And threatened me with death, going in the vault,
  If I departed not and left him there.
PRINCE. Give me the letter, I will look on it.
  Where is the County's page, that raised the watch?
  Sirrah, what made° your master in this place? 280
PAGE. He came with flowers to strew his lady's grave,
  And bid me stand aloof, and so I did.

266. *is privy:* shares the secret.   270. *still:* always.   280. *made:* did.

Anon comes one with light to ope the tomb,
And by and by my master drew on him,
And then I ran away to call the watch. 285
PRINCE. This letter doth make good the Friar's words,
Their course of love, the tidings of her death.
And here he writes that he did buy a poison
Of a poor 'pothecary, and therewithal
Came to this vault to die and lie with Juliet. 290
Where be these enemies? Capulet! Montague!
See what a scourge is laid upon your hate
That Heaven finds means to kill your joys with love!
And I, for winking at your discords too,
Have lost a brace of kinsmen. All are punished. 295
CAPULET. O Brother Montague, give me thy hand.
This is my daughter's jointure,° for no more
Can I demand.
MONTAGUE.   But I can give thee more.
For I will raise her statue in pure gold,
That whiles Verona by that name is known 300
There shall no figure at such rate° be set
As that of true and faithful Juliet.
CAPULET. As rich shall Romeo's by his lady's lie,
Poor sacrifices of our enmity!
PRINCE. A glooming peace this morning with it brings, 305
The sun for sorrow will not show his head.
Go hence, to have more talk of these sad things.
Some shall be pardoned and some punishèd.
For never was a story of more woe
Than this of Juliet and her Romeo.   [*Exeunt.*] 310

297. *jointure:* dowry.   301. *rate:* value.

ANTIGONE

by SOPHOCLES

TRANSLATED BY *Dudley Fitts* AND *Robert Fitzgerald*

THE ANTIGONE OF SOPHOCLES An English Version by Dudley Fitts and Robert Fitzgerald, copyright, 1949, by Harcourt Brace Jovanovich, Inc. and reprinted with their permission.

CAUTION: All rights, including professional, amateur, motion picture, recitation, lecturing, performance, public reading, radio broadcasting, and television are strictly reserved. Inquiries on all rights should be addressed to Harcourt Brace Jovanovich, Inc., 757 Third Avenue, New York, New York 10017.

Photos: From the Norma Film production, 1962, directed by George Tzavellas. Filmed at Alfa Studios, Athens.

Recording of this text (with Dorothy Tutin) available through Caedmon Records, Inc., 505 Eighth Avenue, New York, N.Y. 10018.

In order to understand and to appreciate Greek tragedy, the modern reader needs to know that the Greek tragedians—particularly Aeschylus and Sophocles—wrote plays that reflect a searching contemporary concern with moral and religious questions. The Greek drama of the fifth century B.C. had, in fact, developed out of religious ritual a few years earlier; this origin helps to explain the ritualistic conventions of the plays, the alternation of dramatic episodes of dialogue with the appearance of the chorus, and the generally stylized rhythms of the action. This not-too-remote religious origin explains another characteristic of Greek theater. Plot (or as Aristotle calls it, fable) was relatively fixed, a conventional body of material deriving mainly from two great myths: the events surrounding and following the Trojan War and the story of the downfall of the house of Labdacus, which supplied the plot for *Antigone*. As a result, though individual playwrights often introduced variations, when the audience attended *Antigone* in the spring of 441 B.C., they were well acquainted with the main outlines of the plot. This fact explains why the Greek theater devoted so little attention to exposition and why in the majority of the plays the most crucial event, which has initiated the original tragic action, has already taken place.

The important role of the chorus can also be explained in a religious context, though by the time Sophocles wrote *Antigone* attention had gradually shifted away from the chorus to the main actors. However, like the choric responses in the Christian mass, the odes of the Sophoclean chorus (a chorus of fifteen actors and a leader) are vestiges of music sung by celebrants in a religious ritual. While the action takes place, the chorus observes and in intoning the odes serves as the voice of elders, questioning, admonishing, advising, and expressing collective fear, joy, and grief.

Sophocles' *Antigone* is an exemplary illustration of this Greek theatrical mode. The action represents the end of a long, complex series of events in which Oedipus, former king of Thebes, had unknowingly killed his father, Laius, and equally unknowingly married his mother, Jocasta. From this incestuous union had come four children, the daughters Antigone and Ismene and the sons Eteocles and Polyneices. After Oedipus' discovery of his crimes, he had gone into exile and the rule of Thebes had been entrusted to his two sons in alternating years. Urged on by jealousy and ambition, Polyneices attacks the city with a foreign army during one year's reign of Eteocles. In this war between the brothers both are killed. *Antigone* begins shortly after this violent slaughter with the children's uncle, Creon, the new king, denying the traitorous Polyneices burial, a rite regarded by the Greeks as sacred, its omission being a sacrilege that would condemn the spirit of the buried to eternal wandering rather than grant the comfort of joyful reunion with one's ancestors in the underworld. As the play opens Antigone has already decided, in direct disobedience to Creon's order, to perform the rites and to bury Polyneices' body, quite aware that in performing such acts she may be forfeiting her life.

This incident in the myth illustrates a recurring preoccupation of Greek tragedy: the conflict between political and religious law. In his position as ruler of Thebes, Creon rashly decides to persecute Polyneices beyond the grave for his treason to the state. Antigone with no less impetuosity decides to provide burial rites for her brother, meeting the demands of religious law by ignoring Creon's edict. The collision between these two strong-willed persons is inevitable.

But the tragic forces of the play circle finally around Creon, for he has made the decision to leave Polyneices' body unsanctified by the burial service and must answer the seditious accusation of Antigone and the admonishment of the chorus. And he must resist the prophetic but vain warning of Teiresias. Creon's tragedy, which implicates Antigone, his son Haemon (in love with Antigone), and his wife Eurydice, is the tragedy of late-awareness. Wavering between his overweening pride (the Greeks called it *hubris*) and his suddenly aroused fear, he hesitates a few moments too long. In that short time his decision becomes irredeemable.

Characters

ANTIGONE
ISMENE
EURYDICE
CREON
HAIMON
TEIRESIAS
A SENTRY
A MESSENGER
CHORUS

SCENE: *Before the palace of Creon, King of Thebes. A central double door and two lateral doors. A platform extends the length of the façade, and from this platform three steps lead down into the "orchestra," or chorus-ground.* TIME: *Dawn of the day after the repulse of the Argive* army from the assault on Thebes.*

PROLOGUE

[ANTIGONE *and* ISMENE *enter from the central door of the Palace.*]

ANTIGONE. Ismene, dear sister,
 You would think that we had already suffered enough
 For the curse on Oedipus:°
 I cannot imagine any grief
 That you and I have not gone through. And now—   5
 Have they told you of the new decree of our King Creon?
ISMENE. I have heard nothing: I know
 That two sisters lost two brothers, a double death
 In a single hour; and I know that the Argive army
 Fled in the night; but beyond this, nothing.   10
ANTIGONE. I thought so. And that is why I wanted you
 To come out here with me. There is something we must do.
ISMENE. Why do you speak so strangely?
ANTIGONE. Listen, Ismene:
 Creon buried our brother Eteocles   15

* Greek.

PROLOGUE. 3. *Oedipus:* their father, condemned by prophecy to kill his own father and to have children by his mother.

With military honors, gave him a soldier's funeral,
And it was right that he should; but Polyneices,°
Who fought as bravely and died as miserably,—
They say that Creon has sworn
No one shall bury him, no one mourn for him,   20
But his body must lie in the fields, a sweet treasure
For carrion birds to find as they search for food.
That is what they say, and our good Creon is coming here
To announce it publicly; and the penalty—
Stoning to death in the public square!
                              There it is,   25
And now you can prove what you are:
A true sister, or a traitor to your family.
ISMENE. Antigone, you are mad! What could I possibly do?
ANTIGONE. You must decide whether you will help me or not.
ISMENE. I do not understand you. Help you in what?   30
ANTIGONE. Ismene, I am going to bury him. Will you come?
ISMENE. Bury him! You have just said the new law forbids it.
ANTIGONE. He is my brother. And he is your brother, too.
ISMENE. But think of the danger! Think what Creon will do!
ANTIGONE. Creon is not strong enough to stand in my way.   35
ISMENE. Ah sister!
Oedipus died, everyone hating him
For what his own search brought to light, his eyes
Ripped out by his own hand; and Iocaste died,
His mother and wife at once: she twisted the cords   40
That strangled her life; and our two brothers died,
Each killed by the other's sword. And we are left:
But oh, Antigone,
Think how much more terrible than these
Our own death would be if we should go against Creon   45
And do what he has forbidden! We are only women,
We cannot fight with men, Antigone!
The law is strong, we must give in to the law
In this thing, and in worse. I beg the Dead
To forgive me, but I am helpless: I must yield   50
To those in authority. And I think it is dangerous business
To be always meddling.
ANTIGONE.   If that is what you think,
I should not want you, even if you asked to come.
You have made your choice, you can be what you want to be.

17. *Polyneices:* led the Greeks against Thebes.

But I will bury him; and if I must die, 55
I say that this crime is holy: I shall lie down
With him in death, and I shall be as dear
To him as he to me.
     It is the dead,
Not the living, who make the longest demands:
We die for ever . . .
       You may do as you like, 60
Since apparently the laws of the gods° mean nothing to you.
ISMENE. They mean a great deal to me; but I have no strength
 To break laws that were made for the public good.
ANTIGONE. That must be your excuse, I suppose. But as for me,
 I will bury the brother I love.
ISMENE.   Antigone, 65
 I am so afraid for you!
ANTIGONE.   You need not be:
 You have yourself to consider, after all.
ISMENE. But no one must hear of this, you must tell no one!
 I will keep it a secret, I promise!
ANTIGONE.   Oh, tell it! Tell everyone!
 Think how they'll hate you when it all comes out 70
 If they learn that you knew about it all the time!
ISMENE. So fiery! You should be cold with fear.
ANTIGONE. Perhaps. But I am doing only what I must.
ISMENE. But can you do it? I say that you cannot.
ANTIGONE. Very well: when my strength gives out, I shall do no
 more. 75
ISMENE. Impossible things should not be tried at all.
ANTIGONE. Go away, Ismene:
 I shall be hating you soon, and the dead will too,
 For your words are hateful. Leave me my foolish plan:
 I am not afraid of the danger; if it means death, 80
 It will not be the worst of deaths—death without honor.
ISMENE. Go then, if you feel that you must.
 You are unwise,
 But a loyal friend indeed to those who love you.

      [*Exit into the Palace.* ANTIGONE *goes off, L.*]

[*Enter the* CHORUS.]

---

61. *laws of the gods:* To refuse a man burial was to sentence his spirit to wander forever.

PÁRADOS

STROPHE° 1

CHORUS. Now the long blade of the sun, lying
  Level east to west, touches with glory
  Thebes of the Seven Gates. Open, unlidded
  Eye° of golden day! O marching light
  Across the eddy and rush of Dirce's° stream, 5
  Striking the white shields of the enemy
  Thrown headlong backward from the blaze of morning!
CHORAGOS.° Polyneices their commander
  Roused them with windy phrases,
  He the wild eagle screaming 10
  Insults above our land,
  His wings their shields of snow,
  His crest their marshalled helms.

ANTISTROPHE 1

CHORUS. Against our seven gates in a yawning ring
  The famished spears came onward in the night; 15
  But before his jaws were sated with our blood,
  Or pinefire took the garland of our towers,
  He was thrown back; and as he turned, great Thebes—
  No tender victim for his noisy power—
  Rose like a dragon behind him, shouting war. 20
CHORAGOS. For God hates utterly
  The bray of bragging tongues;
  And when he beheld their smiling,
  Their swagger of golden helms,
  The frown of his thunder blasted 25
  Their first man from our walls.°

PÁRADOS. *Strophe:* the strophe/antistrophe are divisions within the choral odes. 4. *Eye:* sun. 5. *Dirce:* a spring near Thebes. 8. *Choragos:* choral leader. 26. *walls:* Capaneus was willed by a thunderbolt at the moment of his triumph.

STROPHE 2

CHORUS. We heard his shout of triumph high in the air
    Turn to a scream; far out in a flaming arc
    He fell with his windy torch, and the earth struck him.
    And others storming in fury no less than his   30
    Found stock of death in the dusty joy of battle.
CHORAGOS. Seven captains at seven gates
    Yielded their clanging arms to the god
    That bends the battle-line and breaks it.
    These two° only, brothers in blood,   35
    Face to face in matchless rage,
    Mirroring each the other's death,
    Clashed in long combat.

ANTISTROPHE 2

CHORUS. But now in the beautiful morning of victory
    Let Thebes of the many chariots sing for joy!   40
    With hearts for dancing we'll take leave of war:
    Our temples shall be sweet with hymns of praise,
    And the long night shall echo with our chorus.

SCENE ONE

CHORAGOS. But now at last our new King is coming:
    Creon of Thebes, Menoikeus' son.
    In this auspicious dawn of his reign
    What are the new complexities
    That shifting Fate has woven for him?   5
    What is his counsel? Why has he summoned
    The old men to hear him?

    [*Enter* CREON *from the Palace, C. He addresses the* CHORUS *from the top step.*]

CREON. Gentlemen: I have the honor to inform you that our Ship of State, which recent storms have threatened to destroy, has come safely

---

35. *two:* Eteocles and Polyneices.

to harbor at last, guided by the merciful wisdom of Heaven. I have summoned you here this morning because I know that I can depend upon you: your devotion to King Laïos was absolute; you never hesitated in your duty to our late ruler Oedipus; and when Oedipus died, your loyalty was transferred to his children. Unfortunately, as you know, his two sons, the princes Eteocles and Polyneices, have killed each other in battle; and I, as the next in blood, have succeeded to the full power of the throne. 17

I am aware, of course, that no Ruler can expect complete loyalty from his subjects until he has been tested in office. Nevertheless, I say to you at the very outset that I have nothing but contempt for the kind of Governor who is afraid, for whatever reason, to follow the course that he knows is best for the State; and as for the man who sets private friendship above the public welfare—I have no use for him, either. I call God to witness that if I saw my country headed for ruin, I should not be afraid to speak out plainly; and I need hardly remind you that I would never have any dealings with an enemy of the people. No one values friendship more highly than I; but we must remember that friends made at the risk of wrecking our Ship are not real friends at all. 29

These are my principles, at any rate, and that is why I have made the following decision concerning the sons of Oedipus: Eteocles, who died as a man should die, fighting for his country, is to be buried with full military honors, with all the ceremony that is usual when the greatest heroes die; but his brother Polyneices, who broke his exile to come back with fire and sword against his native city and the shrines of his father's gods, whose one idea was to spill the blood of his blood and sell his own people into slavery—Polyneices, I say, is to have no burial: no man is to touch him or say the least prayer for him; he shall lie on the plain, unburied; and the birds and the scavenging dogs can do with him whatever they like. 40

This is my command, and you can see the wisdom behind it. As long as I am King, no traitor is going to be honored with the loyal man. But whoever shows by word and deed that he is on the side of the State—he shall have my respect while he is living, and my reverence when he is dead. 45

CHORAGOS. If that is your will, Creon son of Menoikeus,
  You have the right to enforce it: we are yours.
CREON. That is my will. Take care that you do your part.
CHORAGOS. We are old men: let the younger ones carry it out.
CREON. I do not mean that: the sentries have been appointed. 50
CHORAGOS. Then what is it that you would have us do?
CREON. You will give no support to whoever breaks this law.

CHORAGOS. Only a crazy man is in love with death!
CREON. And death it is; yet money talks, and the wisest
 Have sometimes been known to count a few coins too many. 55

[*Enter* SENTRY *from L.*]

SENTRY. I'll not say that I'm out of breath from running, King, because every time I stopped to think about what I have to tell you, I felt like going back. And all the time a voice kept saying, "You fool, don't you know you're walking straight into trouble?"; and then another voice: "Yes, but if you let somebody else get the news to Creon first, it will be even worse than that for you!" But good sense won out, at least I hope it was good sense, and here I am with a story that makes no sense at all; but I'll tell it anyhow, because, as they say, what's going to happen's going to happen, and—
CREON. Come to the point. What have you to say? 65
SENTRY. I did not do it. I did not see who did it. You must not punish me for what someone else has done.
CREON. A comprehensive defense! More effective, perhaps,
 If I knew its purpose. Come: what is it?
SENTRY. A dreadful thing . . . I don't know how to put it— 70
CREON. Out with it!
SENTRY.   Well, then;
 The dead man—
            Polyneices—

[*Pause. The* SENTRY *is overcome, fumbles for words.* CREON *waits impassively.*]

                    out there—
                        someone—
New dust on the slimy flesh!

[*Pause. No sign from* CREON.]

Someone has given it burial that way, and
Gone . . . 75

[*Long pause.* CREON *finally speaks with deadly control.*]

CREON. And the man who dared do this?
SENTRY.   I swear I
 Do not know! You must believe me!
                    Listen:
 The ground was dry, not a sign of digging, no,
 Not a wheeltrack in the dust, no trace of anyone.

It was when they relieved us this morning: and one of them, 80
The corporal, pointed to it.
                    There it was,
The strangest—
            Look:
The body, just mounded over with light dust: you see?
Not buried really, but as if they'd covered it
Just enough for the ghost's peace. And no sign 85
Of dogs or any wild animal that had been there.

And then what a scene there was! Every man of us
Accusing the other: we all proved the other man did it,
We all had proof that we could not have done it.
We were ready to take hot iron in our hands, 90
Walk through fire, swear by all the gods,
It was not I!
I do not know who it was, but it was not I!

[CREON's *rage has been mounting steadily, but the* SENTRY *is too intent upon his story to notice it.*]

And then, when this came to nothing, someone said
A thing that silenced us and made us stare 95
Down at the ground: you had to be told the news,
And one of us had to do it! We threw the dice,
And the bad luck fell to me. So here I am,
No happier to be here than you are to have me:
Nobody likes the man who brings bad news. 100

CHORAGOS. I have been wondering, King: can it be that the gods have done this?

CREON [*furiously*]. Stop!
    Must you doddering wrecks
Go out of your heads entirely? "The gods!"
Intolerable! 105
The gods favor this corpse? Why? How had he served them?
Tried to loot their temples, burn their images,
Yes, and the whole State, and its laws with it!
Is it your senile opinion that the gods love to honor bad men?
A pious thought!—
                No, from the very beginning 110
There have been those who have whispered together,
Stiff-necked anarchists, putting their heads together,
Scheming against me in alleys. These are the men,

And they have bribed my own guard to do this thing.
[*Sententiously.*] Money! 115
There's nothing in the world so demoralizing as money.
Down go your cities,
Homes gone, men gone, honest hearts corrupted,
Crookedness of all kinds, and all for money!
[*To* SENTRY] But you—!
I swear by God and by the throne of God, 120
The man who has done this thing shall pay for it!
Find that man, bring him here to me, or your death
Will be the least of your problems: I'll string you up
Alive, and there will be certain ways to make you
Discover your employer before you die; 125
And the process may teach you a lesson you seem to have missed:
The dearest profit is sometimes all too dear:
That depends on the source. Do you understand me?
A fortune won is often misfortune.

SENTRY. King, may I speak?
CREON. Your very voice distresses me. 130
SENTRY. Are you sure that it is my voice, and not your conscience?
CREON. By God, he wants to analyze me now!
SENTRY. It is not what I say, but what has been done, that hurts you.
CREON. You talk too much.
SENTRY. Maybe; but I've done nothing.
CREON. Sold your soul for some silver: that's all you've done. 135
SENTRY. How dreadful it is when the right judge judges wrong!
CREON. Your figures of speech
May entertain you now; but unless you bring me the man,
You will get little profit from them in the end.
[*Exit* CREON *into the Palace.*]
SENTRY. "Bring me the man"—! 140
I'd like nothing better than bringing him the man!
But bring him or not, you have seen the last of me here.
At any rate, I am safe! [*Exit* SENTRY.]

ODE ONE

STROPHE 1

CHORUS. Numberless are the world's wonders, but none
   More wonderful than man; the stormgray sea
   Yields to his prows,° the huge crests bear him high;
   Earth, holy and inexhaustible, is graven
   With shining furrows where his plows have gone   5
   Year after year, the timeless labor of stallions.

ANTISTROPHE 1

The lightboned birds and beasts that cling to cover,
The lithe fish lighting their reaches of dim water,
All are taken, tamed in the net of his mind;
The lion on the hill, the wild horse windy-maned,   10
Resign to him; and his blunt yoke has broken
The sultry shoulders of the mountain bull.

STROPHE 2

Words also, and thought as rapid as air,
He fashions to his good use; statecraft is his,
And his the skill that deflects the arrows of snow,   15
The spears of winter rain: from every wind
He has made himself secure—from all but one:
In the late wind of death he cannot stand.

ANTISTROPHE 2

O clear intelligence, force beyond all measure!
O fate of man, working both good and evil!   20
When the laws are kept, how proudly his city stands!
When the laws are broken, what of his city then?
Never may the anárchic° man find rest at my hearth,
Never be it said that my thoughts are his thoughts.

ODE ONE.   3. *prows:* i.e., ships.   23. *anárchic:* lawless.

SCENE TWO

[*Re-enter* SENTRY, *leading* ANTIGONE.]

CHORAGOS. What does this mean? Surely this captive woman
Is the Princess, Antigone. Why should she be taken?
SENTRY. Here is the one who did it! We caught her
In the very act of burying him.—Where is Creon?
CHORAGOS. Just coming from the house.

[*Enter* CREON, *C.*]

CREON. What has happened?
Why have you come back so soon?
SENTRY [*expansively*]. O King,
A man should never be too sure of anything: I would have sworn
That you'd not see me here again: your anger
Frightened me so, and the things you threatened me with;
But how could I tell then
That I'd be able to solve the case so soon?

No dice-throwing this time: I was only too glad to come!

Here is this woman. She is the guilty one:
We found her trying to bury him.
Take her, then; question her; judge her as you will.
I am through with the whole thing now, and glád óf it.
CREON. But this is Antigone! Why have you brought her here?
SENTRY. She was burying him, I tell you!
CREON [*severely*]. Is this the truth?
SENTRY. I saw her with my own eyes. Can I say more?
CREON. The details: come, tell me quickly!
SENTRY. It was like this:
After those terrible threats of yours, King,
We went back and brushed the dust away from the body.
The flesh was soft by now, and stinking,
So we sat on a hill to windward and kept guard.
No napping this time! We kept each other awake.
But nothing happened until the white round sun
Whirled in the center of the round sky over us:
Then, suddenly,

A storm of dust roared up from the earth, and the sky
Went out, the plain vanished with all its trees   30
In the stinging dark. We closed our eyes and endured it.
The whirlwind lasted a long time, but it passed;
And then we looked, and there was Antigone!
I have seen
A mother bird come back to a stripped nest, heard   35
Her crying bitterly a broken note or two
For the young ones stolen. Just so, when this girl
Found the bare corpse, and all her love's work wasted,
She wept, and cried on heaven to damn the hands
That had done this thing.
                    And then she brought more dust   40
And sprinkled wine three times for her brother's ghost.

We ran and took her at once. She was not afraid,
Not even when we charged her with what she had done.
She denied nothing.
                And this was a comfort to me,
And some uneasiness: for it is a good thing   45
To escape from death, but it is no great pleasure
To bring death to a friend.
                    Yet I always say
There is nothing so comfortable as your own safe skin!
CREON [*slowly, dangerously*]. And you, Antigone,
You with your head hanging—do you confess this thing?   50
ANTIGONE. I do. I deny nothing.
CREON [*to* SENTRY].   You may go.   [*Exit* SENTRY.]
[*To* ANTIGONE] Tell me, tell me briefly:
Had you heard my proclamation touching this matter?
ANTIGONE. It was public. Could I help hearing it?
CREON. And yet you dared defy the law.
ANTIGONE.   I dared.   55
It was not God's proclamation. That final Justice
That rules the world below makes no such laws.
Your edict, King, was strong,
But all your strength is weakness itself against
The immortal unrecorded laws of God.   60
They are not merely now: they were, and shall be,
Operative for ever, beyond man utterly.

I knew I must die, even without your decree:
I am only mortal. And if I must die

Now, before it is my time to die,
Surely this is no hardship: can anyone
Living, as I live, with evil all about me,
Think Death less than a friend? This death of mine
Is of no importance; but if I had left my brother
Lying in death unburied, I should have suffered.
Now I do not.
              You smile at me. Ah Creon,
Think me a fool, if you like; but it may well be
That a fool convicts me of folly.
CHORAGOS. Like father, like daughter: both headstrong, deaf to reason!
She has never learned to yield.
CREON.   She has much to learn.
The inflexible heart breaks first, the toughest iron
Cracks first, and the wildest horses bend their necks
At the pull of the smallest curb.
                      Pride? In a slave?
This girl is guilty of a double insolence,
Breaking the given laws and boasting of it.
Who is the man here,
She or I, if this crime goes unpunished?
Sister's child, or more than sister's child,
Or closer yet in blood—she and her sister
Win bitter death for this!
   [*To* SERVANTS]   Go, some of you,
Arrest Ismene. I accuse her equally.
Bring her: you will find her sniffling in the house there.

Her mind's a traitor: crimes kept in the dark
Cry for light, and the guardian brain shudders;
But how much worse than this
Is brazen boasting of barefaced anarchy!
ANTIGONE. Creon, what more do you want than my death?
CREON.   Nothing.
That gives me everything.
ANTIGONE.   Then I beg you: kill me.
This talking is a great weariness: your words
Are distasteful to me, and I am sure that mine
Seem so to you. And yet they should not seem so:
I should have praise and honor for what I have done.
All these men here would praise me
Were their lips not frozen shut with fear of you.
[*Bitterly.*] Ah the good fortune of kings,

  Licensed to say and do whatever they please!
CREON. You are alone here in that opinion.
ANTIGONE. No, they are with me. But they keep their tongues in leash.
CREON. Maybe. But you are guilty, and they are not.
ANTIGONE. There is no guilt in reverence for the dead.   105
CREON. But Eteocles—was he not your brother too?
ANTIGONE. My brother too.
CREON.   And you insult his memory?
ANTIGONE [*softly*]. The dead man would not say that I insult it.
CREON. He would: for you honor a traitor as much as him.
ANTIGONE. His own brother, traitor or not, and equal in blood.   110
CREON. He made war on his country. Eteocles defended it.
ANTIGONE. Nevertheless, there are honors due all the dead.
CREON. But not the same for the wicked as for the just.
ANTIGONE. Ah Creon, Creon,
  Which of us can say what the gods hold wicked?   115
CREON. An enemy is an enemy, even dead.
ANTIGONE. It is my nature to join in love, not hate.
CREON [*finally losing patience*]. Go join them, then; if you must have your love,
  Find it in hell!
CHORAGOS. But see, Ismene comes: 120

  [*Enter* ISMENE, *guarded.*]

  Those tears are sisterly, the cloud
  That shadows her eyes rains down gentle sorrow.
CREON. You too, Ismene,
  Snake in my ordered house, sucking my blood
  Stealthily—and all the time I never knew   125
  That these two sisters were aiming at my throne!
                Ismene,
  Do you confess your share in this crime, or deny it?
  Answer me.
ISMENE. Yes, if she will let me say so. I am guilty.
ANTIGONE [*coldly*]. No, Ismene. You have no right to say so.   130
  You would not help me, and I will not have you help me.
ISMENE. But now I know what you meant; and I am here
  To join you, to take my share of punishment.
ANTIGONE. The dead man and the gods who rule the dead
  Know whose act this was. Words are not friends.   135
ISMENE. Do you refuse me, Antigone? I want to die with you:
  I too have a duty that I must discharge to the dead.
ANTIGONE. You shall not lessen my death by sharing it.

ISMENE. What do I care for life when you are dead?
ANTIGONE. Ask Creon. You're always hanging on his opinions.   140
ISMENE. You are laughing at me. Why, Antigone?
ANTIGONE. It's a joyless laughter, Ismene.
ISMENE.   But can I do nothing?
ANTIGONE. Yes. Save yourself. I shall not envy you.
   There are those who will praise you; I shall have honor, too.
ISMENE. But we are equally guilty!
ANTIGONE.   No more, Ismene.   145
   You are alive, but I belong to Death.
CREON [*to the* CHORUS]. Gentlemen, I beg you to observe these girls:
   One has just now lost her mind; the other,
   It seems, has never had a mind at all.
ISMENE. Grief teaches the steadiest minds to waver, King.   150
CREON. Yours certainly did, when you assumed guilt with the guilty!
ISMENE. But how could I go on living without her?
CREON.   You are.
   She is already dead.
ISMENE.   But your own son's bride!
CREON. There are places enough for him to push his plow.
   I want no wicked women for my sons!   155
ISMENE. O dearest Haimon, how your father wrongs you!
CREON. I've had enough of your childish talk of marriage!
CHORAGOS. Do you really intend to steal this girl from your son?
CREON. No; Death will do that for me.
CHORAGOS.   Then she must die?
CREON [*ironically*]. You dazzle me.
                       —But enough of this talk!   160
   [*To* GUARDS.] You, there, take them away and guard them well:
   For they are but women, and even brave men run
   When they see Death coming.
                         [*Exeunt* ISMENE, ANTIGONE, *and* GUARDS.]

ODE TWO

STROPHE I

CHORUS. Fortunate is the man who has never tasted God's vengeance!
   Where once the anger of heaven has struck, that house is shaken
   For ever: damnation rises behind each child
   Like a wave cresting out of the black northeast,

When the long darkness under sea roars up 5
And bursts drumming death upon the windwhipped sand.

ANTISTROPHE 1

I have seen this gathering sorrow from time long past
Loom upon Oedipus' children: generation from generation
Takes the compulsive rage of the enemy god.
So lately this last flower of Oedipus' line 10
Drank the sunlight! but now a passionate word
And a handful of dust have closed up all its beauty.

STROPHE 2

        What mortal arrogance
        Transcends the wrath of Zeus?
Sleep cannot lull him, nor the effortless long months 15
Of the timeless gods: but he is young for ever,
And his house is the shining day of high Olympos.°
        All that is and shall be,
        And all the past, is his.
No pride on earth is free of the curse of heaven. 20

ANTISTROPHE 2

        The straying dreams of men
        May bring them ghosts of joy:
But as they drowse, the waking embers burn them;
Or they walk with fixed eyes, as blind men walk.
But the ancient wisdom speaks for our own time: 25
        Fate works most for woe
        With Folly's fairest show.
Man's little pleasure is the spring of sorrow.

ODE TWO. 17. *Olympos:* home of the gods.

SCENE THREE

CHORAGOS. But here is Haimon, King, the last of all your sons.°
Is it grief for Antigone that brings him here,
And bitterness at being robbed of his bride?

[*Enter* HAIMON.]

CREON. We shall soon see, and no need of diviners.°
—Son,
You have heard my final judgment on that girl: 5
Have you come here hating me, or have you come
With deference and with love, whatever I do?
HAIMON. I am your son, father. You are my guide.
You make things clear for me, and I obey you.
No marriage means more to me than your continuing wisdom. 10
CREON. Good. That is the way to behave: subordinate
Everything else, my son, to your father's will.
That is what a man prays for, that he may get
Sons attentive and dutiful in his house,
Each one hating his father's enemies, 15
Honoring his father's friends. But if his sons
Fail him, if they turn out unprofitably,
What has he fathered but trouble for himself
And amusement for the malicious?
                    So you are right
Not to lose your head over this woman. 20
Your pleasure with her would soon grow cold, Haimon,
And then you'd have a hellcat in bed and elsewhere.
Let her find her husband in Hell!
Of all the people in this city, only she
Has had contempt for my law and broken it. 25
Do you want me to show myself weak before the people?
Or to break my sworn word? No, and I will not.
The woman dies.
I suppose she'll plead "family ties." Well, let her.
If I permit my own family to rebel, 30
How shall I earn the world's obedience?

SCENE THREE. 1. *sons:* Megareus, another son of Creon, sacrificed himself during battle to appease the gods.   4. *diviners:* those who foretell the future.

Show me the man who keeps his house in hand,
He's fit for public authority.
                              I'll have no dealings
With law-breakers, critics of the government:
Whoever is chosen to govern should be obeyed—
Must be obeyed, in all things, great and small,
Just and unjust! O Haimon,
The man who knows how to obey, and that man only,
Knows how to give commands when the time comes.
You can depend on him, no matter how fast
The spears come: he's a good soldier, he'll stick it out.

Anarchy, anarchy! Show me a greater evil!
This is why cities tumble and the great houses rain down,
This is what scatters armies!

No, no: good lives are made so by discipline.
We keep the laws then, and the lawmakers,
And no woman shall seduce us. If we must lose,
Let's lose to a man, at least! Is a woman stronger than we?
CHORAGOS. Unless time has rusted my wits,
What you say, King, is said with point and dignity.
HAIMON [*boyishly earnest*]. Father:
Reason is God's crowning gift to man, and you are right
To warn me against losing mine. I cannot say—
I hope that I shall never want to say!—that you
Have reasoned badly. Yet there are other men
Who can reason, too; and their opinions might be helpful.
You are not in a position to know everything
That people say or do, or what they feel:
Your temper terrifies them—everyone
Will tell you only what you like to hear.
But I, at any rate, can listen; and I have heard them
Muttering and whispering in the dark about this girl.
They say no woman has ever, so unreasonably,
Died so shameful a death for a generous act:
"She covered her brother's body. Is this indecent?
She kept him from dogs and vultures. Is this a crime?
Death?—She should have all the honor that we can give her!"

This is the way they talk out there in the city.

You must believe me:
Nothing is closer to me than your happiness.
What could be closer? Must not any son
Value his father's fortune as his father does his?
I beg you, do not be unchangeable:
Do not believe that you alone can be right.
The man who thinks that,
The man who maintains that only he has the power
To reason correctly, the gift to speak, the soul—
A man like that, when you know him, turns out empty.

It is not reason never to yield to reason!

In flood time you can see how some trees bend,
And because they bend, even their twigs are safe,
While stubborn trees are torn up, roots and all.
And the same thing happens in sailing:
Make your sheet fast, never slacken—and over you go,
Head over heels and under: and there's your voyage.
Forget you are angry! Let yourself be moved!
I know I am young; but please let me say this:
The ideal condition
Would be, I admit, that men should be right by instinct;
But since we are all too likely to go astray,
The reasonable thing is to learn from those who can teach.
CHORAGOS. You will do well to listen to him, King,
 If what he says is sensible. And you, Haimon,
 Must listen to your father.—Both speak well.
CREON. You consider it right for a man of my years and experience
 To go to school to° a boy?
HAIMON.   It is not right
 If I am wrong. But if I am young, and right,
 What does my age matter?
CREON. You think it right to stand up for an anarchist?
HAIMON. Not at all. I pay no respect to criminals.
CREON. Then she is not a criminal?
HAIMON. The City would deny it, to a man.
CREON. And the City proposes to teach me how to rule?
HAIMON. Ah. Who is it that's talking like a boy now?
CREON. My voice is the one voice giving orders in this City!

96. *school to:* to learn from.

HAIMON. It is no City if it takes orders from one voice.
CREON. The State is the King!
HAIMON.   Yes, if the State is a desert.

[*Pause.*]

CREON. This boy, it seems, has sold out to a woman.
HAIMON. If you are a woman: my concern is only for you.
CREON. So? Your "concern"! In a public brawl with your father!   110
HAIMON. How about you, in a public brawl with justice?
CREON. With justice, when all that I do is within my rights?
HAIMON. You have no right to trample on God's right.
CREON [*completely out of control*]. Fool, adolescent fool! Taken in by
   a woman!
HAIMON. You'll never see me taken in by anything vile.   115
CREON. Every word you say is for her!
HAIMON [*quickly, darkly*].   And for you.
   And for me. And for the gods under the earth.
CREON. You'll never marry her while she lives.
HAIMON. Then she must die.—But her death will cause another.
CREON. Another?   120
   Have you lost your senses? Is this an open threat?
HAIMON. There is no threat in speaking to emptiness.
CREON. I swear you'll regret this superior tone of yours!
   You are the empty one!
HAIMON.   If you were not my father,
   I'd say you were perverse.°   125
CREON. You girlstruck fool, don't play at words with me!
HAIMON. I am sorry. You prefer silence.
CREON.   Now, by God—!
   I swear, by all the gods in heaven above us,
   You'll watch it, I swear you shall!
   [*To the* SERVANTS]   Bring her out!
   Bring the woman out! Let her die before his eyes!   130
   Here, this instant, with her bridegroom beside her!
HAIMON. Not here, no; she will not die here, King.
   And you will never see my face again.
   Go on raving as long as you've a friend to endure you. [*Exit* HAIMON.]
CHORAGOS. Gone, gone.   135
   Creon, a young man in a rage is dangerous!
CREON. Let him do, or dream to do, more than a man can.
   He shall not save these girls from death.

---

125. *perverse:* insane.

CHORAGOS.   These girls?
   You have sentenced them both?
CREON.   No, you are right.
   I will not kill the one whose hands are clean.   140
CHORAGOS. But Antigone?
CREON [*somberly*].   I will carry her far away
   Out there in the wilderness, and lock her
   Living in a vault of stone. She shall have food,
   As the custom is, to absolve the State of her death.
   And there let her pray to the gods of hell: 145
   They are her only gods:
   Perhaps they will show her an escape from death,
   Or she may learn,
                  though late,
   That piety shown the dead is pity in vain.   [*Exit* CREON.]

ODE THREE

STROPHE

CHORUS. Love, unconquerable
   Waster of rich men, keeper
   Of warm lights and all-night vigil
   In the soft face of a girl:
   Sea-wanderer, forest-visitor!   5
   Even the pure Immortals cannot escape you,
   Any mortal man, in his one day's dusk,°
   Trembles before your glory.

ANTISTROPHE

Surely you swerve upon ruin
   The just man's consenting heart,   10
   As here you have made bright anger
   Strike between father and son—
   And none has conquered but Love!

   ODE THREE. 7. *dusk:* Life is viewed here as a single day.

>   A girl's glánce wórking the will of heaven:
>   Pleasure to her alone who mocks us,   15
>   Merciless Aphrodite.°

SCENE FOUR

> [*As* ANTIGONE *enters guarded.*]

CHORAGOS. But I can no longer stand in awe of this,
  Nor, seeing what I see, keep back my tears.
  Here is Antigone, passing to that chamber
  Where all find sleep at last.

> STROPHE I

ANTIGONE. Look upon me, friends, and pity me   5
  Turning back at the night's edge° to say
  Good-by to the sun that shines for me no longer;
  Now sleepy Death
  Summons me down to Acheron,° that cold shore:
  There is no bridesong° there, nor any music.   10
CHORUS. Yet not unpraised, not without a kind of honor,
  You walk at last into the underworld;
  Untouched by sickness, broken by no sword.
  What woman has ever found your way to death?

> ANTISTROPHE I

ANTIGONE. How often I have heard the story of Niobe,° 15
  Tantalos' wretched daughter, how the stone
  Clung fast about her, ivy-close: and they say
  The rain falls endlessly
  And sifting soft snow; her tears are never done.

---

16. *Aphrodite:* goddess of love, or, more accurately, of sexual desire.
  SCENE FOUR. 6. *at . . . edge:* at the point of death. 9. *Acheron:* river of the underworld. 10. *bridesong:* according to Greek custom, bride and groom were accompanied home by singing friends. 15. *Niobe:* distracted by grief for her dead children, she was turned by Zeus into a marble statue whose face is always wet with tears.

I feel the loneliness of her death in mine. 20
CHORUS. But she was born of heaven, and you
   Are woman, woman-born. If her death is yours,
   A mortal woman's, is this not for you
   Glory in our world and in the world beyond?

STROPHE 2

ANTIGONE. You laugh at me. Ah, friends, friends, 25
   Can you not wait until I am dead? O Thebes,
   O men many-charioted, in love with Fortune,
   Dear springs of Dirce, sacred Theban grove,
   Be witnesses for me, denied all pity,
   Unjustly judged! and think a word of love 30
   For her whose path turns
   Under dark earth, where there are no more tears.
   CHORUS. You have passed beyond human daring and come at last
   Into a place of stone where Justice sits.
   I cannot tell 35
   What shape of your father's guilt appears in this.

ANTISTROPHE 2

ANTIGONE. You have touched it at last: that bridal bed
   Unspeakable, horror of son and mother mingling:
   Their crime, infection of all our family!
   O Oedipus, father and brother! 40
   Your marriage strikes from the grave to murder mine.
   I have been a stranger here in my own land:
   All my life
   The blasphemy of my birth has followed me.
   CHORUS. Reverence is a virtue, but strength 45
   Lives in established law: that must prevail.
   You have made your choice,
   Your death is the doing of your conscious hand.

EPODE

ANTIGONE. Then let me go, since all your words are bitter,
   And the very light of the sun is cold to me. 50

Lead me to my vigil, where I must have
Neither love nor lamentation; no song, but silence.

[CREON *interrupts impatiently.*]

CREON. If dirges and planned lamentations could put off death,
Men would be singing for ever.
    [*To the* SERVANTS]   Take her, go!
You know your orders: take her to the vault   55
And leave her alone there. And if she lives or dies,
That's her affair, not ours: our hands are clean.
ANTIGONE. O tomb, vaulted bride-bed in eternal rock,
Soon I shall be with my own again
Where Persephone° welcomes the thin ghosts underground: 60
And I shall see my father again, and you, mother,
And dearest Polyneices—
                dearest indeed
To me, since it was my hand
That washed him clean and poured the ritual wine:
And my reward is death before my time!   65

And yet, as men's hearts know, I have done no wrong,
I have not sinned before God. Or if I have,
I shall know the truth in death. But if the guilt
Lies upon Creon who judged me, then, I pray,
May his punishment equal my own.
CHORAGOS.   O passionate heart,   70
Unyielding, tormented still by the same winds!
CREON. Her guards shall have good cause to regret their delaying.
ANTIGONE. Ah! That voice is like the voice of death!
CREON. I can give you no reason to think you are mistaken.
ANTIGONE. Thebes, and you my fathers' gods,   75
And rules of Thebes, you see me now, the last
Unhappy daughter of a line of kings,
Your kings, led away to death. You will remember
Because I would not transgress the laws of heaven.
What things I suffer, and at what men's hands,   80
[*To the* GUARDS, *simply*] Come: let us wait no longer.
                              [*Exit* ANTIGONE, *L., guarded.*]

---

60. *Persephone:* queen of the dead.

ODE FOUR

STROPHE 1

CHORUS. All Danae's° beauty was locked away
In a brazen cell where the sunlight could not come:
A small room, still as any grave, enclosed her.
Yet she was a princess too,
And Zeus in a rain of gold poured love upon her.   5
O child, child,
No power in wealth or war
Or tough sea-blackened ships
Can prevail against untiring Destiny!

ANTISTROPHE 1

And Dryas' son also, that furious king,   10
Bore the god's prisoning anger for his pride:
Sealed up by Dionysos in deaf stone,
His madness died among echoes.
So at the last he learned what dreadful power
His tongue had mocked: 15
For he had profaned the revels,
And fired the wrath of the nine
Implacable Sisters that love the sound of the flute.

STROPHE 2

And old men tell a half-remembered tale
Of horror done where a dark ledge splits the sea   20
And a double surf beats on the gráy shóres:
How a king's new woman, sick
With hatred for the queen he had imprisoned,
Ripped out his two sons' eyes with her bloody hands
While grinning Ares watched the shuttle plunge   25
Four times: four blind wounds crying for revenge,

ODE FOUR. 1. *Danae's:* The Chorus alludes to three persons who suffered fates similar to Antigone's.

ANTISTROPHE 2

Crying, tears and blood mingled.—Piteously born,
Those sons whose mother was of heavenly birth!
Her father was the god of the North Wind
And she was cradled by gales, 30
She raced with young colts on the glittering hills
And walked untrammeled in the open light:
But in her marriage deathless Fate found means
To build a tomb like yours for all her joy.

SCENE FIVE

[*Enter blind* TEIRESIAS, *led by a boy. The opening speeches of* TEIRESIAS *should be in singsong contrast to the realistic lines of* CREON.]

TEIRESIAS. This is the way the blind man comes, Princes, Princes,
  Lock-step, two heads lit by the eyes of one.
CREON. What new thing have you to tell us, old Teiresias?
TEIRESIAS. I have much to tell you: listen to the prophet, Creon.
CREON. I am not aware that I have ever failed to listen. 5
TEIRESIAS. Then you have done wisely, King, and ruled well.
CREON. I admit my debt to you. But what have you to say?
TEIRESIAS. This, Creon: you stand once more on the edge of fate.
CREON. What do you mean? Your words are a kind of dread.
TEIRESIAS. Listen, Creon: 10
  I was sitting in my chair of augury,° at the place
  Where the birds gather about me. They were all a-chatter,
  As is their habit, when suddenly I heard
  A strange note in their jangling, a scream, a
  Whirring fury; I knew that they were fighting, 15
  Tearing each other, dying
  In a whirlwind of wings clashing. And I was afraid.
  I began the rites of burnt-offering° at the altar,
  But Hephaistos° failed me: instead of bright flame,
  There was only the sputtering slime of the fat thigh-flesh 20

SCENE FIVE. 11. *augury:* foretelling the future by interpreting signs or omens. 18. *burnt-offering:* an animal, food, etc., sacrificed to a god. 19. *Hephaistos:* god of fire.

Melting: the entrails dissolved in gray smoke,
The bare bone burst from the welter.° And no blaze!

This was a sign from heaven. My boy described it,
Seeing for me as I see for others.

I tell you, Creon, you yourself have brought   25
This new calamity upon us. Our hearths and altars
Are stained with the corruption of dogs and carrion birds
That glut themselves on the corpse of Oedipus' son.
The gods are deaf when we pray to them, their fire
Recoils from our offering, their birds of omen   30
Have no cry of comfort, for they are gorged
With the thick blood of the dead.
                                O my son,
These are no trifles! Think: all men make mistakes,
But a good man yields when he knows his course is wrong,
And repairs the evil. The only crime is pride.   35

Give in to the dead man, then: do not fight with a corpse—
What glory is it to kill a man who is dead?
Think, I beg you:
It is for your own good that I speak as I do.
You should be able to yield for your own good.   40

CREON. It seems that prophets have made me their especial province.
All my life long
I have been a kind of butt° for the dull arrows
Of doddering fortune-tellers!
                            No, Teiresias:
If your birds—if the great eagles of God himself   45
Should carry him stinking bit by bit to heaven,
I would not yield. I am not afraid of pollution:
No man can defile the gods.
                            Do what you will,
Go into business, make money, speculate
In India gold or that synthetic gold from Sardis,   50
Get rich otherwise than by my consent to bury him.
Teiresias, it is a sorry thing when a wise man
Sells his wisdom, lets out his words for hire!

22. *welter:* bloody offering.   43. *butt:* target.

TEIRESIAS. Ah Creon! Is there no man left in the world—
CREON. To do what?—Come, let's have the aphorism! 55
TEIRESIAS. No man who knows that wisdom outweighs any wealth?
CREON. As surely as bribes are baser than any baseness.
TEIRESIAS. You are sick, Creon! You are deathly sick!
CREON. As you say: it is not my place to challenge a prophet.
TEIRESIAS. Yet you have said my prophecy is for sale. 60
CREON. The generation of prophets has always loved gold.
TEIRESIAS. The generation of kings has always loved brass.
CREON. You forget yourself! You are speaking to your King.
TEIRESIAS. I know it. You are a king because of me.
CREON. You have a certain skill; but you have sold out. 65
TEIRESIAS. King, you will drive me to words that—
CREON.   Say them, say them!
　Only remember: I will not pay you for them.
TEIRESIAS. No, you will find them too costly.
CREON.   No doubt. Speak:
　Whatever you say, you will not change my will.
TEIRESIAS. Then take this, and take it to heart! 70
　The time is not far off when you shall pay back
　Corpse for corpse, flesh of your own flesh.
　You have thrust the child of this world into living night,
　You have kept from the gods below the child that is theirs:
　The one in a grave before her death, the other, 75
　Dead, denied the grave. This is your crime:
　And the Furies° and the dark gods of Hell
　Are swift with terrible punishment for you.
　Do you want to buy me now, Creon?
　　　　　　　　　　　　　　Not many days,
　And your house will be full of men and women weeping, 80
　And curses will be hurled at you from far
　Cities grieving for sons unburied, left to rot
　Before the walls of Thebes.

　These are my arrows, Creon: they are all for you.

　[*To* BOY] But come, child: lead me home. 85
　Let him waste his fine anger upon younger men.
　Maybe he will learn at last
　To control a wiser tongue in a better head.   [*Exit* TEIRESIAS.]

77. *Furies:* avengers of unpunished crimes.

CHORAGOS. The old man has gone, King, but his words
  Remain to plague us. I am old, too,
  But I cannot remember that he was ever false.
CREON. That is true. . . . It troubles me.
  Oh it is hard to give in! but it is worse
  To risk everything for stubborn pride.
CHORAGOS. Creon: take my advice.
CREON.   What shall I do?
CHORAGOS. Go quickly: free Antigone from her vault
  And build a tomb for the body of Polyneices.
CREON. You would have me do this?
CHORAGOS.   Creon, yes!
  And it must be done at once: God moves
  Swiftly to cancel the folly of stubborn men.
CREON. It is hard to deny the heart! But I
  Will do it: I will not fight with destiny.
CHORAGOS. You must go yourself, you cannot leave it to others.
CREON. I will go.
            —Bring axes, servants:
  Come with me to the tomb. I buried her, I
  Will set her free.
            Oh, quickly!
  My mind misgives—
  The laws of the gods are mighty, and a man must serve them
  To the last day of his life!   [*Exit* CREON.]

PAEAN°

STROPHE I

CHORAGOS. God of many names°
CHORUS.   O Iacchos
                        son
  of Kadmeian Sémele
                O born of the Thunder!
      Guardian of the West
                    Regent

PAEAN: song of praise. 1. *God . . . names:* Dionysos (also called Iacchos and Bacchos), the son of Zeus "the Thunderer" and Semele.

of Eleusis' plain
        O Prince of maenad Thebes
and the Dragon Field° by rippling Ismenos:°   5

ANTISTROPHE 1

CHORAGOS. God of many names
CHORUS.   the flame of torches
  flares on our hills
            the nymphs of Iacchos
  dance at the spring of Castalia:°

from the vine-close mountain
           come ah come in ivy:
Evohé° evohé! sings through the streets of Thebes   10

STROPHE 2

CHORAGOS. God of many names
CHORUS.   Iacchos of Thebes
  heavenly Child
        of Sémele bride of the Thunderer!
  The shadow of plague is upon us:
                come
  with clement feet°
         oh come from Parnasos°
  down the long slopes
         across the lamenting water   15

STROPHE 1

CHORAGOS. Io Fire! Chorister of the throbbing stars!
  O purest among the voices of the night!
  Thou son of God, blaze for us!

5. *Dragon Field:* sacred place. *Ismenos:* a river. 8. *Castalia:* spring sacred to the muses. 10. *Evohé:* a joyous shout to Dionysos. 14. *with clement feet:* show us mercy. *Parnasos:* sacred mountain.

CHORUS. Come with choric rapture of circling Maenads
  Who cry *Io Iacche!*
             God of many names!   20

ÉXODOS

[*Enter* MESSENGER, *L.*]

MESSENGER. Men of the line of Kadmos, you who live
  Near Amphion's° citadel:
             I cannot say
Of any condition of human life "This is fixed,
This is clearly good, or bad." Fate raises up,
And Fate casts down the happy and unhappy alike: 5
No man can foretell his Fate.
             Take the case of Creon:
Creon was happy once, as I count happiness:
Victorious in battle, sole governor of the land,
Fortunate father of children nobly born.
And now it has all gone from him! Who can say   10
That a man is still alive when his life's joy fails?
He is a walking dead man. Grant him rich,
Let him live like a king in his great house:
If his pleasure is gone, I would not give
So much as the shadow of smoke for all he owns.   15
CHORAGOS. Your words hint at sorrow: what is your news for us?
MESSENGER. They are dead. The living are guilty of their death.
CHORAGOS. Who is guilty? Who is dead? Speak!
MESSENGER.   Haimon.
  Haimon is dead; and the hand that killed him
  Is his own hand.
CHORAGOS.   His father's? or his own?   20
MESSENGER. His own, driven mad by the murder his father had done.
CHORAGOS. Teiresias, Teiresias, how clearly you saw it all!
MESSENGER. This is my news: you must draw what conclusions you can
  from it.

ÉXODOS. 2. *Amphion:* His music supposedly charmed the stones to build a wall around Thebes.

CHORAGOS. But look: Eurydice, our Queen:
   Has she overheard us?   25

   [*Enter* EURYDICE *from the Palace, C.*]

EURYDICE. I have heard something, friends:
   As I was unlocking the gate of Pallas'° shrine,
   For I needed her help today, I heard a voice
   Telling of some new sorrow. And I fainted
   There at the temple with all my maidens about me.   30
   But speak again: whatever it is, I can bear it:
   Grief and I are no strangers.
MESSENGER.   Dearest Lady,
   I will tell you plainly all that I have seen.
   I shall not try to comfort you: what is the use,
   Since comfort could lie only in what is not true?   35
   The truth is always best.
                         I went with Creon
   To the outer plain where Polyneices was lying,
   No friend to pity him, his body shredded by dogs.
   We made our prayers in that place to Hecate°
   And Pluto, that they would be merciful. And we bathed   40
   The corpse with holy water, and we brought
   Fresh-broken branches to burn what was left of it,
   And upon the urn we heaped up a towering barrow
   Of the earth of his own land.
                            When we were done, we ran
   To the vault where Antigone lay on her couch of stone.   45
   One of the servants had gone ahead,
   And while he was yet far off he heard a voice
   Grieving within the chamber, and he came back
   And told Creon. And as the King went closer,
   The air was full of wailing, the words lost,   50
   And he begged us to make all haste. "Am I a prophet?"
   He said, weeping, "And must I walk this road,
   The saddest of all that I have gone before?
   My son's voice calls me on. Oh quickly, quickly!
   Look through the crevice there, and tell me   55
   If it is Haimon, or some deception of the gods!"
   We obeyed; and in the cavern's farthest corner
   We saw her lying:
   She had made a noose of her fine linen veil

---

27. *Pallas:* Athena, goddess of wisdom.   39. *Hecate:* goddess of the underworld.

And hanged herself. Haimon lay beside her, 60
His arms about her waist, lamenting her,
His love lost under ground, crying out
That his father had stolen her away from him.
When Creon saw him the tears rushed to his eyes
And he called to him: "What have you done, child? Speak to me. 65
What are you thinking that makes your eyes so strange?
O my son, my son, I come to you on my knees!"
But Haimon spat in his face. He said not a word,
Staring—
   And suddenly drew his sword
And lunged. Creon shrank back, the blade missed; and the boy, 70
Desperate against himself, drove it half its length
Into his own side, and fell. And as he died
He gathered Antigone close in his arms again,
Choking, his blood bright red on her white cheek.
And now he lies dead with the dead, and she is his 75
At last, his bride in the houses of the dead.

       [*Exit* EURYDICE *into the Palace.*]

CHORAGOS. She has left us without a word. What can this mean?
MESSENGER. It troubles me, too; yet she knows what is best,
 Her grief is too great for public lamentation,
 And doubtless she has gone to her chamber to weep 80
 For her dead son, leading her maidens in his dirge.
CHORAGOS. It may be so: but I fear this deep silence.

[*Pause.*]

MESSENGER. I will see what she is doing. I will go in.
      [*Exit* MESSENGER *into the Palace.*]

[*Enter* CREON *with attendants, bearing* HAIMON's *body.*]

CHORAGOS. But here is the King himself: oh look at him,
 Bearing his own damnation in his arms. 85
CREON. Nothing you say can touch me any more.
 My own blind heart has brought me
 From darkness to final darkness. Here you see
 The father murdering, the murdered son—
 And all my civic wisdom! 90

 Haimon my son, so young, so young to die,
  I was the fool, not you; and you died for me.
CHORAGOS. That is the truth; but you were late in learning it.

CREON. This truth is hard to bear. Surely a god
    Has crushed me beneath the hugest weight of heaven.
    And driven me headlong a barbaric way
    To trample out the thing I held most dear.

    The pains that men will take to come to pain!

  [*Enter* MESSENGER *from the Palace.*]

MESSENGER. The burden you carry in your hands is heavy,
    But it is not all: you will find more in your house.
CREON. What burden worse than this shall I find there?
MESSENGER. The Queen is dead.
CREON. O port of death, deaf world,
    Is there no pity for me? And you, Angel of evil,
    I was dead, and your words are death again.
    Is it true, boy? Can it be true?
    Is my wife dead? Has death bred death?
MESSENGER. You can see for yourself.

  [*The doors are opened, and the body of* EURYDICE *is disclosed within.*]

CREON. Oh pity!
    All true, all true, and more than I can bear!
    O my wife, my son!
MESSENGER. She stood before the altar, and her heart
    Welcomed the knife her own hand guided,
    And a great cry burst from her lips for Megareus dead,
    And for Haimon dead, her sons; and her last breath
    Was a curse for their father, the murderer of her sons.
    And she fell, and the dark flowed in through her closing eyes.
CREON. O God, I am sick with fear.
    Are there no swords here? Has no one a blow for me?
MESSENGER. Her curse is upon you for the deaths of both.
CREON. It is right that it should be. I alone am guilty.
    I know it, and I say it. Lead me in,
    Quickly, friends.
    I have neither life nor substance. Lead me in.
CHORAGOS. You are right, if there can be right in so much wrong.
    The briefest way is best in a world of sorrow.
CREON. Let it come,
    Let death come quickly, and be kind to me.
    I would not ever see the sun again.
CHORAGOS. All that will come when it will; but we, meanwhile,

Have much to do. Leave the future to itself.
CREON. All my heart was in that prayer!
CHORAGOS. Then do not pray any more: the sky is deaf.
CREON. Lead me away. I have been rash and foolish.
   I have killed my son and my wife.   135
   I look for comfort; my comfort lies here dead.
   Whatever my hands have touched has come to nothing.
   Fate has brought all my pride to a thought of dust.

   [*As* CREON *is being led into the house, the* CHORAGOS *advances and speaks directly to the audience.*]

CHORAGOS. There is no happiness where there is no wisdom;
   No wisdom but in submission to the gods.   140
   Big words are always punished,
   And proud men in old age learn to be wise.

STUDY GUIDE

Study Guide

A RAISIN IN THE SUN

Act One

SCENE 1

1. What basic conflicts between the following characters are established during the morning routine: Walter Lee and Ruth, Beneatha and Walter Lee, Travis and his parents.
2. How does the legacy from Big Walter set the plot in motion?
3. What are the chronic frustrations in the lives of the Youngers?
4. What values and viewpoints are in conflict in the Younger household?
5. Miss Hansberry said that in Beneatha she was poking fun at her own youthful ideas. What girlish ideas and whims does Miss Hansberry mildly ridicule?
6. In what way is a social revolution occurring within the Younger household?
7. Why is the window plant important?
8. What does the minor crisis at the end of the act foreshadow?

SCENE 2

1. What new viewpoint does the visitor (Asagai) introduce?
2. What personal conflict exists between Beneatha and Asagai?
3. What is the thematic importance of the references to Africa?
4. What is the source of the breach between Walter Lee and his mother?
5. Why does Ruth consider an abortion?

Act Two

SCENE 1

1. What ironies are involved in Beneatha's Nigerian dress and her rejection of blues music as "assimilationist junk"?
2. What does the "brave warrior" scene reveal about Walter Lee?

3. How is the word "assimilationist" used?
4. What values and attitudes does George Murchison introduce?
5. What barriers exist between George Murchison and Walter Lee?
6. What do the Murchisons—father and son—symbolize for Walter Lee?
7. Why does George refer to Walter Lee as "Prometheus"?
8. What is the significance of the Clybourne Park address?
9. How are sunlight and the new garden related to Lena's attitudes toward her children?
10. What is Walter Lee's reaction to the purchase of the house?

SCENE 2

1. Why does Beneatha reject George Murchison?
2. How do invisible people, such as the Johnsons, Big Walter, the Arnolds, and Willie Harris, affect the lives of the Youngers?
3. How does Lena propose, at first, to divide the insurance money?
4. What do Walter Lee's dreams of the future tell us about his values as well as those of the society of which he is a part?
5. Why does Lena change her mind and give Walter Lee part of the money?

SCENE 3

1. What economic and social pressures does Karl Lindner introduce?
2. Why is Lena's gift from her children addressed to Mrs. Miniver?
3. What effect is given by Miss Hansberry's use of music and song throughout the play?
4. What crisis occurs at the end of the second act?

Act Three

SCENE 1

1. What choices for the future do George Murchison and Asagai offer Beneatha?
2. What is the meaning of Beneatha's invective ("Monsieur le petit bourgeois noir") directed to Walter Lee?
3. How does Walter Lee plan to extort money from Karl Lindner? Why does his plan distress the other members of the family?
4. How do Beneatha and Walter Lee differ in their search for identity?

5. How would you rank the four principal characters in order of complexity?
6. At what point does Walter Lee grow "into his manhood"?
7. Why is Lena Younger so solicitous of the window plant even as she abandons the apartment?
8. What is the significance of the play's title?

ALL MY SONS

Act One

1. What relationships and values are established in the opening scene?
2. What is the significance of the fallen tree?
3. How long has Larry been missing-in-action?
4. What mutual dilemma confronts Chris and Ann?
5. How does the domestic conflict over their marriage set the plot in motion?
6. What is the significance of Kate's dream?
7. In what way is Joe's make-believe game with Bert significant?
8. Why is Kate so insistent that Larry is still alive?
9. What facts are revealed about Joe Keller and about Steve Deever, Ann's father?
10. In what ways has the war affected the lives of the Kellers and the Deevers?
11. What is Chris's attitude toward his own war experiences?
12. In what way is George Deever's telephone call a pivotal incident?
13. What tensions does George's impending visit generate among the Kellers?

Act Two

1. Why is it significant and also symbolic that Chris removes the fallen tree from the yard?
2. What is the function of the scene between Sue Bayliss and Ann Deever?
3. Why does Sue Bayliss attack Chris's "phony idealism"?
4. What motivates Joe Keller to offer Ann's father a job?
5. How do the two visitors (Ann and George) bring the action of the play nearer its crisis?

6. What pressures does the absent Steve Deever exert upon the principal characters?
7. What does Deever's hat symbolize?
8. What is George's version of the "cracked cylinder heads"? How does it differ from Joe's account in Act One?
9. What picture of Steve Deever do we get from his son? In what ways does it differ from Joe's description of his business partner?
10. What seemingly insignificant bit of information results in the crisis of Act Two?
11. What truth does Kate finally bring into the open?
12. What is Joe's defense for the shipment of defective airplane engines?
13. What crucial issue separates Joe and Chris at the close of Act Two?

Act Three

1. How are "life's compromises," referred to by Jim Bayliss at the beginning of the act, related to the total meaning of the play?
2. Why does Joe now perpetuate the falsehood that Larry is alive?
3. What statement foreshadows the ending of the play?
4. What does Ann demand in exchange for her silence?
5. Why does Chris refer to his country as a "zoo"?
6. What is Joe's opinion of the morality of a wartime economy? Why, then, does he consider himself exonerated?
7. How does the letter precipitate the crisis and the play's resolution?
8. Why is his father's death a shock to Chris?
9. In his Introduction to his *Collected Plays,* Miller wrote that the theme of *All My Sons* is the question of action and consequence. In what ways do past acts and their consequences collide in the present time of the play?

PICNIC ON THE BATTLEFIELD

1. What is the significance of the play's title?
2. What is the function of the objects on stage, such as the knitting, field telephone, phonograph, camera, umbrella, picnic basket?
3. What attitudes toward war separate the son from his parents? The soldier from the general? The soldier from the stretcher bearers?
4. What common feelings, circumstances, and activities do Zépo and Zapo share? Why are they so alike?

5. What clichés of language and behavior does Arrabal satirize?
6. What is the function of the stretcher bearers?
7. What significance does the corpsman's statement about the dead (". . . they didn't plan it that way") have for the entire play?
8. How does the universe Arrabal depicts differ from that of the more conventional play?
9. Why are the sources of destruction (the captain's orders, the bombs, the bullets) unseen?
10. What are Arrabal's specific criticisms of war?
11. What is the significance of the Tépans's anecdote about the cow who ate their picnic lunch?
12. What is the significance of Mme. Tépan's confusing the beret and the record?
13. Why does Mme. Tépan want her picture taken with the prisoner?
14. Why do the Tépans decide to stop the war?
15. What is the meaning of the pantomime that closes the play?
16. Does the suggestion that an absurd play has neither a beginning nor an end apply to *Picnic on the Battlefield*?
17. In what way is the sight of the Tépans standing beneath an umbrella while bombs fall around them a visual metaphor for the entire play?

GHOSTS

Act One

1. What is the relationship between Engstrand and Regina? In what ways do they resemble one another?
2. What evidence of Engstrand's false piety emerges?
3. What are the hinted relationships between the following characters: Engstrand and Regina, Regina and Oswald, Pastor Manders and Mrs. Alving?
4. What influences Mrs. Alving and her decision about the insurance? What does this decision tell us about her?
5. What does the ominous remark about the fire in Engstrand's carpentry shop foreshadow?
6. In what ways has Engstrand deceived Pastor Manders?
7. Why is it significant that Oswald resembles his dead father?
8. What is the discrepancy between Oswald's childhood memories of his father and the public rumors about Captain Alving?

9. How does the discussion about "illegal unions" reveal the generation gap between Oswald and Pastor Manders?
10. How has Mrs. Alving been influenced by repressive concepts of duty?
11. In what ways is Mrs. Alving's statement that Oswald will inherit nothing from his father ironic?
12. At the close of Act One, what event conjures up "ghosts" for Mrs. Alving?

Act Two

1. How does the information revealed about the past in Act Two highlight the details of Act One? What developments take place in the relationships between Engstrand and Regina, Mrs. Alving and Pastor Manders?
2. What clues are given to Mrs. Alving's battle with ghosts both from "within and without"?
3. What does the scene between Engstrand and Manders reveal about the opportunism of one and the naiveté of the other?
4. In what ways do the gloom of the weather and the absence of sunlight underscore the problem of *hidden* disease, motive, and truth?
5. How does the light imagery support the action of the play? How do Ibsen's stage directions and dialogue associate light and darkness with spoken truths on the one side and concealed and harmful truths on the other?
6. Why does Manders express surprise at finding Mrs. Alving, Oswald, and Regina together in the living room?
7. How does the burning orphanage add to the meaning of the play?

Act Three

1. How does Engstrand blackmail Pastor Manders into giving financial support to his "tavern"?
2. What is Ibsen's implied comment on the moral fiber of the ministry?
3. What irony is implied in Engstrand's renaming his tavern "Captain Alving's Home"?
4. In what ways does Mrs. Alving show tragic awareness of her inadequacies as a wife as well as her responsibility for her husband's conduct and her son's disease?
5. How does Regina prove to be Jacob Engstrand's "spiritual" daughter?

6. At the close of the play, Mrs. Alving confronts a tragic alternative. To what extent is she now free to exercise a choice in Oswald's fate? Is her awareness of her predicament strong enough to overcome her emotional state?
7. How do the five "no's" and one "yes" at the end of the play affect your understanding of what Mrs. Alving intends to do?
8. Why do you suppose Ibsen left the play without specific resolution?
9. Throughout the play "ghosts" are symbols. How does Ibsen use these symbols to develop the theme of the play?

THE MISER

Act One

1. What is the function of the opening scene between Valere and Elise?
2. What does Valere hope to accomplish by adopting a disguise?
3. How do the paired scenes between Valere and Elise and Cleante and Elise define the play's conflicts?
4. What three secrets is the action of the play built on?
5. The device of Valere's pretending to take Harpagon's side against Elise is called a reversal. What does Molière accomplish by the frequent use of such reversals?
6. How does Molière stimulate the audience's interest at the end of Act One?

Act Two

1. What double effect does Molière achieve in his satire on moneylending practices?
2. Does a kind of dramatic justice result from the scene between Frosine and Harpagon? How does it contribute to the development of their characters?
3. On the basis of this scene between Frosine and Harpagon what conclusions can be drawn about the role of the professional "go-between"?

Act Three

1. What is the purpose of the lengthy opening scene between Harpagon and his servants?
2. Does Molière seem to condemn Frosine's point of view on marriage?
3. To what comic advantage does Molière briefly conceal identities; for example, borrower to lender, aging suitor to Mariane? How do these delays contribute to the comic tension?
4. How does Molière use misunderstandings and talking at cross-purposes as sources of comedy?
5. What desired freedom does Cleante's playing proxy for his father in the scene with Mariane permit him?
6. How does Harpagon's loss of his ring foreshadow future events?

Act Four

1. Why does Frosine decide to introduce a "rich widow" to Harpagon?
2. How does Harpagon trick Cleante into revealing his true feelings and to what purpose?
3. How does the comic reversal in this scene resemble other scenes in the play?
4. What more profound disorder does the rivalry in love between father and son reflect?
5. Which scene in this act is the turning point of the play?
6. How does Harpagon's final speech summarize his entire system of values?

Act Five

1. How does the misunderstanding about the pig at the beginning of the act relate to miserliness?
2. What purpose does Valere's and Harpagon's misunderstanding of the "theft" serve?
3. What is the function of Signor Anselme?
4. Why is Harpagon's choice at the play's close consistent and appropriate?
5. What values and social norms are affirmed as well as rejected at the close of *The Miser*?

6. How is the relationship between the themes of love and avarice resolved at the end of the play?

ROMEO AND JULIET

Act One

1. Sampson and Gregory begin the action of the play with a series of bawdy puns. What purpose is served by these sexual overtones?
2. In her conversation with the nurse and her mother in Scene 3 Juliet is seen as a courteous and obedient child. How does this fact make the change in her later conduct more dramatic?
3. Mercutio's Queen Mab speech in Scene 4 is a pure flight of fancy. What purpose does it serve at this moment in the play?
4. When Tybalt tells Capulet in Scene 5 that Romeo, a Montague, is present at the ball, Capulet refuses to take any action and prevents Tybalt from acting. What does this suggest about social laws in Shakespeare's day?

Act Two

1. In lines 17–20 of Scene 1 Mercutio seems to be praising Rosaline. What is his real intent?
2. From the dialogue scene between Romeo and Juliet, what general physical description of the Elizabethan stage can be deduced?
3. There are several references to the moon and the sun in the passionate avowals of love in this scene. How are these used to strengthen the lovers' meanings?
4. Why in Scene 3 does Friar Laurence agree, rather surprisingly, to perform the marriage ceremony for Romeo and Juliet in spite of their fathers' bitter hatred?
5. What effect is achieved in Scenes 4 and 5 by having the nurse act as a go-between in the arrangements for the marriage of Romeo and Juliet?

Act Three

1. In Scene 1 the description Mercutio gives in lines 5–25 of Benvolio's general behavior does not seem to agree with the name

(Benvolio, "well-wishing") Shakespeare has given him. Is there a contradiction here?
2. Romeo's conduct in this scene appears cowardly to Mercutio. Why does Romeo refuse to fight when he has been challenged by Tybalt?
3. In Scene 2 Juliet first longs for Romeo to arrive, then she curses him, then she apologizes for her intemperance. What are the real reasons for this apparent inconsistency?
4. In Scene 3 when the sentence of banishment is conveyed to Romeo he seems to consider it a fate worse than death. Is his reaction a logical one?
5. The passage in Scene 5, lines 1–36, modeled on the *aubade,* or "morning song," contains a good deal of argument about birds. How is this made appropriate?

Act Four

1. In Scenes 3 and 4 there is a great deal of preparation for celebration going on. What effect does this conviviality have on what occurs in Scene 3?
2. Why does Shakespeare end Act Four with Peter and the musicians engaged in general argument?

Act Five

1. At the opening of Scene 1 Romeo remembers a dream he has just had. What preparation does this provide for the rest of the scene?
2. Though Paris has a relatively small part in the play, what conclusions can be drawn about his character?

General

1. As noted in the introduction, accident seems to play a large part in the outcome of the play. How many accidents are there and are they all purely accidental?
2. After the mention of the "star-crossed lovers" in the Prologue, the stars are referred to in various ways up to Romeo's line, "Then I defy you, stars," (V, 1, 24) and finally
                                  Oh, here

> Will I set up my everlasting rest,
> And shake the yoke of inauspicious stars
> From this world-wearied flesh.
>
> (V, 3, 109–112)

From these references is it possible to decide the role of the stars in the play?

3. Friar Laurence appears in five scenes. What is his general function in the play?
4. Shakespeare's young lovers are notoriously strong-willed. What effect does the decisiveness of Romeo and Juliet contribute to the play?
5. Old Capulet seems to us a strict disciplinarian. What motives does he have in attempting to marry Juliet off to the County Paris?
6. The "gap" between generations in this play seems hopelessly unbridgeable. Does any solution other than the one Romeo and Juliet choose suggest itself?
7. According to Renaissance ideals of the family, Romeo and Juliet were violating a fundamental law of parental privilege. Does the play make a statement on this problem?
8. Prince Escalus is prepared to sacrifice both Montagues and Capulets in order to maintain public peace. Does the play support or criticize his actions?
9. In the beginning of Act One Romeo believes himself to be desperately in love with Rosaline, but by the end of the act he has fallen in love with Juliet. Is he merely "fickle," or are there differences in these loves?
10. What changes take place in Romeo's character, even in his language, between the beginning and the end of the play?
11. We learn from the play that Juliet has led a typically protected life, but when she meets Romeo she gives her heart without hesitation. Does Shakespeare make this sudden change convincing? Explain.
12. Several versions of love emerge and are contrasted in the play. What contribution do these contrasts make to the love that develops between Romeo and Juliet?

ANTIGONE

1. What do we learn about the characters of Antigone and Ismene in their first dialogue?
2. How does Antigone's reference to her father Oedipus prepare us for the action that follows?

3. Does Antigone seem to be more interested in following the traditional form of burial or in defying Creon?
4. In the first entrance of the Chorus we are reminded of past events and prepared for rejoicing. What does Sophocles accomplish by this contrast?
5. Creon very quickly makes his personality clear. How would you characterize him?
6. Why does Sophocles make the Guard, the bearer of crucial information, a semicomic character?
7. In the famous ode following the exit of the guard, the Chorus sings the praises of man, but adds a warning on the misuse of man's gifts. How does this prepare us for the entrance of Creon in the scene that follows?
8. Is the final stanza of the ode a warning to Creon or to Antigone?
9. Why is Antigone so vehement in denying Ismene's complicity in the burial of their brother?
10. Haimon's first speech suggests that he is blindly loyal to his father in spite of his love for Antigone. What effect does this expression of loyalty have on his conduct later in the scene?
11. What conclusions may be drawn about Sophocles' dramatic technique from the fact that the lovers Haimon and Antigone never appear on the scene together?
12. To what degree are Creon and Antigone selflessly devoted to principle in their collision of wills, and what part does the expression of ego play?
13. In the visible action of the play very little is made of the love between Antigone and Haimon, but what consequence does it have in the working out of Creon's destiny?
14. Remembering that a distinct veneration surrounded the figure of the "seer," what effect does Creon's treatment of Teiresias produce?
15. In a play of such tragic proportions, Creon alone makes reference to money and bribery. What qualities do these references add to his character?
16. Does it appear that Teiresias has any purpose other than serving as the voice of reason?
17. What finally causes Creon to change his mind?
18. If the first ode is a hymn to the greatness of man and the last a cry for help, what attitude toward man's destiny does the Chorus progressively voice in the course of the play?
19. Is it possible to decide finally whether destiny or a flaw in character is primarily responsible for the tragic outcome of the play?

SUGGESTED TOPICS FOR PAPERS

Suggested Topics For Papers

SHORT OR MEDIUM LENGTH

RAISIN IN THE SUN

The degree to which the problems of the Younger family were the result of their being black. Consider the family as a whole, or any one of its members.
The influence of Joseph Asagai on the Younger family.
The future of the Youngers.

ALL MY SONS

The integrity of Joe Keller's claim that he built up the business for Chris.
The dramatic importance of Kate's statement that Joe hasn't "been laid up in fifteen years." (Act Two)
The significance of "All" in the title.

PICNIC ON THE BATTLEFIELD

The significance of the similarities.
Contrasting versions of war by father and son.
The role of the stretcher bearers.

GHOSTS

The relationship between Pastor Manders and Mrs. Alving.
Our impression of Captain Alving: what it is and how it is given to us.
The significance of the fire at the end of Act Two (realistic and symbolic).

THE MISER

The role of love in the play.
The contrast between Harpagon and Signor Anselme as fathers.
Master and servant relationships.

ROMEO AND JULIET

Contrasting versions of love in the play.
The function of Friar Laurence.
The necessities of the state and those of the individual.

ANTIGONE

The role of the Chorus.
The influence of pride on the outcome.
The conflict of personalities.

LONG PAPERS

1. Fathers, living or dead, have an important role in all the plays. Analyze and compare the role played by the father in three of the plays.
2. Using any plays that seem appropriate, discuss the impact of institutions—business, government, church, law, the army—on the young people of the play.
3. Drama can illustrate ideas in action, can teach, entertain, and arouse emotional responses. Select the play that comes closest to performing all of these functions and analyze the methods it uses to accomplish these ends.
4. Some of these plays are realistic, and some are poetic and symbolic. Choose one in each style and discuss each author's use of the particular method.
5. Although conflict between generations is important in all the plays, each playwright uses this conflict in a different way. Contrast the use made of this generational confrontation in three of the plays.
6. In all of the plays the young people condemn the power structure. Present a reasoned argument for the justice of the power structures in as many of the plays as possible.
7. Assuming that you believe in the ideals of the Women's Liberation Movement, discuss several plays in relation to women's rights.
8. It has been said that character makes drama. In which plays is this statement best illustrated? Cite contributions to the play as a whole by several of the characters.
9. Which of the seven plays appeals to you most? Explain why.